SAINT SAUL

A Skeleton Key to the Historical Jesus

SAINT SAUL

A SKELETON KEY
TO THE HISTORICAL JESUS

DONALD HARMAN AKENSON

McGill-Queen's University Press
Montreal & Kingston

© McGill-Queen's University Press 2000
ISBN 0-7735-2090-2

Legal deposit third quarter 2000
Bibliothèque nationale du Québec

Printed in Canada on acid-free paper
Published simultaneously by Oxford University Press, Inc.

McGill-Queen's University Press acknowledges the
financial support of the Government of Canada through
the Book Publishing Industry Development Program (BPIDP)
for our publishing activities. It also acknowledges
the support of the Canada Council for the Arts
for its publishing program.

Canadian Cataloguing in Publication Data

Akenson, Donald Harman
Saint Saul: a skeleton key to the historical Jesus

Includes bibliographical references and index.
ISBN 0-7735-2090-2

1. Jesus Christ–Historicity. 2. Paul, the Apostle, Saint. I. Title.

BS2506.A38 2000   232.9'08   C00-900386-X

This book was typeset by
Typo Litho Composition Inc. in 10.5/13 Times.

In memory of my parents

Contents

Acknowledgments

Through the years, I've become convinced that editors are to books what tact is to civilized social life: the ingredient one notices only when it is awry. So, having been editorially rejected, deflected, and corrected hundreds of times, I've come to the conclusion that it was almost always for the best, and certainly always for the better.

For singular grace and favour I am grateful to Cynthia Read of Oxford University Press, and to my supernally generous colleagues at McGill-Queen's University Press: Philip Cercone, Arden Ford, Joan Harcourt, Roger Martin, Susanne McAdam, Joan McGilvray, Aurèle Parisien, Bruce Walsh and Roy Ward. Within Queen's University, Dave Turpin, Les Monkman, Tom Thayer and Bill Leggett have served not only as friends and supporters of the Press, but as sources of personal advice and encouragement.

This volume focuses on a set of small, but highly vexed, issues that lie at the heart of the history of Christianity. In *Surpassing Wonder. The Invention of the Bible and the Talmuds* (New York: Harcourt Brace, and Montreal and Kingston: McGill-Queen's University Press, 1998), I presented a very large argument concerning the formation and interrelationship of the texts of the Tanakh, the Christian scriptures and the classic Rabbinical writings. Some of that material which reflects directly on the issue of Christian origins is reprised here in highly condensed form, and for most readers (particularly my ideal reader, the educated layperson) that should be enough. However, experts – who will wish to do their homework before drawing any judgements – should consult the text of *Surpassing Wonder* for full documentation and argumentation of points that are carried over from that volume. Most of the ideas presented here are based directly upon primary texts and can be followed without immersing oneself in the massive literature that surrounds the basic Christian and Jewish documents. I have mentioned where relevant a few of the giants and grotesques of modern scholarship, but mostly I have let the texts and the related arguments speak for themselves.

Donald Harman Akenson
Kingston, Ontario, and Liverpool, England
Feast of the Conversion of Saint Paul, 2000 CE

SAINT SAUL

Prologue

In the present day Quest for the Historical Jesus, the single most repeated assertion of his substance is that Jesus was Jewish. That observation might seem obvious enough, but given the anti-Jewish nature of the Christian scriptures, it is one worth making. However, once it is made, this worthy assertion is given only a brief respectful nod by the Jesus-Questors – rather like a verger briefly reverencing the altar before getting on with his daily roster of duties. Thus, in almost every version of the present day Quest, Jesus comes labelled as being "a Jew" (as if we automatically know what that most protean of terms meant two thousand years ago), and then he is defined as one with such unusual characteristics that he becomes a Jew who has most of the distinguishing marks ascribed to early Christians.

This will not do: it is weak history and worse piety. Running through the present study is a theme so pervasive that it requires statement only a single time: that once we recognize that Jesus was a deeply committed follower of Yahweh – a "Jew" in contemporary parlance – that recognition changes fundamentally the way that we read the relevant historical documents of his era and, most especially, the manner in which historians must assay the early Christian texts.

Virtually every recent Quest for the Historical Jesus depends for its evidentiary bedrock on the material found in the four narrative Gospels – Matthew, Mark, Luke, and John – and tries to extract accurate "facts" or uncover hidden or "primitive" shards of texts from within those Gospels. For reasons that will become clear as my argument develops, this is the wrong place to start, not least because it makes Jesus-the-Jew a derivative of texts whose goal was to modify, minimize, or exorcise his Jewishness (depending on which Gospel one reads) and, perforce, to convert him (however unintentionally) to Christianity and thus from being a follower of Yahweh to being a co-partner.

To break that perceptual-set, we need to start with our eyes elsewhere.

*The World of Saul of Tarsus
and Yeshua of Nazareth*

The Wounded Magus

I

NOTICE THE MAN COMING UP THE STREET. YOU'VE SEEN HIM BEFORE, lots of times, on different streets, various cities, other continents. He's the nearest thing we have to a witness.

What we want is a witness to the life of a man named Yeshua, born in Nazareth who, after his death, was transformed into Jesus-the-Messiah or, if you prefer, Jesus Christ. Our problem is forensic: nobody who knew Yeshua personally put anything down on paper, at least not that we've ever found and this despite a couple of thousand years of looking. And everybody who wrote anything at all plausible about Yeshua's life did so forty to eighty years after his death. By that time, there wasn't much Yeshua left, but there was a whole lot of Jesus in his place. That's not necessarily bad – great art, great dreams, great imaginings can purify the human soul – but we're still a bit curious about the historical Yeshua, the skeleton of everyday reality on which so many rich liturgical vestments have been hung.

So keep your eye on that weird stranger. At first sight, he's the kind of person none of us really wants to meet. He's injured in some way we can't quite define; there's something that makes him uneasy and he transmits that discomfort to every one he deals with. You remember that on other streets, in other cities, he's jumped out at you unexpectedly, or bumped into you as you turned a corner: intense, his head jerking, and saliva droplets spitting out of the corners of his mouth as he tries to tell you something terribly, terribly important. Yet, he's not really menacing, and if you give him a chance to speak, you'll realize that he seems slightly frightening only because you've been trained to fear everybody scruffy, physically bent, burbling. If you can make yourself hold still for just two minutes – an eternity on the street – you'll hear him tell you some things you'll never forget.[1]

That's Saint Saul and he has a lot to say about Jesus-the-Christ. And he'll also tell us a good deal about the historical Yeshua: only he'll say things elliptically, and we will have to decode the cascade of metaphor, word, song that pours out.

There's no shame in not wanting to meet Saul. That's his real name and it's the one we use here; on the street he calls himself Paul, but that's a *nom de guerre*. He can be trying. People he's attempted to talk to have beaten him up, and when he really irritated them, they had him jailed as a public nuisance. He easily could have made Asia Minor's list of the ten people one least would like to have to dinner. Eventually Saul was martyred, which is the polite and Christian way of indicating that he truly got on people's nerves. Even his fellow believers found him impossible at times. Saul and the brother of Yeshua of Nazareth, known as "James the Less" in Christian tradition for complicated exegetical reasons, not as a value judgement on his importance, were often at loggerheads. James the Less was the head of the believers in Jerusalem after Yeshua's death, and he and Saul carried on a decades-long negotiation about what was the ambit of true faith. Brilliant, god-drunk, unpredictable, Saul, who had never met Yeshua of Nazareth in the flesh, was convinced that he knew him better than those who had.

Peculiar, yes; a genius, probably; crazy, no. He is important to us because he is the only person who wrote about Yeshua before the near-East's equivalent of a nuclear blast – the destruction of Jerusalem and its Temple in the Roman-Jewish war of 66–73 CE – changed forever the way people who worship Yahweh think and act. Or, to be strictly accurate, Saul is the only pre-70 writer whose works have survived. They come to us in the form in which he dictated them, or at least in close copies. We need him.

Saul's writing is notoriously jagged, full of metaphors that fly right out of the frame of discussion, packed with contradictions of his own arguments and mined with analogies that backfire. That is no real problem, once one realizes that his mind simply does not work like that of most people, and this because he has his own mode of perception. He sees things as if through the optics of a giant many-faceted diamond. Like the eye of a fly in the animal world, Saul's mind takes in hundreds of overlapping images. He sees things much better than most of us do, but his unusual mode of apperception produces an even more unusual mode of personal expression. He never quite settles on words to explain himself, but produces spiky, intense concepts that to our minds are contradictory. But better this richness than bland and puréed prose, for Saul's prose is nothing if not revealing. To it, we can adjust.

However, we face two problems whose origin is external to Saul's epistles. The first of them is that for nearly twenty centuries, theologians have worked on Saul. Like retro-plasterers, they have filled the lacunae in individual letters, taped the joints between the several epistles, and have tried to sand smooth Sauls's words as they relate to the major issues of Christian theology. This is a valid exercise and it is what theologians are paid to do. Historians, however, will learn more about the historical Yeshua if they take Saul's letters on their own terms, without later theological overlays. Saul is complex enough, without reading him through a confessional filter.

And, secondly, without being impious we have to get away from the Christian church's later opinion (ratified formally in the fourth century), that Saul was writing scripture. The Christian concept of scripture, as a specific canon of writings, somehow divinely instigated, precisely defined in number and nature by ecclesiastical authorities, had great value as a means of institutional control – and the evidence from the mid-second through the late fourth centuries, when scores of "heresies" were floating around, makes it clear that the church fathers desperately needed quality-controls over the content of the fast-evolving Christian creeds. The concept of scripture, however, is anachronistic as far as Saul's letters are concerned. At the time of their writing, they were just letters, nothing more. He was communicating with his friends, encouraging the weak, denouncing his enemies. The letters have a sense of immediacy and of specific occasion that are far distant from the ex-cathedra quality that is usually projected into "the Christian canon." As historical evidence, Saul's writings are no different than any other letters we might find in the same period. Their primary historical value comes from Sauls's proximity to early followers of Yeshua of Nazareth.

Thus, despite the later patina of canonicity, and despite the heroic efforts of generations of theologians to sand smooth Saul's jagged immediacies, as historians we have licence to deal with Saul and with his writings as directly as we can. He is the nearest witness in time to the historical Yeshua and we have to get as close to Saul as possible, with as little conceptual haze as possible between our eyes and his intense, disconcerting visage.

2

In his relationship with Yeshua of Nazareth, Saul has always made observers uneasy. Significant segments of the early Jesus-movement were terrified by this former-persecutor of Yeshua's followers suddenly becoming a convert to their side; some of the early church fathers, devout and devoted believers in Jesus-the-Christ, questioned the appropriateness of preserving Saul's letters as part of the treasury of Christian knowledge; while others, no less devout, believed that his epistles were superior as spiritual documents to all others, including the Gospels.

In modern times (from roughly the era of the French Revolution to the present day), the issue has been: did Saul hijack Yeshua's religious movement? The question is usually phrased more decorously, but that is what it means. Was Saul such a successful hijacker that there's almost nothing of Yeshua left? This is not a frivolous question, for one has to accept the historical fact that (as Dieter Georgi expresses it), "Jesus did not leave any organized movement, let alone a new religion."[2] The Acts of the Apostles describes the way that the disciples scrambled to readjust their world after the crucifixion of Yeshua, and, ultimately they did so with great success. A guild of men and women who had been a minuscule faction among the worshippers of Yahweh eventually became the forebears of an independent world religion. One has to grant Saul his considerable part in this process, especially his turning the energies of many of the faithful towards evangelizing Gentiles, a group towards which Yeshua of Nazareth showed no interest, and indeed, if the Gospels are to be trusted, seems to have disliked quite strongly. (In Mark [7:24–30] Yeshua employs an analogy in which persons of Hellenic culture are compared to curs; and in Matthew [10:5–6] Yeshua tells his disciples not to preach to Gentiles or Samaritans, but only to the "house of Israel.") However, even Saul's own letters make it clear that he was himself just one of many who carried on this activity (the names of Barnabas and of Apollos come immediately to mind and there are several others). So, one can hardly lay on Saul's doorstep the charge that he bears the responsibility for transforming the audience for the teachings of Yeshua of Nazareth from Temple-worshipping Yahweh-followers to Gentiles.

Joseph Klausner, the great Jewish scholar of events of the early Common Era, once observed that "without Paul, Christianity would not have become a world religion with a distinctive theology and a highly developed ecclesiastical organisation."[3] That view, shared by many Christian scholars, is not really an historical statement, however, for it presents Saul's activity as an absolutely necessary prerequisite for the evolution of an independent religion by the followers of the crucified Yeshua; it is a normative statement of what could not happen: no Saul, then no Christianity. Rather than adopt this meta-historical position – which is incapable either of proof or disproof – it is cleaner, and historically undeniable, to state that Saul had a great theological and organisational influence on the Yeshua faith in its early years. Whether or not another figure of equal influence would have emerged had Saul not been on the scene is a side-issue not worth pursuing, for it is something we can never know.

Within Christian circles, the Saul who did exist (as distinct from his imaginary substitute) has been either attacked or apostrophized (mostly the former) for retro-changing the religious views of Yeshua of Nazareth. Paradoxically, he is said to have done this out of loyalty to his master. A gentle, but vigorous statement of this view was composed early in the twentieth century by William Wrede who suggested that the single greatest change Saul made in the beliefs of early Yeshua-followers was to invest with eternal meaning the myriad acts of the master's life. Saul, in his letters, spends very little time quoting directly the teachings of Yeshua, but instead focuses chiefly on Yeshua's life as a series of divine acts – an indwelling of God's spirit, the bodily crucifixion and the cosmic resurrection – through which humanity can obtain salvation. Thus, Yeshua of Nazareth, who appears to have been primarily a religious teacher, is transformed by Saul into a divinity. And thus, many scholars suggest, emerges the religion of Christ.[4]

That view, when expressed softly, can be accepted by a wide band of scholars and believers. For historians it seems to cover the available information fairly adequately and for many believers, it matters not a great deal that Saul re-defined Yeshua of Nazareth as Jesus-the-Christ, since (to their minds) he got it right. Nevertheless, the reader should be aware that there is a strong sector of Christian tradition (mostly Protestant fundamentalists and traditionalist Roman Catholics) which holds that any distinction between the historical Yeshua and Jesus-the Christ is impious and therefore unacceptable. And there is a secular tradition which holds that, yes, Saul re-defined Yeshua of Nazareth and that his doing so was one of the great disasters of western history. The most indignant and articulate exponent of this was Friedrich Nietzsche who claimed that Saul had killed the "Christianity" of Yeshua and had replaced it with a counterfeit version of the Good News, a vision of hatred produced in the fetid confines of a sinister Pharisaic mind. The apostle not only counterfeited Jesus' life, Nietzsche argued, he falsified the history of the people of Israel and, indeed, the entire history of mankind. Saul's presentation of Jesus-the-Christ, therefore, is nothing less than the "original betrayal."[5]

Although it is hard to find anyone sane who agrees in detail with Nietzsche on his theory of Christian origins, he does point, largely through his own impercipience, to two real phenomena. One of these is that, as Victor Furnish has recognized, Saul's "place in the church was won at the cost of his place in history."[6] That is, he was so engagé, so deeply committed to action, that he did not receive the chronicling he deserved. No cold and judicial eye evaluates his words and actions (even the Book of Acts is swept up in his vision). And, secondly, it is in fact impossible to compare Saul and Yeshua, and that holds whether one is trying to prove them consonant with each other or in conflict. As Samuel Sandmel suggested, what one can do is something quite different: compare what the epistles of Saint Saul taught and what the Gospels taught. "Surely Paul's eminence is such that in these comparisons we need not begin defensively with Paul. Indeed, were I a Christian and faced with the need to choose between Paul and one of the evangelists, I would tend on most matters to prefer Paul."[7]

Still, by implication, Nietzsche is right on one point: it's virtually impossible to be neutral about Saul. Today, more than any other part of the Bible, his epistles cause discomfort and unease both to Christians and to persons who, while not Christian, take seriously moral questions raised in the New Testament. In three areas, the great apostle offends modern sensibilities. One of these is his implicit endorsement of the socioeconomic order as it stands. The metonym for this is his acceptance of slavery. One can argue about the nature of slavery in the Roman world (it may have been less brutal than chattel slavery in antebellum America), but he did send the escaped-slave

Onesimus back to his owner. (The Letter to Philemon was a generous document, but it still was a slave-manifest, the shipping statement that accompanied a chattel.) Secondly, Saul is very ambiguous on the proper position of women in the life of the community of faith. He is torn. At some points he seems to tell them to sit still and be quiet (1 Cor. 14:34–35) and that, everything considered, it is best if men have nothing biologically to do with women, celibacy being the highest spiritual state (1 Cor. 7:7). But on the other hand he is quite willing to accept as junior partners – co-missionaries, deaconesses, patronesses – several women of apparently-powerful character: Lydia, Prisca (var: Priscilla), Phoebe and, perhaps, Junia.

Now, on both the matter of chattel slavery and on the question of possible misogyny, judgement is necessarily difficult. Saul of course was a product of his own times (who isn't?) and he cannot be expected to espouse the views of a later era. Crucially, on both the matters of slavery and on the issue of women's place in the church, he is softer (one shudders to suggest "more progressive," that being a term employed by enlightened groups ranging from the government of Albania in the 1950s to the Shining Path guerillas of our own day) than were most of his contemporaries. And if he sometimes offends us, there are always the wonderfully comforting ambiguities of his letter to the Galatians where he suggests (3:28) that in Christ there is neither Jew nor Greek, slave nor free, male nor female. He may mean this solely theologically, or he may have some ideal future sociology in mind, but it is enough to permit his friends to plead his case.

Without ambiguity, however, is Saul's homophobia, and it is nothing less than that. Saul, who spent most of his life in Asia Minor and in the Hellenised portions of the Roman empire, lived in a culture that was considerably more tolerant of homosexuality, especially male, than was that of North America and of western Europe until, perhaps, the 1980s. Therefore, the anachronism-defence disappears. Granted, the situations were not identical, but they are close enough to permit us to hear Saul's words directly, and they are clear. He definitely abhorred lesbianism, which to him is a "vile affection," by which women "change the natural use into that which is against nature" (Romans 1:26). And he is just as repulsed by "men with men, working that which is unseemly" (Rom. 1:27). Now, it is barely possible to argue that Saul is against male and female same-sex relationships not because they are inherently wrong, but because they involve men taking on female roles and females assuming male roles, and this is what is against nature. That is plausible because in his first letter to the Corinthians (6:9), he denounces *malakoi*, which the King James Bible translates as "effeminate(s)." A modern term would be "rent-boys." So, just possibly, Saul is not really against homosexuality but against sexual acts in which at least one of the males has to behave like a woman (that is, be a passive recipient) or in which a woman may behave like a man, with another woman.[8] That goes out the window, however, when one notes the word Saul uses for dominant men who have sexual congress with passive males – a mode of sexual intercourse in which the supposedly natural dominance of the male is preserved. These men are called *arsenokoitai* (1 Cor. 6:9). Generation after generation of translators have tried to paraphrase this term, for it is one of extreme derogation. It means butt-fuckers, and the apostle will have none of it. Despite the tenor of his own times, Saul was unabashedly homophobic and, as *The Guardian* deftly noted, "not much liked by the gay lobby, right?"[9]

So be it. The point here is not that Saul was either right or wrong on his views concerning women, social hierarchy, and same-sex physical relationships; the point is that he touched a number of issues (not only these) that have been matters of burning contention at least since the era of the so-called European Enlightenment. And before that, in the heady morning of the Protestant Reformation, his theology (especially his doctrine of grace) was enough to send armies marching. And one can trace the explosive reactions to his work back to the council of Nicea of the fourth century and right to the council of Jerusalem of the mid-first century. With Saul around, every issue is volatile, and not just intellectually: Saul is the one person in the entire Judaeo-Christian tradition whom one can neither ignore nor pass by bemusedly, giving him the spiritual equivalent of a patronising pat on the head.

My own feeling is that however frequently one encounters distasteful attitudes in Saul's epistles, these moments are irrelevant. They should be treated as epiphenomenal, like a rain shower occurring in the face of a volcanic eruption. Whatever his rebarbarative moments, Saul seems to me to be the character who is most authentically defined of all the figures we find in the Tanakh, the New Testament, and the Talmuds. His only rival is King David, whose life is chronicled as a heart-breaking, fully-rendered biography, one that is shorter than we would wish, but still fuller than any other third-person chronicle. Jesus-the-Christ, by the time we meet him in the Gospels, has become a divinity and deities are notoriously hard to identify with. Saul, however, is a jagged, flawed, and therefore totally convincing human being. And, unlike everyone else in the scriptures and Talmuds, he has left us writings that are not merely ascribed to him by others, but are unassailably his own creation. Saint Saul we meet in person; and when we finally become at ease with his angular personality, he talks to us in his oblique way of the historical Yeshua and starts us on an historical pilgrimage that is pure joy.

3

The ground rules for dealing with Saul, as a conduit to the historical Yeshua are simple and are mostly matters of taste. First, the reader will perhaps be surprised that whenever possible we use the today-unfashionable Authorised Version of the Bible (the "King James Version" – hereafter "KJB"). This is because it is still the best English-language version. Not the most accurate: the best – and we have William Tyndale, its unacknowledged ghost-writer, to thank for that. On points of detail it must be checked against more modern translations, ones whose erudition and finite accuracy surpass it. Those little matters are important, for God is in the details. But God is also in the music. All of the modern English language translations of the New Testament that I have encountered are either written for the tone deaf or, with false-vividness, for the philistine. The Almighty has enough trouble with a world where even the music of the ionosphere is being distorted by human technodreck: at least let his Word sing.

Secondly, the reader will not be ground down by portmanteau footnotes – the sort of thing one respondent at an annual meeting of the Society of Biblical Literature called "porcupine quills meant to protect an underdeveloped epistemology."[10] Although I have read literally rooms-full of books and articles pertinent to the topic at hand, the logical and evidentiary structure laid out here is well within the ambit of any educated non-specialist, and befogging the main issues with technical apparatus whose only purpose is to establish that I have done my homework is to no one's benefit. Some truly fine (indeed, great) minds are found in the field of biblical studies and I am grateful to have been able to learn from some of them. Whenever a direct quotation is used, a unique opinion is referred to, or a rarely-known fact is instanced, appropriate citation is made in the notes to the text. (And, occasionally, when somebody of eminence has produced an idea so silly that it teaches us how *not* to think, that too is documented.) As far as possible, however, my argument relies on primary texts, the Tanakh, the New Testament, the Apocrypha and the major pieces of the Pseudepigrapha, all of which are available in standard form and are conveniently available to anyone who cares about the nature of early Christianity. And even here, the references are mostly to the New Testament, so it's easy to check my line of argument.

Because a discussion of the Apostle Saul's evidentiary relationship to the historical Yeshua must intersect with a long tradition of biblical historical scholarship which has avoided Saul, as if he were the carrier of some form of spiritual cholera, it is impossible just to jump into a delineation of what Saul's writings imply about the historical Yeshua. Instead, Saul has to be interwoven in a way that shows how the "historical Jesus" traditionally has been approached, and how Saul should help, indeed, be a source-of-first resort. So, rhetorically, this book works the way the early transatlantic cables did: Saul's evidence, like a ribbon of high-tensile steel, weaves in and around the other material, appearing and disappearing, but always, by virtue of its strength and ductility, being the strand that determines the direction and depth of the entire enterprise. Even when Saul and his writings are not being directly discussed, they are the heart of the exercise.

Exciting Times: The Religious World of Saul of Tarsus and Yeshua

I

SAUL AND YESHUA LIVED IN AN ERA THAT WAS THE MOST INVENTIVE, most imaginative, most ideationally fecund in matters of religion of any time that is adequately recorded in human history. Even if we limit our time horizon to the century covered, roughly by years 30 BCE to 70 CE, and even if we limit our geographical vision to Eretz Israel and to the Diaspora communities in the Near East that owed their allegiance to Judaism, even so the perpetual swirl of new ideas, new sects, and the splintering and recombination of old ideas and older factions, is dizzying. Take the twentieth-century American propensity to create new religious movements and to borrow and combine disparate concepts, and compress that amount of creativity into a population one-fiftieth its number, most of its members living in an area the size of Massachusetts, and one has an idea what it must have been like. Try to conceive of a mental world so rich with ideas, prophets, factions, priests, savants, and god-drunk fanatics that it was the equivalent of a night-sky kept alight by thousands and thousands of fire-flies, brief-lived, incandescent, luminous. That's what Yeshua and Saul witnessed.

Understandably – but unfortunately for historical understanding – the religious authorities of both the Christian and the Jewish faiths, as they developed after 70 CE, have had a strong interest in playing down the fecundity of the century immediately before the Temple was destroyed, and this has constricted scholarship until very recent times. Both faiths base their claims to authenticity upon a spiritual genealogy that goes back, from the Second Temple era, to the time of Solomon's Temple, back to Moses and his Torah, and finally, back to the creation of the human race. The faith-documents of each religion have presented the last century of the Second Temple as much more solid in religious terms, much more disciplined, and much less imaginative than it really was. The reason for this is that both Christianity and Rabbinic Judaism required a solid pre-Destruction link in their own genealogy. In the Jewish case, it was required if the spiritual pedigree of the post-70 Rabbis were to be traced, through the Second Temple era, back in time to Moses, their spiritual progenitor. And Christians needed a virtually monolithic "Jewish" faith of the early first century, for they defined many of their key concepts as negations of what they claimed were "Jewish" beliefs and practices. So, until very recently, the marvellous fluidity of the era was lost. Even today, only a minority of scholars (though a growing one) refuse to take for granted what the misleading conventional wisdom dictates concerning the period in which Saul and Yeshua lived.[1]

There is a famous statement in the Jerusalem Talmud, attributed to Rabbi Johanan, that the reason the Chosen People were exiled and their Temple destroyed was that, in the years before that catastrophe, there had arisen twenty-four parties of heretics.[2] Of course, in religious controversies, "heretic" is a term used for one's opponents, and when religious history eventually is written by the winning side, "heretic" refers to those who lost. But if we scrub the word "heretic" (and its blame-casting), and replace it with "faction," "religious party," even "cabal," (almost any word except "sect" or "cult," which are heavily loaded terms), then Rabbi Johanan was right. His report meant, in everyday language, that there were lots and lots of Judahist religious groups flourishing in pre-70 CE times, each in some way related to all the others, each in some sense part of Judahism, but each different and, increasingly, each given to self-invented variations of belief and practice. *Multiple Judahisms* (to adapt Jacob Neusner's seminal terminology) prevailed: not one single faith.

Of course, Rabbi Johanan's use of "twenty-four" is not a real number, but rather an expressive one: twice the number of the original twelve tribes. It means that there were more forms of Judahism than could be counted. Many of these religious parties left their mark on the historical record, either by virtue of their actions or because their speculations or rules of discipline were written down and subsequently either preserved or, in our own time, rediscovered; but this written permanence can only have been achieved by a small fraction of the full number of groups. Many must have coalesced, met for a time, and then dissolved, leaving behind no religious writings and no notices of their brief careers.

Still, just listen to the names of a few of the groups that were in operation during the combined lifetimes of Yeshua and of Saul, each claiming to be the true embodiment of the Yahweh-faith. In addition to the priestly establishment that ran the Temple and which, from Maccabean times onwards, was strife-ridden, and variously intertwined with the civil authorities, there were the big factions: the ascetic Essenes, the Sadducees (distinguished by their traditionalism and their refusal to accept the newly-fashionable belief of the resurrection of the individual soul, and perhaps the body, after death), and the Pharisees (the group Saul said had trained him in Judahism, and the faction closest to Yeshua in belief and style of religious argument). But what does one make of the "Knockers," and their tandem cohort "the Awakeners?" Later Rabbinic authorities thought that they were distinguished by their insistence on using humane killing methods in Temple sacrifices, instead of the ritual throat-slitting that was required practice. There was the "Fourth Philosophy" that, according to Flavius Josephus, was founded by one Judas the Galilean shortly before the beginning of the Common Era and seems to have been Pharisees-with-an-attitude, in that they accepted most Pharisaic purity conventions but would literally die rather than call any man master. And then there were the Zealots and the Sicarri, holy terrorists of whom we know much less than we think. Various brigands proliferated, some of whom had charismatic powers and strong religious beliefs. If only we could interview one Hezekiah (late 40s and 30s BCE), or the unnamed, but infamous, Galilean cave brigands (30s CE), Eleazar ben Dinai (30s to 50s CE), Tholomaios (40s CE), Yeshua, son of Sapphias (60s CE) or John of Gischala (mid-60s CE). And, how does one interpret the strange sects that seem to be represented in the documents found at Qumran and Masada (the "Dead Sea Scrolls")? And where did the various prophetic movements fit, such as the movements of Theudas, and of "the Egyptian" (for whom Saul was at one time mistaken: Acts 21:38). Some of the frequent revolts against civil (and, sometimes, religious) authorities clearly had overtones of cleansing-the-faith: the seizure of the Jerusalem Temple amidst demands for a new high priest, at the time of Herod the Great's death (4 BCE) and the monarchical movements that followed soon after this rebellion, one in Galilee led by a man named Judas, one in Transjordan headed by a certain Simon, one in Judea led by the massive Athronges, a former shepherd. In each case the leader took on a royal crown or related apparel, actions which in the context of the Judahist faith (wherein true kingship was created by Yahweh), inevitably had religious implications. All that deals only with Eretz Israel. One could go on, and when done, begin all over, charting the immense variations of Judaism found in the Diaspora (such as, for example, the sacrificial Temple found at Leontopolis in Egypt), and the syncretistic mixings with various Greek and Roman religions (the possibility of there having been a Second Temple Judahist form of Gnosticism opens an immense range of beliefs, as do interrelationships with Hellenic mystery cults).[3] Even then, defining all those groups, we would know only a tiny bit of the rich speciation of the Yahweh-faith in its most luxuriant hour, the last century of the Second Temple.

Yet, crucially, even a full recognition of the fact that there were scores and scores of Judahisms in operation in the lifetimes of Yeshua and of Saul, understates the real richness that they, and anyone in the Judahist tradition who was seriously interested in the nature of ultimate reality, enjoyed. For the true richness was not that Saul or Yeshua could have joined any of a large number

of Judahist factions (in fact, Yeshua did, becoming a follower of John the
Baptist for a time; and, of course, Saul became a follower of Yeshua), but
rather that they could virtually bathe in a spume of ideas. The Judahist world
of the late Second Temple era was a fountain of unmatched primary ideas and
a history of the covenant with Yahweh (found in Genesis through Kings of
the Tanakh), and of newer concepts (Messiah, resurrection) and of new figures (the personification of angels and of Satan as a primal force), and of new
visions (those in the Book of Enoch, for instance), exceeded in their mind-
blinding flashes anything previously articulated within Judaism. And new
spiritual disciplines arose (the Dead Sea Scrolls are full of rigorous spiritual
mortifications). Neither before nor since was the Yahweh-faith this blessed
with such a heaven-circling rainbow of inventive minds.

Because the great lottery of history selected as winners, after the mini-
apocalypse of 70 CE, the heirs of the Pharisees (who became the progenitors
of Rabbinic Judaism) and the heirs of the Yeshua-faith (who also had some
relationship, albeit much less close, with the pre-70 CE Pharisees), as the two
survivors of the myriad Judaisms of the later Second Temple era, it is easy
to focus too closely on their beliefs as defined after 70 CE. Because they won
the unpredictable lottery-for-survival, it is easy to let that narrow our vision to
what those two factions believed and then, effectively, to push those observations backward in time, making them dominant before the Destruction, when
actually they were not. It is only with the false-omniscience of hindsight that
anyone can explain the narrowing of the scores of branching possibilities
down to two versions, and this reduction being contingent on an event (the
devastation of 70 CE) that was unlikely, unpredictable, and, for all practical
purposes, random.

In the present context, that is a debilitating mistake, because Yeshua and
Saul had conveniently available to them an immense menu of ideas, one so
rich that it not only has eluded full scholarly analysis, but has literally defied
full description. Here the trick is to forget the various factions and to treat the
complexes of ideas that floated around between the multiple parties of Judahism (the ideas sometimes being borrowed by one group from another, sometimes being virulently denounced), as entities-in-themselves. That is helpful,
because the practice of religious thinkers in the later Second Temple era was
wonderfully mix-and-match. There were scores of interesting components
lying around the shop-floor of the Judahist religious world, and these were
put together in inventions so ingenious that it makes one shake one's head in
continual wonder.

Of course, the kernel of the Yahweh-faith was the covenant between the
Almighty and one branch of humankind, the people who call themselves the
Chosen People. Granted, almost all religions imply some kind of a deal be-
tween the invisible forces of the universe (the gods) and the people under the

dominion of those forces. In virtually all religions, mankind proposes, God disposes. What distinguishes the covenant with the ancient Hebrews is that it provided its adherents with an explicit system of if-then thinking. *If* you will do this, *then* I will bless you, Yahweh says, and *if* you disobey me, *then* I will punish you. This, when translated into person-to-person relations, provides both a way of expressing and calculating social morality and law, and also creates a strikingly modern sense of history: *because* the people did "X," *then* "Y" happened to them. The covenant is defined in the primary texts of the Hebrew scriptures: the books of Genesis-Kings, which form a unity, taking the world from Creation down to the Babylonian exile. For religious thinkers of Saul's and Jesus' time, the covenant was a flexible concept. This plasticity came from the Genesis-Kings text, wherein the covenant begins as unconditional, something Yahweh just does: "I do set my bow in the cloud and it shall be for a token of a covenant between me and the earth" (Gen. 9:13). Later, that version is displaced by a specific bargain made with Abram (whose name changes to Abraham), that in return for obedience, he shall become the progenitor of a great nation and that Yahweh and Abraham's "seed" shall have an everlasting relationship (Gen. 17:6–8). The seal of this bargain is a form of male genital mutilation, circumcision (Gen. 17:11). Later, a new version of the covenant is written, when Yahweh talks to Moses from a burning bush, and, later, on Mount Sinai, gives him the details of Torah, and eventually the 613 commandments of divine law. Still later, the covenant is again renegotiated: the holy mountain is moved from Sinai to Mount Zion, Jerusalem, the seat of the monarchy of King David, and the covenant becomes a deal with the kingdom of Judah.[4]

Anyone who knew the scriptures – and everything we know about Judahist religious thinkers of the early Common Era suggests they knew the scriptures very well indeed – understood that there were two imponderables behind the concept of covenant: (a) to whom did it apply? (b) what did it require? The answers to these questions had changed considerably over time (as the scriptures record) and, in the early Common Era, when there was no royal Davidic monarchy, the terms of definition obviously were open to discussion. That this is the case is indicated by the fact that one can instance literally dozens of attempts to redefine the covenant in the last century of the Second Temple era: these are found in contemporary documents among the Dead Sea Scrolls, the Pseudepigrapha, the Apocrypha, and, indeed, in the "Writings" section (the Kethuvim) of the Tanakh. Further, the Rabbinic Jewish literature that was codified in the years 200–600 CE carries references which, at minimum, suggest that in the first century of the Common Era a very lively debate was taking place concerning Halachic matters, the behavioural-legal requirements of the covenant with Yahweh. All of which is to say that when Saul (certainly) and Yeshua (probably) began reflecting on the big issues – what is the covenant and to whom does it apply and what are its central demands? – they were working within the tradition of Judahist thought which permitted wide-ranging speculations about the base-rules of the faith.

The primary scriptures of Judahism – Genesis through Kings – are not abstract or philosophical in nature, and Yahweh is defined not by syllogism, but by his behaviour. In practice, this means by how he behaves when making and enforcing his deal with the Chosen People. Here, it is crucial to realize that although Yahweh gets all the good lines in the Tanakh, in fact there are a fair number of deities whom the Chosen People also worship. These, of course, are sanitized as foreign gods by the post-exilic editors of the books of Genesis-Kings, and those who worship these "false gods" are reported as being punished. But anyone with a bit of shrewdness about human behaviour has to suspect that either the Chosen People were terrible spiritual recidivists, or that they actually paid deep respect to Asherah, Baal, and the various "El" gods who keep appearing in the scriptures. At minimum, for a long time Yahweh is distinguished not by being the only god, but by being simply the toughest deity on the block. He defeats the gods of Israel's enemies. By the beginning of the Common Era, he is presented as the only real god and, in the thinking of those Diaspora worshippers who were well read in Greek philosophy – such as the great Philo Judaeus – Yahweh increasingly becomes an abstraction.[5]

So, although the Yahweh-faith in its most conventional forms (such as embodied by the priestly establishment) did not encourage speculation about Yahweh's nature – obedience was the watchword – the very nature of the covenant with Him and the material contained in the earliest scriptures provided a subterranean mandate to try to define more accurately the nature of divinity. The key here is to realize the amazing range that speculation assumed in late Second Temple times: ranging from Hellenized theology that turned Yahweh virtually into a Platonic form, to a dark, weighty, demanding ascetic force worshipped by the desert communities of the Dead Sea region, to a boss-god, the number one deity of those Diaspora groups who came to some accommodation with local deities. (An instantial case is the post-exilic community of Elephantine in upper Egypt, which maintained its traditional Yahweh figure as god and in their temple also had a female god as consort).[6] And, as Salo Baron once noted, it was to be expected that in many Diaspora situations, the god of Judahism came to be thought of as more or less identical with the supreme local deity.[7] Now, undeniably, many (indeed, probably, most) of the speculations about the nature of Yahweh that proliferated in later Second Temple times were eventually suppressed by Rabbinic and by Christian authorities, and, in most cases, their nature went unrecorded. At the time, however, throughout the length and breadth of the Judahist world, people were discussing ideas and introducing practices that, after 70 CE, were to be declared literally unthinkable.

If many of the variations of Second Temple Judahism were determined by the varying ways religious thinkers responded to the classic questions concerning the nature of the covenant, the templates for some totally new ideas – responses to new questions – were being cast. Some of these ideas were taken up later by Christian and Jewish authorities (sometimes by both.) I say "new": here I mean ideas that (as far as presently available evidence indicates) either had not previously been part of the religious life of the Chosen People, or had, when redefined, become effectively new. These constructs were new to Judaism, not necessarily to other religions of the Near East. Most of them appear after the rededication of the Second Temple in 164 BCE, and the rise of the Hasmonean dynasty and the roughly 120 years of Judean independence. And in the early Common Era these ideas circulated and, like components strewn around the floor of some great do-it-yourself garage, they were put together in strange and wonderful combinations by religious inventors. Finally, in the first generation or two after the Temple was virtually levelled, the most serviceable of these new ideas were fit together with the most durable of those that came from early times (and, especially, those that are found in Genesis-Kings), to form the basis of two enduring religious systems, the Rabbinic Jewish faith and Christianity.

Before looking at those new concepts, some of which are quite dazzling, others merely puzzling, a warning is necessary: at this point we are on the edge of encountering one of the pivotal evidentiary questions that lies at the heart of any discussion of the historical Yeshua. The question is, what did Yeshua believe? The problem arises because almost all of the descriptions of his worldview were put together after 70 CE, at just the time the Yeshua-faith was emerging to become Christianity. So, just at the moment the Christian writers (especially the author-editors of the Gospels) were sorting out for their own Christian communities what they believed about Jesus-the-Christ and where this fit into the boundaries of the Yahweh-faith, they were simultaneously setting down authoritative versions of what Yeshua of Nazareth believed about the nature of the Almighty and about the universe, seen and unseen. One becomes very nervous about the final product when one notices a simple fact about the Gospels: the author-editors of the Four Gospels *never* overtly disagree with Yeshua. So, on the surface the situation is this: the Gospels agree with Yeshua. However, any alert historian will immediately suggest an alternative statement of the situation: Yeshua is made to agree with the author-editors of the Gospels. That, obviously, is a problem. Push it aside for the moment, but keep in mind that it is an issue that bedevils every quest for the man behind Christianity.

As an example of the way new (or in this case newish) ideas could circulate within later Second Temple Judaism, we should first look at the book of 4 Maccabees.[8] This is the narrative of the martyrdom in roughly 167 BCE, of two faithful followers of Yahweh, the one, an eighty-nine year old scribe,

Eleazar, and the others a mother and her seven sons. All in this case are killed by Antiochus IV Epiphanes, the psychotic Syrian despoiler of Jerusalem and profaner of the Temple. The book of 4 Maccabees is a beautifully polished piece of expository prose, written by a follower of Yahweh, whose first language was Greek, sometime between 63 BCE and 70CE. Whether his home was in Alexandria in Egypt or in Antioch in Syria has been a matter of scholarly debate; almost certainly it was not Jerusalem or any place in Palestine. The text is a surprising, seductive, very artful construction. It begins by announcing itself as a philosophical argument, of the graceful sort in which the author employs the word "I" without either embarrassment or being self-vaunting. Purely Greek, one might think. But, very quickly, the author breaks away: Reason is described as being the force that makes one choose a life of Wisdom, and that, the author argues, is exactly what the Law does. So, at minimum, the highest Greek virtues are equated with the highest Judahist virtues. Indeed, the rhetorical force of the early pages leaves the distinct impression that obedience to Yahweh's law is a subsuming virtue, encompassing, at least for the Chosen People, all the Greek virtues, and more.

This opening sequence established, the author steps back and, as if we were viewing a cinematic sequence shot with an ever-widening lens, we realize that his opening piece of Greek philosophy is really a plinth on which a set of compelling dramas are enacted. There are two martyrdoms. One of these is taken from 2 Maccabees (written pre-125 BCE) and describes in gruesome detail the killing of the eighty-nine-year-old scribe Eleazar by Antiochus Epiphanes, for his refusal to eat pork. Not only does the old man refuse, but when kindly guards suggest that he fake eating pork by substituting some other meat of his own choosing, he adamantly rejects the idea. He dies horribly on the rack (2 Macc. 6:18–31). In 4 Maccabees, this account is conflated with another tale of martyrdom taken from the same historical moment and same source (2 Macc. 7:1–41), that of seven brothers and their mother (all unnamed) tortured by Antiochus. These stories are run together in 4 Maccabees, expanded, and are outfitted with details of the tortures: they are so graphic as to pull one ineluctably forward, reading more and more, while being ashamed that one is doing so. It is a tiny masterpiece of the pornography of violence, and is the more compelling because the author creates dialogue for the martyrs and their tormentors, lines that are good enough to take from the page right into a Greek or Roman amphitheatre.

Yet, 4 Maccabees ends not with the symmetry of Greek expository prose (which, in the usual instance, would have required a return to high philosophical discussion), but rather with an invocation of a whole skein of faithful martyrs, children of Israel, who had maintained their faith in the Law of the Almighty and thus had controlled their own weaknesses and passions. The book's last word is simply "Amen."

The great achievement of 4 Maccabees as a piece of persuasion is that it turns upside-down what a Greek-influenced audience of the time (and a modern audience as well) would have expected. The path one expects is an argument that would justify following the Law of Moses because that Law was consonant with abstract Reason and Virtue in Greek philosophies. Instead, by slapping the reader violently with historical events, the point is made that actual (not abstract) good behaviour, actual control of the passions, actual rejection of the flesh's weakness, are primary, and that these are obtained by faithfulness to the Law. If the abstractions of Reason and Virtue possibly bring one to engage in the same kind of proper behaviour, then it is the Law of Moses that is accrediting the concepts of Reason and Virtue, not the other way around. Thus, the book of 4 Maccabees simultaneously implies the compatibility of the mind of Greece and the religion of Yahweh, while establishing the primacy of the latter.

Within this text – read it, it's too compelling to miss! – two ideas are taken for granted, ones that are not found in the original Genesis-Kings portion of the Old Testament, but which in the two or three centuries before the destruction of the Second Temple were taken up by a variety of Judahist religious groups. One of these is *the doctrine of the immortality of the individual soul*. Here the concept is unfocused (does the immortality of the soul imply the resurrection of the body?), but it unmistakably is affirmed. (See 4 Macc. 14:5–6, 16:13, 17:13, and especially 18:23–25.) Secondly, *the idea that individual human blood sacrifice could act as an antidote for the sin of others* is introduced. The martyrs became "as it were, a ransom for the sin of our nation" (4 Macc. 17:21). "Through the blood of these righteous ones and through the propitiation of their death the divine providence rescued Israel, which had been shamefully treated" (4 Macc. 17:22). The martyr Eleazar, just at the point of death as his flesh is being burned from his bones, turns his eyes heavenward and cries out, "You know, O God, that though I could have saved myself I am dying in these fiery torments for the sake of the Law. Be merciful to your people and let our punishment be a satisfaction on their behalf. Make my blood their purification and take my life as a ransom for theirs" (4 Macc. 6:27–29). This is not the same thing as the doctrine eventually created by Christianity – that of a divine man-god's blood being spilled for the salvation of individuals – but one senses what is in the air: among certain Judahists, concepts of ransoming from bondage, and of propitiation for sin through the spilling of blood, are flickering about, like St. Elmo's fire, from one religious group to another. Eventually this fire is captured, lightning in a bottle, and is used with great effect by the inventors of Christianity.

Earlier, I mentioned that the general trend within Judaism of the Second Temple era was towards an increasingly clear form of monotheism (all the time granting that significant factions of the Yahweh-faith had gotten off the historical train at points of their own choosing and were affirming earlier forms of the deity, as found in the books of Genesis-Kings). This trend towards an increasingly abstract definition of Yahweh's character had its advantages (it placed Yahweh above the vulgar fray of the pagan gods), but it was less satisfying emotionally to many (probably most) Yahweh-worshippers than the old days, when Yahweh was presented as an idiosyncratic, but awesome, personality. So, in what can be considered as the emotional equivalent of Newtonian physics, the thinkers, the religious inventors of the later Second Temple era, compensated for Yahweh's becoming increasingly remote by introducing an entire range of figures and concepts that were, if not palpable, at least conceivable in human terms.

Here, as an example, note the text of one of the lowest-temperature religious books to be produced in later Second Temple times, the Book of Jubilees. (The reader accepts, I hope, that the reasons I am using actual contemporary texts as illustrations of the points that I am arguing are, first, that they are hard evidence, and, second, that the texts are like the photographic plates used by subatomic physicists: they freeze in a moment in time sets of events that, over time, are in frenzied interaction.)

The Book of Jubilees deserves to be much better known than it is, particularly because it was widely used in later Second Temple times, and because it reveals certain very important points about the history of the period. Its title refers, in the first instance, to time that is metered in "jubilees," that is, periods of forty-nine years (seven "weeks" of seven years), that are followed in the fiftieth year by a major sabbatical. It is a big book and appropriately enough, it is divided into fifty chapters. Like many other essays in religious invention of this period, it adopts the outlines of an existing text, but Jubilees does this not so much to revise the content of the original text as to honour it. The Book of Jubilees, therefore, deals with historical material found in the Pentateuch, but begins by repairing what had long been one of the problems of the so-called Books of Moses: although from the mid-fifth century BCE onwards some (but not all) Judahists ascribed the first five books of the scriptures to Moses, references to Moses' alleged authorship were muddy at best within the text. The key invention of the Book of Jubilees takes care of that problem immediately. The author begins with Moses going up the mountain to obtain the stone tablets from Yahweh and then he has Moses spend forty days and forty nights in the presence of the Almighty. God tells him, "Set your mind on everything which I shall tell you on this mountain, and write it in a book ..." (Jub. 1:5).[9] Later, the Almighty deputes an angel to write down for Moses the history of the world from creation onwards (Jub. 1:27). This is a bit confusing, but the sum is simple enough: this book, the Book of Jubilees, comes directly from Moses, for either it was dictated to him by Yahweh or it was dictated by God to an angel who then passed the book on to Moses.

Therefore the credentials of the Book of Jubilees – its provenance, as it were – are much stronger than those of the Pentateuch.

Put so explicitly, this implied claim sounds shrill and slightly egomaniacal. Yet, in tone, the Book of Jubilees is remarkably matter-of-fact and almost devoid of rhetorical excesses. The new beliefs it introduces are limited. Whoever wrote it was a good tinkerer, a minor historical revisionist, but not a great inventor.[10]

The importance of Jubilees lies in the way it forces us to read other texts. The Book of Jubilees was excluded both from the Hebrew Bible and from the Christian deutero-canonical writings. It was preserved on the periphery of Christianity, the only full version being in Ethiopic, which itself was a translation of a Greek version that was taken from a Hebrew original.[11] With that skein of translation, and with the book's being preserved in full only in Christian sources, as an indicator of Judahist thought in the later Second Temple period the text might well be treated with suspicion. Yet, portions of the Hebrew original turned up in several of the caves near Qumran[12] and the Hebrew fragments correspond surprisingly closely to the Ethiopic version.[13] This suggests that the Christian curators of pre-Christian Jewish manuscripts took their responsibilities very seriously. Until the 1950s, the Book of Jubilees was considered by most Jewish scholars to be a Christian forgery. Yet, it was found in five of the eleven Qumran caves, which means that it was among the most-copied and widely-distributed of the extra-biblical manuscripts in the Qumran collections.[14] Further, the idea of the Book of Jubilees (and, therefore, one infers, some form of the text itself) was known to Paul and to the authors of Luke, Acts, James, Hebrews, and 2 Peter.[15] Indeed, outside the Pentatcuch and the Prophets, Jubilees may have been among the most widely read Judahist texts in the early years of the Common Era. (Although the Book of Jubilees is cited in the Damascus Rule of the Essenes[16] this does not mean that it was a document of any specific religious party.)

The author, it seems, is a learned and concerned member of the Judahist community, who is at peace with his co-religionists on most matters. So, if we juxtapose the calm and steady tone of the Book of Jubilees with the fact that the volume was very widely read, and therefore represents something more than a product of a single sect, then we have something unusual: a quietly normal piece of religious writing, produced by a well-informed, concerned, but not agitated, follower of Yahweh who lives in the home land. Yet note what he is willing to do, and without hesitation or embarrassment: *rewrite what was supposedly the most sacred, most inviolable parts of the Hebrew scriptures*. He does nothing less than correct the Books of Moses. Jubilees is, therefore, a Parallel-Torah, superior in authority (because it actually was transmitted, so the text says, by the hands of Moses) to the older one.

This casts a very large shadow over the traditional idea that the Hebrew scriptures (at least the Pentateuch and the Prophets) were inviolable sacred writ well before the Common Era. The Book of Jubilees (and several of the other texts I have discussed in *Surpassing Wonder*) indicate that one could be sharply critical of the Pentateuch and the Prophets and still remain within the fold. It is as if the several re-inventors of Judahist historical traditions all subscribed to the admixture of old loyalty and new revisionisms that is asserted in the opening words of one of the great inventive documents in the English language, the Prayer Book of 1549: "there was never any thing by the wit of man so well devised, or so sure established, which in continuance of time hath not been corrupted." Since time's passage corrupted things, re-invention and revision purified.

In Jubilees, this re-invented Book of Moses, the author had two radical revisions in mind, one involving law in the narrow sense, and the other accomplishing a theodicy. The first of these, a Parallel-Torah, is intended to turn the old Torah only a few degrees and this according to a restricted priestly interest. The usual title of the book, "Jubilees," points to this material. The reference to the Jubilees year comes from a Pentateuchal text (see Lev. 25:8–10), and refers to a major sabbatical to be taken every fiftieth year (after seven *x* seven years). Clearly, the author is concerned with liturgical time-keeping. The *idée fixe* that runs through Jubilees is the necessity of sorting out the Judahist religious calendar so that the various major religious festivals (Passover, Atonement, Unleavened Bread, Tabernacles and Weeks) all fall on the same date and on the same day of the week each year. The author believes that these festivals were created by the patriarchs (this is a new invention, which the Pentateuch does not contain). The author of Jubilees makes it a religious imperative to reject the lunar religious calendar (which had a 354-day year and therefore no regularity of days of the week) and replace it with a solar calendar of 364, which was divisible by seven into fifty-two weeks, and therefore was regular.[17] The author of Jubilees cares greatly about this matter, for he has Yahweh tell Moses to inform the people that unless the solar calendar is employed "… they will mix everything, a holy day as profaned and a profane one for a holy day, because they will set awry the months and sabbaths and feasts and jubilees" (Jub. 6:37). Probably to most present-day readers, the details of liturgical time-keeping seem of secondary importance, if not downright petty, but that casts into even sharper relief this fact: that it was permissible in later Second Temple Judaism to further a devotional viewpoint by revising the basic historical narrative of the Chosen People. And it is hard to think of any bigger revision within the tradition than inventing words of Yahweh to Moses.

The priestly figure behind the Book of Jubilees also rewrote the history of the Chosen People, from Creation to the Exodus, to deal with a matter that he never would have dared to formulate explicitly. It is an issue so flesh-searing that even Philo, the first person in the Judahist tradition to handle abstract ideas in a theological fashion, did not touch it. This is *the issue of the origin of evil* and the ineluctable question that follows from considering it: the nature of Yahweh. The problem that the inventor of Jubilees has is that he cannot believe that evil came into the world by an act of the Almighty, or that Yahweh would be involved in specific actions that tempted the Chosen People into infidelity, or that Yahweh would act in a way that was precipitate, high-handed, and callous.

The primary Judahist texts, the Genesis-Kings unity, deal with this potential problem with straightforward ease. They report that Yahweh acts as his own agent and they show him doing all sorts of things that are unreasonable, and by any rational standard, unnecessary. The Yahwist tradition, as articulated in Genesis-Kings, does not require that one believe Yahweh is both all-powerful and all-good. He can, at times, be a very nasty piece of work indeed, but he still is our God: that is the message.

By the time the Book of Jubilees is written, this is no longer universally acceptable. Many followers of Yahweh *now demand that he be both God and good*. The inventor of the Book of Jubilees gets Yahweh partially off the hook by introducing a cast of characters whose existence limits the Almighty's direct agency in the world. Therefore, he no longer can be charged with acting capriciously or callously (Jubilees avoids the question of who is ultimately responsible for the action of this new cast of characters; the book's inventor is satisfied to get Him off the primary charge). The *new set of intermediary figures are angels, and their opposite, demons*. Angels certainly are found in the primary text of Judahism, Genesis-Kings, but there, for the most part, the Almighty runs his own errands. However, in the Book of Jubilees, angels become the agents of Yahweh's will, doing everything from bearing messages to controlling the forces of nature to interfering on earth to protect certain chosen individuals from mishaps. That is half of the equation: moral physics dictates that if there be angels, then there must be demons. They too are found in the primary narrative of the ancient Hebrews, but there they are circumscribed in their behaviour and eccentric in characteristic.[18] By contrast, in Jubilees, the demons are a unified type and they act in the world in a manner antipathetic to the way the angels behave. This means that not God, but they, are immediately responsible for the evil that befalls mankind.

There is more. The symmetry that Jubilees creates concerning angels and demons requires playing out on a higher plane. And here the inventor of Jubilees introduces Satan, although by another name. This is "Mastema," who is chief of the evil spirits. This figure is not found in the Hebrew scriptures, at least not as a figure who heads the forces of evil in both the visible and the invisible world and is an implacable foe of Yahweh and almost his equal.[19]

Jubilees is the earliest documented case of *Satan becoming a specific and powerful individual*, one who has an invisible army that fights against Yahweh and his invisible army.[20] Mastema (introduced in Jubilees 10:8) becomes the general of the army of evil. It is he who plots the test of Abraham, by inducing Yahweh to tell Abraham that he must offer up his son Isaac (Jub. 17:16). And it was Mastema who hardened the hearts of the Egyptians during Israel's captivity and facilitated the Egyptians' pursuit of the children of Israel as they left their place of bondage (47:9–12). Such a radical rewriting of the history of the Chosen People frees Yahweh from the responsibility of having to arrange the Egyptian bondage and similar events, as is reported in the Pentateuch. Thus, a semi-theodicy is accomplished.

It is only "semi" because Mastema and his demons engage in evil by permission of Yahweh. This is explicitly stated in Jubilees, not merely a point of inference. Mastema received his influence only by directly petitioning the Almighty. As "chief of the spirits" he was concerned by the possibility that Yahweh might bind up all the demons and dispose of them. He petitioned, "O Lord, Creator, leave some of them before me, and let them obey my voice ..." (Jub. 10:7–8). The Lord replied by sending nine-tenths of the demons to "the place of judgment" and leaving the remainder to serve alongside Mastema in his work of corrupting the sons of men (Jub. 10:9). Even if this revision of the Pentateuch leaves Yahweh with clean hands, in the sense that He no longer directly inveigles the Chosen People to commit evil, He nevertheless has given licence for evil to exist.

The inventor of Jubilees is no theologian: the concept of theology as a form of thought detached from narrative was totally alien to him and to his readers. Therefore, he uses the only tool that he has in his workshop to try to fix the machinery: he continues to invent new historical narrative, and in the middle of his discussion of the life of Abraham he briefly extends his narrative into the future. He describes a future generation that will arise and states that a great judgement will follow. In the end, there will be "no Satan and no evil one" (Jub. 23:29). This is not an apocalyptic passage, but rather a projection into a narrative future of a partial solution to the problem of evil that exists, and cannot be resolved by the author of Jubilees through his use of a narrative of time past. The book, though of limited success as a theodicy, stands "at the head of a mighty tradition that was to subsist for some two thousand years, and still subsists today,"[21] an initial milestone in the introduction of the figure of the devil into Jewish and Christian cultures.

The Book of Jubilees' rewriting of crucial portions of the Pentateuch is an example of the willingness within some sectors of later Second Temple Judaism to treat the primary history of the Chosen People as something to be revered, but also something that was plastic and transformable. One could easily produce a dozen solid examples of this practice from pre-70 CE times, and there are several dozen more examples that are as yet unsubstantiated in their dating, but which are potentially within the same period of origin. The most important of the historical inventions that can firmly be attributed to the period before the destruction of the Second Temple are as follows: a re-worked Pentateuch found in the Qumran caves, the Apocryphon of Joseph; the Genesis Apocryphon, a radical revision of the Creation story and the patriarchal narratives; the Book of Enoch, discussed below; the Book of Giants, which deals with a period when imperfect angels mated with human beings and produced giants on the earth; the very fragmentary Book of Noah; the Testament of the Twelve Patriarchs, said to be the last words of each of the sons of Jacob, a document which exists in a full version containing later Christian interpolations, but which also is found in fragments in pre-Christian versions in the Qumran caves; four books that either purport to have been written by Moses or to capture the teachings of Moses not found elsewhere, and known as the Words of Moses, Pseudo-Moses, the Apocryphon of Moses, and Pseudo-Moses Apocalypse; the Letter of Jeremiah, an item of 100 BCE or earlier that purports to be a missive sent by the prophet to the Babylonian exiles; Third Maccabees, of approximately the same period, an intermingling of various biblical traditions with more recent matter concerning the Diaspora people in Alexandria; Pseudo-Philo, an early Common Era retelling of the primary history of the Chosen People, from Adam to David; the Lives of the Prophets.

Perhaps the most memorable texts to develop within later Second Temple Judahism were those that combined *visions of the heavens, of the future, and of divine imposition of future righteousness* – in other words, *the genre of apocalypse*. The only example of this form that was accepted into the Old Testament was the Book of Daniel, the heart of which was written in response to rapine by Antiochus Epiphanes, referred to earlier in relation to 4 Maccabees. The text circulated widely in the world of Second Temple Judaism (several copies were in the Qumran library, for example), and it is clearly influential in forming the New Testament view of future-time, especially as found in the Book of Revelation. Crucially, although Daniel is a one-of-a-kind production within the Tanakh, other apocalyptic texts swirled through the world of Judaism in the time of Saul and Yeshua. Sometimes the various apocalyptic texts interacted with each other, thus indicating that apocalypticism was not a secret, mystery-genre, but part of a very public array of speculations. Here the most revealing exhibit is the Book of Enoch (sometimes called "First Enoch"), which is a rolling anthology of Second Temple apocalyptic visions: it is divided into five separate books and contains a dozen distinct apocalypses.[22] These date from roughly 300 BCE to 70 CE, and all of the material was part of the thought-world of the early Common Era. Crucially, the later portions of the Book of Enoch interact with the Book of Daniel.

Portions of Daniel bring to the fore the concept of *the resurrection of each dead individual and the eternal judgement of each person*. (See Dan. 12:1–2.) This is very different from the predominant view of the Old Testament which propounds the concept of the collective judgement of the Chosen People, which occurs in real-time, not in an indeterminate future-time. Whether or not most adherents of the Yahweh-faith accepted this new view, even as late as the mid-first century of the Common Era, is impossible to determine. A common-place historical belief is that the Pharisees believed in the resurrection of the dead (and thus, presumably, in the eternal judgement of each soul), and that the Sadducees did not.

One of the most interesting parts of the Book of Enoch is that a big segment of it – the so-called "Book of Similitudes" – tries to complete a dramatic scene that the author of Daniel leaves unfinished.[23] This occurs in chapter seven of Daniel, where a transcendent judicial-monarchical figure appears, "whose garment was white as snow, and the hair of his head like the pure wool: his throne was like the fiery flame, and his wheels as burning fire" (Dan. 7:9). This is the "Ancient of Days," and he has the ultimate dominion over all peoples, nations and languages, forever (Dan. 7:14). That is final enough, but not sufficiently detailed. We want to know more, so the Book of Similitudes (which comprises chapters 37–71, inclusive, of the Book of Enoch) proceeds to tell us what happened before, during, and after that scene in Daniel when the Ancient of Days appears.

What the deeply mystical inventor of Similitudes does with the components that Daniel has left to him to work with is quite astounding. To fill us in about the Ancient of Days, the author blends together motifs that are found in Daniel and in three other major sources and adds his own original twist. One of these sources is Psalm 2, wherein Yahweh, on his heavenly throne, laughs at the world's rulers and sends his adopted son to reign on Zion, his holy hill. The Book of Isaiah (specifically, First Isaiah), chapter eleven provides another source of predictions of a future kingdom to be set up "out of the stem of Jesse" (Is. 11:1). This nationalistic prophecy puts forward the case for the primacy of Judah and of Jerusalem within the Hebrew polity after the Assyrian conquest of the tribes of Israel. It is a wonderfully rich prophecy in its visual imagery and it contains the famous image of the wolf lying down with the lamb. A third source is Second Isaiah (Isaiah 40–55), specifically chapter forty-nine, a prophecy concerning the restoration of the Chosen People after the Babylonian exile. It has a "Redeemer of Israel," a "Holy One," as the active agent of Yahweh's will. However, merely parsing its grammar of invention would obscure the explosive alchemy of the Book of Similitudes. Nothing could be more misleading than a clinical description of the work: a set of four parables each containing several visions granted to Enoch, filling in many of the lacunae left by Daniel, chapter seven.

That is accurate enough, but it is akin to describing James Joyce's *Finne-gans Wake* as a very long Irish short story about the history of the world from the fall of Adam to the resurrection of mankind. The Similitudes has a cast of characters that includes every higher entity, whether human being or angel or demon, who ever has existed. The human multitude alone consists of "ten million times ten million souls" (Enoch 40:1). They stand before the throne at judgement day. They serve as a massive Greek chorus, as a resonating board for the pronouncements of the major players, and as a pliable medium upon which the powerful characters work their will.

The distant comparison of the Book of Similitudes and *Finnegans Wake* is apposite, not only because each starts before human time, but because each is a cyclical composition. Indeed, Joyce would argue that *Finnegans Wake* doesn't start or end; it just keeps going round and round. And that's also the way the Book of Similitudes works. Although one has to read such inventions linearly (one word follows another on the page), in fact the pictures that emerge are not like frames in a cinema film, but, instead are more like a deck of photographs that can be endlessly reshuffled to give a different story each time. In the case of the Book of Similitudes, the characters in one vision often seem to show up in another, under a different name. But it may only seem this way, because the inventor of these visions does not make equilibrations or specify identities across visions. So we are forever on tenterhooks as we see characters tumble from one gyring vision to another. Or do we? And the same holds for "plot," if that is the correct word. The several visions ascribed to Enoch in the Book of Similitudes can neither be taken as forming a sequential series of events, nor as happening coterminously; and one cannot declare them to be either mutually incompatible or to be capable of harmonization. At one moment they are one thing, then, another.

Consider the characters. They include two fairly off-hand mentions of Messiah (Enoch 48:10 and 52:4), in which Moshiah is a figure of authority, but passive. The really active figures are, first, the archangels: Michael, of course, and Raphael, Gabriel and Phanuel (En. 54:6, 60:4, 71:8–10). Among other tasks, they are responsible for throwing evil kings and potentates into the fiery furnace at the end of time, a prototype of hell. Second, myriad good angels serve under the generalship of these archangels. Third, however, the figure of Satan is explicitly introduced as a primary figure of evil (En. 53:4). This figure, almost equal in strength to Yahweh, is a character we saw earlier in the Book of Jubilees, which almost certainly was known to the inventor of the Book of Similitudes. Satan is a relatively new invention as far as the tradition of Yahweh is concerned, for in the Hebrew scriptures he is a subordinate and biddable messenger of the Almighty. Not here. Whether or not Satan is the same entity as "the Evil One" (En. 69:15) is, in the fashion characteristic of the Book of Similitudes, left to the reader to determine. The text lets one have it either way. Fourth, no fewer than twenty-one evil angels are named. They have deliciously mephitic names, noisome of sulphur: Kokba'el, Azaz'el, Baragel, and so on. Part of their noxiousness is that their very names involve incorporation of the god-name "El." Fifth, each of these chiefs of the fallen angels has a phalanx of fallen angels at his command (En. 69:1–3). Added to this, sixth, is a female monster named Leviathan who lives in the ocean (En. 60:7–8) and, seventh, a male monster, called Behemoth who lives in an invisible desert located east of the Garden of Eden (En. 60:8).

Opposed to the forces of evil is an eighth set of characters (in addition to Messiah and to the angels already mentioned). These are power figures on the side of the light: "the Righteous One" (En. 38:1–2), the "Son of Man" (En. 46:3), and "the Elect One" (En. 49:2). Now, when turning from one vision to another, it is impossible to tell whether or not these are names for the same figure or for someone entirely different. The absence of verbal equilibrations as between these figures means that the names, and the association of those names, tumble from one vision to another. Momentarily, they juxtapose themselves so that, for example, "the Righteous One" and "the Son of Man" seem to be synonymous, but then the rhetorical drum turns another rotation, another vision starts, and the two names come to represent separate, entirely different entities. The same things happen with the God-figures who comprise the ninth bundle of characters. Yahweh is not present in the text under that name, which is hardly surprising, given that the text has been preserved in Ethiopic. However, there are various figures who could be the Almighty. These include the "Lord of the Spirits, who created the distinction between light and darkness" (En. 41:8); the "Antecedent of Time" (En. 47:3 and 55:1), who is directly derivative from the "Ancient of Days" of the Book of Daniel, and the similar figure, the "Before-Time," who at one point is identified with the "Lord of the Spirits" (En. 48:2). All these god-figures seem consonant with each other, if not quite congruent, in contrast to the figures of the Son of Man, the Messiah, the Chosen One, and the Elect One, which are never really joined.

The series of visions in which all these characters play their parts is cyclical, in the sense that the visions circle back, one on the other. Each vision provides its own distinct answer to the question, "what really happened in Daniel, chapter seven?" For modern readers, the most difficult aspects of the Book of Similitudes to come to terms with are (1) its assumption that one can start any place in the book and read one's way around it; or, indeed, that major items can be read in random order, an assumption, incidentally, that holds for Similitudes' cross-time counterpart, *Finnegans Wake*; (2) its assumption that even as one reads a specific vision, one has knowledge of all the others; and (3) its assumption that the cumulative effect of reading all of these visions is not hindered, but indeed augmented, by the ambiguous relationship between the varied visions and that any contradictions are not distractions, but are enrichments, for they are indications of the multiplicity of truth granted to those who experience (not merely read: experience) the book.

This carousel of apocalyptic tales operates on a time scale that is adapted at one end from the Book of Genesis (the tales start before human time) and at the other end from Daniel, and perhaps other apocalypses that are now lost, and these go past the end of time. What is striking, and new, is the ground-base belief that the Almighty (whatever he may be called in the specific vision in question) not only knows everything, but has known everything since before the beginning of time. (See esp. En. 39:11.) Further, the very act of knowing every occurrence from before time to past the end of time means that the Almighty is himself eternal: "There is no such thing as non-existence before him" (En. 39:11). This is very close to being a theological argument, although it is not articulated as such. It means that the Almighty is (a) omniscient, (b) the ground of existence in which all things, good and evil, exist, and (c) it implies a pre-determinism of all life, angelic, demonic, and human, from before time to the days which follow the end of time. The Book of Similitudes, in addition to being a very complex body of literature, is well in advance of most pieces of Judahist writings of the late Second Temple era in its theological sophistication.

All that recognized, forget the analysis. Pick up a copy of the text and whirl with it until it takes you into the Dervish-like state of enlightenment that it commands. Let yourself be carried off by the "wind vehicle" which takes you to the west, where you can see all the secret things of heaven. See there the great mountains of copper, of silver, of lead, and of coloured metals (En. 52:1–4). Fly across the "deep valley with a wide mouth," where all the human race brings gifts and tributes, but yet the valley does not become full (En. 53:1–2). Observe Michael, Raphael, Gabriel, and Phanuel seize the wicked rulers of the earth and throw them into the furnace of hell (En. 54:1–6). See those who were oppressors on earth drown by rising flood waters (En. 54:10). Spin around again and observe, in light so bright that it scarcely can be faced, the righteous ones passing before the Lord of the Spirits and on to eternal life (En. 58:1–4). Spin back before time and observe the storerooms where hail, mist, and wind are kept. Observe the storeroom of the sun and the moon, from which, with each cycle diurnal and monthly, they exit and then return (En. 41:1–5). Spin again and see the Son of Man who will open all the hidden storerooms, both physical and spiritual, and who will depose kings from their thrones and crush the teeth of sinners (En. 46:3–5). Spin, spin, there is so much more to experience in the cycles that flash by: Sheol being emptied with the resurrection of the dead (En. 51:1–2), angels preparing ropes that will hoist the righteous to heaven (En. 61:1–3), and the ultimate light-refracting structure, a multi-crystal structure built into the heavens, with tongues of living fire issuing forth light from the interstices, where one crystal abuts its neighbour (En. 71:5–6). Spin, spin, spin!

And then, finally, crash to earth. The apocalyptic ecstasy cannot be long sustained, even in a masterpiece such as the Book of Similitudes. The visions are too demanding, our senses too prone to overload. We have to be protected from an intoxication from which some devotees never return.

But consider what the Book of Similitudes means to the history of late Second Temple Judahism. It suggests that in at least one stratum of the Yahweh-faith, a vocabulary, a set of symbols, a proto-typology, and a set of beyond-time narratives were emerging: these were based on scriptural origin-als, but were much richer in their inventiveness than anything we have yet encountered in the later Second Temple era. If we can momentarily put the brakes on the carousel that is the Book of Similitudes, we can see that there are many components of the sort that will later be used by Rabbinic Judaism and by Christianity to develop their own official views of what happened be-fore time began and what will happen when time comes to an end. I strongly suspect that there were other, parallel, now-lost apocalypses in circulation prior to the end of the Second Temple period. It is hard to see how something so evocative as the Book of Similitudes, so soundly based on a deep bank of apocalyptic motifs, could be a one-of-a-kind production. The Book of Simil-itudes may have been the best of its sort (we never will know, really), but it must have come from a rich tradition of para-biblical invention. To find a document such as the Book of Similitudes and to declare it to be singular, and thus interesting but of limited consequence, would be the equivalent, say, of discovering a full version of *Carmen* in a musical culture which previous scholars had believed knew only plain-song, and therefore dismissing it as anomalous. I think the Book of Similitudes testifies that there existed in the general religious environment of late Second Temple Judahism a bank of apocalyptic concepts in addition to, and different from, the rather limited range of constructs we find in the Tanakh, where the Book of Daniel is the only true apocalyptic conduit.

2

Saul and Yeshua, then, lived in interesting religious times, and so did anyone within the disparate Judahist tradition who paid any attention to the increas-ing variegation of the Yahweh-faith. Reflect on some of the new ideas – com-ponents that could be used in making a wide variety of belief-systems – which were being forcefully articulated in the early Common Era, the time of Yeshua and Saul: the doctrine of the immortality of the individual soul; the concept of the resurrection of the dead and the eternal judgment of the indi-vidual; the idea that individual human blood sacrifice could act as an antidote for the sins of other human beings; a need for theodicy, the explanation of how evil comes into the universe; the demand that God be not only great, but good; a new set of intermediary figures, angels and demons, now active, unlike their largely-passive position in the Hebrew scriptures; Satan (under various names) becomes a specific and powerful individual, unlike his character in the Tanakh; the genre of the apocalyptic flourishes, with visions of the heavens and of the imposition of divine righteousness in the future world. And all of this intermixed with the myriad age-old possibilities that stem from the primary narrative of the Chosen People: the protean nature of Yahweh, and the issues of *halachah*, the almost infinite number of ways to interpret the 613 commandments of the Hebrew scriptures.

Rich, indeed, so rich that we need to be very clear what our recognizing the spiritual excitement of Yeshua and Saul's world does *not* mean. First, I am not suggesting that anyone in the Second Temple era bought into all of these new ideas, or even all of the old ones. They were available, but were put together in hundreds of different ways, some components being used in one system, others in another; and even when the same components were employed, the actual final piece of religious machinery could vary greatly. Second, the texts that I have cited are not put forward as sources for later developments (although they well may have contributed somewhat); they are put forward as particularly clear examples of the array of hundreds of ideationally-rich texts from the later Second Temple period which we know from the surviving Dead Sea Scrolls, the Nag Hammadi finds (the large Gnostic library discovered in 1945), the Pseudepigrapha and the Apocrypha, and which, in turn, are only a tiny proportion of what must have been an exponentially greater flood of innovative religious production. Remember: what we do have survived a devastating war (that of 66–73 CE), nearly twenty centuries of neglect, and in some cases systematic suppression by post-70 CE Christian and Jewish authorities who were very concerned with cleaning up the sight-lines for their respective religious pedigrees.

At this point in our conspectus of the religious world of Saul and of Yeshua, it is wise to turn down the temperature slightly. The ideational units that we have been discussing were red-hot, high-intensity items that apparently were well-known (if not necessarily accepted) by many different Judahist groups of the time. Here we should examine some ideas that, though potentially explosive, were low temperature, by virtue of their being low-intensity, vaguely-defined and handled by only a small minority of the multiple Judaisms that proliferated in the Second Temple era. That these concepts eventually came to be employed by Christianity, as it wrote out its own scriptures after the great Destruction of 70 CE, should not make us read backwards into the early Common Era either a ubiquity or a prepotency for these ideas.

The hardest concept for persons brought up in the Christian tradition to deal with is Messiah. The term *MSYH*, which the Masoretic Text indicates was pronounced, roughly "Mosheeah," is often transliterated as "Mosiah." (There are wars among modern Jewish groups about which is the right

English-language transliteration; in choosing "Moshiah," I am not making any judgement as between them, merely choosing a reasonably accurate version.) Moshiah appears thirty-eight times in the Hebrew Bible (that is, in the Old Testament), and means "Anointed One." Of course there is no capitalization in the Hebrew text, but it is fair to read Moshiah as "Anointed One." Also, Moshiah usually appears without an article in front of the term. Translators from Hebrew frequently use either the general "an Anointed One" or "the Anointed One" to move the term into idiomatic English. However, in the latter case – when a definite article is employed – it most emphatically must *not* be taken as meaning "*the* Anointed One" in some transcendent sense. If "the Anointed One" is employed, it means: the one person appointed at a specific time for a specific task. The reference is to a precise situation, not to a history-transcendant typological figure.[24]

The litmus indicator here is that thirty-six of the thirty-eight times Moshiah appears in the King James translation of the Tanakh, it is used correctly to mean "Anointed One." However, in two instances – Daniel 9:25 and 9:26 – a new word suddenly appears: the term "Messiah." This is a bastardized form of the Greek "Messias" which was created in the late 1550s by the translators of the Geneva Bible.[25] Neither "Messias" nor "Messiah" functions as a neutral transliteration of Moshiah. "Anointed One" would have done quite adequately in the King James rendering of the Book of Daniel; here the insertion of the new term "Messiah" perforce implies the insertion of a new idea into the Hebrew text, and one alien to the original. It is nothing less than a rewriting of the Hebrew text, to insert a much later idea, a reference to Yeshua of Nazareth whom Christians define as Jesus-*the*-Messiah, or Jesus-the-Christ.

Were this not the King James Bible, one could ignore the mistranslation, or even enjoy it. However, before noting the marvellous creativity in the Christian invention of Yeshua as "the Messiah," we need a baseline of judgement determined by what the term Moshiah meant when it was used in pre-Christian times. Here the probative material is found in virtually every other English-language translation of the Bible. Therein, Moshiah is called "Anointed One" in most cases. This contradiction to the KJB translation of Daniel 9:25 and 9:26 is found in the following translations of the late nineteenth and the twentieth centuries: the New International Bible, the Living Bible, the Revised Standard Version (various editions), the Tanakh of the Jewish Publication Society, the Anchor Bible, the Jerusalem Bible, the New English Bible, the Revised English Bible, the Modern Readers' Bible, and one could go on. The point is that the King James Bible got it very wrong, and later translations, though they get the translation right, are still overshadowed by that greatest of seventeenth-century texts.

In the Book of Daniel, the apocalyptic sections concerning the "seventy weeks" is not about the coming of a Messiah in the Christian sense, but about an Anointed One, a purely Judahist idea. It is hardly a recondite piece of exegesis to note that in Daniel's chapter nine, the Anointed One does not exist except as a conjoint entity with the Temple. This is not to make the simplistic statement that the reference is to a holder of the High Priestship, although that is part of the reference. In fact, the reference to an Anointed One works only when there is a High Priest within the context of the Temple. Moshiah in Daniel's "seventy weeks," then, personifies the situation in which a covenantal relationship between Yahweh and his people will flourish: when the liturgical-sacrificial system operates with its two major components intact, an authentic High Priest, and a purified, daily-sacrificing Temple. Moshiah here is the divinely sanctioned system whereby the Chosen People and Yahweh touch and mutually affirm their covenant.

Putting aside, then, the "Messiah" reference in the KJB version of Daniel, the question remains as to whether or not there is any reference in the Old Testament to Messiah, in the sense that Christians later use the concept, to mean a redeemer or saviour both of individual souls and of the righteous as a collective group. No. There are passages that are later re-invented (and quite brilliantly) by the creators of Christianity, but in the Tanakh they do not carry those meanings.

In those parts of the Tanakh that predate the Maccabean revolt (that is to say, almost all the Hebrew scriptures), the term Moshiah (anointed one) is used in three very tight contexts. One of these applications is to kings. For example, King Saul is referred to as Moshiah of Yahweh (I Sam. 12:3) and King David is described as Moshiah of the God of Jacob (2 Sam. 23:1).[26] In this, and other royal usages, the monarch's being anointed signifies that he is a servant of Yahweh. That this use of Moshiah has no reference either to Moshiah being a redeemer or to his being an apocalyptic leader of the Chosen People is indicated in Second Isaiah (that is, Isaiah 40–55), wherein the phrase "Moshiah of Yahweh" refers to King Cyrus of Persia who grants the children of Israel a boon (Isaiah 45:1). Secondly, Anointed One is used to refer to both the holder of priestly offices in general (Leviticus 4:3 applies the term Anointed One to the generic office of priest) and more importantly, to the High Priest (as the Book of Daniel exemplifies). Thirdly, Psalm 105:15 issues a warning:

Do not touch My anointed ones;
Do not harm My Prophets.   (Jewish Pub. Soc.)

This comes close to equating the prophets with the several Anointed Ones.

One cannot avoid the conclusion that, although the concept of Messiah is present in the Hebrew scriptures, it is there only as a limited and peripheral idea. In each of its usages Moshiah implies a person anointed either by, or on behalf of, Yahweh as a specific office holder or a person with a specific task, such as prophesying. Certainly, Messiah is not a major part of the Hebrew scriptures, much less their ideational spine. Moshiah is not at any point associated with a future redeemer or saviour.

However, because Moshiah as a concept became fairly significant in later Rabbinical Judaism, and became absolutely central to Christianity, strenuous efforts have been made to find Messianic references in places where the word "Moshiah" is not employed. (One of the most famous of these passages in the Old Testament, where theologically-determined exegetes wish to find Messiah, even though the term is not used, is the "Suffering Servant" passage in Second Isaiah.) Here the central point is one of method and of logic. It hardly seems sensible to deal with Messiah in the Hebrew scriptures by refusing to accept those places where Moshiah is actually used as a term to refer to kings, priests, and prophets, and yet look for the "real" references to Messiah only in places where the scriptures do not introduce the concept. Granted, there are such things as sub-texts and arguments-from-silence, but the forcing of Moshiah into places where the writers did not use the term is surpassing strange. As William Scott Green has noted, this forced exegesis seems to "suggest that the best way to learn about the Messiah in ancient Judaism is to study texts in which there is none."[27]

Yet, if Messiah has little to do with the eventually-canonical Hebrew scriptures, conceivably the idea could be central to the later development of Judahist extra-canonical thought, during the years between the Maccabean revolt and the destruction of the Second Temple. And, perhaps, this could occur even in the sense that is totally absent in the Old Testament, of Moshiah being a future redeemer. Perhaps. Let us look first at the biggest body of data, the Pseudepigrapha, the Apocrypha and the Dead Sea Scrolls.

Although the case is slightly stronger here than in the Tanakh, it still is not very powerful. For instance, if one takes as a data base all the (as yet) known extra-biblical Judahist writings composed after 167 BCE and before 70 CE, other than the Dead Sea Scrolls, only two documents refer to Messiah.[28] One of these is the portion of the Book of Enoch that we viewed earlier, called the Book of Similitudes (chapters 37–71). This, most scholars believe, is the last portion of the Enoch-anthology to have been written. In two places (48:10 and 52:4), the term Messiah is used, but in a strangely subordinate form: as if referring to an archangel rather than to an independent figure. In the first instance, a judgement is announced against those who "have denied the lord of the Spirits and his Messiah," and in the second, an angel explains to Enoch that at the final judgement Yahweh will cast a number of judgements, which will "happen by authority of his Messiah …" Apparently, in the latter case, Moshiah would not be an active participant in events, but rather, the guarantor of their authenticity.

In the extra-canonical Songs of Solomon, hymns number 17 and 18, there is found praise of "the Lord Messiah," a future super-king of the Davidic line who will destroy Judah's enemies and purge Jerusalem. Whether the voice here is closer to old-time classical prophecy or to later Second Temple apocalyptic rhetoric, is open to question. The clear point is that Messiah is a king who will reign in the manner of a powerful and righteous monarch. This is not a piacular or redemptive figure, but an Anointed One, in the same sense that King David was.

That is all. Moshiah as a proper noun does not appear elsewhere, although the verb form "to anoint" occurs on a few occasions. If Messiah as a concept was central to the thinking of the followers of Yahweh in the late Second Temple era, they found very effective ways to keep this a secret.

The Qumran Scrolls are equally revealing, and also in a negative sense. The term is clearly located in four of the Qumran fragments and ambiguous references that may be to Moshiah are found in two or three more. In the War Scroll (a central exhibit among the Dead Sea Scrolls) the term is employed in the plural. Victory over Israel's enemies will come "by the hands of your Anointed Ones" (War Scroll 11:7). In the "Damascus Document" or "Damascus Rule" (another major Dead Sea text), Moshiah is employed in the plural to refer to the prophets[29] (CD 2:12 and 5:21–6:1). Another usage in the Damascus Document is in the formula "Messiah of Aaron and Israel" (CD 12:23–13:1, 14:19, and 19:10–11). The "Messiah of Aaron and Israel" is an apocalyptic figure who ends the "time of wickedness" (CD 12:23), and he will "atone for their sins" (CD 14:19). This atonement is either for the sins of the whole Chosen People, or of the members of the religions faction that produced the document: the text is unclear. A small fragment found in Cave Four of the Qumran caves talks of a time when the entire heavens and earth shall listen to Yahweh's Moshiah and he will honour the devout individual "and call the just by name."[30] If (and it is a big "if") this fragment stems from the same belief-system as does the Damascus Document, then that text's references are to Moshiah redeeming, not the entire Chosen People, but only a fraction, comprised of those individuals who are devout and just by factional standards.

Three characteristics of the apparently Messianic usage of the crucial Dead Sea text, the Damascus Document, are noteworthy. First is the way that this Moshiah – whom one would expect to be central to the discussion – is only mentioned briefly, almost with a passing nod. The concept of Messiah is there, certainly, but the Damascus Document almost says that, really, it's no big deal. This is very curious indeed. Secondly, there is the matter of the title "Messiah of Aaron and Israel," or, more accurately, "Anointed One of Aaron and Israel." This seems to apply directly to a future High Priest, for it is to Aaron that the competing high priestly lines traced their ecclesiastical ancestry. So the future Moshiah will be a High Priest with the proper creden-tials. This position, that Messiah will be a proper High Priest, is buttressed by a fragment from Qumran Cave No. 11 (again *if*, and only if one accepts that this document comes from the same belief system as does the Damascus Rule). This fragment is an apocalyptic piece in which Melchizedek is pre-sented as the active agent of God, and Moshiah as the messenger of Melchizedek. Messiah is identified as the man "anointed of the spirit about whom Daniel spoke" (11Q Melchizedek 2:18). The reference almost cer-tainly is to the high priest who is forecast in Daniel's prophecy of the "sev-enty weeks." Thirdly, in what seems to be a related Qumran document, one given the name "Rule of the Community," or "the Community Rule," there is a fleeting eschatological reference to the way the religious community in question was to be run "until the prophet comes, and the Messiahs of Aaron and Israel" (Rule 9:11). Note the plural. From this many scholars have con-cluded that not one, but two Messiahs would appear to redeem the righteous. This belief in two Messiahs is injected thence into the Damascus Document, with the assertion that "Messiah of Aaron and Israel" really means Messiah*s* of Aaron and Israel, and is best differentiated as meaning "Messiah of Aaron" and "Messiah of Israel."[31]

This is not bad scholarship, but it certainly is confusing eschatology. What, indeed, did the texts in the Qumran library – the best source we have on late Second Temple variants of documents – mean when they referred to Mes-siah? We must remain confused, because the authors of the documents were confused. The concept of Messiah in the Qumran documents is neither cen-tral, nor is it very well thought out, and these judgements hold whether one wishes to read the Qumran manuscripts as independent and unrelated items, or as texts that dovetail into one another.

Yet, consider the context in which these Qumran documents were found: in a late Second Temple library that included copies of various complex texts that were basic to the Judahist tradition. These ranged from entire sets of what later became the canonical Hebrew scriptures (save for the Book of Esther) and big and complex volumes, such as the Book of Jubilees and the Book of Enoch. This means that whoever wrote the four Qumran documents I have referred to above almost certainly knew how to frame complicated and important concepts within the tradition of Judahist religious invention. Yet, despite this knowledge, the concept of Messiah is left so vague as to be almost evanescent. (That we cannot be sure whether the belief was in one or in two Messiahs is vague indeed.)

This leads to a simple conclusion, but one that most biblical scholars – especially those whose background is the Christian tradition – being dead keen to find any Messianic reference, resist: that *the concept of Messiah was only of peripheral interest to later Second Temple Judahism.* Even if one speculates that future scholarship on the Qumran libraries may produce from the remaining fragments as many as half-a-dozen more possible references to an Anointed One, or Anointed Ones, it still would not shake the basic point.[32] As indicated by the contemporary texts – the Dead Sea Scrolls, the Apocrypha, and the Pseudepigrapha – Messiah was at most a minor notion in Judahism around the time of Yeshua of Nazareth. Most of the Chosen People were not awaiting the Messiah.

A second idea that, eventually, the post-70 Christians relate to Yeshua of Nazareth is not found at all in Judahist documents, although it was very common in "pagan" religions in the early Common Era: the idea that a god could become incarnate in a human being (or, vice versa, that a human being, through his glorious achievements, could transmute himself into a god.) This was the case with several of the Roman emperors, some of whom were declared to be divine after their death, others before. Julius Caesar, who was killed in 44 BCE, was divinized and his adopted son Augustus called himself "son of god."[33] One suspects that when, in 79 CE, Vespasian the former tax collector, who, as Roman general, had initially commanded the anti-Jerusalem campaign of 66–73 CE, and who, with his son Titus was celebrated on a coin bearing the legend "Judea Captured," was deified upon his death by the Roman senate, both Christians and Jews would have joined in outrage. This is not to say that the idea of divine incarnation could not be borrowed with great effect from pagan sources; merely that the evidence that we at present possess indicates that it was not part of the tradition of Judahism, even in the faith's most arcane versions.

Nor was the idea that a divinity (or, Yahweh, if one sticks to strict monotheism) could in some way impregnate a human being any part of the beliefs expounded by any known Judahist source document of Saul and Yeshua's time. The belief that post-Destruction Christianity eventually articulated was new to the Yahweh faith, "the totally novel belief," in Geza Vermes' words, "in an act of divine impregnation …"[34] Such a belief would have raised no difficulties with most contemporary cultures. For instance, one can point to the Egyptian construct of the goddess Isis and her son Horus; and the Greek myth that the virgin Danae, impregnated by Zeus, gave birth to Perseus; and there are several others. Perhaps some day in the future, when the Christian equivalent of the Dead Sea Scrolls is uncovered, it will be possible to pinpoint from which pagan religion the Virgin Birth was borrowed. That, though, will not make the fundamental textual problem go away: unlike almost every other motif in the New Testament, this one is not an interpretation of the Hebrew scriptures or of the diverse religious literature of the several Judahisms of the later Second Temple period. Moreover, as Ulrich Luz points out, the Torah implies that the idea "that God and human beings can sexually interact is the pinnacle of sacrilege."[35] The case he points to is the scene in the book of Genesis where, after the flood, the "sons of God" (KJB) or "divine beings" (JPS) had sexual relations with human women, producing thereby a race of giants. Yahweh, seeing this wickedness, decided to destroy humankind. Eventually, he changed his mind, and let Noah survive (Gen. 6:1–9).

In the New Testament, the author-editors of the Books of Matthew and of Luke (both post-70 CE) were the proponents of the notion of the Virgin Birth of the Messiah. How do they make their case palatable? Matthew's chief implement is an Old Testament proof text. He describes Mary's having been "found with child of the Holy Ghost" (Matt. 1:18) and then explains:

> Now all this was done, that it might be fulfilled which was spoken of the Lord by the prophet, saying,
> Behold, a virgin shall be with child, and shall bring forth a son, and they shall call his name Emmanual, which being interpreted is, God with us. (Matt. 1:22–23)

This is a reasonably accurate version of Isaiah 7:13 and 7:14, which states:

> And he [Isaiah] said, Hear ye now, O house of David; Is it a small thing for you to weary men, but will ye weary my God also?
> Therefore the Lord himself shall give you a sign; Behold, a virgin shall conceive, and bear a son, and shall call his name Immanuel.   (KJB)

Except that: in the Hebrew text the word is *ALMH*, meaning "young girl." In Matthew this term is *parthenos*, something quite different. In the original, "young girl" does not carry any connotation of virginity in the medical sense, and almost all of the recent translations of the Hebrew scriptures, Christian and Jewish alike, have abandoned the concept of virgin in the sense of one who has never had sexual intercourse with a male.[36]

Yet, if the concepts of human incarnation of deity, of divine impregnation, and of virgin birth were not part of the idea-set of any of the Judaisms of the late Second Temple period (at least as far as presently available evidence indicates), some potentially-related concepts were around, circulating on the margins, and these were later of considerable use to Christians. (Again, whether or not Yeshua himself accepted these ideas – or whether they were projected onto him by his later followers – is one of history's big questions.) These are the three related concepts of: the idea of the *Kingdom of God*, of the *Son of God*, and of the *Son of Man*. Each of these is a relatively new concept which blossoms only after the Maccabean revolt of 167 BCE. Each of these ideas has been the subject of hundreds of books and many of these works are distinguished pieces of scholarship. However, the bibliodensity of the writings is apt to obscure a fundamental fact: that in *none* of the texts known at present is there indicated an identity *at the time of the later Second Temple* of the concept of Messiah and of Son of God, Son of Man, and of the coming of the Kingdom of God.[37]

Consider first the idea of the Kingdom of God, in the future and apocalyptic sense, as distinct from a triumphant nationalistic kingdom for the Chosen People that would exist in real time and on the present earth.[38] Another phrase for this concept is the "Kingdom of Heaven." There is, first of all, no mention of the Kingdom of Heaven in the Hebrew scriptures, nor, as yet, has it been found in an explicit form in the para-biblical literature of the later Second Temple era. There is, however, a concept of the "Kingdom of Yahweh" (translated as "Kingdom of the Lord" in the KJB), found twice in the Tanakh. In the first of these instances (1 Chron. 28:5) the reference is to the enthronement of Solomon, and in the second occurrence (2 Chron. 13:8) the context is historical, namely the dynastic war between Abijah and Jeroboam. The only other pre-70 CE reference to the Kingdom of God (or the Kingdom of Yahweh) is in the Psalms of Solomon which were written between 63 BCE and the Temple's destruction. There (in 17:3) it is declared that "the kingdom of our God is forever over the nations in judgement." This is an important (albeit unique) Second Temple reference, because it is found in the same psalm in which the term Moshiah is employed to describe the descendant of King David who will purify Jerusalem and will place the Gentile nations under his yoke. This future kingdom could be this-worldly, or otherworldly and occurring at the end of time (the psalm is unclear), but certainly the propinquity of the concepts of Moshiah and of the Kingdom of God is intriguing.

That, however, is all there is in terms of direct reference. Given the large body of biblical and para-biblical writings, three direct references (only one of which appears in association with perhaps-apocalyptic visions) is a very small body of data. The natural reaction of those who are committed to the belief in the ubiquity, or at least the centrality, of the Kingdom of God as a pervasive idea in the Hebrew scriptures and in the "inter-testamental period," is to frame a litany of *inferred* references to the apocalyptic Kingdom of God. That is exactly what we saw taking place when it was pointed out how rare the concept of Messiah is: inferred evidence replaced direct, and modern interpolations were interspersed into the ancient text. The same thing happens with the apocalyptic Kingdom of God. It is said to be found in the interstices of text after text, just waiting to be liberated from the cramped confines of what the text actually says.

Normally, one would not obstruct the attempts to liberate the sub-text from the primary text; after all, close and subtle reading usually increases our understanding. But in this case one must resist, for the inferential reading is all tilted very heavily in one direction: namely to find reference to the Kingdom of God in as many places as possible and to tie these references to a future apocalyptic, end-of-time state, and, further, if at all possible, to tie all these references to the appearance of Moshiah. In other words, an entire herme-neutic industry has invested itself with the task of destroying the following historical realities: that, *in Second Temple times*, (1) the concept of the King-dom of God was not much used; (2) when it was employed, it was not clearly articulated; and (3) it was not yet bonded to the idea of Moshiah or to the genre of apocalypse.

A parallel set of conclusions holds both for the concept of Son of God and of Son of Man. Take, first, Son of God. Unless one chooses to assume that every time the kingship of Judah or of Israel is mentioned, the holder of the office is "a" (or even "the") Son of God – this in the manner of many king-doms of the Ancient Near East – then the concept is virtually absent in the Hebrew scriptures. The Book of Samuel has the prophet Nathan relating these words of the Almighty concerning King David: "I will be his father, and he shall be my son" (II Sam. 7:14). One of the Psalms has the voice of King David saying, "the Lord hath said unto me, 'Thou art my Son; this day have I begotten thee'" (Ps. 2:7). Another Psalm, of Ethan the Ezrahite, reports Yahweh's words that King David is the Almighty's "first-born," and "higher than the kings of the earth" (Ps. 89:27). Elsewhere, the prophet Hosea calls the Children of Israel "the sons of the living God" (Hos. 1:10). This is within the context of a prophecy concerning their future state, where these sons of God "shall be as the sand of the sea, which cannot be measured nor numbered" (Hos. 1:10). None of these references is apocalyptic and, though meaningful, the phrase "Son (or sons) of God" is not used as a focal point around which to construct a narrative, a prophecy, or a hymn. One must conclude that either the concept of Son of God is peripheral to the Hebrew scriptures, or that it is so well understood as never to require articulation, an alternative that seems unlikely indeed.

However, in the extra-biblical literature of the later Second Temple era, there is one small fragment, no more than a tiny dot on an otherwise barren landscape, which suggests how the concept was developing in at least one band of Yahweh's followers. This is an Aramaic fragment found in Qumran cave number four, which has been given the unrevealing name "Aramaic Apocalypse." It consists of little more than 200 decipherable words, but among these is reference to an eternal king who "will be great over the earth." "He will be called son of God and they will call him son of the Most High." Crucially, this kingship is welded tightly to the concept of the future apocalyptic kingdom. "The sword will cease in the earth and all the cities will pay him homage … His kingdom will be an eternal kingdom."[39]

Manifestly, this is a much different conception of Son of God from that found in the Hebrew scriptures: it involves a single person, a future king, who will rule a world at the end of time. Because this is one small fragment and because its social context and authorship are completely unknown, we should not overread it. However, it seems to suggest that among some groups – perhaps a small band of enthusiasts, or perhaps the idea was held more widely, as a folk-belief – the concept of Son of God had moved from being associated with a real-world monarchy to being attached to an apocalyptic imperium, a future-world kingdom. In the present state of biblical studies concerning the later Second Temple era, there is no direct evidence of this God's-son construct being bonded with the idea of Moshiah, but such a union would be a natural occurrence eventually, and did in fact occur after the year 70 CE.

The information on the related construct, "Son of Man," is richer. Nevertheless, it is barely present in the Hebrew scriptures, except as a general designation for a human being. This holds with two exceptions. One of these is the Book of Ezekiel, wherein the prophet is addressed by Yahweh ninety-three times as "Son of Man." The term here is specific to the prophet Ezekiel and has no generalizable or time-transcendant quality.

In contrast, the other important usage, in the Book of Daniel, chapter seven, is a reference to a super-human being, one who exists beyond historical time. This chapter probably (but not absolutely certainly) is part of the portion of Daniel written after the desecration of the Temple by Antiochus Epiphanes. It contains a vision of four world empires and the rise of the "little horn." These empires are destroyed, however, and thereupon appears the Ancient of Days, a figure of snow white hair, white garments, regnant on a snow-white throne. Thousands of souls stand before him for judgement. And then Daniel sees "one like the Son of Man" (Dan. 7:13, KJB) who joins the Ancient of Days and is given "dominion, and glory, and a kingdom, that all people, nations and languages should serve him: his dominion is an everlasting dominion, which shall not pass away, and his kingdom that which shall not be destroyed" (Dan. 7:14). Who is this person "like the Son of Man?" He is not the Anointed One of Daniel's chapter nine (for the Anointed One's role is specific to Jerusalem). And he is not a human being, at least if one permits the text to take itself seriously, for this figure is *like* the Son of Man (KJB). This is not a later translator's interpretation, but an accurate indication that the author-editor of the Hebrew text consciously employed a simile. Given that "Son of Man" in the Hebrew original has no article attached to it, and given that "Son of Man" in the scriptures usually simply means a human being, the Jewish Publication Society's version is a more accurate translation than is the King James Bible: "one like a human being." The logic that follows from this is that if the figure is "like" a human being, it is not one. Most probably, the text refers to an angelic messenger whose form resembles that of a human being. The Archangel Michael, who is strongly privileged in Daniel (it is he who, in chapter twelve, carries the great cosmic battle to deliver the Chosen People), and if this figure is not Michael, it is an angel of similar power and prestige.

From the viewpoint of religious invention, the great virtue of the Book of Daniel is that it is capable of being endlessly reshaped. It has provided components that several varieties of Christianity and of Rabbinic Judaism later used to great effect. However, here we would like to know how Daniel's "Son of Man" vision was employed among the followers of Yahweh before the Second Temple was destroyed and consequently the meaning of all Hebrew texts was thereby irrevocably altered. There is one major opportunity to see how it was employed in the Second Temple era and this has already been referred to: the portion of the Book of Enoch that is known as the Book of Similitudes. There, as vague, separate, but undeniably extant, entites are: Moshiah (En 48:10 and 52:4), the "Son of Man," (En 46:3) and figures that are reasonably close in nature, but are never joined: the Chosen One and the Elect One. The context in which these characters operate is the end of time, the era of judgement. The Book of Similitudes, then, suggests that much of what later becomes the basic conceptual matrix of Christianity – the idea of Moshiah, of Son of Man, of the time of judgement – were circulating in close proximity to each other. It was an easy bit of religious rhetoric for later Christians to redefine them and to apply them to Yeshua. Or, indeed – and here we are back at the nub of the whole quest for the historical Yeshua – for him to assimilate them and to apply them to himself.

3

In emphasizing the extraordinary ideational richness of later Second Temple Judaism and in noting the myriad Judahist factions and parties in Eretz Israel and the Diaspora, I have been implicitly documenting a point that neither the Christian nor the Jewish authorities of (to take an arbitrary date), 200 CE would have accepted, nor would most of their followers since then: that there was *no* direct line of historical probability (let alone inevitability) either from the people of Judah who returned to Jerusalem in 538 BCE to the Rabbis who began to emerge dominant after 70 CE and who, by roughly 200 CE had founded Rabbinic Judaism, the form that now dominates the Jewish world; nor was there a direct line from the post-Exilic followers of Yahweh to the form of Christianity that was brought into existence after 70 CE by the writers of the Christian Gospels. The great religious figures of the later Second Temple era – Hillel, Shammai, John-the-Baptizer, Yeshua, Saul – lived in an historical era when scores of versions of the Yahweh-faith battled with each other for primacy, or at least for possession of their own unassailable ecological niche. And in that era, the dozens of major ideational components that were lying around the shop floor were put together into literally hundreds of possible Judahisms. And that conclusion is dictated even by our severely-decimated set of contemporary texts.

That Christianity and Rabbinic Judaism eventually became the two surviving systems from the multiplicity of Judahisms was the result of a grand-chance lottery. By a combination of good luck and of their being pre-adapted to the post-70 CE world (more of that in a moment), they survived and eventually prospered. Believers may, if they wish, see this as God's hand working in human time, but in the cold world of the professional historians, the result has to be described as being the product of a highly unlikely, largely non-linear course of events.

One must underscore the fact that, as denizens of their own time, neither Yeshua nor Saul was pinned down by the ideological rails that the post-70 CE exponents of the two faiths tried to drive through the Second Temple era. No more were they constricted by the attempts of twentieth-century "secular" scholars who tried to limit the dimensions of the religious world of the early Common Era. Two examples will suffice, each involving a scholar of genuine, if imperfect, genius. The touchstone of the modern effort to restate in secular terms the historical claims of the early Rabbis and early church fathers was the work of George Foot Moore, whose *Judaism in the First Centuries of the Christian Era* (New York: Schocken, two vols, 1927–30) was distinguished by knowledge not only of early Christian thought but (unusually, for his time), considerable virtuosity in post-70 Rabbinic texts. Moore developed the concept of "normative Judaism" as the historical engine that drew all other constructs in its train. The problem was that Moore paid serious attention primarily to the Rabbinic texts that were set down in the years, roughly, 200–600 CE. These documents included a great deal of material that was said to have originated before the great Destruction of 70 CE, but he approached these data uncritically. Fundamentally, his idea of Judaism as it existed in later Second Temple times was (1) a form that was situated in Eretz Israel, not the Diaspora, and (2) was essentially Rabbinism writ small, which is to say, Pharisaism. Everything else was merely deviant from this normative form. As scholars of the 1930s and 40s pointed out, Moore's fictive "normative Judaism" did not work as history, because (a) it left out several well-documented forms of Yahweh-worship that operated within Eretz Israel and were anything but marginal and (b) ignored forms of belief and worship in the Diaspora which were, in fact, in line with the "normative" constructs which Moore presented. The normative-deviant dichotomy did not cover the situation at all well.

The second effort was that of E.P. Sanders, who in 1977 proposed a way around the failings of George Foot Moore's work, namely the existence of a pattern of belief that he denominated "covenantal nomism," and which, he argued, covered not only Palestine but most of the Diaspora and did so for the period, roughly, 200 BCE to 200 CE. This, *the* "Jewish" faith of the period was comprised of eight beliefs:

> (1) God has chosen Israel and (2) given the law. The law implies both (3) God's promise to maintain the election and (4) the requirement to obey. (5) God rewards obedience and punishes transgression. (6) The Law provides for means of atonement, and, atonement results in (7) maintenance or re-establishment of the covenantal relationship. (8) All those who are maintained in the covenant by obedience, atonement and God's mercy belong to the group which will be saved.[40]

Thus, apparently, the desire to have a single "Jewish" faith in the later Second Temple era was satisfied.

Not really. Although Sanders's *ad hoc* readings of various texts are among the subtlest and most insightful one encounters, his hypotheses are nowhere given what is usually called "operational specificity." That is, no way is defined for a third party to examine a specific form of Judahism and find out if a given characteristic was actually present. This is not a tiny problem: Sanders admits that not every religious document which is part of "covenantal nomism" will have every one of the characteristics listed (so, then, which, if any, are necessary requisites?) and, further, he points out, as an example, that the Book of Enoch (which is central to the tradition Sanders is defining) is notably "defective." That is, it does not have the elements mentioned, yet "one can see enough to justify the assumption that the elements which are not mentioned are presupposed"![41] Now, one is hardly pettifogging if one has difficulty with an evidentiary system that (a) either finds the desired phenomenon or (b) postulates that its existence, though not visible, is to be assumed.

And, alas, that is only a small portion of the problem. Although Sanders is presenting a complex set of hypotheses, he does not honour the most basic protocols of hypothesis testing. Not only are his sub-hypotheses not operational, but he has no null-hypothesis. One of the agreed rules by which scholars present ideas concerning human behaviour is that they specify their hypotheses in such a way, so that *if* a given datum appears, *then* we all agree that the hypothesis is disproved. Also, this "null hypothesis" is so framed that the scales are always slightly weighted against any new idea, otherwise no-proof, no-datum, or "not proved" would be taken as permitting a new idea to float into the realm of accepted wisdom. (A simple example: if someone hypothesized that the sun rose in the west, and, on a heavily cloudy day one was unable to observe any movement of sunlight whatsoever, this "not proved" does not mean one can say "tests have shown it possible that the sun rises in the west.")

Even if one were to work out ways of making the "covenental nomism" thesis reasonably testable – say, by demanding the verifiable articulation of specific beliefs or of visible liturgical patterns, and not just "presuppositions" on the part of groups that claimed to be part of the Yahweh-faith – I suspect one would come up with two results: first, that most of the factions and their documents would not affirm all the requisite concepts of covenantal nomism as Sanders has listed them and, second, one would find branches of the Yahweh faith that actively reject some of the specified criteria. *There simply was no uniform Judahist faith in the world of Yeshua and Saul.* This has to be taken as the historical situation until testable, falsifiable evidence indicates otherwise.

One path around this uncomfortable situation is to agree that, indeed, there was no single Judahist orthodoxy, but that despite the multiple Judaisms of the time, there existed "orthopraxy," that is, a common set of actions, based on a single legal system that prevailed among Judahists everywhere. Again, no. As Bruce Chilton and Jacob Neusner note, one can scarcely infer a shared legal code from the general prohibition on pork and a few shared feasts in the liturgical calendar. "Such evidence as we have of diverse Jews' laws points in the opposite direction. What these sets of laws shared in common in part derives from the Scripture all revered. What turns up in a number of contexts in further measure proves so general or so fragmentary as to yield no trace of a single, systematic and comprehensive law common among Jews."[42]

Although I think it is a specious exercise to try to define for the early Common Era what "lowest common denominator Judaism" may have been – specious because a set of religious beliefs and practices makes little sense when ripped out of its societal context, and to do this for the scores of Judahisms simply destroys historical reality – the following are the only four items of consequence on which I can find agreement among all the Judahisms of the century before the Destruction: (1) the name of the world's greatest deity – and, to most, but not all of his followers, the only deity – was Yahweh. (2) The first five books of the Tanakh – the "Books of Moses" – were of unique spiritual authority. Most Judahists would have accepted several other texts, some of which eventually became part of the Tanakh, but also others that did not. (3) Israel is a chosen people. And (4) the Temple, either in its physical form as Herod's Temple, or in a spiritualized form (as put forward by some of the Dead Sea texts), was the central icon of the faith, something so revered that to describe it as Judaism's aniconic idol is justified.

Actually, even attempting to list the elements of "lowest common denominator" Judaism in the era of Yeshua and Saul is an act of historical vandalism, and I do so only to illustrate the poverty of the approach – and, thus, I hope, to innoculate the reader against that sort of thinking. Granted, each of the four characteristics listed above is fundamental to each of the many

Judahisms of the Second Temple era, but those characteristics acquire meaning only within the context of the richness, the inventiveness, the spirit-soaring, truth-wrestling, god-fearing, heaven-touching, earth-spattering revelation which each Judahism captured for its own.

4

The end of the world's greatest period of religious inventiveness, the later Second Temple period, came with a crash, literally.

This is the appropriate moment, therefore, to survey the nature of the one central icon of the myriad Judahisms of the pre-Destruction era, the Temple itself, and its functionaries, priests and their liturgical actions, especially the ritual killing of animals. The Temple goes back far into the Yahweh-faith, to the reign of King Solomon who in the mid-960s BCE began to build a permanent sacred structure to replace the temporary edifice that the Chosen People had carried with them on their wanderings. Yahweh could be limned only in the covenant, and, after Solomon's time, the covenant could be touched only in the Temple. There, in the Holy of Holies, in the tabernacle in which the early Israelites had travelled with their god in the Ark of the covenant, Yahweh was physically present (see Exodus 29:42 and 33:9). There, under priestly auspices, were killed all manner of beasts, their blood being a direct offering to Yahweh, for the propitiation of sins and for a reaffirmation of the covenant with him.

This architectural wonder was destroyed by the Babylonians in 587–586 BCE, was rebuilt on a more modest scale in 538 BCE (ff) and, then totally replaced by Herod the Great's massive Temple. This was begun in 20/19 BCE and final details still were in progress in the early 60s of the Common Era, not long before it was fated to be demolished. This Temple (which by a convention respected in scholarly circles is called the "Second Temple," although actually it was the third), loomed over all the Judahisms of this, the "later Second Temple era" by virtue of its physical characteristics – it possibly was the largest religious building in the western world (depending upon how one assesses Egyptian funerary structures). And it was not cold architecture: the Temple was the equivalent of an industrial site, full of priests and acolytes and, at major feast times, especially Passover, it probably was the largest abattoir in the then-known world.[43] But, however imposing it was physically, the Temple was infinitely more powerfully symbolically. It was the one aspect of Judahist praxis to which every adherent had to respond.[44]

Reformers and revolutionaries could reject the priesthood of Maccabean times as corrupt (the authentic high priestly line had been displaced).[45] And some visionaries went further and sought nothing less than a new Temple, perhaps on earth, perhaps in the heavens.[46] The Temple could be rejected, denounced, embraced, or eulogized. But it could not be ignored. It was not a mere motif, but the pivot around which the Yahweh-faith revolved. As Jonathan Kirsch rightly argues, concerning the Tabernacle, the node of the Temple: "the Mosaic code specifies that all sacrifices to Yahweh (and various other ritual acts of high importance) must take place at the entrance to the Tabernacle, a commandment with profound implications in the politics of ancient Israel, since it established Jerusalem, the presumed site of the Tabernacle, as the only place where Yahweh could properly be worshipped."[47]

It is impossible, therefore, to express the horror which the destruction of the Temple in 70 CE engendered. Flavius Josephus in his *The Jewish War* gives as evocative a contemporary account as it is reasonable to demand, but it misses something. The burning of the Temple and the destruction of Jerusalem by the Romans is somehow diminished by the very fact that Josephus can even talk about it. He was a former general and his very concern with the clash and splatter of battle obscures the reality that the destruction of the Second Temple was not a military event, but apocalyptic. An entire grid of belief – based on the location of the god-house, the place of sacrifice to Him, the place where the covenant between Yahweh and his people was daily reaffirmed – vanished. And so too did all the metaphorical aspects of the Temple as an architectonic symbol of ultimate reality.

To use the word "trauma" to describe what occurred would be to miniaturize the event. A Krakatoa-magnitude eruption blasted stone from stone; darkness covered the land; and the rich world of multiple Judahisms came to an end. Although we today take it for granted that the Yahweh-faith would somehow be re-invented and would survive without its physical focus point and without the rituals that there perpetuated the contract with Yahweh, that is a wildly ahistorical assumption. It was an improbable achievement bordering on the miraculous, that not one, but two, of the Judahisms of the pre-Destruction era adapted and flourished in the new world, wherein there was no Temple. Just as the Temple had not been a mere motif among pre-Destruction Judahisms, the mastering of the terrifying problem – how to continue the contract with Yahweh even though his house was destroyed – was not the solving of a mere riddle, but the single most important prerequisite for survival.

The post-70 world – the world that saw the creation of the Christian scriptures and of the Rabbinic texts – was so different from that of Saul and of Yeshua as to be beyond mere comparison: one religious universe had ended, another had begun. Helmut Koester is certainly correct when he notes that the letters of Saul were written "two decades or more before the first extant Gospel literature,"[48] but even this understates the distance between those epistles and the narrative Gospels: Saul's letters come from one universe; the Gospels from its successor.

What we know today as the Christian and the Jewish faiths were the two forms of the myriad pre-70 Judahisms that survived and prospered after the great disaster. They did so because of three shared characteristics: each was lucky, each was pre-adapted to post-70 events, and each, after 70, had leadership which collectively acted with wisdom and indeed genius.

As for luck, Jewish tradition has Rabbi Yohanan ben Zakkai, the leader of the Pharisees and the conduit to post-70 Rabbinism, being smuggled out of besieged Jerusalem in a coffin[49]; and Christian tradition posits that before the final destruction of Jerusalem, many Christians fled to the town of Pella which was across the Jordan River.[50] Whether or not these traditions should be taken literally is unclear, but they enhull an important point, that, unlike some of the other Judahist factions (the Zealots for example), neither group was wiped out in the Jewish-Roman war, nor was either group (in contrast, apparently, to the Sadducees), organisationally broken.[51]

The pre-adaptation to the hard times that reigned after the Jewish-Roman War involved at least some of the Pharisees (who evolved into the founders of Rabbinic Judaism) and at least some of the Yeshua-followers who had begun before the Destruction to assert a form of Yahweh-worship that, potentially, did not require the existence of the physical Temple. In the case of the Pharisees, they already were developing a form of "separated" everyday life, in which the head of each family acted in his home as a priest, ordering and living a life of strict ritual holiness.[52] And some of the Yeshua-followers – most notably, as we shall see, those associated with the Apostle Saul – had begun to conceive of the Temple as an invisible and eternal structure and the only necessary sacrifice to be the once-for-all death of Yeshua of Nazareth. After 70 CE, each group built on these foundations. The genius of each case, Jewish and Christian, was that its post-70 leadership articulated a Temple religion, but one in which a visible and tangible Temple no longer was necessary. They transcended. The world of the two faiths that crystallized after the Destruction was very different from the world of multiple Judahisms which had formed Saul and Yeshua.

5

In underlining the discontinuity that the events of 66–73 CE introduced into the Yeshua-faith, I am not making a negative statement, at least not in the sense that skeptics of early Christian developments sometimes employ to put down the faith for its lack of early evidentiary material. Actually, belief in the truth of the Christian revelation transcends historical details. However, merely as an historian I am making several positive observations: that is, arguments for which there is strong evidence in the historical record. These arguments are apt to be resisted by those historians and historically-based theologians who work in the historical Jesus field, in part because of their radical implications when taken as a whole. And, in part, because, despite recent lip-service to the concept of Jesus as a Jewish figure, a strong residual bias towards getting Christianity out of its Semitic phase as quickly as possible remains. This harkens back (I think almost completely unconsciously on the part of most Jesus-Questors) to the origins of their work in the largely-Teutonic enterprise of "Higher Criticism," which several twentieth-century Jewish scholars denominated "the Higher Anti-Semitism."

So, I have suggested (1) that the pre-70 CE Judahist world was one of the richest religious cultures ever to exist. Many Judahisms, not just a single one, existed. The Yeshua-faith was a sub-set of the Judahist world, and inevitably, given the fecundity of that world, there would be several Yeshua-faiths. (2) There is very little conceptual apparatus in the Christian faith that we encounter in the post-70 CE Christian scriptures (which is to say the New Testament, with the exception of the Pauline letters, which are pre-70 CE) that did not come from the stock-room of late Second Temple Judahism. The skilful rearrangement of the pieces is breath-taking, but at its core, the religion that eventually rules much of the Gentile world is unmistakably a repackaging of late Second Temple Judahism. (3) As I shall document later, the Yeshua-movement until 70 CE was dominated by Jerusalem and, indeed, by the surviving members of the family of Yeshua of Nazareth. It had not in any significant sense broken free of the centripetal pull of Mount Zion. (4) After 70 CE, the historical evidence is overwhelming that the varieties of Judaism declined sharply. By the time of Bar Kochba's revolt (132–35 CE), Christianity and Rabbinic Judaism were the two major surviving versions, although a few small bands of variant believers staggered on, until they were put down as "heretics" by one of the two main survivors, or until they simply straggled into extinction, parched wanderers in a waterless desert.

Now, (5) this pattern implies that, although the greatest event in the life of most believers in Jesus-the-Christ was the "resurrection experience" (however defined), the greatest event in the stewardship of those who were called to be the custodians and interpreters of the narrative of his ministry was the destruction of the centrepoint upon which all their theologies depended: the house of Yahweh, the Jerusalem Temple. That is, the author-editors of the New Testament – call them the "writers" if you wish – had to frame a story that included not only the life and death of Jesus of Nazareth and the resurrection of Jesus-the-Christ, but they had to do so to an audience who knew that the Temple had been pulverised, and who desperately wanted a way to continue to enact the eternal covenant with Yahweh. They needed an invisible Temple.

This (6) leads us to a point that is crucial. The really important moment in the invention of the religion that becomes "Christianity" is the event that causes the Christian scriptures, and especially the Four Gospels, to be composed. Of course, all the books of the New Testament use Jesus-the-Christ as their main figure. But in the present historical exercise, we must have the courage to turn the matter around, uneasy as that may make us. Specifically, we must realize that although all of the scriptural discussions of Jesus seem to be dependent upon him, in fact his existence as an historical entity depends upon the scriptures: *no writers, then no Jesus*. So the crucial moment in the evolution of the Yeshua-faith into full-fledged Christianity is the creation of the New Testament, and the core documents are responses to a world turned awry by the Roman-Jewish War. That will be discussed in more detail in a moment, but here my goal is to get the reader to overcome momentarily the immensely seductive power of the Christian scriptures and thus to overcome the parallax that otherwise precludes our using them as historical documents. Put simply, because the New Testament mostly tells about events before 35 CE, it leads us to keep our focus on those alleged early events, and thus to miss the point that the creation of the texts themselves is of equal, or greater, importance. We have to keep using the post-70 CE situation as a framework, or it will be impossible to view the scriptures' evocation of earlier events in a realistic perspective.[53]

· 3 ·

Avoiding Words that Make Us Lie

I

ONE OF THE BIGGEST CHALLENGES IN DEALING WITH THE EARLY days of the Jesus-faith is to avoid saying things we do not mean. Whether we do so consciously or unthinkingly, using the wrong words wears ruts of fallacy deep into our unconscious. Language teachers sometimes refer to "false-friends," words that are familiar in one language, but which, when they (or very similar packages of sound or orthography) are found in another tongue, mean something entirely different. Unfortunately, the present-day vocabularies of the Jewish and the Christian faiths are so full of false-friends that they almost seem to be designed to lead us astray.

We need to guard ourselves against words that give false continuity. Frequently, in their attempts to assert the spiritual genealogy (and thus the legitimacy) of their own beliefs, religious authorities have papered over great historical changes. Often this is accomplished by using one word to cover two or three distinct historical phenomena. This practice is especially misleading when the phenomena being discussed are separated by time, and also by quantum shifts in the character of the religious practices and beliefs involved. No biologist would insist on using the word "mammal" to cover all predecessors of human life forms; but the vocabulary of the "Judaeo-Christian tradition" often obscures abrupt declensions in the evolution of beliefs, by using terms that effectively deny any shift has occurred. A simple, practical rule: different things have to be called by different names.

Equally, we have to avoid "Whig words." This is a reference to the work of the distinguished historian of England, Herbert Butterfield who, in 1931, pointed out that most of the political history of England in his lifetime had been written as a smooth and inevitable progression towards the democracy of his own times, the Whig party of the early nineteenth century being presented as the touchstone of this enterprise. Thereby, a march of wisdom was supposedly chronicled.[1] As a set of mind, the Whig-mentality is particularly misleading in dealing with early Christianity, for it judges the authenticity and the importance of an early practice according to how it fits into the seemingly-inevitable progress towards the form of Christianity that eventually triumphed. Here not only are the subtleties of connotations important, but also the more basic matters of what language is employed for significant names and events. When modern scholars systematically employ Greek-derived names and terms instead of Hebrew-derived terms that have an earlier historical root, they are implying (however unconsciously) the existence of an historical "progress" towards the Jesus-faith as a Gentile religion. Few historical evolutions could have been less automatic, less a matter of a smooth progression, and we need a vocabulary which reflects the massive contingencies and permits us to discuss unhindered the cascade of surprises that produced the final outcome: a faith outside of Judaism.

And we need to avoid "semantic nests." Sometimes a term comes to refer to an overarching entity and, simultaneously, some of that entity's components. When that happens, meaning slides out of control.

At minimum, avoiding a fallacy-inducing vocabulary will help us get fewer things wrong. At best, it will have a positive impact, making things clearer and thus helping us get more things right. The words that I suggest we use as an agreed vocabulary in our discussion – this in a small covenant between author and reader – are mostly older words, or ones derived from the earliest situation of the Jesus-faith. Two or three could be called "neologisms," but not, I think, in the nasty sense of that term. "Neologism" is an academic attack-word for the process of making up new terms for their own sake and most often it refers to the proliferation of unnecessary technical terms, whose chief result is to make the subject at hand seem more complicated than it really is – and, correspondingly, the author to appear smarter than he or she really is. I hope that is not what's involved here, for mostly I am suggesting simplifications and, when possible, old words. Even if the reader dislikes the terms I am proposing, and even if ultimately my entire subsequent argument is found unacceptable, at least the reader will have saved a lot of time and misunderstanding by our having abandoned from the outset the semantic shell-game that characterises so much biblical scholarship.

Most of the words that need careful use have been employed already, in chapter two. This way of proceeding is similar to that employed in language immersion programs: it is best to see where and how a piece of vocabulary fits in context before turning to a lexicon. My fair hope is that a few simple words will permit us to get closer to the way the people of Saul and of Yeshua's time thought about religion than will the theologised constructs that usually are taken for granted and which automatically funnel us unthinkingly down certain predetermined lines of historical belief.

2

Start with Yeshua. That's his name, not "Jesus." It's what his father and mother and his brothers and sisters called him and it's how his followers knew him. Probably the name was pronounced in the rough regional dialect of Galilee as "Yeshu,"[2] but in Jerusalem, the epicentre of his religious life, it was fully articulated. Not Jesus: Yeshua. After his death, some of his follow-ers moved into the pagan world and there they employed the Hellenised form of his name but, if the Gospels are accurate, Yeshua never in his adult years left Eretz Israel (that is, the Holy Land). So, even if one accepts that there was a considerable degree of surface-level Hellenisation in the land, it is unlikely (nearly to the point of nil-probability) that, in a religious world which circled around the Jerusalem Temple, whose priests enacted ancient Semitic rituals, and whose scholars studied Hebrew-language texts, a devout and thoughtful religious leader would have changed his name from Hebrew to Greek. This is an extremely simple point, but not a petty one, for it alerts us to the smoothest, most deceptive vocabulary shift in all the writing about the invention of Christianity: by changing Yeshua's name to a Greek cog-nate, the writers of the Christian texts made the Gentilisation of the faith seem to be something that was part of the inevitable flow of spiritual progress, and, most misleadingly, that this process was intended by Yeshua. No. That won't do. Yeshua spent his life as a devout (if troublesome) adher-ent of the Yahweh-faith of the late Second Temple era. It must have pained the author(s) of the Gospel of Matthew to record Yeshua's direct order to his disciples – "Go not into the way of the Gentiles, and into any city of the Samaritans enter ye not: But go rather to the lost sheep of the house of Israel" (Matt. 10:5–6) – but the commandment apparently was so well known in Christian traditions of the last quarter of the first century that it could not be erased, though it clashed with the church's actual practice. Continually, we must bring to consciousness the fact that "Jesus" was not a Christian (he never heard the word "Christian," much less embraced it), was not intentionally involved in founding a Gentile religion, and was com-pletely loyal to the Yahweh-faith, which he wished to purify, not destroy. So, we use the name he called himself: not Jesus, Yeshua.

Had Yeshua ever heard anyone refer to his earthly father as "Joseph," he would have understood, for that is a reasonable Greek transliteration of *YSF*, most accurately written in English as "Yosef." But if he had heard his mother referred to as "Mary," brothers as "James," "Joses," "Judas" and "Simon," he would have thought the speaker either terribly affected or a bit touched.

His mother was "Miriam," his brothers were "Yacov," "Yosef," "Yudah" and "Shimon" (in the most likely modern-English spelling), names deeply anchored in the Hebrew scriptures. Here the difficulty is with the customary English-language transliterations (see Matthew 13:55 and Mark 6:3), not the Greek texts. Still, the result is the same as when we hear the Greek text talk about "Jesus," not Yeshua: the totally non-Gentile nature of his world and of his worldview is obscured. In all these instances, we are encountering (in English-language discussions) an early precursor to propaganda in the original sense of that word. "Propaganda" in origin is a religious term, stemming from the *Sacra Congregationio de Propaganda Fide*, an agency established within the Roman Catholic church in the latter half of the sixteenth century (and later formalised in 1622) to deal with the burgeoning number of "heathen" nations that were being discovered as Europe strip-mined the New Worlds its explorers were encountering. One of Propaganda's tools was the control of vocabulary so as to make the Church's version of religious truth, and the Church's right to define that truth, more easily assimilable by cultures that were not otherwise prepared to see Christianity as the natural outcome of a divine plan. The customary anglicisation of the Semitic nomenclature of Yeshua's life is largely Protestant in origin (the Roman Catholic church was not much given to encouraging Bible reading among the laity until the second half of the twentieth century), but it is propaganda nevertheless.

The divinity whom Yeshua served was not some Greek abstraction or Roman demi-god. He (and it was a male, no doubts there) was the tribal god of the Chosen People and he had several names, the most sacred of which was represented by the four letters *YHWH*, now frequently referred to as "the Tetragrammaton." Nobody knows for certain how this name was pronounced by the ancient Israelites, since vowels were not added to the Hebrew scriptures until well into the Common Era. Even then, the vocalisation of the holy name was not permitted and whenever *YHWH* appeared in the text, the scribes placed the vowel-letters for the word "Adonai," (meaning "Lord") underneath the consonants for *YHWH*. Thus, every time the name of the deity was to be uttered aloud, it was pronounced "Adonai." (From this arises the misleading English-language transliteration "Jehovah." Almost universally in scholarly circles the convention is to pronounce this, the prime divine name, as Yahweh.) Now, whether or not the taboo on uttering the divine name was universally operative in Yeshua's time, is not clear, but the point is that anyone devoted to the faith of the Chosen People knew God's real name: Yahweh. So when we read of Yeshua referring to the deity (and there is only one deity for Yeshua), no matter what name the New Testament says was on his lips, in his mind there had to have been the omnipresent divine name, Yahweh. When the New Testament has Yeshua use the term "the Lord" (*Kyrios,* e.g., Mark 5:19), it not only scrubs the Semitic background of

Yeshua's thought from the text, it simultaneously opens the way to a huge slurp in meaning, for Yeshua himself is frequently referred to as "the Lord," and it often becomes difficult to tell if the Lord God (Yahweh) or the Lord Jesus Christ is the point of reference. The implosion of meanings is not accidental. Significantly, the New Testament writers, when quoting the Old Testament, change the divine name from Yahweh to "the Lord" or to "God" (*Theos*).[3] Since this does not occur in the Greek translations of the Hebrew scriptures which predate Christianity, it has to be taken as an intentional management of vocabulary by either the framers or the copyists of the New Testament.[4] By changing the name of God, they were attempting to do nothing less than change God's nature, from a Semitic deity – who, over time, had come to be seen not just as the most powerful of the world's gods, but, finally, as the only one – to something more compatible with Hellenistic and Roman civilisations – which demanded on the one hand, a god who could take human form and could operate in a world where gods frequently did just that, and on the other hand, a god who could be treated as a great philosophic abstraction. Yahweh just didn't fit. However, while granting the success of the New Testament's framers in re-defining divinity, we have to keep clear: this was done after Yeshua's death and cannot be projected into his own reflections and beliefs. Yeshua believed in the ancient god of Israel, Yahweh.

With the reader's permission, I should like to use one term somewhat differently from the way it usually is employed by specialists in the very early history of ancient Israel. This is "Yahweh-faith." To specialists who deal, say, with events between roughly 1600 BCE and 800 BCE the term refers to the "Yahweh cult," which was one of the many cults of ancient Palestine, and the one which eventually became dominant in the life of the Chosen People. Here, when dealing with items in the 200 years or so before and after the beginning of the Common Era – the period usually called "late Second Temple Judaism," and "early Christianity," and "early Rabbinic" eras – the term "Yahweh-faith" is employed as a convenient umbrella-reference for all of the variant forms of Judahism whose followers worshipped Yahweh and this includes the followers of Yeshua of Nazareth.

Now, Saul. He is a most exasperating man, and nowhere moreso than on the issue of his name. In none of his surviving letters does he refer to himself other than as Paul (*Paulos*). This Hellenic name (meaning, roughly, "small," or "little"), functioned in the three-name Roman legal system as his cognomen, that is, as his last, or family, name. His cognomen was the public expression of his proudly-held Roman citizenship. His sense of being "Paul of Tarsus" was like that of a successful nineteenth-century English merchant who was quite pleased to be So-and-So "Esq.," even though the feudal rank of esquire (a knight's youthful shield-bearer) was vestigial: public respectability has to be asserted or it ceases to exist. He also had a Semitic name which, curiously, we discover only in the post-70 CE Acts of the Apostles and then in a staccato, passing fashion. Without any preparation we are told that "Saul" (usually, *Saulos/Saulou/Saulo*, occasionally in direct address *Saoul*) as a young man was present at the stoning of Stephen, the first martyr of the Jesus-faith, and that the victim's clothes were laid at Saul's feet (Acts 22:20). Thereafter, Saul is back-filled into the narrative of the post-crucifixion era as a persecutor of the followers of Yeshua. He then undergoes a world-famous conversion on the road to Damascus (Acts 9:4–9) and becomes an evangelist for the faith. Saul is last heard of in a notably clumsy editorial baton-pass – "Saul, who also is called Paul" (Acts 13:9) – and thereafter everything has to do with "Paul."

A sequence of obvious questions arises. Why does the author-editor of the Acts of the Apostles introduce this additional name, Saul, instead of sticking with Paul throughout, especially since the apostle himself seems to have disliked the name? The unavoidable answer is the obvious one: in Christian tradition, it was well established that Paul had another name and the actual name was well known. King Saul was the equivalent of the patron saint of the tribe of Benjamin, of which our apostle proudly asserted membership (Rom. 11:1, and Phil. 3:5). So, accepting that the Greek form of the Hebrew name was Saulos, what was its social context? Perhaps it was one of Paul's first two names, like the first and second name in modern European naming systems. Possibly, but a better case has been made for this being an alternative name, part of a double-naming system. The analogy here is to the two-name system used in imperialised societies, where there is one name taken for public use and an ethnic name used within the family and clan. Thus, in effect, a Gentile name and a "Jewish" name, each to be used in different situations. A family thereby kept alive both its public position and its cultural inheritance.⁵ And Saul is a fine name for use by a Diaspora family that wanted to affirm its religious and cultural heritage. King Saul had been the first monarch of Israel. And Saul ("Shaul") was the name of the founder of one of the clans of the tribe of Simeon (Gen. 46:10; Exod. 6:15). This Saul was the son of a Caananite woman and an Israelite father, and hence the name was an especially apposite tag for someone of the Yahweh-faith whose life occurred at the intersection of two cultural worlds. Hence, one would like to know why did the apostle not employ this name when identifying himself in his letters? It was not accidental, certainly.

A reasonable, but not compelling, suggestion is that his letters were all to communities outside Eretz Israel. Even when he was writing to communities that had significant proportions of Yeshua-followers who, like the apostle himself, had been brought up in the Yahweh-faith ("Christianised Jews," in a totally anachronistic phrase), these communities were living in a Graeco-Roman world and therefore his use of his legal name, Paul, was appropriate.

That may be accurate, but it lacks explanatory force. Why did he not – just once – allow a Semitic usage that would have been familiar and thus a comfort to many who heard his letters read? I think the best answer is the elegantly uncomplicated one proposed by T.J. Leary: that "Saulos," despite its Hebrew origins, had a slang meaning in demotic Greek that would have been impossible for the apostle to live with. "Saulos" meant "slut-arsed" and referred to the swinging gait of prostitutes.[6] Given his adamant condemnation of homosexuality, one can hardly expect the apostle to accept a name that would liken him to the mincing posteriors of rent boys and queens.[7] His dignity could take the word play that would come from Paulos – little guy, short-stuff, things like that – but Saulos, never.

So in employing here his Hebrew-derived name – Saul in its English-language version – am I not being really disrespectful? No, for despite the apostle's own discomfort with the name, at our distance in time it has no negative overtones and, more importantly, "Saul" constantly reminds us that the great apostle has to be viewed as a fervent adherent of the Yahweh-faith of his time. He was not a twentieth- or fourth- or second-century Christian, but a zealous (if radical and radically inconsistent) believer in the Yahweh-religion of the Second Temple era. Here, the reader should understand that in emphasizing that the Apostle Saul makes sense only within the Jerusalem-centred religion of his own time, I am running counter to a stream that dominated liberal Jewish scholarship until very recently. "The conventional Jewish view," writes Arnold Jacob Wolf, "is that Jesus was a fairly good Jew, but Paul was an anti-Semite who created Christianity. The problem is that Paul was at least as Jewish as Jesus ... One cannot any longer say that he was the founder of Christianity, unless one realizes that somehow Jesus gave him a lead, an entering wedge for a new religion. Religions are not invented out of nowhere. Paul did not create the Jesus of the New Testament."[8] In fact, in the last decade Jewish scholarship has come to recognize that however heterodox his ultimate conclusions, one has to see him as part of the swirl of late Second Temple beliefs and to deal directly with "this amazing Jew, who so strongly emphasizes his Jewish (indeed Pharisaic) background ..."[9] In other words, Saul.

3

Sometimes historical clarity and accuracy are served by the assertion of certain terms – such as the names of the two contemporaries, Yeshua of Nazareth and Saul of Tarsus – and at other times by deletion. Two pivotal words that we will not use to refer to the historical situation before 70 CE, when the Temple, the centrepiece of the Yahweh-faith was destroyed, are: "Christianity" and "Judaism," and their derivative forms "Christian," "Jew" and "Jewish." That is a very tough line indeed, but the reasons for it are dead-simple.

Christianity and Judaism are present-day religions, separate, but sharing a single belief: each believes that it goes back almost forever, to Yahweh's covenant with ancient Israel. One (or both) beliefs may be true spiritually, but that is something historians are not competent to judge except on the basis of evidence in the visible world. What is clear historically is that each of those sister-faiths, in the form in which we recognize them today, came into being as responses to the ancient world's equivalent of a nuclear explosion, the virtual levelling of the great Temple during the Roman-Jewish war of 66–73 CE. The Temple had been the agreed orientation point, the centre of all the religious variants (including the Yeshua-faith) that worshipped Yahweh as their god. Two sets among the scores of Yahweh-worshipping groups survived, adapted radically and swiftly, after 70 CE: those who eventually formed "Rabbinic Judaism" (the common antecedent of almost all of the branches of modern Judaism) and Christianity (whose Gospels were articulated in the last three decades of the first century). This entire process is described and documented in great detail in my *Surpassing Wonder: the Invention of the Bible and the Talmuds* (1998), and here we must take that material as read. The economical point is that we cannot use "Christian" or "Jewish" to describe pre-70 groups, because doing so presupposes a false continuity which, in each case, will lead us to lie to ourselves.

Consider "Christianity" as a term. It is not employed (as far as extant records reveal) by third parties, in this case Roman observers of the empire, until well into the second century. The first usage of the term is by Pliny the Younger who, about 112 CE, reports to the Emperor Trajan about a potentially troublesome group he was investigating, believers in Jesus Christ, called Christians. A little later (c. 115) Tacitus refers to Christians.[10] The awareness by these Roman officials of Christians as a sect separate from mainline Judaism is very significant in documenting the eventual split of the Jewish and Christian faiths after the destruction of the Second Temple in 70 CE. The context for this recognition by outside observers of the distinctiveness of the Christians – and of their having a collective name that was sufficiently well-known to be used in official reports on the state of the Roman provinces – was not merely the increasingly sharp self-definition of the believers in Jesus-the-Christ. It was also the product of a growing militancy within the mainline Yahweh-worshipping communities, a restiveness that eventually resulted in widespread rioting in several cities of the Diaspora in 115–117 CE. This mysterious and ill-chronicled upwelling involved Rome, Egypt, Cyprus and Cyrene, and probably thousands of Jewish deaths. One should take this torrid social venting (and the period of growing tension that preceded it) as the backdrop for the first recognition by outsiders that within the world that had once been the Yahweh-faith of the Second Temple there now were sharply divided groups, and one of them bid fair to become a separate religion. At roughly the same time, some members of the Yeshua-faith were using the term "Christian" to describe themselves. Saint Ignatius, bishop of Antioch, uses the word Christian seven times in letters that are traditionally dated around 110 CE and it is also used as self-description in the anonymous "Teaching of the Apostles," usually known as the *Didache* and dated very vaguely: anywhere from 70 CE to the end of the second century. The point is that almost certainly some of the Yeshua-followers had taken up the name "Christians" as a self-designation by the early second century.[11]

But do not jump too fast: it would be a big mistake to assume that the name was accepted by all (or even most) followers of Yeshua even in the early second century and it certainly would be a mistake to project its widespread acceptance by them back into the first. This fact is made abundantly clear by articulating a single probe: "how often does the New Testament use the term 'Christian?'" Answer: only three times (1 Peter 4:16, Acts 11:26, and 26:28): not in the four Gospels, not in the Book of Revelation, not in the Pauline letters. If the followers of Jesus-the-Christ were conscious of themselves as "Christians," they certainly did a good job of keeping it quiet.

Undoubtedly they had a name for themselves – "Believers," "Disciples," "Followers of the Way" are frequent suggestions – but there clearly was no single name and no single sense of shared corporate identity. Now, if this is demonstrably true in the later first century, it follows ineluctably that one cannot lay a single corporate name on them before the great Destruction of 70 CE, and, in no circumstances can one employ a name – "Christian" – which implies both a self-consciously defined chasm between them and others of the Yahweh-faith before 70 CE, and a straight-line continuity with the religion that develops after 70 CE and eventually evolves into the Christianity of our own times. Whatever they were, the first two or three generations after Yeshua's death were not "Christians."

So, what were they called in Second Temple times? We really do not know, and I doubt if they had a single collective name for themselves, nor a sense of corporate identity that embraced themselves all as a single religious family, distinct from other Yahweh-worshippers. In the late fourth century, Epiphanus, bishop of Salamis (c. 315–403) suggested in an historical discussion of the early Yeshua-followers that before they ever were called "Christians," they were called (in English transliteration) "Jessians." This he thought may have been in honour of Jesse, the father of King David; in later gospel accounts, Jesus of Nazareth is from David's royal line. Alternately, Epiphanus suggested, the name came from the Greek "Jesus,"[12] and was a name we would today interpret as light slang: "Jesus-ers." Epiphanus also suggested that before anyone called them "Christians," the Yeshua-followers were known as "Nazarenes" (not Naziraeans and not Nazarites, each of which is something very different), in obvious reference to Yeshua's being from the town of Nazareth. Significantly, that name came to be applied to all followers of Yeshua, both Gentiles and those of Israelite origin.[13]

Later, roughly in the middle of the first century, the term "Christian" was applied – almost certainly by outsiders – to Yeshua-followers who lived in Antioch-on-the-Orontes in Syria (Acts 11:26). This must have been a somewhat derogatory term, meaning, roughly, "Christers." Clearly, the name was not accepted for quite a long time thereafter: it was employed by only two of the New Testament writers. None of the Pauline epistles employs the term, from which one infers that it was alien to the great missionary as a descriptor of his own activities. And the Acts of the Apostles points out that when he was arraigned before the Roman official Felix, probably in the early 60s CE, Saul was called "a ringleader of the sect of the Nazarenes" (Acts 24:5), and this, manifestly, was how the Yeshua-followers were known in Jerusalem.

Here, we should be clear about what I am *not* suggesting. I am not saying that merely because a group does not have a single concept for itself, we cannot adopt or invent one (although we do need to be wary of doing something that implies a unity that really was not there). Nor am I suggesting that because outside observers do not have a single term for a given body of individuals, that it could not be a single entity. Nor, even, am I suggesting the converse – that if a disparate group of individuals employed a single umbrella-name to cover themselves, it means they share in common the characteristics we actually want to know about. There is nothing doctrinaire here, but a judgement that *in the specific historical exercise at hand* we should not use a given word – "Christian" – to deal with collective events before, at the earliest, 70 CE. Up to that point, the Yeshua-followers have not developed a single self-definition, have not broken with the Temple-controlled Yahweh faith, and certainly have not become a Gentile religion. All that is misleadingly implied if we apply the term "Christian" to pre-Destruction events. A blanket of false-continuity with the later history of the Christian church will befog, and probably preclude, our catching sight of either Saul or Yeshua.

So, it's a small matter, but very helpful: "Yeshua-followers, or "Jesus-followers," the "Yeshua-faith," or the "Jesus-faith" refer to the period before the Temple is destroyed and the physics of the religious world changed utterly. And, after that occurs, the word "Christian" gradually becomes appropriate. When, exactly, is a judgement call, but by the beginning of the second century new beliefs had been articulated, new scriptures had been written, and Gentile domination had become obvious, and thus a clear continuity with the next eighteen centuries of Christianity had begun.

4

"Judaism" and "Jewish" present the same fundamental problem, albeit in a very different form. The fundamental problem is that *in the present historical investigation,* we will not be able to see or discuss with sufficient clarity the religious world of the leaders of the Yahweh-faith with whom Saul and

Yeshua interacted if we bring with us the words "Judaism," "Jew," and "Jewish" as terms of description and explanation of the pre-70 situation. Here, the minute I write those words, I realize that editors will shudder and publishers run for cover. Nobody wants to irritate the Jewish book public who, per-capita, buy more books than any other group, save the Irish (in their homeland) and the Icelanders (in theirs). In fact, my observation concerning the sensitivity of the issue, may confirm that I have a reasonable point. If there is a disposition to view as a single and necessary historical path running from ancient Israel through the early Common Era, past the destruction of the Temple, through the creation of the Talmuds, and thus through the creation of Rabbinic Judaism down to the present day, then this is a commitment to an historical explanation that is dictated prior to the historical evidence and can be maintained only independently of it. My position is that one can understand the miracle that is Rabbinic Judaism only if one realizes how different it is from pre-Destruction practices – and recognizing this helps one understand not only the development of the modern Jewish faith (which is not really our focus in this book), but of Christianity (which is.)

The actual words here are very tricky. The preferred self-designation of the Chosen People was (and among the devout, still is) "Israel" and its derivatives: not "Judah" and its derivatives. That is good-quality propaganda, in the sense I referred to earlier. The history of the ten tribes of Israel comes to an end with Israel's destruction by Assyria in 722/721 BCE. Yet its rival Judah and Benjamin (the southern kingdom, known collectively as "the kingdom of Judah") did not repudiate the religious heritage of Israel, but instead embraced it. The scriptures produced by the scribes of Judah subsume into the history of Judah all the desirable aspects of the history of its ancient rival Israel. It is a brilliant feat of cultural imperialism, for it appropriates to Judah the entire heritage of the Yahweh-faith and all the historical and mythological tapestry associated with Israel, and leaves behind only the talismanic word "Israel," and that word's usage is controlled entirely by the scribes of Judah.

Judah wins big, yet we have no word for its particular version of the Yahweh-faith. As a term of convenience, I have suggested elsewhere (see *Surpassing Wonder*) that we recognize Judah's victory and use the term "Judahism." This is very different from later, post-70 CE "Judaism"; and these "Judahists" lived in a very different religious world from post-Destruction "Jews." From the return from the Babylonian exile (beginning in 538 BCE) until 70 CE was a distinct world, religiously luxuriant, unlike anything that had come before or was to come after. In that period: (1) Judah existed in one form or another as a recognizable geo-political unit, sometimes as a country, sometimes as a colony. (2) The religious and political life of this entity centred on Jerusalem. (3) In Jerusalem was the so-called "Second Temple" (the First Temple, King Solomon's, had been destroyed in 587/6 BCE), which actually was two successive edifices, that of Zerubbabel (begun 520 BCE) and that of Herod the Great (begun about 20 BCE) which was probably the largest, most architecturally overpowering religious edifice in the entire ancient world. (4) The religion of Judah circled around the Temple like a trained falcon gyrring around its master and it was virtually impossible for any Judahist (that is, any Yahweh-worshipper of the period) to think either about Yahweh or about religious duty without the Temple being in the forefront of consciousness. (5) During this same era the basic scriptures of the Tanakh (the so-called "Old Testament") were compiled from ancient sources, edited, and augmented by the insertion of new material. Indeed, entire new books were written and accepted as being in some sense authoritative (mostly these are in the "Writings," the last portion of the Tanakh). (6) And an amazing array of new ideas, new sects, new visions appeared, in a grand swell of religious fecundity, rarely if ever matched in human history.

All that disappeared after 70 CE. The Temple was destroyed, Jerusalem was mostly rubble, Judah as a political entity disappeared from the face of the earth, most of the religious leaders moved to the countryside and, ultimately, to Diaspora lands. The fecundity of religious thought of the pre-Destruction era was replaced by consolidation and by the rigour of the men who created first the Mishnah and then the two Talmuds, the great rule books of subsequent Jewish life. And, most importantly, the Rabbinic religious leaders essayed the same task that the Yeshua-followers faced: to invent a Temple religion for a world in which the physical Temple no longer existed. They, like their Christian counterparts, succeeded, brilliantly.

But one can see how misleading it is to use a single term to span the years and the religious practices that run from ancient Israel through the high years of Judah's rule, through post-Destruction Rabbinic times, down to the present day. Granted, the [anglicized] Greek *Joudaios* and the Latin *Judaeus*, derived from "Judah," have a long run, going back in the Greek case to the third century before the Common Era, and it is not linguistically misleading when English-language translators have Yeshua or Saul talking about "the Jews." But it is historically misleading to present-day readers, and this is the case even if one accepts the actual words employed as being precisely reported. Leland J. White, editor of the *Biblical Theology Bulletin*, summarizes the entire situation succinctly: "Invested as they are with the cultural overlay of the contemporary world, the terms [Christian] *Church* and *Judaism* signify entities non-existent in the first-century Mediterranean world. There were no 'Jews' or 'Christians,' or 'Judaism' or 'Church' – as present-day people understand these terms ..."[14]

Thus, without offence to anyone, I hope we can use "Yahweh-faith," the term that I suggested earlier, when we require an umbrella term to cover the cascade of spiritual variants that tumble from the original covenant of Yahweh and ancient Israel. "Judahism" covers the era from the return from Babylon until 70 CE. In that period there were scores of Judahist factions (some of which we will deal with later). The term "Yeshua-faith" (and its verbal variations) covers the group that is the chief focus of our attention. And, after the Temple's destruction and the re-alignment of the religious world, we can begin to talk about Christians, and about Jews.

By limiting ourselves that way, we can do something very positive historically: we can let the people of Yeshua's time escape from the segregation imposed upon them by later belief-systems. We can let them talk to each other.

The Front-Edge Quest

· 4 ·

The Search for a Distant Dominion

I

SAUL AND YESHUA, THEN, LIVED IN ONE WORLD, THE VERDANT
realm of the multiple-Judahisms of the late Second Temple era. The writers
of the Christian Gospels, however, lived in a totally different world, one in
which Eretz Israel was increasingly arid spiritually: physically degraded, its
religious centre, the Temple, destroyed. As S.G.F. Brandon put it, in a classic
formulation, the catastrophe of 70 CE was "probably the next most crucial
event for Christianity, after the Resurrection experiences."[1] The followers of
the Yeshua-faith wandered spiritually, like the Chosen People had wandered
in the desert. Eventually, they came to rest in Gentile lands, both emotionally
speaking, and, for the most part, in literal geographic terms as well. In the
course of this intense period of confusion, re-orientation, and consolidation
(roughly four decades were involved in this wandering, not unlike the forty
years experienced by the children of Israel), a wonderful array of documents
appeared, all of them dealing with Jesus-the-Christ. For most persons of faith
this is enough.

However, some believers, and a fair number of students of history, would
like to know more about the historical Yeshua, what his main characteristics
and beliefs were before he was transmuted into the figure of faith, Jesus-the-
Christ. By definition we will never know as much as we want about Yeshua
of Nazareth: no figure of fascination in human history has ever been documented to the point of satisfaction; no matter how much we know, we always
want to know more. But surely, we can get behind the church's literature, all
of which, except for Saul's epistles, is a response not only to the memory of
Yeshua-of-Nazareth's message, but also a communal reaction to the much
more recent trauma of the great Destruction.

Perhaps. The task is much bigger than purely literary, however, because, as
I have argued, Yeshua and Saul (the only pre-Destruction documentary witness to the Yeshua-faith), lived in one world, the writers of the New Testament documents in a totally different one. Later historical observers live in

neither: we inhabit a third world, but not one that has clear sight-lines on either of the earlier two.

Here, we need to observe for a time the participants in what is usually called "the quest for the historical Jesus." They have come in all denominational stripes, and have carried some very heavy intellectual and theological baggage. Our perspective is simply that of the professional historian. We are committed to assaying evidence according to the rules set down by the historical profession, which mostly implies the combination of high evidentiary standards with a slightly distant, somewhat bemused view of how the human race operates, not least when it tries to tell its history to itself.

If the practical goal of the Yeshua-quest is to get back before the Destruction of 70 CE, there are a variety of ways. The least credited is derivative from the parrot-on-the-shoulder school of biblical inspiration. A very large group of Christians believe that the scriptures were directly dictated by God to scribes, so that there is no difference between Yeshua-of-Nazareth and Jesus-the-Christ and that to get back to the earliest moments of Christianity all one has to do is read the texts and believe them literally. This may ultimately be correct (God does have licence to work in strange ways), but will only be verified in a land that is beyond merely worldly evidence.

However, out of this group has grown a variety of "evangelical" scholars who, while not taking all the New Testament details as literal, assume them to be in some sense accurate. These scholars include both Protestants and Catholics. A quick summary would be that their locus of institutional affiliation is the Southern Baptist Convention of the United States and the portions of the Roman Catholic Church whose beliefs, if not liturgical practices, are those of pre-Vatican II. The incarnation of Jesus is taken as an historical starting point and they build from there. Again, this sort of thing is beyond the rules of historical debate in the sense we conduct it in the secular world (how does one operationally define a demi-god?), but on one front, the evangelicals are players in the game. They are very coruscating, often insightful, frequently amusing, in their detailing of flaws in logic and deficiencies in the secular historical method employed by their "liberal" opponents. ("Liberal" in evangelical circles has the same ring that "communist" did in the halls of midwestern state legislatures in the 1950s). Hence, because of their keeping a baleful eye on humanist-skeptic-academic-foreign influences such as myself, I have a good deal of respect for them.[2] This respect turns to admiration when one watches evangelical scholars do what is sarcastically called "harmonization" by their "liberal" critics – that is, trying to sand away the rough edges of the often-contradictory parts of the New Testament texts. However unproductive these efforts are (the Christian scriptures are full of contradictions and this is one of their most interesting points, for it tells us what Christians were arguing about in the late first century of the Common Era), the evangelicals understand something extremely important about the New Testament: that it is indeed a single artifact and before taking it to pieces, a sensible reader will first try to come to terms with how it works as a cohesive entity. (A bit more of that later.)

That said, the classic evangelical approach to the historical Yeshua is simply to deny the problem as I have defined it above. The authorship of the books of the New Testament is taken to be that which the church at some period placed on their spines – Matthew, Mark, Luke, John, names of authority – and it is asserted that, being mostly apostolic in origin, the books of the Christian scriptures were written in the 30s and 40s of the Common Era. Thus denial solves the problem: the world of Yeshua and the world of the scripture writers become one, by fiat.

This does not work and it is not a matter on which the historical evidence is ambiguous. For example, we do not know who wrote *any* of the four Gospels. The names were not assigned until roughly the middle of the second century of the Common Era. Putting on authoritative names – John and Matthew were two of Yeshua's disciples, Mark was a follower of Saul, and Luke was one of Saul's converts – made the anonymous works more authoritative in an era, the mid-second century, when a miasma of traditions about Jesus-the-Christ were afloat, and these names helped to privilege one set of texts out of an array of a dozen or so rival "gospels."[3]

This naming process ("pseudepigraphy" in the technical language of the trade) was not mendacity on the part of the second century Christian leaders. Rather, it is an indication of a different concept of authorship than we employ in the present-day world. It was very common in the biblical tradition to ascribe books to earlier figures, this being a validation of the power that the texts themselves inherently carried: the obvious example being that the first five books of the Hebrew scriptures are called the "Books of Moses," when they contain no clear indication of authorship of the entire corpus by Moses.

Moreover, despite their reference to events before the birth of Yeshua, the books of the New Testament *in the form in which we at present possess them* were all written with the destruction of the Jerusalem Temple as their *raison d'être*. (The one set of exceptions, of course, are the epistles of Saint Saul, the most under-used source in the Yeshua-quest.) The motif that holds the New Testament together as a triumphant unity is the knowledge of each and every one of the authors and editors that a vast catastrophe had happened and that a new religion was a-borning. Consider, for example, the Synoptic Gospels – Matthew, Mark and Luke, so named for their "seeing together" on many matters. Each is a response, in various degrees of fulness, to the problem that confronted all Judahisms (including Christianity): namely, how to knit together the fragments of the late Second Temple Yahweh-faith, now blown apart by the religious equivalent of a direct hit by a meteor. None of them makes full sense unless that common purpose is recognized.

Moreover, each of the Synoptics contains within it specific acknowledgements that the Temple has been destroyed, woven into the individual texts within the same grammar of biblical invention that one observes in the Old Testament. Mostly this is done in the form of a "prediction" that is made after an event, a technique found elsewhere in the scriptures and which is most successfully employed in the Book of Daniel. For example, in Luke, after Jesus' triumphal entry into Jerusalem, Jesus is reported as weeping for the fate of Jerusalem:

> For the days shall come upon thee, that thine enemies shall cast a trench about thee, and compass thee round, and keep thee in on every side,
> And shall lay thee even with the ground, and thy children within thee; and they shall not leave in thee one stone upon another; because thou knewest not the time of thy visitation.   (Luke 19:43–44)

That is a very good précis of what happened during the siege of Jerusalem in the Roman-Jewish War of 66–73. One can grant the author his poetic licence: the Temple, having been destroyed mostly by fire, had a few stones still standing – as Josephus records, two towers and a stretch of the western wall were left intact as a protection for the Roman garrison.[4] The Gospel of Luke returns to this theme:

> And as some spake of the temple, how it was adorned with goodly stones and gifts, he said,
> As for these things which ye behold, the days will come, in the which there shall not be left one stone upon another, that shall not be thrown down.   (Luke 21:5–6)

And the author-editor of Luke, unable to shake the tragic siege of Jerusalem of 69–70 from the forefront of his consciousness, returns to it yet again:

> And when ye shall see Jerusalem compassed with armies, then know that the desolation thereof is nigh.
> Then let them which are in Judaea flee to the mountains; and let them which are in the midst of it depart out; and let not them that are in the countries enter thereinto.   (Luke 21:20–21)

Yes, flee! The remembrance of the siege, the Temple's destruction, and the necessity of flight into the countryside for safety was the common heritage of all who, like Luke's author-editor, had to re-invent a religious world in which the spiritual metropole was missing.

The same trauma, the same massive task of re-invention confronted the author-editor of Matthew. One can see that he is brooding on the issue, even when his attention seems to be focused on other matters. For example, in the middle of the Parable of the Marriage Feast (which in Luke 14:16–24 is a calm, non-violent story), the author-editor of Matthew has the literary equivalent of post-traumatic flashback and introduces into the feast a violent (one would almost say zealot) element who attack the servants of the righteous and then are themselves destroyed:

> And the remnant took his servants, and entreated them spitefully, and slew them.
> But when the king heard thereof, he was wroth: and he sent forth his armies, and destroyed those murderers, and burned up their city.   (Matt. 22:6–7)

Matthew reports Jesus' predictions about the Temple in essentially the same words used in Luke, quoted above:

> And Jesus went out, and departed from the temple: and his disciples came to him for to shew him the buildings of the temple.
> And Jesus said unto them, See ye not all these things? verily I say unto you, There shall not be left here one stone upon another, that shall not be thrown down.
>   (Matt. 24:1–2)

Clearly, the author-editors of Matthew and of Luke knew of the siege of Jerusalem and of the destruction not only of the Temple, but of virtually the entire city. So too did the author of the Gospel of John, who has Jesus saying, while in the Temple, that "this temple" would be destroyed (John 2:19). When employed in the Synoptic Gospels, this is the basis of a "prediction" by Jesus that the Jerusalem Temple would be destroyed. Here, however, the author-editor of John uses his knowledge of the Temple's destruction more subtly. In a nice piece of stagecraft, he has Jesus and "the Jews" engage in cross-talk, the Jews believing that Jesus is referring to Herod's Temple which was forty-six years in the building (2:20) but, as we are informed in an off-stage voice, Jesus "spake of the temple of his body" (2:21). John, therefore, has Jesus-the-Christ replacing the Temple with his own person, something that he scarcely would have propounded unless he were writing after the Temple had been demolished. This is a dating point. But a more telling dating point is the entire structure of the Gospel of John, which is nothing less than the description of a temple religion without the Temple. It has been well-argued that the sub-structure of John probably was the Jewish religious calendar and that the stories of Jesus are placed in patterns that follow the probable order of the lectionaries used by the Judahist faithful.[5] The Temple was gone and both Christianity and the embryonic Jewish faith (which was the replacement of the Judahism of the Second Temple) were engaged in the same process of re-invention.

Of course their knowledge of the destruction of the Temple became central to the thinking of all of the Gospel writers and to their exposition of the life of Jesus. It is true to the tradition of biblical invention that they should place the most important facts in the mouth of the most important figure: Jesus. Moreover, it is wonderfully skilful. By having the baleful and bewildering knowledge of the crash of the Temple-based Judahist religious system transformed from a disaster-report into a prediction uttered by Jesus, an inexplicable tragedy was turned into a predicted-event. An uncontrollable social and cultural catastrophe became controllable, for Jesus had predicted it, and therefore the event was part of a tightly controlled divine plan. This is a splendidly successful piece of work, biblical invention at its best.

And it is a fluorescent-orange buoy, a visible marker for the historian in what is otherwise an ill-marked and muddy river of time. The only objection that can be made is the fundamentalist argument – that Jesus said whatever is found on his lips in the Gospels – and that assertion cannot be answered, or indeed rationally dealt with, by an historian. It is a faith held prior to historical scrutiny, and though it may warm the human heart, it does not illuminate the mind. If one cannot accept what is one of the most historically documentable points about the invention of the New Testament – that the Gospels of Matthew, of Luke, and of John in their present forms were written after the fall of Jerusalem in 70 CE – then one might as well stop reading at this point.

Thus far, I have not discussed Mark. That Gospel is best approached tangentially, through Matthew. Jesus' prediction that the Temple would not be left one stone on another, cited above (Matt. 24:1–2, and doubled in Luke 21:5–7), is directly asserted in Mark:

> And as he went out of the temple, one of his disciples saith unto him, Master, see what manner of stones and what buildings are here!
>
> And Jesus answering said unto him, Seest thou these great buildings? There shall not be left one stone upon another, that shall not be thrown down.   (Mark 13:1–2)

Further, Matthew, in the story of Jesus before the Sanhedrin, has him being accused by two false witnesses, who said:

> ... This fellow said, I am able to destroy the temple of God, and to build it in three days.   (Matt. 26:61)

This is found in duplicate in Mark: where the false witnesses claim

> We heard him say, I will destroy this temple that is made with hands, and within
> three days I will build another made without hands.   (Mark 14:58)

A Temple made without hands was exactly what the former Judahisms tried to build after 70 CE. So important is this to Mark's author-editor that he repeats it, with great ironic effect, while Jesus is on the cross:

> And they that passed by railed on him, wagging their heads, and saying, Ah, thou
> that destroyest the temple and buildest it in three days,
> Save thyself, and come down from the cross.   (Mark 15:29–30)

This is yet another example of what might be called the judo-technique of the Gospel writers: they turn the force of their misfortune, in this case the destruction of the heart of the Judahist symbolic system, and use it for their own advantage. The specific literary form is irony: by virtue of their historical knowledge that the Temple indeed has been destroyed, Matthew and Mark here are able to produce a text wherein the reader experiences the fact as foreknowledge: one reads it and says, yes, Jesus was right, the Temple was doomed – and then, triumphantly – and it was replaced by Jesus himself. It is what, in professional sports, is called a great inside-move, quick, subtle, efficient. Had the correspondence occurred in our own lifetimes, we might wonder if the author-editors had all attended an editorial round table. Each, of course, used the ironic foreknowledge at the appropriate point in his own narrative.

The point worth pressing here is that if the author-editors of Matthew, John, and Luke, both in specific textual reference and in the general structure of their works, each indicate a clear consciousness that the Temple had been destroyed, and thus their books are written subsequent to that event, then the same argument holds for Mark: that Gospel, too, shows knowledge of the wasting of Jerusalem, and it too is structured so as to invent a Temple religion for a world without the Jerusalem Temple. The reason for pressing this point is that some scholars who otherwise are very strong on evidentiary criteria in their work, turn away from those criteria when it comes to Mark: they want the text to be earlier than the Roman-Jewish War and the Temple's destruction, for they believe Mark was the first Gospel to be completed and, obviously, if the first one is post-70 CE, so are the others. If that is the case (as it demonstrably is) then, save for the writings of Saul, we have no canonical Christian text that provides direct access to the historical events of the period before the trauma of 70 CE. Thus, one is forced to contemplate the still-swirling dust of Jerusalem that obscures the horizon, forever interposing between the Christian Gospels and the historical Yeshua.

2

Naturally, one understands the desire to get back before 70 CE, but it has to be done without cutting corners: such as simply declaring that one of the Gospels indeed is pre-70. That won't work without a preliminary bonfire of the verities, including the rules of historical evidence. However, there is a possible way to the pre-70 world. This is to employ outside sources ("para-biblical," "extra-biblical," or "extra-canonical" are the terms sometimes used), which have their origins in the Yeshua-faith, but which are (one hopes) demonstrably pre-Destruction in their provenance.[6]

This is to introduce the crucial concept of *third-party evidence*. In common historical practice, three sorts of evidence are distinguished: "first party," which is provided by an individual himself; "second party," which comes from the associates of the first party or, alternately, from a cohort who was in some way an opponent of the first party: involved persons in other words. And "third-party" evidence usually comes from someone who is distant emotionally from the first party. These are not watertight categories; they are terms of merely rough description. And there is no reason that any one of the three sorts of evidence is necessarily more accurate than any other. Each has its value, and each can be misleading, depending on the specific historical context. Third-party evidence sometimes is called *independent attestation*, and that term bears note, because it is misused among Yeshua-questors. The various reports of the life of Yeshua of Nazareth that are found within the single source, the New Testament, and which are definitely second-party sources (the writers of the Gospels, for example, were nothing if not deeply committed to the Yeshua-faith) are sometimes wrongly labelled "independent attestation," because they do not quite agree in detail with each other. That yields a sense of false security, based on a terminological side-slip. Reports from within the Christian canon that were written after the Destruction are not independent attestations: they all are second party, the attestation of enthusiastic adherents. Truly independent attestation means third-party attestation, evidence produced by someone who was not deep into the Yeshua-faith, or deeply opposed to it: someone such as a Roman civil administrator or a Greek or Roman historian who, though finding Yeshua and his followers a bit *infra dig*, had no great interest in fabricating anything about their cause. The kind of person we are looking for is one who observed them rather the way a nineteenth-century traveller in the Middle East noted customs, persons, and folk beliefs that were interesting, but not really all that important: such reporters might get details wrong, but they have no motive for forging a big lie.

If one asks for third-party evidence concerning either Yeshua of Nazareth or the early Yeshua-faith after his demise, one discovers that (in addition to

Saul, for whom we have direct first-party evidence), of the people we know from the Christian scriptures, only four players are confirmed. (One excludes here figures such as Herod the Great, the various Roman emperors and civil governors; people within the Christian narrative are our interest.) This is a small number, but, I think, heartening, because the four figures found in first-party and in independent sources are exactly the ones that a shrewd reading of the scriptures would lead us to predict would leave footprints; and this implies that the endoskeleton of the canonical scriptures is structurally sound). And these are the four figures who, when considered as vectors in the earlier evolution of the Yeshua-faith, provide the structural basis for a reading of history which is consonant with our knowledge of the multiple-Judahisms that swirled around in late Second Temple times.

The first two active participants in the New Testament tradition for whom there exists third-party attestation are John-the-Baptizer and Yeshua of Nazareth, and for these attestations one has to be immensely grateful as it puts paid to a good deal of tiresome Victorian speculation that the whole business of the New Testament was fictional. John-the-Baptizer is clearly identified and discussed for three paragraphs in Flavius Josephus's *Jewish Antiquities* (18:116–19). The Baptizer is described as a prophet who exhorted his fellow Judahists to live a righteous life and to engage in baptism as a preliminary cleansing, prior to being found acceptable to God. Herod Antipas put the Baptizer to death, according to Josephus, because such an eloquent preacher well might have turned the crowds who followed him into seditious mobs. Public opinion was so enamoured of him that, when later, Herod Antipas lost a battle and a large part of his army, it was interpreted as Yahweh's taking vengeance on Herod for his killing of the holy man. While we must grant that Josephus has his failings as an historian,[7] he provides an independent attestation of John-the-Baptizer's existence and basic character. Good evidence, as far as it goes.[8]

The same holds for that concerning Yeshua of Nazareth. Here too the one account based on contemporary information collected concerning pre-70 CE comes from Josephus. Interestingly, his report on Yeshua is shorter than that on John-the-Baptizer, seemingly suggesting that in the pre-Destruction period with which Josephus was directly familiar – his own birth is taken as 37 CE – the Baptizer movement was more important than that of Yeshua. In any case, one of the references Josephus makes to Yeshua is clearly authentic. The passage (in *Jewish Antiquities* 20:200) refers in passing to the execution of Yacov – "James" in modern English – who was killed, probably in 61–62 CE – and identifies him "as the brother of Jesus who was called the Christ." A second reference in the same book (18:63–64) clearly has some Christian interpolations and, at minimum, is strongly tainted.[9] Still, one solid confirmation by a third party of Yeshua's existence has considerable probative power.

This is so because third-party attestation of the existence of Yeshua-of-Nazareth and of John-the-Baptizer gives us licence to use second-party sources – the Christian scriptures – to define the possible relationship between the first-century religious leaders. Here it is important to realize that the second-party sources all tilt one way: they were written by post-70 Christians, not by post-70 disciples of the Baptizer. So (a) one naturally expects them to subordinate John-the-Baptizer to Yeshua of Nazareth and yet (b), if they include references to the Baptizer it is because his memory was too strong among Yeshua-followers and their descendants to be erased and thus (c) if these references are found to be laudatory, this can only be because in the collective memory of the emerging Christian faith, John-the-Baptizer was on the same side as Yeshua in the battle for good (if not holding quite the same rank in Yahweh's army). Hence, I think we can legitimately meld the second- and third-party evidence to give the following picture of the basic social physics of the earliest Yeshua-faith:

1 John-the Baptizer was a prophet who practised baptism.
2 Yeshua of Nazareth possibly was his kinsman, most likely a cousin. This suggestion is usually derided by most biblical scholars, because it is based on the famous, and slightly comic intra-uterine salute by which the pre-natal Baptizer recognises the superiority of the pre-natal Yeshua (Luke 1:41). We should keep an open mind on this matter (it is peripheral in any case), because it fits well with what we later learn about the post-crucifixion Yeshua-faith, that Yeshua's family ran the Jerusalem church as a family franchise.
3 In any case, the moment of Yeshua's religious animation came when he was baptized by John (see Mark 1:9–11; Matt 3:1–17; Luke, 3:21–22; and, probably John 1:32).
4 This is the start of Yeshua's career as a professional religious. I think, however, we should resist calling this moment a conversion. The classic definition of conversion is Arthur Darby Nock's: "By conversion we mean the reorientation of the soul of an individual, his deliberate turning from indifference or from an earlier form of piety to another, a turning which implies a consciousness that a great change is involved, that the old was wrong and the new is right. It is seen at its fullest in the positive responses of a man to the choice set before him by the prophetic religions."[10] As applied to the late Second Temple era, that definition is misleading, for within the world of multiple Judahisms, changes of factional affiliation and belief were not made because the Yahweh-faith was considered wrong (and some new one right); but rather because new, better ways were perceived of affirming more clearly, more truly, more purely the rightness of the old-and-forever faith. I do not think that Yeshua (or Saul, or hardly

anyone in the pre-Destruction era) was "converted" in the modern sense of the term. Instead, they became energized, activated, and animated within the boundaries of the continuing religious system that was the world of multiple Judahisms. Yeshua, under the influence of John-the-Baptizer, did not reject the Yahweh-faith, but suddenly saw a new and better way to embrace it.

5 By virtue of his being baptized by John (the ritual *mikveh* being a standard form of cleansing in the multiple Judahisms of the time), Yeshua became a disciple of the Baptizer. The Gospels do not dwell on this circumstance, but it appears (from John 3:26) that Yeshua spent some time with John, beyond the Jordan River, as a disciple and perhaps as a field curate in the Baptizer's movement.

6 Crucially, Yeshua moved away from the Baptizer (it appears that this occurred amicably), and took some of the Baptizer's followers with him. In one version this happens within three days of the baptism of Jesus (John 1:35–39), but in another Yeshua begins to preach on his own only after John-the-Baptizer is put in prison (Mark 1:14; Matt 4:17). Both the indebtedness of Yeshua to John-the-Baptizer and the amicability of the split seems confirmed by New Testament texts in which Yeshua strongly praises the Baptizer (Matt 11:11; Luke 7:27).

7 In the manner of the world of multiple Judahisms, the movements of Yeshua of Nazareth and of John-the-Baptizer continued to develop alongside one another, rivals to be sure, but sympathetic ones. Two intriguing references occur in the Acts of the Apostles (18:24–19:7). In the first of these, one Apollos, an Alexandrian of the Yahweh-faith, preached in Ephesus, and Corinth and converted many to the Yeshua-faith. He taught fervently and faithfully the things of Yeshua, but knew "only the baptism of John" (18:25). In the second incident, Saul discovers in Ephesus certain individuals – twelve of them, no coincidence in biblical writing – who had not heard of the Holy Ghost, yet had been baptized – probably by Apollos, although this is uncertain (19:2–3). Saul rebaptizes them in the name of Jesus Christ and immediately they prophesied and spoke in tongues, a sure sign of the presence of the Holy Spirit. Now, whether Apollos himself was a disciple of John-the-Baptizer, or a disciple of Yeshua who also believed in the necessity of baptism as done by John-the-Baptizer, is a question that is not very significant: what does count is that, clearly, at least one form of the beliefs of the Yeshua-faith and those of the continuing disciples of John-the-Baptizer were, in the mid-50s, still compatible one with another. That fits with the general context in which the early Yeshua-faith operated: in the late Second Temple era, various Judahisms not only separated themselves from each other, but some acted syncretically with others, and this clearly is one such instance.

8 Ultimately, after 70 CE, most of the followers of John-the-Baptizer were subsumed into newly-emergent, somewhat aggressive Christianity. However, the Baptizer's faith did not entirely disappear and, indeed, has continued alive in a very attenuated form into our own century, in the Mandaean religion found in small enclaves in Iraq and Iran.

Such, then, are the basic physics that relate two of the three major characters in the pre-70 world of Judahism, individuals whose existence and basic religious character are attested by third-party sources. The third individual of similar documentary reliability is Yacov, brother of Yeshua. He is reported by Josephus to have been an adherent of the message of his late brother and, for that faith, having been brought up before the high priest Ananus II and the Sanhedrin in the early 60s CE. He was condemned to be stoned to death (*Jewish Antiquities*, 20:200–03). This manifest injustice so offended the sense of the ordinary citizens of Jerusalem that, according to Josephus, King Agrippa removed Ananus from the high priestship. What counts most about Yacov is that, when merged with the first-party evidence (the letters of Saint Saul) and the second-party (the rest of the New Testament), the following structural relationships become clear:

1 Soon after his brother died, Yacov, having seen the visions of the resurrected Yeshua (1 Cor. 15:7), was given the authority of an apostle, and this despite the Gospel of John's claim, that while alive "neither did his brethren believe in him [Yeshua]" (John 7:5). (This seems hard to fit with the author-editor of Acts reporting that Yeshua's family waited in the upper-room after the crucifixion – Acts 1:14 – but each writer clearly thinks that he has the story right.)
2 Yacov became the leader of the Yeshua-followers in Jerusalem. This was the single most significant position in the world of Yeshua-followers, for it was at the centrepoint of the Judahist world, Zion and its great Temple.
3 Saul (as we shall see) chafed against the hegemony of the Family Firm in Jerusalem, but he agreed to send tribute money to the Jerusalem church. This was labelled money for the poor of the Jerusalem church, but it was a cognate of the Temple tax owed annually by all adherents of the Yahweh-faith, and now payable by believers from the hinterlands to the keepers of the keys to Yeshua's heritage. (More of that in chapter seven.)
4 Despite Saul's face-saving measures that label Yacov merely one of the "pillars" of the Jerusalem headquarters of the Yeshua faith (Galatians 2:9), there was no doubt who was the main player. Yacov's authority over Peter and Barnabas, for example, is clear (see Gal. 2:12) and so too was his primacy at the Council of Jerusalem wherein Saul had to obtain a licence in order to continue preaching his version of Yeshua's words (see Acts chapter 15).[11]

5 The life of each man, Yacov and Paul, was determined by their adherence
to a faith in Yeshua of Nazareth each man acquired only after the death of
Yeshua. And, until their own respective deaths (in the same historical era,
the early-to-mid-60s, before the Destruction), they were natural rivals, the
heads of two separate, but allied forms of the Judahist religion.

Notice that one can no more think of John-the-Baptizer and not think of
Yeshua of Nazareth, than one can think of Yacov without referring to Saul.
Each is a natural dialectical relationship. Saul, who is not referred to in third-
party sources based on pre-70 information (at least not with a degree of accuracy that gives me confidence), has to be counted as one of the four players
whose existence and character is bed-rock solid: in his case because of his
first-person letters which make him in Jurgen Becker's apt summary "the only
figure in early Christianity about whom, because of direct self-testimonies,
we can learn biographical and theological details."[12] (On the dimensions and
authenticity of the canon of Saul's letters, see chapter six.)

In structural terms, what the New Testament tells us about the relationship
of its four most-surely-real characters is (a) that John-the-Baptizer came first
and that Yeshua was his disciple; (b) that Yeshua became his own master,
and, following his death, both Saul and Yacov became his disciples; (c) that
at least some of the followers of John-the-Baptizer kept to his version of the
Yahweh-faith; and (d) that, therefore, from roughly the late 20s CE to the
mid-60s there were three forms of Judaism which were particularly close to
each other, as rivals and, at times, as allies: those of Saul, of Yacov, and of the
followers of their spiritual cousin, Yeshua's betimes mentor, John-the-
Baptizer. Doubtlessly, there were more forms of the Yeshua-faith within the
envelope of multiple Judahisms of the pre-Destruction era, but these are well
documented. The picture fits comfortably with the knowledge that we possess about the myriad plasticities of belief that existed before the catastrophe
of 70 CE.[13]

3

That is good solid history, a joining of third-party and first-party sources with
those second-party sources which (when read with a skeptical eye) marry
with them. If we were dealing with most topics it would be sufficient to stop
here. Because of the vast investment western culture (and, increasingly, a
considerable segment of industrializing eastern culture) has in the religion of
Jesus-the-Christ, scholars are impelled to push onward, perhaps past the point
of good sense. Our problem is that a description of the physics of pre-70s versions of the Yeshua-faith as forms of the multiple Judahisms of the time, is
emotionally unsatisfying. The necessary depersonalization that characterizes
social physics is exactly what the Yeshua-questors and the faithful long to
escape. Everyone wants precision; everyone wants passion. What did Yeshua

really say; what did he really do? That thirst is easy to understand, but hard to assuage. Consider how much more we could infer about the life of the historical Yeshua if we had confident knowledge of these two simple facts: could the historical Yeshua converse effectively except in Aramaic? And could he read or write in any language?

So, it is natural that scholars should attempt to outflank the central evidentiary problem: the need for sources that take us out of the arid world of the post-70 years and give us access to Yeshua's followers, and maybe even to Yeshua in the rich days of multiple Judahisms.

Here we enter the world of the big risk. We encounter a particularly aggressive cadre within the battalion of Questors for the historical Yeshua. They have no tribal name, but "liberal biblical scholars" is close to being an agreed, if irritatingly undefined label. This is a collection of individuals who, for reasons that are often well-articulated in scholarly terms, place little credence in the direct historical accuracy of the canonical Christian scriptures; yet, in an attempt to jump back into the world prior to the great Destruction, they often embrace a bizarre range of possible-pre-70 "gospels." In doing so many (most in my view) do so with a verve of affirmation for the authenticity of para-biblical texts that has its source in emotions and beliefs which are anterior to the evidence and operates independently of it. This situation is dispiriting to a professional (secular) historian, because one really wishes to find pre-70 CE "gospels" that will take us back into the world of Yeshua and Saul, and thus let us become acquainted·with the faith of some of Yeshua's followers before the Temple's destruction forced either the demise or the huge re-write of all Judahist beliefs, not merely those of the Yeshua-followers.

That sounds vague, so here we should examine a specific case. It is a metonym for a larger issue: how competently the keener enthusiasts for the new allegedly-pre-70 CE texts have employed the tools of historical evidence. The case is that of the "Secret Gospel of Mark," often shortened to "Secret Mark." (The name was given to it by modern scholars.) The path here is interesting. In 1960 Professor Morton Smith of Columbia University, a well-known and highly respected New Testament scholar, reported at a meeting of the Society of Biblical Literature that, in 1958, he had made an extraordinary discovery. This was a previously-unknown letter of Clement of Alexandria (not to be confused with Clement of Rome), a pivotal church father of the late second century. This in itself was sensational, for no letters of Clement of Alexandria have been preserved in original form. But there was more. In the newly-discovered letter of Clement were quotations from a previously unknown "secret" Gospel of Mark, which, Clement allegedly said, was preserved separately from the public version and was available only to a select circle of early Christians.

There was, however, no ancient manuscript or anything close to it. In 1958, Morton Smith had been cataloguing the library of the Marsaba monastery, located about eighteen kilometres southeast of Jerusalem. There, he reported, he had come across an edition of six letters of Ignatius that had been published in Amsterdam in 1646. In the end-papers was found a modern copy of a letter by Clement of Alexandria. It was in a handwriting which Smith later identified as being roughly mid-eighteenth century. Notice here that the modern provenance of the printed book and the relatively-recent handwriting mean that if the item was the product of a forger, he was engaged in the relatively easy task of obtaining a printed book and of using inks and handwritings that are accessible at the present day, quite a different task from forging an ancient document. Apparently only Smith (now dead) ever saw the "original."

After his sensational announcement in December 1960, Smith, showing a restraint in equal parts admirable and unusual among biblical scholars, became reticent. He did not publish the text until 1973 and then he produced two major volumes, the one highly scholarly, the other a headline grabber: *Clement of Alexandria and a Secret Gospel of Mark* (Cambridge: Harvard University Press, 1973) and *The Secret Gospel: The Discovery and Interpretation of the Secret Gospel According to Mark* (New York: Harper and Row, 1973).

Although controversy followed these publications, it is fair to say that most New Testament historians who are not in religious-right institutions accepted the authenticity of the Clementine letter and (with due allowances for Clement's capacity for polemics) agreed that a Secret Gospel of Mark had once existed and that the fragment immersed in the newly-found and unique Clementine letter was also authentic. Several of the "liberal" biblical scholars who, as I mentioned earlier, tend to be very keen on para-biblical material, have argued that the fragments of Secret Mark not only pre-date the writing of the Gospel of Mark, but were part of a secret gospel that was employed by the later writers of the four canonical Gospels. Indeed, the affirmers of the authenticity and importance of Secret Mark form a small *Who's Who* of one wing of the Jesus-questors. To take only three instances: perhaps the single most influential scholar to dive unreservedly into Secret-Mark scholarship was Helmut Koester. His influence has been immense, his scholarly production prodigious. A veteran of what his acolytes termed with lapidary tactfulness in a Festschrift service "the German armed forces between 1943 to 1945," he studied in the post-war years with Rudolf Bultmann at the University of Marburg. After a time as a Lutheran pastor, he took a doctorate in theology and in 1959 was appointed an associate professor at Harvard, where he came to occupy two endowed chairs simultaneously. A prolific writer, he also trained dozens of graduate students. He was even more influential organizationally. He became the editor of the *Harvard Theological Review*, and also the effective godfather of the International Q Project, the most expensive and extensive attempt at reconstructing a pre-70 gospel.[14] Here the point is that Koester not only judged Secret Mark to be authentic, but worked it into a scholarly theory of the origin of the Christian gospels that scholars still actively debate. He posited that Matthew and Luke used an early "Proto-Mark" which then became Secret Mark and then was made into a special version of Mark by the Carpocratian Christians. Another version, he says, became part of a large Gospel of Mark of which the canonical version is an abbreviation.[15]

A second, highly-visible scholar is John Dominic Crossan, co-founder of the Jesus Seminar, and the 1990s' most prolific writer on the "historical Jesus." In his massive *The Historical Jesus. The Life of a Mediterranean Jewish Peasant* (1991), he authenticates Secret Mark, and infers that canonical Mark is a censored version of Secret Mark. He further suggests that there was an additional book, "Erotic Mark."[16] He has recently (1998) affirmed Secret Mark as one of "four extracanonical gospel texts that I judged to be crucially important for understanding the Jesus tradition."[17]

And thirdly, we should note that the Jesus Seminar, which includes virtually every player in the "liberal camp" – John S. Kloppenborg, Robert T. Fortna and Marcus Borg being the ones apt to be most familiar to general readers – has put its stamp of authority on the book, affirming (in 1998) that it is an independent document and that, possibly, it is an early version of the Gospel of Mark as found in the New Testament. In either case, the existence of Secret Mark shows that the Gospel of Mark was found in two versions; thus, the Seminar suggests that other Gospels may have done so as well.[18] (For a general discussion of the intriguing methods of the Jesus Seminar, see Appendix A.)

So, the announcement made by Morton Smith in 1958 had led to forty years of scrutiny of the text of Secret Mark, a good deal of lively debate about where it fit into Christian tradition, and an affirmation of its authenticity by many of the leading scholars who examine and pass judgment on para-biblical texts. Thus, Secret Mark may – just may – be authentically pre-70 CE and thus the conduit we so desperately desire to get us directly into the world of Yeshua and Saul.

Is that why we are looking at Secret Mark, to get us into the world of multiple Judahisms and perhaps learn something directly about the historical Yeshua? Alas, if only that were the case. Instead, we examine the Secret Mark issue because it is a rare moment, a clear adjudication point that allows laymen – anybody with a literate interest in the Bible – to judge the competence of the leading scholars in the field: not the technical competence in small matters, but on the big matters; and to determine, not to put too fine a line on it, whether they have at least as much common sense as God gives to a goose.

For look: Secret Mark is a forgery and not one that requires forensic methods and high magnification to detect. Anyone who could not spot it as a forgery from a height of 3,000 feet should not be allowed to make authoritative pronouncements on the authenticity of texts that relate to Yeshua of Nazareth. The closest thing to Secret Mark in the secular world in recent times was the case of the Hitler Diaries in 1983, and those documents' credentials were a good deal stronger than those of Secret Mark.[19] Merely note the obvious flags: (a) the only person ever known to have seen the document in question was Professor Morton Smith; (b) there are no known letters of Clement of Alexandria preserved in their original form. Although some of his theological works survive, the nature and content of Clement's letters are known only through their being cited in other men's writings; (c) the text in question was produced not on a first- or second-century piece of writing material, but in the end leaf of a book made of seventeenth-century paper; (d) this obviated the need for ancient handwriting and no one flinched when the text was adjudged to be that of a mid-eighteenth-century hand. (The hand-writing expert was, not surprisingly, Professor Morton Smith); (e) though, in the actual event, no one but Smith ever saw the document, the inks would, of course, have been eighteenth-century inks, chemicals readily obtainable.

One could go on with major issues of authentication, but the point is clear: anyone with even the most modest competence in dealing with the provenance and verification of texts of any era would immediately recognize that we have here a simple recipe for fraud. Any country-road antiques dealer would recognize the signs at once.

But, as a test of the competence of the allegedly leading-edge North American scholars, what makes this simultaneously frightening and revealing is that *even if one knew nothing of its diagnostically-fraudulent provenance*, one still would immediately recognize it not only as inauthentic, but as part of a very nasty, but very funny, knife-sharp joke.

Indeed, until one gets the joke, the actual text of the "fragments" of Secret Mark seem disappointing. The text consists of two small portions, one of thirteen verses, the other of only two. (I am here using the translation by Helmut Koester found in *The Complete Gospels*, compiled by and published by the Jesus Seminar.)[20] The first fragment tells a story that scripture readers have heard before, in a slightly different form. Jesus at Bethany is called by a woman whose brother has died. This is a rewriting of the tale of the raising of Lazarus (John 11:1–44). But notice the twist. The writer of this new tale replaces the foul-smelling and asexual Lazarus with a young man who, when revived, "looked at Jesus, loved him, and began to beg him to be with him" (Secret Mark 1:8). "Then they left the tomb and went into the young man's house." This is reported with straight face, and then, as a wry footnote, the text continues, "Incidentally, he was rich" (Secret Mark 1:9). So, Jesus agrees to baptize the young man and, at evening, he comes to Jesus for baptism, dressed only in a linen cloth. That detail is a give-away to the subtext of the fragment: in New Testament studies, from the late 1950s onward, a knowledgeable coterie made a sort of esoteric secret of the belief that baptism in the early church was conducted with the candidate in the nude.[21] Having, after nightfall, baptized the rich and enthusiastic young man, Jesus "spent the night with him, because" – and here the joke goes over the top – "because Jesus taught him the mystery of God's domain" (Secret Mark 1:12). What we have here is a nice ironic gay joke at the expense of all of the self-important scholars who not only miss the irony, but believe that this alleged piece of gospel comes to us in the first-known letter of the great Clement of Alexandria.

There is more. In the short, two-verse, second fragment, the joke is reprised, and, again, the writer sets things in train and then steps back so that we can watch the scholars bang themselves over the head with their own tools. The set-up here is another half-dressed young man, who long has puzzled scholars: a young man who in the Gospel of Mark, with only a "linen cloth cast about his naked body" follows Jesus after he is arrested. When the arresting-party turns on the young man, some of them grab his linen garment and he runs away naked (Mark 14:51–52). In the second fragment of Secret Mark, the reference is to "the young man whom Jesus loved" (Secret Mark 2:1). And, Jesus explicitly refuses to see either the mother of the young man or Salome (Secret Mark 2:2), about as explicit a rejection of the heterosexual world as the writer could get away with, without winking too broadly. Thus the writer has set scholars a cute little puzzle: was the young-man-whom-Jesus-loved the young man from the arrest story in Mark, or a young man from Bethany? The setting of two canonical texts against each other, and turning the whole thing into a false-puzzle for biblical scholars to solve, and all within the context of a gay joke, is no small achievement.

Whoever set this skilled and amusing bit of post-modern scholarly theatre in train must have been immensely diverted by the way it played. Once one understands the burlesque of scholars and scholarship that is the basis of the joke, it's highly amusing to watch the hubris of Harvard University Press, as it promotes Morton Smith's big treatise on the topic, over 450 pages of esoteric commentary, which concludes with two very fuzzy photographs of the only known sighting of the great discovery: clearer pictures of the Loch Ness monster are available. And watching front-edge scholars build Secret Mark into their theories of the life of Yeshua and of the early history of New Testament texts, must have been diverting to the author of the burlesque, whoever that may have been. Although no one has stepped forward to claim authorship, Morton Smith (who died in the early 1990s) has to be the most likely prankster, and he could only have enjoyed watching the most powerful figures in the liberal wing of the Quest establishment – Harvard, the Q Project, the Jesus Seminar being their intellectual bases – take the bait.[22]

Why is this entire skein of events so consequential? In part, because it empowers ordinary literate readers and, particularly, persons with historical training who are apt to be bullied by the academic posture and confused by the technical complexities of the present-day Questors for the "historical Jesus." While granting respect to the professionals in the field for their technical abilities (especially linguistic skills), one should not be frightened by their accomplishments. As we have just observed of some of the most powerful, most influential persons in the so-called "liberal" wing of the field, they are far from being omniscient or, often, even ordinarily shrewd. Vain, yes; credulous, yes; shrewd, no.

Although I could extend the list of those who inhale the narcotic fumes of Secret Mark to include probably two-thirds of the North American-based Jesus-questors, the point is more general. At present the "quest for the historical Jesus" is in a remarkably productive phase. Each year, one or two major historical studies of Yeshua appear and some of these are by scholars of real ability and high technical qualifications. This wave of material is said to comprise the "third Quest" for Yeshua, the first having terminated with the monumental works of Albert Schweitzer, the second being a post-World War II phenomenon, and the third, taking place in late 1980s and the 1990s.[23] The "third Quest" is distinguished not so much by any new methods, but, in North America, by a mega-project mentality (the Jesus Seminar and the Q project being the best-known examples) and by a generally high level of self-confidence: a pervasive, shared, but largely unarticulated belief that we can indeed know a lot about the Yeshua of history and that the forays of professional biblical scholars are just the thing to bring that knowledge back.

Here beware. Although there exist many very solid scholars who are not besotted with the gimcrack false-antiquities of the sort exemplified by Secret Mark (for instance, two of the most rigorous of the Yeshua-questors, John P. Meier and E.P. Sanders), as a professional historian I nevertheless find that the methods of many of those who search for the historical Yeshua make me uneasy and, sometimes, downright queasy. This is particularly true of those who keep declaring that this-or-that previously-unappreciated second- or third-century "gospel" is pre-70 and thus, unlike the New Testament, provides a direct entry into the world that Yeshua lived in. That sours the natural sense of optimism that anyone who has paid attention to the last fifty years of work on previously-unknown ancient texts should have: since the end of World War II, we have been granted the wealth of the Nag Hammadi finds, the wonders of the Cairo Genizah discovered in 1896 but yielding their secrets only more recently, the Bar Kochba letters, the Qumran Library, the Masada texts and all the other Dead Sea Scrolls. This treasure trove of original material discovered in the last fifty years is greater than the sum total of the previous 500 years of new biblically-related material. My faith (and it is faith) is that a Christian lode similar to that of the Dead Sea Scrolls will eventually be disinterred: this because all branches of late Second Temple Judahism had the same motives to hide, and thereby preserve, their spiritual patrimony from the apprehended horror that became every day more palpable, as the Roman-Jewish War of 66–73 slouched to its terrible conclusion.

But my proleptic optimism about the future discovery of truly new texts from before the Temple catastrophe does not extend to the retro-dating of items we already possess. Here, we should turn to another of the exhibits that is at present being put forward as a pre-70 text compiled by followers of Yeshua of Nazareth, namely the Gospel of Thomas. (That the enthusiasts for this text are generally the same ones who endorse the authenticity of Secret Mark is not entirely heartening, but it should not automatically disqualify the Thomas document.) There are also other documents that are claimed to be pre-70 CE (such as the fugitive "Epistle of Barnabas").[24] One of the virtues of the so-called Gospel of Thomas is that no scandal-of-origin is attached to it and, further, by virtue of its content, the strongest case can be made for its pre-70 CE status of any of the extra-canonical writings. Indeed, in 1993 the Jesus Seminar published a big-splash book entitled *The Five Gospels*.[25] The overt agenda of this volume (which presented an assessment of the sayings ascribed to Yeshua in all "five gospels") was, first, that the Gospel of Thomas has as much claim to be a scripture as do the four canonical Gospels and, second, that it had independently evolved from early sources and was neither derivative from, nor interactive with, Matthew, Mark, Luke or John. The covert agenda was even more ambitious: when read within the context of the scholarly literature of the Jesus Seminar and its outriders, the inferences one inevitably drew were (a) that there is some possibility that the Gospel of Thomas actually was pre-Destruction in origin, that (b) in any case, it is based on a pre-Destruction original and (c) that its form – that of a compilation of sayings – with no narrative about Yeshua, is a pristine pre-70 genre.[26] (As we shall see as we go along, there is a strong impulse among the liberal wing of Yeshua-questors to get rid of narrative and leave only sayings as original, or at minimum, pre-70 texts; why this should be the case escapes me, but it is a curious reality of the historiography.)

Enthusiasm for the document is not limited to the Seminar, and the document deserves attention. The Gospel of Thomas receives its name through its being ascribed to Didymus Judas Thomas who, in the Syriac branch of the early Christian church, was revered as an apostle and as a twin brother of Jesus.[27] The book is pseudepigraphic, but that is commonplace within the tradition of biblical invention and certainly does not discredit it as a potential source of information on the historical Yeshua. The Gospel of Thomas was part of the trove of Gnostic documents found at Nag Hammadi in Egypt in 1945. Alone among these items,[28] the Gospel of Thomas has some potential of giving an independent view of the historical Yeshua. The Gospel of Thomas, as found at Nag Hammadi, was a fourth-century Coptic manuscript, and probably would not have garnered much scholarly attention, except that it has a precursor: three Greek fragments from the late second century which, though not identical, are from a close variant edition.[29] This means that the fourth-century Coptic document was based on a Greek source that was written, at the latest, in the second half of the second century, and the Greek manuscript is one of the earliest Christian manuscripts still in existence. Manifestly, the Gospel of Thomas is important.

But important as what? An examination of the translation of the Coptic text[30] presents a curious case. The reader should not be put off by the text's prologue stating that "these are the secret sayings that the living Jesus spoke …" nor by an emphasis on stripping to the buff (see sayings 21 and 39) for this is not a Secret Mark all over again. (In fact, I suspect that whomever forged Secret Mark took one of his cues from the Coptic version of the Gospel of Thomas). However, there are significant portions of the book that are remarkably misogynistic and quite out of tune with the respect which Yeshua shows to women in the canonical gospels. For example, the words of Thomas are these (114:1–2):

> Simon Peter said to them, "Make Mary leave us, for females don't deserve life."
> Jesus said, "Look, I will guide her to make her male, so that she too may become a living spirit resembling you males. For every female who makes herself male will enter the domain of Heaven."

That is about as far as one can go in directly rejecting the idea behind the *Magnificat* (Luke 1:46–56). Similarly, the Gospel of Thomas (saying 15) ascribes these words to Jesus:

> Jesus said, "When you see one who was not born of woman, fall on your faces and worship. That one is your Father."

What these alleged sayings of Yeshua are supposed to mean defies easy explanation.

The largest portion of this, the "fifth gospel," is made up of sayings that have their parallels in the four canonical Gospels. Now, it is possible to speculate, first, that the four canonical Gospels are based on an early version of the Gospel of Thomas. Even the keenest enthusiasts of the text do not do

that; second, one could suggest that Thomas developed completely independently from the Four Gospels and that the overlap with them is because the
"five gospels" used common sayings of Yeshua that were floating around the
Near East after his death. The Jesus Seminar adopts this approach. I dearly
wish it were a compelling argument, because then the canonical sources
would be matched on many matters by non-canonical sources and the probability of the sayings being the actual thoughts of Yeshua would be made
much more likely. Alas, given the actual date of the documents we have
(they are, remember, fourth-century originals), a much more likely explanation is a third one: simply that the bulk of the Gospel of Thomas (that is, the
sayings of Yeshua which aren't totally off-the wall, such as those quoted earlier), is a *Reader's Digest* condensation of the sayings of Yeshua found in the
canonical Gospels.[31]

The Gospel of Thomas, then, is a significant indication of how one distinctive branch of Christianity (Gnosticism, which eventually was declared heretical) took the Gospels and re-invented them during the second- through
fourth-centuries for their own branch of the faith. This is a fascinating piece
of church history, but as attestation of what Yeshua of Nazareth said (it is a
"sayings" gospel), the Gospel of Thomas has no historical proof-value: the
portions that are evidentiarily independent (the Gnostic sections) are so fanciful and so obviously late additions as to be of no probative strength, and the
parts that are historically plausible are derivative.

Nevertheless, the scholarly work on the Gospel of Thomas is illuminating,
for it illustrates a particularly invasive phenomenon among biblical scholars –
namely, *downward-dating-creep*. When one observes this pattern with any
Christian document, it is a warning light to the observer: watch carefully and
count the spoons. The Coptic Gospel of Thomas is from the second half of
the fourth century. The tiny fragments of the Greek version are dated 200 CE,
or a bit before. However, within the scholarly community there is an almost-
magical belief in low numbers, and this despite the existence of the well-
known fact in secular history that later texts are often more accurate than
earlier ones. However, in biblical studies, setting the dating of a document as
early as possible gives it more heft and, not incidentally, thereby helps one's
career. Therefore, although there is no compelling reason to suggest that the
Gospel of Thomas was composed at any particular date before that dictated
by its calligraphy (late second century), the Jesus Seminar, which was particularly keen on its content, stated that "Thomas probably assumed its present
form by 100 CE ..."[32]

That still makes it subsequent in formulation to the usually-accepted
dating of the Four Gospels, 70–100 CE (a matter that we will come to later),
so anyone who wishes to make this document seem prepotent has to take the
dating game one step farther. Stephen J. Patterson, who did a translation of

the Coptic Gospel, argued that its composition in its present form should be placed in the period 70–100 CE. This, primarily because he believed it did not derive from the canonical Gospels, but from the same oral traditions on which these Gospels rely.[33] Here, forget for a moment that Ockham's razor would lead one to suggest that the data are most economically covered by the suggestion that the Gospel of Thomas was based on the canonical Gospels, rather than that Thomas and the canonical Gospels share common, unspecified, oral traditions. Instead, merely note the downward-dating-creep. There is no causal relationship, either in logic or in empirical demonstration, between the Gospel of Thomas's allegedly being based upon oral traditions (rather than upon written sources) and its being written down at the same time the Four Gospels were being set down in their final form. The oral traditions, if they were alive in 70–100, were not suddenly extinct in, say, 110 CE. The chronology suggested by Patterson is in fact a clever debating trick but nothing more: the proposed dating (which is taken to imply support for the oral-composition theory) is in fact derivative from that theory.

Remember that we are here limiting ourselves to a discussion of biblical and para-biblical texts as we at present possess them. For future reference, however, note that there is yet another stage in the dating game and one should be alert to it when, later, we deal with hypothetical texts. The real devotees of the Gospel of Thomas go farther and state that "an earlier edition may have originated as early as 50–60 CE."[34]

Thus, we have moved from viewing a complete document of the fourth century, to a set of fragments from the end of the second, to a postulated origin at the beginning of the second century, to an hypothesized origin between the destruction of the Second Temple and the end of the first century, and, finally to an hypothetical source, of which there is no known physical evidence, said to have been produced between the mid-first century and the Temple's destruction. Granted, it is theoretically possible (although very highly improbable) that these ever-descending datings are historically correct: but the warning light that is set off by downward-dating-creep should be heeded not only here, but with particular assiduousness when one encounters (as we will in the next chapter) hypothetical documents which are said to have been framed before 70 CE. These fictive documents merit special attention because, without presenting any verifiable text, they propel the discussion into an era prior to the invention of the primary history of Christianity as found in the Four Gospels and the Book of Acts. Hence, these hypothetical documents automatically obtain a privileged position in the chronology of Christian invention that is equal to that of the earliest actual Christian documents that we possess, the letters of Saul. Warning light.

John P. Meier, who is the leading "conservative" (in terms of his use of evidence) among the Yeshua-questors, provides as close to a definitive summary of the situation as one can find: "I think we have probed enough representatives of the overheated imaginations of various second-century Christians to show that critics like Crossan, Koester, and James M. Robinson are simply on the wrong track. These apocryphal gospels are very important, but they belong in a study of the patristic Church from the second to the fourth century ... In recent years we have been witnessing the "selling" of the apocrypha ... under the guise of New Testament research and the quest for the historical Jesus. This is a misuse of useful material. There is nothing here that can serve as a source in our quest for the historical Jesus."[35]

That is neither inaccurate nor unkind, and if we substitute "perilous adventure" for Meier's description of the Yeshua-quest as a "precarious venture,"[36] one catches accurately the spirit of most of the Yeshua-questors. They are courageous; they have a sense of high intellectual adventure. They are trying to traverse a wide and uncharted ocean in order to find a rich prophesied-land on the far side. It is not unnatural that they keep telling themselves that they see a landmark on the horizon, and, if that one turns out to be a wisp of cloud, well, there's another possible landfall, just a bit farther on. They long to be able to step off their uncertain and pitching vessel and, even if it's just for a brief time, to put their feet on solid land. When they cannot find any, they allow one of their leaders to declare that solid terra is dead ahead, just a few feet, maybe just inches, below the surface. They get to that point, step off, and plunge in far over their heads. The depths, it seems, always overwhelm.

· 5 ·

Minting New Gospels

I

IF THE SEARCH FOR PREVIOUSLY UNKNOWN (OR KNOWN, BUT unappreciated) documents that take us directly into the world where Yeshua of Nazareth and Saul of Tarsus lived has to be judged fruitless (as yet), there is another angle of attack open to Questors for the historical Yeshua. Many of the Questors believe that they can get back into the world of later Second Temple Judahism by detecting within documents that are demonstrably post-70 CE core texts that are earlier. The task is deceptively simple: if there are no extant pre-70 texts, then build some and sell them. Here the mental agility of the scholars is impressive and the suasive intensity that is invested in promoting some of these texts is quite remarkable. We will examine two examples of this activity at its weakest, and then we will turn to the one that really counts, namely "Q."

The first contender for pre-70 status (which is to say, pre-Four Gospels) is part of the "Gospel of Peter." This item is the by-product of an archaeological dig conducted in Egypt in 1885–86 by French scholars. In a Christian monk's grave was found a small document amidst a set of other items whose earliest dating was the eighth century. However, it appears probable (but not quite certain) that the "Oxyrhynchus papyrus" fragments of c. 200 (discovered in 1897 by Bernard P. Grenfell and Arthur S. Hunt) contain a witness to this putative Gospel of Peter. The title "gospel" comes not from the work itself, but from a mention of what possibly may be this same work by Eusebius. The text itself purports to be by Simon Peter. The text consists of only sixty verses, arranged in fourteen tiny chapters. It focuses on the crucifixion and employs in almost every sentence implicit references to the Tanakh.[1] The Gospel of Peter's version of the Passion narrative is well within the degree of factual variance found in the Synoptics (meaning Matthew, Mark and Luke) and in the Gospel of John: its main new idea is that the elders, priests, scribes and Pharisees recognize what a mistake they have made in crucifying Jesus (Peter chapters 7 and 8) and, while Jesus is in the tomb, he is taken up to heaven by two undefined figures, and then, confusingly, comes down again and enters the tomb (Peter chapters 10 and 11). I find convincing John P. Meier's assessment of the scholarly literature and primary evidence concerning the Gospel of Peter: namely that it is a second-century pastiche of material from the Four Gospels (mostly Matthew) with a bit of imagination thrown in.[2] The fascinating point, however, is the way that a major New Testament scholar, John Dominic Crossan, suggests that the extant document actually is based on a hypothetical one: an item he denominates the "Cross Gospel." Not surprisingly, this is presented as being mid-first-century and thus prior to the Synoptics and to the Gospel of John. Crossan takes the hypothesis one step farther and theorizes that the "Cross Gospel" was one of the sources of all four of the canonical Gospels, and that, later, the Cross Gospel was expanded into a full Gospel of Peter, the fragments of which we now have.[3]

Why this later Gospel of Peter never made the canon is not explained, except by suggesting that it was put together quite late, after the canon was already primarily set: this nicely elides the problem which stems from our having only a late-second century dating for the document that we actually possess.

The deeper problem, however is one of reasoning. *If* one takes a second-century text (which is the artifact we are beginning with) and finds that portions of it resemble closely some first-century texts (in this case the death of Yeshua as told in the New Testament), *unless* one has strong evidence that the second-century text was totally independent in origin and therefore not influenced by the earlier text, then the grounds of presumption are obvious: the second-century text is based, either directly or indirectly, on that of the first century. Or, to keep it to the case in hand, the "Cross Gospel" that is supposed to be hidden within the second-century Gospel of Peter is not pre-70, is not the plinth on which the Four Gospels' story of the death of Yeshua is built, but instead is derivative from the canonical Gospels, and this presumption holds until strong evidence of a different case is put forward. The curious point historiographically is that the main (and almost the only) proponent of the Cross-Gospels-as-basis-of-the-Passion-story reverses the logical grounds of presumption and thereby makes its being the earliest Christian document and an independent source both his basic assumption and (not surprisingly) his conclusion. The intensity of John Dominic Crossan's belief in the existence, independence and priority of his Cross Gospel is palpable, but it carries no historical weight.[4] The Cross Gospel stands as a useful example of the dangers of turning one's wishes into horses.

Another virtually clinical example is found in the positing of a "Signs Gospel" as a readily identifiable, pre-70 part of the Gospel of John. That gospel traditionally has been folded into two portions, the Book of Signs (chapters 1–12) and the Book of Glory (chapters 13–21). The first depends for its narrative force upon the wonderful deeds ("signs") conducted by Jesus in his ministry, the second upon the Passion narrative. Once this is noted, it is not unnatural to look for an earlier source behind each segment. In practice, however, scholarly efforts have been focused upon the first portion, the Book of Signs, and from that effort has emerged the "Signs Gospel." This hypothetical reconstruction stems from a sensible exercise: "*if* we hypothesize that a written source underlies the first half of the Gospel of John, *then* that source *might* look as follows." There are enough hiccups in the Book of John ("aporia" is the technical term), where the story does not flow well, to encourage an examination of these rough spots as nodal points in the final rewriting of John by its editor-author(s): the more so because these aporia usually are associated with specific wondrous events caused by Jesus.

Fair enough: provided one keeps in mind that in no contemporary text is there an indication that such an early signs document actually existed; and, further, this Signs Gospel has to be reconstructed from a single source, the Gospel of John. It thus lacks the rigour that one has when, for example, Matthew and Luke are found to use virtually identical wordings, and thus indicate that either one of them used the other or that they had a third source in common. The creation of the Signs Gospel is a totally hypothetical exercise and yields a narrative "gospel" with almost no sayings of Yeshua. It has been brought to its highest development by Robert T. Fortna, who has produced a Signs Gospel[5] that focuses on six sets of miracles or wondrous actions attributed to Yeshua, plus a symmetrical opening and closing framework. The result is seductive, and that is the point. Recall that Fortna derives the Signs Gospel from the Gospel of John. The formula is:

Gospel of John
minus
whatever the scholar excises and rearranges
equals
the Signs Gospel

Then note Fortna's very first interpretive footnote to his hypothetical construction: "As in a few other scenes, here the author of the canonical Gospel of John has considerably altered the Signs Gospel ('SG'), making its recovery, both as to original wording and to order, uncertain at points."[6] Really: the author of the canonical John has altered the Signs Gospel! Is not the Signs Gospel a hypothetical construct put forward by Robert Fortna? It is: hence, the so-very-revealing footnote means that the author of the canonical Gospel of John, writing in the first century, has considerably altered a hypothetical gospel put forward by an historian in the last portion of the twentieth century.

Even the most addicted of post-modernists will be impressed by this apparent reversal of time's arrow: for nearly two millennia time runs backward.

Fortna's self-hypnosis with his self-created gospel is useful because it shows so explicitly a mesmerization that frequently (not always: frequently) betakes those scholars doing textual reconstruction, and if Fortna's reification is extreme, it is only extreme in its being so obvious. Almost inevitably, once hypothetical constructs are confused with historical documents, chronological time gets badly bent. Fortna, in the introduction to his Signs Gospel, raises the possibility that it is "the earliest gospel."[7] At least one scholar has gone so far as to suggest that the Synoptic Gospels depend upon the fictive Signs Gospel,[8] which is about as far as one can go in finding the causes of the visible world in the invisible.

Neither the character of the "Signs Gospel" nor of the "Cross Gospel" is enspiriting. However, a third, much more significant effort – the reconstruction of "Q," as one of the sources of the Synoptic Gospels – brings us into an arena of first-class minds and work that frequently respects the evidentiary standards of history as a scholarly discipline. We can address "Q," however, only after looking at the way the New Testament texts that deal with the earthly existence of Jesus-the-Christ are arranged.

2

In the Christian scriptures there are three bodies of potential information on the historical Yeshua: the letters of Saul, the Synoptic Gospels (Matthew, Mark, and Luke: the Acts of the Apostles is frequently seen as a continuation of Luke, but it is of little material use in relation to the historical Yeshua); and the Gospel of John. The material in the rest of the New Testament, while valuable in charting the evolution of the Christian faith, has so little that is demonstrably referential to the historical Yeshua as to be virtually epiphenomenal. Of the three main sources, we will save the epistles of Saul until later. They receive scant attention by the Yeshua-questors (wrongly, I think, but that is a matter for later discussion) and, in any case, they are not part of the mix of narrative post-Destruction texts that comprise the Four Gospels. Each of these canonical Four Gospels is a narrative, is anonymous (with later pseudepigraphic attribution by second-century Christians), and none of them includes any claim to have been written, even in part, by an eyewitness to Yeshua's life. This is not overwhelmingly worrisome – later historical collations often are more accurate than eyewitness narratives – but, understandably, biblical historians wish to get behind the editing process of these Four Gospels and thereby to recapture some of the raw data upon which the Gospel historians based their narratives. In practical terms, this is a two-part issue. The Synoptic Gospels – so called because they provide a "seeing together" – have a great deal in common and are markedly different in character from the Gospel of John.

Commonly, John is dated 90 CE or so, although the reason for doing this is hard to intuit. The bracketing dates for the composition of the Johanine text as we have it are 70 CE (the destruction of the Temple is referred to) and somewhere between 125 and 150 CE, which is fixed by an Egyptian papyrus fragment of the Gospel.[9] Given those hard date-lines, it is difficult to find any compelling reason that would make one opt for the middle of the range, except that it is the middle of the range.[10] I suspect that the basic reason the Gospel of John is dated when it is is that the prevailing opinion among biblical scholars is that John is less historically informative than are the Synoptics.[11] And there is a form of magical thinking among biblical historians: (a) if a text is earlier than another text, it is more accurate and (b) if a text is more informative than another one, then it is earlier. Because the Synoptics are usually dated 70–85 CE, then, by this mode of reasoning, the Gospel of John has to be after 85 CE, and is usually dated 90 CE, or so. Like many slips in historical approach, this mindset (or, more accurately, this emotionalset) is difficult to deal with because it usually is not explicitly articulated. Once it is stated outright, however, it dissolves. Here is what is actually being proposed, articulated in an inference called a "hypothetical syllogism:"

1 If one text has more details (is "more informative") than another one, then it is earlier. (If A, then B.)
2 If one text is earlier than another one, then whatever historical detail it has will be more accurate. (The document will be "more informative.") (If B, then C.)
3 And this leads us to conclude that if one text has more details, then its details are more accurate. (If A, then C.)

The conclusion is logically valid but methodologically absurd, for it leaves a purely internal feature of the text to guarantee something substantial about the relation of the text to the external world. Thus, even if one accepts that the Synoptic Gospels are superior as sources of information on historical matters than is the Gospel of John; and even if one accepts the prevailing dating on the Synoptics – 70–85 CE (both matters which I think are very much "not proved") – it does not necessarily determine the dating one endorses for John.

The problem of the potential relationship of the Synoptic Gospels and the Gospel of John is probably the most vexed question among scholars who try to establish the stratigraphy of the Christian scriptures: did John use Matthew, Mark or Luke? Probably most New Testament historians today believe, by a small majority, that John did not use the Synoptics,[12] but this is not a matter for an opinion poll. The real problem is that the variance in historical details are so ubiquitous as between the Synoptics and John – details, not central motifs – and the difficulty of finding formulations in John that could possibly derive from the Synoptics is so great, that one must leave the question open: which is necessarily to opt for the null hypothesis.

The third body of texts in the Christian scriptures that potentially provide information on the historical Yeshua of Nazareth are (in addition to the Gospel of John and Saul's epistles) the Synoptic Gospels: Matthew, Mark and Luke. Studying the literature on these Gospels as composed by historical scholars of the Bible is a pleasure, because it introduces one to some of the most nimble minds in the scholarly profession. There is real intellectual joy in watching these minds grapple with the "Synoptic Puzzle,"[13] which is the question of how the overlapping portions of these books are related to each other, and thus, what was the genealogical line of descent of the three documents.

The "traditional" dating of the Synoptic Gospels among New Testament scholars is 70–85 CE, although a case sometimes is made for the late 60s (during the Roman-Jewish War) for the first of them. The latest hard-date for the completion of the Synoptics is roughly 140 CE when physical evidence becomes available. However, that last date is usually rejected, because none of the Synoptic Gospels show any knowledge of the widespread Jewish revolt in Rome, Egypt, Cyprus and Cyrene of 115–117,[14] which would have fit very well with the concerns of the various author-editors of these texts. Each of the Synoptics is a response, in various degrees of fulness, to the problem that confronted all Judahisms (including Christianity), namely, how to knit together the fragments of the late Second Temple Yahweh-faith, now blown apart in 70 CE by the religious equivalent of a direct hit by a meteor. None of them makes full sense unless that common purpose is recognized.

What scholars are trying to do above all is to answer the question, "Which of the three Synoptic Gospels came first?" Here, as in all historical work, one must be careful not to frame the puzzle so that it tilts the discussion unfairly in a particular direction. For example, one way to state the fundamental content-relationships as between the three books is this. One can say "Of Mark's 661 verses, some 430 are substantially reproduced in both Matthew and Luke. Of the remaining 231 verses, 176 occur in Matthew and the substance of 25 in Luke. Only 30 verses in Mark do not appear in some form in either Matthew or Luke."[15] This is an accurate statement, and a now-traditional formulation. Or one can formulate the data in percentages: "the bulk of Mark is found in Luke (55 percent of it …) and in Matthew (90 percent of it)."[16] But notice that each of those formulations of the Synoptic Puzzle, while accurate, makes Mark the centre of our attention and thus insensibly leads us to give precedence to one major possibility: that Mark is the central element in the puzzle, and automatically, one privileges the idea that Mark came first historically. The exact same data can be covered in a set-up question that produces quite a different set of presuppositions. One could say that "the text of Mark employs, in its version of the scriptures, 176 verses-worth of material found only in Matthew, and 25 found only in Luke. Some 430 verses come from both Matthew and Luke and only 30 from some unknown source." And one could add "90 percent of the material that Mark employs is found in Matthew." Those formulations, obviously, tilt the enquirer towards Matthaean priority. Neither one is an example of good historical question-framing, but a variant of the first one, the tilt towards Mark, is found in most introductions to the textual relationships of the Synoptic Gospels.

If, for the moment, we limit our attention to the three biblical texts as we at present have them, and exclude all exogenous textual variables (hypothetical gospels and the like), and also exclude all matters of historical context, then we have a textual puzzle, involving three texts and eighteen possible relationships. The most supple discussion of the logical possibilities (and a book that anyone who enjoys really tough, focused historical arguments should read), is found in William R. Farmer's *The Synoptic Problem* (1976).[17] The eighteen possible relationships are defined by set-theory and by one additional limiting assumption: that borrowing from one text to another was a one-way phenomenon. That is, if the author-editor of Matthew borrowed from Mark, this excludes the possibility of the author-editor of Mark having borrowed from Matthew. And, of course, this also excludes the three Synoptic author-editors all having borrowed from each other. Without such an assumption, any literary dependence of one upon another would be impossible to demonstrate. Although it is congenial to think of the author-editors of the Synoptics exchanging draft Gospels with each other, rather like short-story writers at an artists' colony, the scene is an unlikely one: the basic assumption shared by virtually all biblical scholars, of one-way borrowing, is realistic.

To be potentially viable in solving the Synoptic Puzzle, any set of arrangements must be able to handle two conditions that are found in the actual Synoptic texts: (1) it must be able to explain those instances wherein all three texts agree and (2) it must be able to handle those instances where two of the Synoptics agree with each other and disagree with the third. Disagreement here can be either overt or from silence. It is a real condition, for there are occasions in the texts wherein, on some issues, each Synoptic Gospel is in conflict with the other two. To handle this situation adequately, the potential arrangement of texts must permit not only indications of agreement, but testimony to disagreement. What is *not* required is (3) that the explanatory system be able to handle those instances wherein the three Synoptics are in complete disagreement with each other. Such instances are explicable only (a) by the introduction of an exogenous *Urtext* for each book, or *Sondergut* – the now-preferable term for "special material" which does not necessarily have to come from a single source – but (b) the initial assumption, that the explanation should arise from a closed system, excludes such external interference.

Given these assumptions, (the Synoptic Puzzle's "rules"), there are eighteen possible relationships among the three texts. (These are diagrammed below.) Crucially, William Farmer reduces the number of potential textual relationships from this eighteen to six. This can be done because, first, six of the theoretically-possible relationships as sketched below are inadequate. These consist of the six instances wherein there is a single independent source and the author-editors of the other two texts either incorporate its material in their own work or reject portions of the original texts. This sequence is diagrammed as follows:

Matthew	Matthew	Mark	Mark	Luke	Luke
↓	↓	is copied in whole or in part by: ↓	↓	↓	↓
Mark	Luke	Matthew	Luke	Matthew	Mark
↓	↓ which, in turn, is copied in whole or in part by: ↓	↓	↓	↓	↓
Luke	Mark	Luke	Matthew	Mark	Matthew

They lack the necessary explanatory power because they cover only the instances wherein all three Synoptic Gospels agree with each other or in which those in line 1 agree with line 2, as against line 3, or those in line 2 agree with line 3, as against line 1. What this set of arrangements does not cover is the agreements that occur between a text in line 1 and one in line 3, in disagreement with line 2.

Now, a second set of three possible relationships must also be discarded. These are the instances in which there is a single independent original source and the author-editors of the other two sources each deal directly with that first source, either accepting or rejecting some portion of the original.

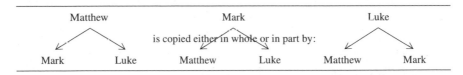

These three possibilities are inadequate because, although they provide for instances of agreement among all three texts, and for instances when either one of the texts on line 2 agrees with the original text on line 1 as against the other text on line 2, it does not provide for the instances wherein the two texts in line 2 agree in having material which is not in the original text on line 1. (Remember, they are copying, so the only two options of the author-editors of the texts on line 2 are [a] to incorporate an item that is in the original text or [b] reject it.)

A related set of three possibilities also is insufficient. These are the ones in which there are two independent texts and these are copied (or not), depending on the taste of the author-editors of the third text.

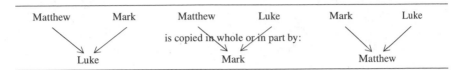

These three possibilities would explain the items on which the Gospels on line 2 agree with one of the Gospels on line 1, against the other Gospel on line 1. It would not, however, account for instances in which the two independent sources on line 1 agree with each other or in which all three Synoptics agree with each other. (And remember, this is a closed logic-system and the assumption is that the works on the top line are independent of each other; were they to agree, there would be no way to demonstrate that they were independent – how would one know they were independent, rather than one having copied the other, as in the original six examples given? – and thus the relationship would violate the assumption of the puzzle, which one cannot do in such logic games.)

Therefore, of the eighteen possible relationships among the texts that set-theory provides for us, twelve have to be eliminated as insufficient to bear the evidentiary weight they are supposed to bear. They cannot possibly do the job, and that conclusion holds irrespective of the actual details of the texts involved. That is a hard point to take in, but no matter how glorious the poetry, narrative or spiritual advice the individual texts may contain, it is irrelevant to the job at hand. Either the machinery can support the weight of the textual relationships or it cannot.

Each of the remaining six possibilities, however, is adequate. Here, one assumes that the first text is independent, and the author-editor of the second text is assumed to have had access to the first (and thus freedom to decide whether or not to copy each individual section of the first text), and the author-editor of the third Gospel is assumed to have had access both to the original independent text and to the second Gospel (and, thus, to have been able to decide on acceptance or rejection of each item in each of those two texts).

Matthew	Matthew	Mark	Mark	Luke	Luke
↓	↓	is copied either in whole or in part by:	↓	↓
Mark	Luke	Matthew	Luke	Matthew	Mark
↓↓	And each of the above is copied either in whole or in part by:		↓↓
Luke	Mark	Luke	Matthew	Mark	Matthew

These six possibilities cover both the instances in which all three Synoptic Gospels agree with each other, and also all possible variations of two-against-one disagreements.

The great beauty of William Farmer's formulating this closed explanatory system is that there is no tilt in its structure in favour of any specific set of arrangements. It is a set of six hypotheses, which cover all the possible relationships. None of these is privileged. One can test the hypotheses one after another: with Mark as the earliest Gospel, with Luke, with Matthew, and with each of the other Synoptic Gospels in the two derivate positions. It is a lovely piece of logical machinery.

This machinery could be associated with any theory of biblical priority, but in the world of biblical scholarship it is usually the basis only of one viewpoint, the *Matthew-hypothesis*.[18] This almost always takes the form of the theory that Matthew was the first Gospel, that the author-editor of Luke used it, and that the author-editor of Mark subsequently used both Matthew and Luke. This is a textual stratigraphy that is upsetting to most Questors for the historical Yeshua, for Matthew is undeniably post-Second Temple, and for Luke and Mark to be even later than Matthew is not of any help in getting behind the 70 CE curtain. However, *within the boundaries of the logical system he has defined*, I find William Farmer compelling. Within his system, his Matthew-hypothesis is much more robust, much more in synchronization with the data as found in the Synoptic Gospels than is the idea that Mark came first.

Yet, the Matthew-hypothesis, while paid lip-service (it is hard to ignore entirely an intellect as powerful as Farmer), is largely ignored by biblical historians, and not entirely for good reasons. One problem is that many scholars find it unattractive because the hypothesis is unfairly saddled with a great deal of dogmatic baggage. The early church fathers saw Matthew as the earliest and the best of the Gospels and from the time of Augustine onwards this was the overwhelmingly dominant view.[19] It became the official position of the Roman Catholic church, and in 1911 the Biblical Commission of the Roman Catholic church affirmed that Matthew was the first Gospel and that it went back to apostolic times. "In deciding the priority of St. Matthew's gospel in its original language and substance, the Biblical Commission has solemnly disapproved of any form of these theories which maintain that St. Matthew's original work was not a complete gospel or the first in the order of time."[20] At that time, historical analysis of the biblical text was almost entirely limited to Protestant scholars, and this endorsement of the Matthew-hypothesis, combined with a dogmatic assertion that Matthew went back to Jesus and his disciples, virtually guaranteed that the Matthew hypothesis was the least likely to gain ascendancy in twentieth-century biblical scholarship. This specific dogmatic handicap no longer exists – the church now permits

Catholic scholars to follow the evidence on this issue – but there is still a segment of followers of the Matthew-hypothesis who endorse it not because of
its logical power, but because of a belief external to the issue of the Synoptic
Puzzle: namely that by endorsing Matthew's priority, they are somehow
catching hold of a text whose traditions extend back to Jesus.[21]

That has nothing to do with the actual Synoptic Puzzle and is the sort of
theological misuse of an historical hypothesis that turns scholars away.
Matthew, in its present form, certainly was written after the destruction of
the Second Temple, and, if the Matthew-hypothesis puts it earlier in the line
of invention than Luke and Mark, that still does not propel it to a date earlier
in time than 70 CE.

Crucially, the Matthew-hypothesis makes sense only if it is assimilated in
the terms defined by its strongest proponent, William R. Farmer, as a neat
solution to a closed-boundary logic problem. Whether Matthew is earliest,
latest, or median in order of invention among the Synoptic Gospels, it still is
post-70, for on that issue the book's contents are unambiguous. This point
was well made by the brilliant classicist (and sometime politician) the late
J. Enoch Powell, who argued not only that Matthew was the first of the Synoptic Gospels to come into being, and that it was the source of the other two,
but that its origin was well after 70 CE and represents a period in which the
Christian church already had firmly established its own liturgical system
quite independent of both imperial Rome and of the various now-scattered
Judaisms. Hence, the year 70 would be the earliest moment for composition,
under this interpretation, but one could easily argue that it represented a
Christianity of one or two decades later.[22]

In that form – in solving most satisfactorily the logical teaser, the Synoptic
Puzzle, and in respecting the clear post-70 date of the Synoptics compilation
in final form – the Matthew-hypothesis is very appealing. Yet it has received
little attention and even less support. The deepest reason, I would speculate,
is because its apparent virtues become emotional drawbacks. *If* the Matthew-
hypothesis is correct as far as inter-textual relationships are concerned, and
if Matthew itself is demonstrably post-70, and *if* the other two Synoptic
Gospels are virtually dependent upon Matthew, *then* biblical historians are
locked into a world of sources that are post-70 CE: and they have no obvious
way of escaping, no way of breaking back into the pre-70 period. I think that
the Matthew-hypothesis is frightening to biblical historians chiefly because
it is perceived as a hope-destroying mechanism: we will *never* know what we
want to know of the historical Yeshua, it seems to prove, ruthlessly. So badly
do searchers for early Christian roots (and especially Questors for the historical Yeshua) want to break past the influence of the catastrophic end of
Second Temple Judaism, that they treat the Matthew-hypothesis as if it
were a threatening character on an urban street: they look away and avoid

eye-contact. Or they appeal to "scholarly consensus" and pass quickly on to more congenial considerations.

That won't do. The Matthew-hypothesis has severe drawbacks and I think that it is not in fact the best available hypothesis, but nothing will be gained by avoiding the issue. In my view, the problems with the Matthew-hypothesis lie in its primary operational assumption: that the Synoptic Puzzle should be defined and solved as a closed-boundary logic problem. That is fine for artificially-constructed brain-teasers, but it is not a sensible assumption if one is dealing with a set of historical documents. These documents have historical referents outside of the logical puzzle, and such referents are not merely adventitious, but are directly related to the matter which the logical puzzle has been constructed to deal with. Historians are not permitted to assume historical patterns and events out of existence.

Here things get tricky. Some proponents of the Matthew-hypothesis point out that it has some direct historical benefits, and that these flow from the magisterial logical solution of the Synoptic Puzzle, rather like the revenues of an appanage accruing to the members of a ruling house. Specifically, it is argued that the Matthew-hypothesis efficiently explains the bi-modal character of the Gospel of Mark, which is said to be a mixture of conflicting viewpoints within Christianity. Mark is put forward as a set of compromises between the Gospel of Matthew, which strongly emphasizes the traditions of Peter and of Jerusalem, and of the Gospel of Luke, which is oriented more around Saint Saul and around the Diaspora of Christianity. This by-product of the Matthew-hypothesis is a potentially useful historical suggestion, but it really has no discriminatory power: the bi-modal character of Mark can just as easily be fit into a theory that suggests Mark was the first of the Synoptic Gospels to be written and that the author-editors of Matthew and of Luke simply disaggregated Mark, each plucking out and emphasizing the aspects he preferred.

Where historical patterns breach the closed-boundary assumption of the Matthew-hypothesis is at a more fundamental level: to have the fullest and most textured Gospel coming first, and the leanest coming last, runs completely counter to the pattern of biblical invention that operates in the Hebrew scriptures (the primary model of the Christian scriptures) and the wide body of para-biblical texts of the later Second Temple era. The grammar of biblical invention facilitates the invention of new texts, but only according to some fairly strict operational principles. Usually, one changes the meaning of a text by expanding it, and in the expansion alters by a few points of the compass its meaning. Or, occasionally, the biblical inventors turn an old text at a 90-degree angle to its original meaning, by redefining the term: thus, the Moshiah of the Tanakh, meaning an anointed figure of priestly, kingly or prophetic rank, became an expected saviour through Christian re-definition. That is very rare.

In very exceptional instances – the replacement of the "young girl" of Isaiah's prophecies with the Virgin of Matthew and Luke – a 180-degree change in meaning is accomplished through brass-necked assertion of the new definition. However, the one way that the grammar of biblical invention does *not* operate is through straightforward deletion of previous texts. Later canonical regulation acted by deletion and censorship, but that was a very different matter than the original invention of texts. As far back as the primary unity of Genesis-Kings, we can observe the manner in which slices of older texts are preserved, even when they are intertextually contradictory. They often are tamed, but they are not thrown out.[23] (The argument I am making in this single paragraph is documented in considerable detail in the text of my *Surpassing Wonder*, especially pages 64–269.)

This is relevant to the Matthew-hypothesis, because, for it to apply to the real historical world – as distinct from its dominating a closed-boundary logical system – the Matthew-hypothesis implies that the author of Mark threw out some of the most important material in Matthew and Luke: most especially the stories related to the Virgin Birth. If one assumes that the author-editor of Mark was writing last and with full knowledge of Matthew and Luke, then one is encountering a total deviation from the rules that have governed all other instances of biblical invention. He is directly rejecting an earlier text, rather than re-inventing it. This, in theory, could have occurred (Mark could have been based on Matthew, with the Virgin Birth deleted as historically inaccurate or as theologically repugnant) except that to have done so would inevitably have made Mark a failure: for, if the author-editor of Mark had knowledge of the Gospels of Matthew and of Luke, so did his audience, or at least they soon would have, for Matthew and Luke were hardly secret documents. Therefore, the Markan narrative would have been judged to have been inadequate, since it left out some of the most electric portions of Matthew and Luke. If Luke and Matthew already were in existence, only someone with no sense of how biblical narrative worked could have written Mark: and anyone who reads the Gospel of Mark knows that its author-editor was one of the canniest of biblical inventors.

The closed-boundary definition of the Synoptic Puzzle nicely tidies up the playing surface by excluding exogenous texts from the discussion. That makes the Puzzle easier of solution, but there are indeed places where the three Synoptic Gospels all disagree with each other, and the Matthew-hypothesis, being a closed-boundary explanation, cannot handle those instances. Here again the real world breaches the walls of the logic system.

Thus, on balance, I prefer the *Mark-hypothesis*, even though it has a number of potential drawbacks.[24] It is basically simple, but includes some elegant moves. Its fundamental point is that since about 50 percent of the Gospel of Mark is also found in the Gospel of Luke, and about 90 percent of the Gospel of Mark is found in the Gospel of Matthew – and thus, inevitably, Matthew and Luke share material that is found in Mark – the best way to explain this situation is to infer that a significant portion of the text of Matthew and of Luke is based upon Mark.

So much of the subsequent course of investigation depends upon whether one follows the Matthew-hypothesis or the Mark-hypothesis, that I must repeat the phrase: "on balance," the Mark-hypothesis seems to me to fit the way the long-term process of the creation of texts worked within the tradition of the Yahweh-faith. However, all judgements about historical matters are really estimates of probability. Historians' adjudicative vocabularies are notoriously fuzzy. Whereas a scientists would say that an event had, say, a 100,000-to-one chance of having occurred, we would say it was a "certainty." Fair enough, but where does "certain" begin? And, what does "unlikely" cover: anything with less than a 50 percent probability of having occurred? If so, it's a pretty large term. Hence, to use a manner of speaking that is alien to historical discourse, but which communicates clearly my sense of the balance of probabilities on this pivotal matter, I'd be willing to bet two-to-one on Mark's being first. Or, to put it another way, the reader should realize that, though I think that on balance the Mark-hypothesis is the best possibility of being historically accurate, I also believe that there is a one-in-three chance that I am wrong.

3

My reason for talking like an odds-maker is not merely cautionary, although a little humility on such a big question as the matter of priority in the Synoptic Gospels might be useful all around. Rather, my direct purpose is to point out that in the scholarly world there are not one, but two, promising versions of the Mark-hypothesis. This despite the fact that one of the two – the one that leads to the hypothetical gospel "Q" – receives almost all the attention. So, when I suggest in the discussion that follows that I find the robustness and fecundity of each of the two versions of the Mark-hypothesis to be dead-equal, I am suggesting that each is unlikely. That's how historical evidence works. To return to our odds-making. If, crudely, the odds are two-to-one that the Mark-hypothesis is right, and if there are two mutually exclusive versions of that hypothesis, then the odds, roughly, are only one-in-three for either of them. This is worth remembering as one encounters the remarkable sense of odds-on certainty of many of the scholars who work on the complexities of "Q." They have the kind of self-confidence that makes bookies rich.

Now, "Q" is so well known that it is not at all well known: an acquaintance with it is expected of an educated person just as an acquaintance with *The Iliad* is expected. And so one encounters *The Atlantic Monthly* languidly misquoting the erudite John Updike as having "simply asserted 'Matthew = Mark + Q' as though the question of Synoptic authorship was settled and could be reduced to a quasi-mathematical formula," and subsequently being sharply rebuked by the novelist.[25] Educated people know about such things. But what is usually "known" about "Q" is that it is part of a "two-source" explanation[26] of how the Synoptic Gospels came into being: Mark and "Q" provide the material for Matthew, Mark and Luke.

Actually, the generally-accepted version of the Mark-hypothesis requires a minimum of four sources, because, although most of Matthew and Luke can plausibly be traced either to Mark or to "Q," each of them has material unique to itself. Thus, to account for the three Synoptic Gospels, one requires: (a) Mark; (b) "Q"; and (c) a source of "Special Material" that is unique to Matthew; and (d) a source of "Special Material" that is unique to Luke. In a previous generation the prevailing speculation was that items "c" and "d" were now-missing documents; but today most biblical scholars prefer to see them as being multiple special sources (*Sondergut*, in the present-day technical term), so that the Mark-hypothesis in the form that involves "Q" is a multiple-source hypothesis.

Here, walk slowly. It is possible to look at Mark, and then at Matthew and at Luke and to be taken by the idea that their relationship may give us the key to something very rare in textual studies, an experimental laboratory. If Matthew and Luke are dependent upon Mark, then we can turn the whole sequence on its head and pretend that we do not know of Mark: we can pretend to derive portions of an unknown document – we will call it Mark – from two known sources.

Why bother? Because this *process* which we can observe – and which is not necessarily an hypothetical process, but possibly a real historical one in which we have lab notes on all three artifacts in the process – gives us a template that we can then apply to a related situation: namely that approximately 200 verses are held in common by Luke and Matthew, but are not found in Mark. We can derive that source – biblical scholars usually call it "Q," which probably stands for "Quelle"[27] – by a process parallel to that by which we pretended to deduce large portions of Mark. "Q" is a fictive document, to be sure, but the legitimacy of the process whereby this conceptual entity was inferred, was established by the way Mark was heuristically derived, in our imaginary laboratory experiment, from common elements of Matthew and Luke. Unlike the so-called "Signs Gospel," which is said to underlie the Gospel of John, "Q" is based upon a set of inventive processes whose reality is confirmed by the documents themselves.

So, the basic sources of the Synoptic Gospels are taken to be Mark and "Q." This arrangement has the virtue of following the way in which the grammar of biblical invention amplifies and transforms texts (by expansion, not by reduction), and also has the virtue of not pretending to be a closed-boundary explanatory system: from the very beginning, the outside world – in this case, in the form of "Q" – is allowed to play a part in the Synoptic Puzzle.

Simple enough. However, because "Q" has become such a focus of scholarly attention in the last one-third of the twentieth century, and its recovery has become a large-scale project of industrial proportions, the concept has lost meaning even as it picked up adherents.[28] Basically, there are four interpretations of "Q" and each of them is conceptually incompatible with the others. The first is rarely articulated very clearly, and is more of an attitude than a methodological position. This is the attitude that what really counts for Christian theologians is biblical literature, considered as a genre, and that historical hypotheses do not have a constitutive function. Instead, these hypotheses – of which "Q" is one – help us to read the Christian Gospels in a more discerning way and, in some sense, to get more out of the texts.[29] The second is that "Q" is most useful as a concept if it is considered to be an *heuristic fiction*, the equivalent in the humanities of a model in the sciences. Scholars who approach "Q" this way see it as an aid to thinking, a way of expressing one of the many possible ways the New Testament may have developed. They do not see "Q" as a potentially real document, any more than a psychologist expects that a transverse section of the human brain will find a "super-ego" or conscience. But, like those heuristic psychological fictions, "Q" can be used as a conceptual tool that bundles together some disparate phenomena and makes them slightly more understandable. Scholars who adopt this approach are not at present terribly influential in "Q" research, but their long-range research in hermeneutics will, I suspect, be substantial, for they are good at remembering that behind all the conceptual trees there still is a real forest. Thirdly, there are those scholars who treat "Q" as an *hypothetical construct*. That is, they say that, no, we cannot infer from present sources a "real" document "Q," one that will be the equivalent of actually finding an ancient text of "Q": however, they add, once we have defined the limits of what actually can be known about "Q" (more of that in a moment), then a useful hypothetical document can be created. Fourth, the most enthusiastic group – the one that makes a goodly portion of its livelihood from "Q" research – believes that a *real document* is recoverable and that this document is equal in its historical reality to that of the four canonical Gospels and that in many ways it is superior substantively to those four texts. (That the four positions I have just defined are distinct and incompatible categories in historical logic is clear, but, scholars being scholars, some few manage to straddle two of these positions simultaneously.)

The reticulation of "Q" research has reached such a level of theory-upon-theory-upon-theory that one instinctively sympathizes with the observations of John P. Meier. He is a Catholic scholar and is generally recognized as the leading student in North America on the question of the historical Yeshua. He accepts that "Q" has some considerable value, but also says:

> I must admit, though, that the affirmation of Q's existence comes close to exhausting my ability to believe in hypothetical entities. I find myself increasingly skeptical as more refined and detailed theories about Q's extent, wording, community, geographical setting, stages of tradition and redaction, and coherent theology are proposed. I cannot help thinking that biblical scholarship would be greatly advanced if every morning all exegetes would repeat as a mantra: "Q is a hypothetical document whose exact extension, wording, originating community, strata, and stages of redaction cannot be known." This daily devotion might save us flights of fancy that are destined, in my view, to end in skepticism.[30]

Obviously, Meier is not one of the "Q" enthusiasts. Members of that group, those who feel that "Q" is a "real document" in some sense, resent the use of the word "hypothetical" to refer to "Q." For example, Stanley D. Anderson, in his introduction to the initial volume (1996) of *Documenta Q*, which will be the massive database of the "International Q Project," under the general editorship of James M. Robinson, Paul Hoffmann and John S. Kloppenborg, expresses this perfectly: "the reconstruction of Q is not in fact as hopeless or hypothetical a project as is sometimes imagined."[31] For the enthusiast, "hypothetical" is a dirty word. Burton L. Mack, one of the most energetic promoters of "Q" as a real entity, comments, "You still hear that: *only a hypothesis*." He adds impishly: "There will be a text! It's going to have a Library of Congress number!"[32] John Dominic Crossan announces that "I prefer to call Q the *Q Gospel*."[33] Although most enthusiasts do not use that term, they need not: "Q" is automatically redefined as the Q Gospel, the second term being taken as implied in the first. The joy of dealing with this "gospel" is apparent in Burton Mack's exclamation. "Q will put us in touch with the first followers of Jesus. *It is the earliest written record we have from the Jesus movement, and it is a precious text indeed.* (emphasis mine) ... Q puts us as close to the historical Jesus as we ever will be. Thus the importance of Q is enormous. It has enabled us to reconsider and revise the traditional picture of early Christian history by filling in the time from Jesus until just after the destruction of Jerusalem when the first narrative gospel, the Gospel of Mark, was written."[34]

The phobia concerning the word "hypothetical" evinced by "Q"'s most earnest advocates is unfortunate because it reduces considerably the power of their case by reducing the wattage of their thinking. "Hypothetical" is part of the common currency of professional historians, social scientists and, indeed, all branches of human studies which attempt as part of their activities to find out what most-likely happened in some sequence of human events. A variety of probative techniques exist for evaluating any given historical sequence, but the two basic ones are: (a) find some direct evidence that an event occurred, a document existed, a person performed a certain action; or (b) develop a hypothetical network of indirect data and relevant concepts that give a high degree of probability that the occurrence in question either happened or did not, or that the artifact in question either existed or did not. Now, the one thing everyone who has anything to do with "Q" agrees on is that there is (as yet) not a single atom of direct physical evidence for the existence of the document "Q." Therefore, it is an hypothetical entity. So the central issue that the "Q" advocates should be addressing is the degree of probability that the hypothetical construct "Q" is apt to conform to an actual real-world document when (in the fulness of time) that text becomes available. Are they putting together an hypothetical construct which they know has certain limiting features (as compared to the real world) or is this construct put forward as an attempt at the full case?

The most unfortunate aspect of the distaste for the term "hypothetical" is that it seems to have spilled over to the concept of "hypothesis." Properly used – that is, not just as a sloppy mis-synonym for speculation or guess – "hypothesis" and "hypotheses" are among the main tools in any rational examination of human behaviour. They permit falsification (that is, verifiable proof or disproof) of a theory or of a prediction that has no visible direct evidence. They tell, in advance, what we will find if a given hypothesis is verified true and what we will find if it is not. Without hypotheses there is no way to go any farther in observing human history than statements drawn directly from eyewitnesses or from primary documents. Yet, the curious situation is that I cannot discover any moment in the modern development of the "Q" theory (say, from, roughly 1970 onwards) when the proponents of the theory have actually defined the criteria by which we will know if their theories are confirmed or falsified. They have not employed hypotheses, much less operational hypotheses, that an external observer could replicate: a very curious situation indeed.

In Appendix B, I express some misgivings that a professional historian is apt to have about the present-day "Q"-industry. However, I wish to make it clear that despite the hubris of the enthusiasts of "Q," their basic goal is not quixotic, merely too loosely defined. That said, recall here that there is another version of the Mark-hypothesis, one that the "Q" followers do not deal with effectively. This is the alternative source-viewpoint put forward most forcefully by the English scholar Michael D. Goulder. Goulder, and his predecessor of the 1960s, A.M. Farrer, are so very unlike the present-day "Q" industry as to be almost unfathomable to the "Q" scholars. Part of the problem is that Goulder and Farrar are, well, too English. The Teutonic school, in considerable part through the influence of the great Rudolf Bultmann's student, Helmut Koester, has blossomed into America's unique biblical mega-projects, the Jesus Seminar and the International Q Project. ("International" is a word Americans use when permitting the occasional Canadian and European into their enterprises). These New World magnates just don't understand the English. The Brits, for instance, mostly work alone. And they usually express themselves cautiously and, when on the attack, use the stiletto rather than the cheque book. Thus, two of the sharpest, shortest, most radical criticisms of the last 40 years – Farrer's "On Dispensing with Q"[35] and Goulder's "Is Q a Juggernaut?"[36] have gone unanswered, presumably because they are too obliquely witty to be taken seriously and too lethal to be faced squarely. And Goulder, as a one-man Disloyal Opposition to the "Q" industry, has the dismaying characteristic of being very precise in his hypotheses and rigorous in his standards of proof. These virtues are easily drowned out by special pleading and general large-group harrumping. All this is a mistake, because "Q" needs sharpening if it is to have any continuing value.

Earlier, I affirmed that I would bet on the side of the Mark-hypothesis – that is, that Mark was the first of the three Synoptic Gospels and was used by the other two. But I also said that there were two versions of the Mark-hypothesis and these seem to have equal chances of being correct. One of these, "Q," is so overpoweringly well known that many very knowledgeable biblical scholars would be hard pressed to articulate the second version of the Mark-hypothesis. Here it is, as stated in conversation by E.P. Sanders. "I believe that Luke and Matthew copied Mark and that Luke also copied Matthew." That certainly cleans up the playing field. "I think it accounts for the majority of the parallel material in Matthew and Luke."[37]

Review for a moment. William R. Farmer convincingly demonstrated that, considered as a closed-boundary problem, Matthew, Mark and Luke could be related in only six ways that explained both similarities and divergences in the texts. The Mark-hypothesis has two variants in Farmer's system and a third, which is "Q." These are:

1 in the classic "Q" model, Mark and "Q" form the basis for the three Synoptics (with allowance for some special material from outside).
2 Or, deleting "Q": Mark came first and was copied by Luke, and then Matthew was put together using the material from Mark and Luke (with a little creativity and a bit of special material by each author-editor along the way).

3 Or, again deleting "Q": Mark came first and was copied by Matthew and then Luke used the material from Mark and Matthew to form his own Gospel (with, again, a little special material and some modest creativity by each author-editor as he copied portions of previous manuscripts).

Now, I remain impressed with the classic "Q" model (even if its elaboration in the last twenty years has turned it into a novella, beyond scholarly verification), because it *may* provide a generalizable insight into how scripture-making took place at the time of the Temple's destruction: the quick blending together of narrative and sayings material into the three Synoptic Gospels under the pressure of the great Destruction. That does something extremely rare in biblical studies – namely, to join together sensibly the internal history of Christianity and the history of the external world in which the new faith was emerging.

For the second version of the Mark-hypothesis, noted above, I have found no strong argument based on inter-textual material.[38] However, that for the third, as articulated by Michael Goulder, is quite powerful. It works as follows, and involves cases in which at least two of the three Synoptic Gospels have material that is close enough to be considered, if not identical, of high affinity. There are three classes of such relationships:

1 Primary Agreements (that is my term) in which Mark, Matthew and Luke all agree. These mostly are matters of narrative, but not entirely. The explanation for these primary agreements in all three version of the Mark-hypothesis is that Luke and Matthew borrowed from Mark.

2 Secondary Agreements (again my term), which are the items on which Matthew and Luke agree concerning material which is *absent* in Mark. It is this material that in the classic "Q" model is made the basis of the hypothetical "Q" document, consisting mostly of sayings.

3 Minor Agreements – this is the generally-employed scholarly term, and it is a very important one – in which narrative sections that are included in Matthew and Luke agree *against* the witness of Mark. These are where the stiletto is hidden.

Michael Goulder is a rigorist and he operates by the same rules that professional historians do. His point concerning the Minor Agreements (of Matthew and Luke as against Mark's narrative) is that for them to occur, the author-editor of Luke has had to have had access to the text of the Gospel of Matthew. Otherwise how would one explain the instances of agreement? (Recall here Farmer's diagrams; one fits perfectly.) So, if one were to find that Luke agrees with Matthew as against Mark in a number of cases (enough to indicate this was not a random phenomenon), then these cases will have falsified the classic "Q" hypothesis (and its modern derivatives as well) by making "Q" totally unnecessary. If the author-editor of Luke knew Matthew, then that explains not only the Minor Agreements question, but the Secondary Agreements as well. Therefore, "Q" becomes redundant.

Michael Goulder is completely right to demand that the "Q" hypothesis be put in a form that can be falsified, and technically right that one single case of a Minor Agreement between Matthew and Luke as against Mark is sufficient to falsify "Q" (as Goulder says, if the hypothesis is that all swans are white, one needs find only a single black swan to falsify it). However, in a field given to special pleading, one needs several confirmatory cases (and also, as I suggested above, to protect against random interference in the data set). In his massive study of the Gospel of Luke (1989) Goulder provides these in spades,[39] but to my mind equally compelling is the fact that Morton Enslin, working completely independently of Goulder, and only peripherally con-cerned with the "Q"-issue (he focussed upon the Synoptic relationships in themselves), produced nine significant instances in which Luke directly used Matthew against Mark.[40]

All this would be intellectually impressive, but rather sterile, had not Goulder (and Enslin) provided in their expositions for the idiosyncrasies and creativity of the texts' author-editors. The scholars are not being impious when they argue that the author-editors of Matthew and Luke were creative individuals who were willing inventively to intervene in their respective texts. That is the historian's recognition of real-world behaviour, not mere paradigmatic thinking, for if there is one point that I established with literally hundreds of historical examples in *Surpassing Wonder*, it is that the people who made the scriptures and the ancient para-scriptural texts were not pas-sive. Within a sense of very strict guidelines as to what was permissible, they acted on their own, bringing in a good story they had heard one place, an uplifting saying from elsewhere. Perhaps, in this new context, that agency by the author-editors explains all those niggling idiosyncrasies that the classic "Q" model imputed to Urtexts, and which the present "expanded-Q" model assigns to *Sondergut*.[41]

4

So, we are at an impasse. None of the new "gospels" that we surveyed in chapter four (Secret Mark, the Gospel of Peter, the Gospel of Thomas) are pre-70 CE and one of them is an obvious hoax. Further, the attempt to mint new gospels from old ones (the Signs Gospel, the Cross Gospel) fails the most basic evidentiary tests. Whether or not "Q" will ever be defined with sufficient rigour to make it historically useful is hard to guess. And, although the various solutions to the Synoptic Puzzle are of great intrinsic intellectual interest, they do not at present help very much in our making the first step in searching for the historical Yeshua: getting back into the world where he lived, that of the Second Temple *before* the Destruction. All these exercises leave us on one side of time's great wall, the Roman-Jewish War of 66–73, and Yeshua and his early followers out of sight, on the far side.

Hence, at the risk of being labelled a Luddite, I conclude that the most likely way to gain access to the historical Yeshua – to the limited extent this is possible – is through the canonical New Testament.

*A Skeleton Key to
the Yeshua-Faith*

· 6 ·

Saul's Life and Letters

I

IN MINNESOTA IN MY YOUTH, I SPENT A FAIR BIT OF TIME WITH AN old Swedish-Baptist preacher. He could have been sent to us by the casting director for any of Ingmar Bergman's early films, except he wasn't as much fun. He was compelling, though, in a way that could easily have been mistaken for self-importance. Everything he said, he said slowly, and he expected you to listen to the end of whatever point he was making, even though you were cocksure what that would be. But he fooled you, and sometimes to his own quiet delight, himself, just often enough to keep you coming back: raising the kind of half-anguished, half-smartassed kind of questions that priests and pastors and rabbis have been putting up with from shortly after Creation. He did not read a great deal by the standards of his vocation, but what he read, he studied very carefully indeed. One day, on winter holiday from Yale College, I talked to him about a then-fashionable commentator on the New Testament whom we were studying. He had not read the man, he said, and probably never would. He paused: long. And then added. "In my life, I have frequently found that the Bible throws a good deal of light on the commentaries."

That is the way it is with the letters of Saint Saul. There exist an Armada's-load of theological and exegetical commentaries, ranging from the arcane to the inane, with the great bulk in between being sensible, earnest, and often convincing, at least until one reads the next one, which is equally sensible, earnest, convincing, and totally in conflict with what one has just read.[1] Because so much of the violent history of Christianity is related to how enthusiasts read Saul's epistles – entire countries were laid waste in the sixteenth and seventeenth centuries, in part because of disagreements about what the authentic channels of Grace were – and because the letters of Saul were often misread as licences to anti-Semitism, here we shall limit our discussion of theology and of non-historically orientated exegesis and stick as closely as we can to the original texts and also to the recent historical discussions of Saul. These, in contrast to most of the recent work on the historical Yeshua, are generally low temperature, evidence-based, and operate by the probative rules of historical scholarship. So, for the purposes of this chapter we will focus on history, not theology, and will keep to the simpler matters of historical interpretation. The speculative and messy ones are reserved for later chapters.

Paula Fredriksen has written that Saint Saul "cannot take us as close to the historical origins of the Jesus movement as we might expect, and wish, he would. But his letters do come from someone irrefutably acquainted with the leaders of the original community. And they do come directly from Paul himself, without the vicissitudes of oral transmission that makes criticism of the Gospels so complicated. In this sense, then, the Pauline letters are the primary source for the Christian tradition *par excellence*."[2] They are the best sources, undoubtedly, but we have to keep reminding ourselves of some basic ground rules. First, when these letters were written, they were not scripture. Later, well after the destruction of Jerusalem, the emerging Christian church defined them as authoritative, and eventually as canonical. But Saul wrote them as forms of communication, in no fundamental way different from the communications of, say, a Roman mentor to his young prodigy. Reading Saul's epistles without the parallax of nearly two millennia of reverence is hard, perhaps impossible, but it is worth trying. They are the letters of a man to his best friends and, sometimes, his most distrusted allies. Secondly, if we try to deal with Saul on his own terms, we are not to become simple-minded: our volitional innocence is not the same thing as real naiveté. Saul, as revealed in his letters, was a feral creature. He would appear in one town or city after another, sometimes leaving footprints the size of craters, at other times, no marks at all, save a half-sentence in a later letter as the only mark of his coming and going. To the historical observer he is maddening, for he appears when least expected and he ducks out of sight just when we think he will be most useful. He is a close witness to the earliest Yeshua-faith, but a difficult one.

We should repeat here Paula Fredriksen's lapidary phrase, that Saul's letters come to us "without the vicissitudes of oral transmission," and the reason the Apostle Saul's letters, whatever their difficulties, must be the heart of the quest both for the historical Yeshua and the earliest Yeshua-faith becomes clear. Prior to being written down – *and Saul's is the first writing-down* – the Yeshua movement and its message "is not only alive; it is also changeable, fluid. It exists only in the minds of those who belong to it – there are no texts – and therefore it tends to mean whatever someone wants it to mean. This is where the village divides." A shrewd observation, but the reader should recognize that, though applicable to the early Yeshua-faith, the description actually refers to a situation in the late twentieth century on the small island of Tanna in the Vanuatu complex near Australia. There the locals worship a god-figure, one John Prum (variant: Frum), a benevolent American trader or perhaps a renegade soldier from wartime, who left them one day in the 1930s or '40s, having done much good, and promising to come again to set the world aright. The islanders keep alive his words, to the extent they can remember them, regulate themselves by a liturgical calendar, and on high holidays dress in their version of vestments, in this case khaki trousers, body-paint in the shape of the American flag, and carry "rifles" made out of bamboo. They march with military precision, but when the rituals are done, they argue about the true nature of John Prum and what faith in him means.[3]

Now, I fully realize that to draw any analogy between a modern situation and one of the early Common Era is to invite a rabid response from biblical specialists. They are forever telling us that "biblical history" is not like modern history. It works by different rules. These are never specified, but what the subtext of this observation communicates is clear: keep off the grass, it's our turf, and not public property. But, in fact, the biblical specialists are dead wrong, and on two counts: present-day professional historians are quite sensitive to changes over time in the meaning of words, social customs and artifacts and they strive hard not to write the past as a pale simulacrum of the present. And, given that sensitivity, there are nevertheless some moments in time when major features of historical events repeat themselves and we can learn from those repetitions.

The John Prum movement is just a small speck on history's big chart – and no one will be more surprised than its leaders if it turns into a world religion – but it should sensitize us to the fact that any new faith (or a radically new version of an old faith) will be especially fluid until it is set into text. Until then, multiple versions of the faith will proliferate promiscuously, spreading outwards from the original version, each claiming, of course, to be the original. This will continue, though at an abated pace, once fixed texts are introduced, until eventually a consolidation phase (heresy hunting) begins. That is relevant to Saul and his version of the Yeshua-faith, because we must continually remind ourselves: although Saul's letters are the first text of the Yeshua-faith, at the time of their writing *they represented only one version of what was already a multiple-version Yeshua-faith, within the complex of multiple Judaisms.*

This is to restate and update the situation that we surveyed in chapter two. The pioneering arguments of Jacob Neusner, that the Yahweh-faith of the later Second Temple era consisted of multiple Judaisms, is now widely accepted. The Yeshua-faith was one sub-phylum within the panoply of those Judaisms. Only after the devotional world of the time was reordered following the religious equivalent of a nuclear blast – the destruction of the Temple and the near-levelling of Jerusalem in 70 CE – was the plural world of Second

Temple Judahisms gradually replaced by the binary world that we have today come to think of as the natural order: the hegemony in the western world of the Rabbinic Jewish and the Christian religions. Before that, however, the worship of Yahweh was composed of many Judahisms, and when we note in Saul's letters that there is evidence of at least half-a-dozen different versions of the Yeshua-faith floating about in the 50s and 60s of the Common Era, we are *not* observing splits within Christianity, but rather, fractures within late Second Temple Judahism, something very different indeed.

2

If Saul is the earliest window we have into any of the several forms of the Yeshua-faith in the era when its followers were like those of the John Prum movement, intense, impressionable, avid to learn more facts and words of their master, but lacking an agreed philosophical or theological plinth on which to mount their master's image – then we would expect the letters of the Apostle Saul to be the heart of any search for the historical Yeshua. After all, the only hope of finding out what Yeshua was actually like is to deal analytically with what his followers thought he was like.

Yet, here we encounter one of the strangest aspects of all the literature on the "Search for the Historical Jesus": almost nobody wants to deal with Saul. Although to a professional secular historian, the obvious course of action would be to start the Quest with Saul's letters, and to use this source (which is not only the earliest in the New Testament, but the only one whose author is known) as the meter stick against which to gauge other sources: not that Saul is always right, but he should be looked at first. Yet, almost nobody does this. Saul is looked at as a last resort, usually, and often not at all. The resistance to Saul as an historical source – which often runs over into direct denigration of his value to the Yeshua-quest – is so widespread as to be nearly universal. This is puzzling, and it gives one the feeling of having missed a very important committee meeting where all the crucial decisions have been made, but no reasoning for the decisions has been minuted. One has to guess why.

Saul's slighting by the "liberal" wing (again, to use an imprecise, but recognizable, word) is more understandable than that by the more conservative scholars. The scholars of the Jesus-Seminar-Q-Project-new-and-hidden-gospels camp have two reasons not to like Saul, the one theological, the other a matter of precedence. It is fair to suggest that most of the liberal wing not only have a scholarly admiration for the "Gospel Q" but a positive theological valence towards it. Hence, it is worth enumerating the theological (or theologicalizable) characteristics of "Q" and relating them to Saul. According to one "Q" scholar, the distinguishing characteristic of "Q" is that it is a collection of sayings with (1) no passion-crucifixion narrative; (2) no resurrection;

(3) no birth story; (4) a stress on the Son of Man; (5) a stress on eschatology; (6) a depiction of Jesus as a wisdom teacher; (7) an emphasis on John-the-Baptizer; (8) a contrast with "this generation" and (9) a stress on the Gentile mission.[4] And that is part of the problem. Saul, though never presenting Yeshua in narrative form, believes strongly in the crucifixion and in the resurrection (in his own special definitions, to be sure). He does not employ the concept of Son of Man and, indeed, implicitly rejects the theological assumptions on which the term is based. Saul does not depict Yeshua as a teacher of wisdom, but as Moshiah. And he has no time for John-the-Baptizer. Manifestly, if one is keen on the theology implied in "Q," that of Saul is an affront and his import is to be minimized. Thus, John S. Kloppenborg and Leif E. Vaage celebrate in "Q" the "discovery" of a form of early preaching, "one which had no special place for the death of Jesus and which, unlike Paul, did not view the vindication of Jesus through the apocalyptic metaphor of resurrection."[5]

Equally important, Saul's letters are an historical affront to the putative chronological precedence of "Q" (and to that of the other various hidden or allegedly newly-discovered works.) As I discussed in chapter five (and in Appendix B), even if one accepts the premises of the "Q" industry, there is no reason to date "Q" any earlier than one dates the Gospel of Mark, except that there is a strong emotional pull for declaring an earlier date. Until the 1990s, most scholars working on "Q" were willing to see "Q" as being, perhaps, mid-first century. In the 90s, however, downward-dating-creep (a red light flashes yet again) has been pervasive and the attempt to delineate a stratigraphy in the maximum version of "Q" (the version being produced by the International Q Project), has insensibly pushed putative datings earlier. Thus Helmut Koester suggests that the "entire development of Q" occurred within "the first three decades after the death of Jesus."[6] The implied meaning is clear: the bedrock layers of "Q" predate the letters of the Apostle Saul (which most scholars suggest are from the 50s and 60s CE). Thus, Burton Mack can assert, "the earliest layers of the teaching of Jesus in Q are the least embellished of any of his sayings in any extant document."[7] Hence, it is easy to understand why Saul's epistles are not treated with much warmth: despite the industry's enthusiasm, Saul's letters are extant documents, "Q" is not. And the Apostle Saul, whatever his limitations, certainly described one form of the Yeshua-faith, a form he knew directly. This is in contrast to what Kloppenborg and Vaage describe approvingly as "Helmut Koester's clairvoyant description of the varied texture of formative Christianity and of Q ..."[8]

Somewhat more surprising is the flaccidity of the enthusiasm for Saul's letters among the more "conservative" Questors for the historical Yeshua. (Conservative here refers to those whose evidentiary methods are more traditional and rigorous, their speculations less innovative than the liberals'.) For example, the doyen of conservative scholars, John P. Meier, in his magisterial reassessment of the entire quest for the historical Jesus, passes quickly by Saul: "Outside of the Four Gospels, the New Testament yields precious little about Jesus. By sheer bulk the most likely source of information is Paul, the only writer of New Testament material who without a doubt comes from the first Christian generation. Since the center of Paul's theology is the death and resurrection of Jesus, the events and sayings of the earthly Jesus simply do not play a large role in his letters. More to the point, his letters did not aim generally at imparting initial knowledge about Jesus, which was presupposed – and recalled only when necessary."[9] Other conservative scholars view things similarly.

As for the evangelical scholars, Saul is important theologically (especially on the nature of Grace), but his letters are not examined often for historical insights. When one leans into the more fundamentalist wings of the Christian tradition, one finds Saul being mentioned less often than the (clearly pseudonymous) "John" who is supposed to have written the Book of Revelation. Saul, it seems is eschatologically challenged, apparently being one horseman short of an apocalypse.

Perhaps the most unsettling aspect of the position of Saul within the vast literature on the New Testament is that he almost always is put in the wrong place chronologically. That is a large generalization, I realize, and I can only illustrate it, rather than prove it. But, as illustration, take a look at one of the finest pieces of collective scholarship of this century in any field in the humanities: the massive, six volume, *Anchor Bible Dictionary*.[10] One can read it for months and be continuously impressed, entertained, enlightened. Here, however, the signal point is that in most (not all, most) of its individual articles the chronology is banjaxed. When one examines most subjects, one notices that the usual trajectory of discussion is, first, Old Testament reference, then the Synoptic Gospels, then John, then the Epistles of Saint Saul, and finally, other canonical scriptures. And this is not singular: it is the way most discussions of Christian topics are presented the world around. Saul's letters are used to confirm or expand upon material – the Four Gospels – that was produced later than the letters. It should be the other way around. Saul came first, and to the extent one wants to interrelate the various sections of the New Testament, the later sources (such as the Gospels) should be employed as confirmation or expansion of the earlier (the epistles). Indeed, here we have an instance of the fallacy that runs throughout so much of biblical scholarship, both Old and New Testament, Christian and Jewish, namely the unspoken assumption that the earlier an event referred to, the earlier the text that refers to it. When put that clearly, the position is impossible to endorse. But, when one asks about the career of Yeshua of Nazareth, most scholars start out with the material that has the earliest references and act as if it is the earliest material. No: the epistles of Saul have to be read first. He is the author of the only statements concerning the Yeshua-faith that pre-date the end of Second Temple Judahism in 70 CE and the wholesale reorganization of the religious universe that thereupon followed. Read him first.

3

But what do we read? In its final form, the New Testament includes fourteen epistles that at one time or another have been attributed to Saint Saul: Romans, 1 and 2 Corinthians, Galatians, Ephesians, Philippians, Colossians, 1 and 2 Thessalonians, 1 and 2 Timothy, Titus, Philemon, and Hebrews. Since the Protestant Reformation, however, and its accompanying focus upon close examination of the scriptures, compelling questions about the authenticity of about half the letters have been raised. For example, in the sixteenth century, Martin Luther not only rejected Hebrews as an authentic epistle of the great Apostle, but relegated it to an appendix at the back of his epoch-making German translation of the Bible. (This, in turn, led the Roman Catholic church in 1546 at the Council of Trent to declare all fourteen letters to be authentic, including Hebrews.)[11]

A fair summation of the present state of scholarly opinion (Catholic, Protestant, Jewish, and unaffiliated) is that it categorizes the epistles as follows:

1 Certainly not written by Saint Saul: Hebrews.
2 The "Pastoral Letters," not written by Saul, but by a later acolyte, using his name: 1 and 2 Timothy and Titus.
3 "School of Paul," or "Deutero-Pauline": Ephesians, Colossians, and 2 Thessalonians.
4 The "authentic letters," consisting (in what is frequently taken to be their chronological order), 1 Thessalonians, 1 and 2 Corinthians, Philippians, Philemon, Galatians, Romans.

For our purposes, the four categories can be collapsed into two: those epistles that are "authentic" (and which thus can be used as a source of information on Saul's views on the historical Yeshua) and those letters which are not authentic (and thus cannot be employed, at least without an unacceptable amount of special pleading).

Since this authentic-inauthentic division is crucial, it is proper to understand the nature of the manuscript tradition of the epistles and how textual scholars have proceeded in sorting out the wheat from the chaff. The earliest manuscript to hold a portion of one of Saul's letters is a fragment of the Chester Beatty Papyri (P-46). This dates from the early third century and is a portion of the Epistle to the Romans (15:33–16:1). In later third-century papyri in the same collection are portions of 1 Thessalonians, Galatians,

Romans, Philippians, Corinthians, plus parts of Hebrews, Ephesians and Colossians.[12] The Christian scriptures had two separate forms, the so-called "Western text," perhaps compiled in Rome, or, less likely, Eretz Israel, and the Alexandrian text, which is generally taken to be more accurate. Each of these has variant readings of Saul's letters and some of the tightest textual scholarship being done today involves a sorting out of these differences. As far as dating is concerned, the key point is that from the fourth century we possess virtually-complete versions of the New Testament (including Saul's epistles). There are fragments of the Alexandrian collection dating from the 200s CE and of the Western text of the New Testament from the 300s CE.[13] This, combined with the Chester Beatty fragments, indicates that the period between Saul's writing his letters and direct evidence for their physical existence is about 200 years. That is a significant period of time, but it is very short by the standards of ancient history, wherein it is common to have the earliest physical evidence of a text a millennium or more after its probable date of composition. Several church fathers of the second century refer to collections of Saul's letters. Clement of Rome, writing in what is usually dated as about 95 CE, frequently paraphrases the writings of Saul.[14] Particularly important is the reference from within the New Testament to the Pauline corpus. This occurs in the pseudepigraphic Second Epistle of Peter which dates from late in the first century of the Common Era or, at latest, the first thirty years of the second. There (3:15–16) the author adopts the voice of St. Peter and refers to "Our beloved brother Paul" and to all the wisdom he has "written unto you." An unambiguous reference to "all" of Saul's epistles makes it clear that a collected edition was extant. Moreover, the letters are referred to clearly as "scripture," a sign that they were in some circles already venerated half a century after their production.

None of this implies that the copies of the letters which were circulating were perfect. Indeed, the work of modern scholars, which argues convincingly that nearly half the material written in Saul's name was not actually by him, makes it obvious that the corpus was played with – all in the best of causes, of course, the edification of the faithful. However, at minimum, the physical evidence and the early citations make it clear that in Saul's writings we are dealing with a phenomenon that occurred early in the history of the Yeshua-faith and which many Christians of the latter decades of the first century took very seriously indeed. I have never encountered any plausible argument that Saul either was a figment of a highly creative religious imaginer, or that he did not, in historical actuality, produce at least some epistles that were by his own hand or that any of the authentic letters were not pre-70 CE in origin.

Three theories about how the corpus of letters came together have dominated biblical scholarship for the last two centuries. To use modern terms, they are the evolutionary model, the big-bang model, and the stepwise model.[15] As the name implies, the evolutionary model suggests that the corpus of Saul's letters aggregated gradually, like a pearl acquiring layer after layer of luminescent material. The proposition is that individual groups of the Yeshua-faith not only were proud of possessing their own letter or letters from Saul, but that they learned of other groups which had their own letters. And so they traded copies, and slowly several separate congregations acquired a reasonably full set of his writings. Since Saul was an authoritative figure, letters written in the style-of-Saul were admitted to the corpus, so long as they fit with the great Apostle's attitude and theology. The second proposal is that, in fact, Saul's letters were not much prized and that it was not until the author of Acts – who did not have a copy of any of the epistles – made a hero of Saul, that strenuous efforts were made to find the now-fugitive copies of his writings and to put them together. Thus, the "big-bang," the sudden appearance of the corpus. According to one of the more popular versions of the big-bang theory, the collection was done by a disciple of Saul who collected as many items as he could, and then bundled them together with his own capstone summary, which we know as the Book of Ephesians.

The drawbacks to each of these models are that neither one has any positive documentary evidence in its favour and each has a strong argument against it. As far as the various versions of the big-bang model are concerned, they demand that Saul and his letters be neglected to the point of virtually having been lost. If this is the case in, say, 80–85 CE (which the model suggests), then it is hard to see how someone like Clement of Rome could, in roughly 95 CE, have granted authority to Saul so easily and employed both overt and sub-textual references to Saul's writings with the same ease of longtime familiarity that he had with the Hebrew scriptures. As for the evolutionary model, the major objection is that if the authority of Saul's person and writings were a constantly growing phenomenon, incrementally increasing each time an epistle was copied by some small group and circulated to other believers, then why is Saul unreported in the four Gospels and why are there no direct quotations in Acts of his writings? (That there may have been indirect usage is another matter; here the point is that such covert usage would hardly indicate any great authority for his words, much less for a collected edition of his letters.)

Jerome Murphy-O'Connor, among others, has argued the case for a stepwise theory. In his version, three partial collections emerged (the details are not here important) by roughly the same means that the evolutionary model posited and then, later, in a manner borrowed from the big-bang theory, they were combined.[16] Murphy-O'Connor's case is well-reasoned and thoroughly plausible, but there are simply not enough data to confirm it. Nor can there be within the information derivable from presently-known documents. We have Saul's letters, but how they came to be preserved and embraced within the canon of the New Testament is a mystery about whose nature we can only guess. (Saul, indeed, could have retained copies himself and that could have been the basis of the corpus.) I think Jurgen Becker has put his finger on the reason for that mystery, when he notes that "apart from Paul, no one in the first early Christian generation felt the need to choose the written form of proclamation. In this, Paul is the conspicuous exception."[17] This apparent uniqueness on Saul's part means that he did not fit easily into the way most of the Yeshua-faith kept its collective memory and proclaimed its beliefs. Since the medium of his memory system and proclamation methods were so very different from those of most of the other versions of the Yeshua-faith, one can understand why the mode of the collecting of his letters went unmemorialized: what is unprecedented is often unrecorded.

How do biblical scholars distinguish in the corpus of letters ascribed to Saint Saul those that they validate as "authentic" and those that they do not? And how confident can we be of their judgement? There is no code of agreed methods among scholars, or anything close. The situation is very much catch-as-can, each scholar proceeding in his or her own unique approach. However, to summarize briefly, my reading of more than 200 studies relating to the authenticity of the various letters leads me to this conclusion: that one has to be extremely impressed with the work done in the field in the last half-century and feel quite confident in the authenticity of the seven letters usually credited to Saul. (Mind you, I would give more credence to 2 Thessalonians than do most of the writers and, also, I think a fairly good case can be made for Colossians as an authentic prison letter, but the consensus data-base we will use in this study is very well argued indeed, and I do not intrude my own views.)

Now, here is how the authentic-inauthentic forensics operate in the field of Saul's letters. Although there is no agreed methodology among biblical scholars, if one examines the work of those who are serious players, one finds that there is a collective methodology that runs beneath the surface of the entire field. The first step in understanding this shared method is to recognize that we are dealing with a case of *reversed presumption*, which is unusual, but not unprecedented in historical work. As I mentioned earlier, the usual rule is that an alleged event or situation is presumed not to have occurred or existed unless there is positive evidence for its occurrence. That is, the standard historical rule is that the grounds of presumption are negative and that a neutral case is disproof. However, in certain unusual situations, the grounds of presumption can be reversed: it can be proper to presume that an event occurred unless there is proof otherwise. We are justified to presume, for example, that winter occurs annually in Siberia, unless proved otherwise. In the case of Saul's letters, the unstated collective rule among scholars is that the fourteen epistles assigned to Saul in the New Testament are genuine, unless demonstrated otherwise. Therefore, the collective task which biblical historians have assigned themselves is not to find positive evidence that Saul wrote any given letter, but rather to find negative evidence: that he did not do so.

Why should the letters of Saint Saul be a justified instance for reversing the usual grounds of historical presumption? Not, certainly, for mere convenience, although the reversal indeed is extremely convenient: for, the positive evidence – things such as salutation and signature phrases, site-specific references, late first-century attestation by Clement of Rome and deep second-century affirmations by the church fathers – concerning the corpus of Saul's writings spreads itself quite evenly over the entire body of putative work. Hence, it has no power to discriminate as between individual items. Negative evidence does. One can use the method-of-subtraction (which is to presume every letter ascribed to Saul to be authentic and then delete items that are shown not to fit with the others). But this works only if we can realistically argue that it is highly likely that a goodly portion of the body of letters is genuine. We accept this as the probability because "a," the early church fathers and the subsequent moulders of the canon of the New Testament were convinced not only that Saul wrote a number of religious epistles, but that they were preserved; and, as discussed earlier, the manuscript preservation of letters believed to be by Saint Saul is strong. Still, this would not reverse the usual grounds of presumption, except for fact "b," that the letters of Saul within the New Testament tradition as it evolved were (and are) an "embarrassment," in the technical sense of the term. They do not fit comfortably. They are letters, whereas the basic New Testament form is the historical narrative (as in the Four Gospels and, as in the Book of Revelation, the narrative of future history.) They are personal and direct. The bulk of the New Testament is impersonal, written by a third-person narrator to an undefined and anonymous audience: very different from Saul's case where a first-person letter is directed to specific individuals. Saul's writing is theological and conceptual, while the heart of the New Testament is historical and narrative in form. And, most importantly, the letters of Saint Saul contradict many of the most basic beliefs of the post-70 CE Christian faith, especially as found in the Gospels. (This is discussed in chapter seven and following.) These dissonances were contained and somewhat dampened in the New Testament, but they could not be silenced. So, in including a set of writings that make a hash out of some of the rest of the New Testament's propositions, the early church fathers and the later framers of the Christian scriptures were effectively saying: these letters are for real; for better or worse, as uncomfortable as portions of some of them may make us, they come from Saint Saul.

Given this reversal-of-presumption, the way that textual scholars work on the authenticity-inauthenticity question makes great sense. Ideally, the historians of the Bible's development would discover a single discriminant axis: a single test that could be run on all of the fourteen possible texts and which would give a yes-no answer for each. Unfortunately, no such axis runs through the entire body of Saul's work. Instead the scholars collectively have developed what one might label a "complex of imperfect combined discriminant axes." That is a very ugly phrase, so I hasten to explain.

Since there is no axis-of-discrimination that runs through the whole body of Saul's writings that gives yes-no readings on the authenticity issue, biblical scholars necessarily use imperfect discriminators: axes of discrimination that work in some (often most) of the cases, but not in all. They use a complex of several of these for the obvious reason that no single discriminator does the complete job. What makes the process mystifying – and which is almost never explained by any of the practitioners – is that each scholar adds together the results derived from each of these imperfect axes of discrimination in his or her own way. Each scholar not only chooses which of the imperfect discriminators is appropriate for the epistle or epistles to hand, but synthesizes the results into a complex that, eventually, provides the basis for the scholar's saying, "this is not authentic," or, "since the evidence against authenticity is not strong, we judge this letter to have been written by Saint Saul."

The process is somewhat demystified when we examine the most common of the discriminatory axes employed by specialists in the field. (My comments on the limits of each method are not meant to be diminutive, but only to indicate that no single mode of discrimination can be employed to give all the answers):

1 *Language*. Efforts are made to develop a data base on how Saul used language and then to find deviations from the central patterns in that base. Granting that there always will be a few outliers in any data-set, it nevertheless is reasonable to conclude that an epistle which employs linguistic patterns which deviate from the patterns of the bulk of the letters *in significant numbers of instances* is not by Saint Saul. The specific linguistic indicators most often employed are: sentence structure, use of parallelisms, sectional or paragraph organisation, opening and closing formulas, pet words, and words that are used only once in a given corpus of literature (*hapax legomena*).[18] The limiting dimension here is that some of the reputed letters of Saul are so small – a few hundred words in some cases – that the characteristics that might indicate inauthenticity have no room to develop. Although most biblical scholars are not trained in quantitative techniques, the linguistic method is essentially statistical and is limited by the same factors that limit any statistical exercise, including the necessity of having a data set to examine that is large enough to make the non-appearance of diagnostic items a matter of substantive quality, not of the random exclusion of the diagnostic item from a small-sized data set.[19]

2 *Ecclesiastical-administrative references.* Generally, if the epistle in question is found to have references to positions or activities that eventually became fixed as church offices – deacons, bishops and the like – the letter is held up to the light and the watermark scrutinized. This is a difficult area, because the meaning of the terms for church functions changed over time, and very rapidly in the early generations. In addition, since Saul's letters are the earliest documents of the Yeshua-faith, what appears to be an anachronistic reference in one of them may instead be authentic and may simply be the earliest reference to the position or activity.

3 *Saul's tone of voice and his personal references.* This is a very muddy area. However, in what is largely a technical discipline, there still exist scholars whose chief talent is that they are really good readers. This is an increasingly rare ability in almost all fields of the humanities and social sciences and one honours it. When a really brilliant reader says, effectively, "that's not the Apostle's voice," or "all those names in the text are bogus," one listens. The drawbacks are that such intuitive assessments are difficult, if not impossible, to replicate; and, who constitutes a brilliant reader, and who is just blowing smoke is not always apparent.

4 *Theology.* If a given epistle has a theological viewpoint markedly different from the bulk of the corpus – or, rather, from the bulk of the corpus that is not ruled inauthentic on other grounds – then it is disqualified. In principle this is fine. The method's limitation is that it almost precludes the possibility of our documenting that Saul developed, or veered sharply, theologically during the course of his career as a missionary of the Yeshua-faith. This is unfortunate because the one thing we know most clearly about Saul is that he was capable of great theological swings: his movement into the Yeshua-faith was nothing if not a radical swerve. And his epistles make clear that he was extremely emotionally volatile, and labile emotions can form the basis for oscillating notions.

6 *Chronology of Saul's life.* The massive issue of the pattern of Saul's life is discussed in sections 4 and 5, which follow. Obviously, if an epistle ascribed to Saul contains a reference to events after his death, the epistle almost certainly is inauthentic. Most chronological issues, though, are not so clear, and the use of Saul's personal chronology as a discriminator puts one inside a spinning cage: the chronology of Saul's life is in considerable degree determined by how one arranges the various epistles and, particularly, which ones are excluded from the chronology.

7 *The Roman Standard.* Although this is usually not articulated, the degree to which the epistle in question conforms to the contours of the Epistle to the Romans is a pervasive criterion.[20] Romans is taken (correctly, certainly) to be authentic, so using it as a meter stick is sensible. In doing so, however, one is using as a standard one of the world's truly great pieces of

religious literature to assay other pieces that are mostly merely craftsman-like and, in places, downright incomprehensible. Lest this sound disrespectful of the entire corpus, let me state my own view: that the Epistle to the Romans is the single most compelling, most fluidly argued, most supplely articulated piece of expository prose in the entire body of religious literature in which it is situated, which is to say, in the Tanakh, the New Testament, the Mishnah, and the two Talmuds. It is a monumental achievement, and that is why using it as a criterion has its limitations: no one else gets close, and certainly not Saul himself.

If one is comfortable with the method and application of these methods to the body of letters ascribed to the great Apostle (and I think one should be, for the scholarship is impressive), it is nevertheless fair to remain aware of some finite issues on which we have to settle for unanswered questions and the occasional guess.

One of the most intriguing of these matters for an historian is the speculation concerning letters Saul actually may have written, but which are now lost. Saul was an active proponent of the Yeshua-faith for roughly two decades before his first known letter. It is scarcely credible that, around the year 50 CE, he started writing. The earliest letter, 1 Thessalonians, is that of a practised correspondent, and when one picks it up, one has the feeling of having opened a set of correspondence files in the middle. A lot has come before.

We know from internal evidence in the surviving letters that various post-50 CE letters were lost. In 1 Corinthians 5:9 Saul says, "I wrote unto you in an epistle not to company with fornicators." This is sometimes called the "previous letter," for it antedates First Corinthians, but has left no direct trace. Another lost epistle – often called the "painful letter" – is referred to in 2 Corinthians (2:3–4). This may be the same letter referred to later in 2 Corinthians, where Saul notes that "for though I made you sorry with a letter, I do not repent, though I did repent: for I perceive that the same epistle hath made you sorry, though it were but for a season" (7:8). And, if one credits that Colossians was written either by Saul, or by a disciple of his who knew his correspondence patterns well, then there was also a letter from Saul to the church at Laodicea (Colossians 4:16).

Equally, one would like to know what the other side of the correspondence looked like. Certainly some letters were sent to Saul (the Corinthian-correspondence makes that clear), but in the case of the more upbraiding of the Apostle's epistles, one wonders if the recipients really had any chance of getting a word in edgewise. When Saul was on full tilt at his exhortations, I suspect that the recipients reacted in the same way university students do when they receive a scolding e-mail from mom and dad: delete the item and wait until they cool off.

Among the secondary literary matters biblical scholars deal with is the extent to which later insertions have been made into otherwise-authentic epistles. In my reading of the literature, there are no suggestions that have probative force concerning any major insertions in the authentic letters, such as the introduction of references to liturgical practices or theological beliefs or intra-church relationships that developed after Saul's death. The only pericopes that seem to me to have any chance of actually being interpolations are 1 Thessalonians 2:14–15, 2 Corinthians 6:14–18, and part of Philippians 1:1. Even here the arguments are not, in my judgement, strong, and even were these to be interpolations, they are not major matters of substance.

More suasive are the suggestions that some of the authentic letters of Saul are, in fact, compilations of two or more epistles. This is not unlikely, given that some of the letters must have gone through several copyings and, further, that some of the original manuscripts became tattered, portions lost, before they could be transferred to larger collections. Hence, a later copyist became essentially an editor and put a loose fragment into a larger letter where it seemed to him to fit. For example, a case can be made that Romans 16:25–27, which seems to be an interruption in a fixed epistle-closing formula, comes from elsewhere (its theology and voice are those of the Apostle, but the interruption is jarring). Other scholars suggest that the entire portion of the final chapter of Romans which precedes this closing formula (that is, Romans 16:1–23) is from a different (and now-unidentified letter), for the verses close a theological discussion with what seems to be the payment of social obligation. Second Corinthians is the most likely to be a pastiche because, against the background of a fairly joyous epistle that celebrates Saul's triumph over adversity, the reader suddenly hits a vitriolic rebuke against paganism: 2 Corinthians 6:14–18. (This, as mentioned above, may not be authentic, but an interpolation.) Then, a bit later, one encounters a long, stern lecture (2 Cor. 10–13) to someone unnamed.

There are other, minor suggestions, but those are the main places where scholars suggest with some argumentative force that separate epistles may have been taped together. These are intriguing textual puzzles, but as far as the mission of the present study is concerned, the possible joining of two or three letters into one has virtually no effect. If Saul wrote it, he wrote it, and though we lose context when a fragment is joined to a larger epistle, Saul's basic beliefs about Yeshua are unchanged.

I find it admirable that the great majority of modern textual scholars of Saul's letters are careful to avoid being cavalier with his material. One finds much less of the confident straightening out of Saul's sometimes-chaotic rhetoric today than in the literature of, say, half a century ago. Today we accept that the great Apostle had a lot on his mind. When he concentrated he could write like an angel (as he did in the Epistle to the Romans) but, as the self-defined vicar-general of much of Asia and Europe, he was constantly worried about discipline in his far-flung flock, and all the time he had to carry on a desperate fight for his own legitimacy with the leaders of the Jerusalem church. At times, Saul reminds one of a vice-principal of a large urban high school who has to teach a daily class in calculus to the college-bound stream, then, as head of discipline he breaks up a fight in the hall, and next he finds he has to fill in for a shop teacher who has gone home with a migraine. After school he coaches the offensive line of the football team, and finally at night he has to appear before a special session of the city council and give a polished argument for continued funding for the art and music classes. So we honour the canon of Saul's letters by accepting their sometimes-distracted, sometimes-staccato quality as part of the warrant of their authenticity, the words of a man on a mission.

I propose that we take the seven authentic letters, and concentrate on them and on their most obvious characteristics so as to uncover the outline drawing for what was the first fresco, the first depiction of the historical Yeshua. It may feel slightly unfamiliar to accept the "scholarly consensus" on what constitutes the seven authentic letters of Saul, for in this book I have indicated that, usually, the scholarly consensus on biblical matters is not intellectually impressive. However, here we take the consensus as given, for three reasons. The first is that the recent critical literature on this issue is of a notably high quality. Second, the seven excluded items actually do not contain much, if anything, that directly contributes to the inferences we can draw from the seven authentic letters. And the third reason is rhetorical. Given that we wish to develop an outline of one of the several variant forms of the Yeshua-faith in the era when that faith was still one of the multiple Judahisms of the late Second Temple era, we do not want to distract attention from the main issue at hand; nor raise resistance from skeptics of the whole idea of an historical Yeshua. Therefore, instead of conducting a dozen little arguments on (for example), whether or not fragments of Colossians are really by Saul, or if there are echoes of genuine teachings of Saul in the letter to the Ephesians, we will here take the minimum "scholarly consensus" as defining our data field.

4

Naturally there exists a large body of scholarship on the chronology of the life of Saint Saul. Its single most important substantive point is that Saul's life as a follower of Yeshua occurred entirely – and for historians, therefore, most inconveniently – between the two most crucial dates in the development of the Yeshua-faith: the crucifixion of Yeshua of Nazareth and the destruction of the Second Temple in 70 CE. Saul, as a believer, operates entirely after the crucifixion and he has no inkling of the massive trauma all forms of the Yahweh-faith soon will suffer with the devastation of Yahweh's house. What we lose in detail, however, we pick up in the innocency of Saul's outlook: for he is the only (as yet) known Christian writer who tells about Yeshua and about the Yeshua-faith, without his having to bend the story to fit the awful foreknowledge of the destruction of the seemingly-eternal centre point of the world of Judahism.

The point of contention that dominates present-day historical thought concerning the chronology of Saint Saul's life was raised modestly, almost obscurely, in 1936 in the *Journal of Religion* by the appropriately-named John Knox. This was followed by another modest article in 1939 and by a scholarly book published in 1950 by a devotional press.[21] Considering that at the time he wrote, study of the life of the great Apostle was dominated by imposing authority-figures – persons such as W.L. Knox, C.H. Dodd, and Arthur Darby Nock – John Knox was proceeding with exemplary courage.[22] His trenchantly-accurate observations were exactly the kind of behaviour that frequently ends a career. Knox, with politesse, introduced a question that is so fundamental that it needs to be framed rudely: as a source for the life of Saint Saul, should the Acts of the Apostles be largely torched?

That question has hung over studies of Saul and his writing like the grey ash cloud from a distant volcano. Biblical scholars have either tried to ignore the issue entirely (which can be done if one limits one's topic to commentary on limited segments of the epistles or focuses on a band of theological issues whose character is independent of historical circumstances), or they have had to make a decision on the issue and adjust their statements accordingly. The primary pieces of scholarship on the question are impressive indeed, and could with great benefit be assigned in post-graduate seminars in history departments as examples of the most fundamental of historical exercises, the formation of a chronology from primary sources. The pivotal works are by John Knox, John Hurd, Robert Jewett, Gerd Luedemann, Jerome Murphy-O'Connor.[23] In addition to these are many less comprehensive chronological studies of high value, and also some major studies that deal with the matter of Saul's life course as ancillary to other issues.[24]

In order to focus on the pivotal issue of how we should use Acts as an historical source for the life of Saint Saul, we first need to clear the pitch of a good deal of detritus. Approach to the central issue is hindered by a set of mannerisms concerning the Acts of the Apostles that are common among biblical scholars. One of these is to refer to the author of Acts as "Luke." Now, it is true that the book of Acts begins (1:1) by strongly implying that it is a continuation of the text we now refer to as the Gospel of Luke. Whoever the author-editor of the Gospel of Luke may have been, applying the term "Luke" to the author-editor of Acts is tenuous at best. Indeed, using the name "Luke" for the author-editor of the third Gospel is misleading, for we do not have the vaguest notion who wrote that Gospel. In the mid-second century references in Colossians (4:14) and 2 Timothy (4:11) – both sources which are now excluded from the authentic epistles – and (perhaps) a reference in Philemon (1:24) were used to put a name on the otherwise-anonymous third Gospel. This was imaginative, for although the references in the various epistles ascribed to Saul might be stretched to give a name the church could apply to the author-editor of the Acts of the Apostles (which indeed has a lot to do with Saul's missionary work), these references have no direct applicability to the third Gospel. Still, the spreading backward in time of the putative author of Acts (for whose actual authorship there is not a dot of evidence), to the author of the third Gospel, was the invocation of contact-authority, a phenomenon frequently studied by anthropologists, but not usually indulged in by textual scholars. If, in the present day we are stuck with the appellation "Luke" for the third Gospel, we should not use the name "Luke" as if we know who the author-editor of either the third Gospel or of the Acts of the Apostles actually was. Use of a fictive author moves inexorably from being a figure of speech to a narcotic that makes us think we know more than we do. This holds even if (as probably is the case) the third Gospel and the Acts of the Apostles are in the majority of their content constructed by the same person or persons.

Similarly, the mannerism of referring to "Luke-Acts" as if it were a single book is highly misleading. Though one accepts that the bulk of the two compositions are by the same author-editor(s), one is hesitant to accept even the judgement of the authoritative canonist Brevard Childs that "the literary evidence is unequivocal that the books of Luke and Acts once formed a two-volume work by the same author."[25] While accepting that the same author-editor framed both works, our naming the work "Luke-Acts" and assuming it was an integrated two-volume composition misses the obvious points that the genres of the third Gospel and of Acts are markedly different, and that the Acts of Apostles includes several discontinuous segments (to be discussed in a moment) that bespeak a contributor to the composition who was not part of the framing of the third Gospel.[26] "Luke-Acts" as a term misleadingly implies that not only were the same primary author-editors in charge of constructing the works, but that the resulting products were a unity.

Truer to the actual situation would be the statement that the author-editor(s) of the third Gospel and of Acts produced two separate, but related works. This not only permits a recognition of the generic differences between the two volumes, but also covers the possibility (I think it is a probability) that a significant period of time separated the writing of the two books. So: not "Luke-Acts," but the Book of Acts and the Gospel of Luke, separate entities; and not "Luke" as author of either book, but instead we refer to "the author-editor of Luke" and "the author-editor of Acts."

Here, I would not blame the reader if he or she thinks I am becoming pilpulistic. However, we absolutely must clear our work space of misinformation before looking at the relationship of Saul's letters and the Book of Acts. The present-day use of "Luke" as author of Acts and of "Luke-Acts" as indicating a unified two-volume work gives a spurious contact-authority to the Acts of the Apostles as an historical text. And that tilt is the last thing we want in relating Acts to Saul's writings. If we are to face with integrity the possibility that Acts may have to be largely or totally disregarded, then we owe it to the material to wipe it clean of distortions that would lead us, however unconsciously, to prejudge issues that should be examined unimpeded.

The conceit that both the third Gospel and the Acts of the Apostles were written by a "Luke" who was a companion of Saul on some of his missionary journeys is a nice piece of creativity, but it has virtually no chance of being historical: for the author-editor of Acts, though an admirer of Saul, and perhaps privy to some accurate oral traditions about the great Apostle, has not had access to the one body of information any companion of Saul would have had: his letters. Indeed, the Book of Acts shows a complete ignorance on the part of its author-editor of Saul's corpus of writing. Not one direct quotation is identifiable as being from Saul's epistles[27] and, further, the author-editor gives no indication of an awareness that the letters even exist.

In fact, Acts is an extended ideological message. Its goal is to show that Saul was the leading figure in the expansion of the faith after the death of Yeshua of Nazareth. And, secondly, it attempts to minimize evidence of the vitriolic splits among various branches of the early Yeshua-faith. This it essays chiefly by minimizing the split between Saul and the Jerusalem church, headed by Yacov, the brother of Yeshua.

Students of the New Testament have spent generations trying to harmonize two incompatible accounts of Saul's life and mission: that found in Acts and that implied in the letters. The points where serious incompatibilities arise are: (a) the degree to which Saul had persecuted the followers of the Yeshua-faith in his early life; (b) in particular whether he had persecuted the so-called "Jerusalem church"; and (c) whether he had been complicitous in the murder of Stephen; (d) the circumstances of Saul's change from one form of Judahism – from a form of Pharisaism, to the Yeshua-faith – and whether or not the road-to-Damascus "conversion" was part of the occurrence; (e) the number of missionary journeys Saul made; (f) the number of visits he made to Jerusalem; (g) the nature of the "Jerusalem Conference" and (h) the character of the agreement sorted out there which gave Saul licence to continue to preach; (i) the nature of the collection that Saul was required to raise in support of the "Jerusalem church" and (j) the degree of animosity as between Saul and the central body of the faithful in Jerusalem, headed by the brother of Yeshua. These, and other significant variances between Acts and the letters of Saul are discussed in the studies I have referred to earlier, and from this literature one central fact emerges: on several major matters on which there is information in both of the sources, Acts and the letters cannot be reconciled.

Therefore the immediate question that arises is, whom do we believe? To take a specific case, in Acts, the pre-Yeshua-faith Saul is said to have persecuted the followers of Yeshua in Jerusalem (8:1–3) and to have given his tacit assent to the murder of the saintly Stephen (7:58). Concerning the situation in Jerusalem and its environs, the statement that "as for Saul, he made havoc of the church, entering into every house, and haling men and women committed them to prison" (8:3), cannot be reconciled with Saul's own statement that until after his adhesion to the Yeshua-faith he was "unknown by face unto the churches of Judaea which were in Christ" (Galatians 1:22) and that they had only heard of his persecution of believers – meaning that he had done so in some other place, but not in Jerusalem. Saul's statement is the more convincing because it is not a response to the accusation in Acts, but a statement made twenty to thirty years before the Acts of the Apostles was written. Saul puts it forward as an autobiographical fact that fits in a letter to a local congregation. Fine: so in this instance, we accept Saul's words over those of the author-editor of Acts.

Do we do this in all cases? The strongest arguments for always taking the words of Saul's letters over those of Acts are made by John Knox, in his classic (1950) book and, most forcefully, recently by Gerd Luedemann (1984). This seems to me convincing, but we should understand why we adopt this method. Emphatically, it is not because Saul was incapable of either consciously lying or of unconsciously misrepresenting what had occurred. He was, after all, very human indeed. *Nor* is it because the author-editor of Acts, having a strong set of ideological motives, invariably misrepresented the facts: some portions of Acts concerning Saul certainly are accurate. Some of the factual statements in Acts fit with Saul's letters closely. And, if the author-editor of Acts got these matters right, even though he did not have access to Saul's letters, then whatever sources he used were not entirely without merit, nor was his ideological bent so strong that he destroyed all facticity. But, as an historical source, we must choose Saul's letters over Acts for reasons of probability of accuracy and because of the issue of lack-of-third-party-verifiability. First, it is probable (but not inevitable) that in general a set of first-person letters, written before the great Destruction of 70 CE will be more accurate about the life of the individual who wrote the letters than will be a second-hand account written twenty to thirty years after the person's death, unless the later account is a piece of deeply researched historical writing, which Acts is not (the epistles of Saul were not even recovered by the writer of Acts). This is made the more likely because the first-person letters were written before the great catastrophe of the levelling of Jerusalem and the destruction of the geographic focal point of the faith, an event which bent radically everyone's angle of vision. Secondly, in any specific instance, unless there is independent third-party evidence to help us adjudicate the clashing "facts," then one goes with the first-person, earlier material than with a later, second party. In fact, third-party information is so rare as to be virtually nonexistent. Therefore, the rule has to be that Saul's letters take evidentiary priority over Acts. This is merely a statement of evidentiary method, not of devotional adherence to the epistles and, while using them as the prime source, one would do well to accept that on some issues, Saul probably has misled us (and maybe himself). But this is a con that we cannot detect.[28]

Many (probably most) biblical scholars in the English-speaking world (and, increasingly, in European circles) who have an interest in biblical historical matters now accept John Knox's view that when the two sources clash (and when there is no external determinative source, which there almost never is), then Saul reigns. Simultaneously, most scholars would accept that the Acts of the Apostles contains valuable material of a "traditional" sort (this being the biblical scholars' word for what modern historians comprehend under the related categories of oral history and folklore). Sorting out the useful from the misleading traditional material is the difficulty. However, very few scholars would disagree that the material in Acts can be used to amplify material on incidents that are first reported in Saul's letters. As long as the stories are in alignment, the folklore and oral history contained in the Book of Acts has utility.

However, there remains the bulk of the material in Acts that concerns Saul and which is not aligned with items in the Apostle's letters. Most present-day scholars still resist the unspoken argument that John Knox's methods force into being: if one adopts Saul's own epistles as the standard of factual accuracy, and if on a significant number of occasions the narrative in the Acts of the Apostles has to be judged significantly inaccurate, then, should not the entire Acts of the Apostles, insofar as it deals with Saul, be excised as a direct data source *except* for those portions that are directly confirmed by material in Saul's letters? Certainly that is what we would do in secular history. If, for example, a glossy magazine published during World War II was later found to have gotten most of the major facts of the conflict wrong, would we not chuck it out as a direct source of historical data? As information on what people wanted to believe, on the character of government propaganda, or as other indirect data, we would of course keep it. But as information for a chronology of the war it would be worthless without external confirmatory evidence (which, in the case of Acts and Saul, we do not have). Out it would go.

Yet, most historians of Saul's life – fine scholars such as Robert Jewett (1979) and Martin Hengel (1991) – keep using portions of Acts so long as nothing in Saul's epistles contradicts the Acts-material in question. What is wrong with that?

Everything, actually. The practice implies an amazingly gullible evidentiary double-standard: (1) when the Acts of the Apostles is contradicted by the letters of Saul, the letters are taken as accurate and the Acts of the Apostles as inaccurate; and (2) when they agree, Acts is taken as an historically useful amplification of the letters. Each of these procedures is solid, but procedure (3) most certainly does not follow: that when, as occurs on most matters of chronology and facticity, there is neither contradiction nor affirmation, the Acts are taken as being trustworthy. Consider what that method of evidence-cum-faith would mean in everyday life: if you caught a co-worker lying to you a fair amount of the time – not all the time, for sometimes he or she says things that are indeed true – but in a significant portion of instances, on occasions when his or her word could not be checked, would you automatically accept as your presumption that the uncheckable utterances were true? Not if you valued your own position. It probably is impious to depict the author-editor of the Acts of the Apostles as intentionally lying, so substitute the word "inaccurate" in the analogy and the case is clear: in the absence of affirmative evidence of the accuracy of a statement in Acts concerning the life of Saint Saul, the assumption has to be that any given statement is not to be trusted (it is not necessarily wrong, just not to be trusted as historical evidence). Therefore, one has arrived at a position wherein one (a) accepts the portions of Acts that are confirmed by Saul's letters and (b) distrusts – on the basis of the canons of historical method – all other statements. Since that leaves as useful parts of the Acts of the Apostles only those portions that agree with Saul's letters, one has in essence incinerated most of the parts of Acts that describe Saul's missionary activity. One can continue to use Acts as an independent source of information on the evolution of ideology and tradition in the post-70 CE Yeshua-faith, but not as data on what happened to the first generation's greatest Apostle.

None of us likes to be told that we have been building temples upon quicksand, so it is hardly surprising that the ineluctable implications of John Knox's methods have been largely ignored. Were they to be accepted, a lot of people would be out of work. But, more than that, faces are averted from this situation because of what it may – just may – imply about the third Gospel. Recall that Luke and Acts are frequently joined by scholars as Luke-Acts and that a contact-authority melds the two. Now, if much of the data in Acts – which were generated in an era relatively close to the lifetime of the author-editor of Acts – are adjudged to be inaccurate by reference to the first-person contemporary evidence (Saul's letters), then it might seem very likely that the material on which the author-editor of the two volumes had less recent sources of knowledge (that is, the material about Yeshua of Nazareth) is even more apt to be inaccurate. That, I think, is where the real fear, resistance and denial lies.

All these problems hold if one insists on the Acts of the Apostles being a unified document. If, however, one is willing to contemplate its being not the pavement-smooth product of the "Luke" who allegedly wrote "Luke-Acts," but instead, like most of the scriptures (both Hebrew and Christian), a compilation and composition by one or more author-editors, then in theory portions of Acts relating to Saul still may have value as an historical source independent of Saul's letters. In particular, commentators long have pointed to the inconsistency with the rest of Acts of four so-called "we" sections of the book. These are sections that relate to Saul's missionary work and in which the narrative's tone takes a bit of a bounce, for material appears that instead of being presented by a distant narrator, refers to what "we" did. This is done fairly smoothly (Acts, even with inserts, is a lovely piece of narrative writing), but still it is noticeable: in 16:10–17 (dealing with the trip to Macedonia and the first recorded European convert, the woman Lydia); 20:5–15 (the return to Troas and Saul's raising from a death-like state a young man who had toppled from an upper window, having fallen asleep as the Apostle droned on); 21:1–18 (from Miletus to Tyre to Jerusalem, with a warning from the Holy Ghost of what "the Jews" intended to do to Saul and, finally, a meeting with Yacov and all the elders of the Jerusalem branch of the Yeshua-faith); and 27:1–28:16 (the journey as a captive to Rome by way of Malta, where a poisonous viper bites Saul's hand, but, the Apostle suffers no ill effects).

Emphatically, one does not here jump naively to the assertion that the "we" sections are historically accurate. Manifestly, there is a good deal of folklore in these passages (healings, a seeming raising-from-the-dead, several signs of Saul's more-than-just-human state, all of which parallel stories one finds in the Synoptic Gospels about Jesus), but folklore often has at its heart factual accuracy. Here the point is that *if* the "we" sections come from a different source (apparently a different author) than does the material in the rest of Acts, *then* those sections escape from John Knox's logical steam-roller: for none of the four passages contains any of the substantive clashes with the epistles that I mentioned earlier and, further, with a bit of nimbleness, each of the journeys mentioned can be worked into a chronology of Saul's life that uses the letters as its evidentiary spine. Therefore, one could segregate out from the Acts of the Apostles these four "we" passages and keep them as independent evidence, potentially accurate in substance, if a bit gilded in detail. Except for those sections that are confirmed by Saul's letters, the rest of Acts (insofar as Saul is concerned), as a source of direct historical evidence has to be jettisoned.

That sounds incredibly drastic, and, if one's interest in life is to create a biography of Saint Saul, it is. One loses a lot of good stories and pieces of tradition that one wants to be trustworthy but which, alas, are not: Saul as persecutor of the Jerusalem followers of Yeshua and as a consenting witness at Stephen's martyrdom; the conversion of Saul on the road to Damascus; his shaking off the dust of his feet at Antioch; his speeches before accusers. Most importantly from an historical standpoint, however, this refusal to accept unconfirmed material in Acts (except for the spine of the "we" sections) means the abandonment of the material in the six verses most treasured by chroniclers of Saul: Acts 18:12–17. This is a seemingly minor passage that has Saul appearing before Gallio who was the proconsul in charge of Achia, the Roman province in Greece whose capital was Corinth. This man, Junius Gallio, was memorialized in an inscription at Delphi which gives the dates of his proconsulship. Making allowances for slippages in language, if the events in Acts 18:12–17 are taken as automatically trustworthy, then most scholars suggest that Saul was up before Gallio sometime in the period 49–52 CE. The date is treasured because all the relative chronology of Saul's life suddenly can be hung on a real-world "absolute" date. It is usually cited as the sole absolute dating point in the entire mass of material related to the great Apostle. We want it to be accurate, very, very much.

But remember the rule: because of the demonstrable inaccuracy of Acts on many issues on which it can be checked, the grounds of presumption have to be that this event did not take place. Of those events unconfirmed in Saul's letters, it is no different from any other of the events reported in Acts, so no matter how desperately we desire the convenience of an absolute date, it has to be set aside as untrustworthy (again: not necessarily as untrue, but as not commanding trust).[29]

However, if one is interested chiefly in a meta-task, the employment of Saul's life as a source of information on the historical Yeshua (and secondarily, on what early believers affirmed about Jesus-the-Christ), then the excision of Acts (save for the less folklorish portions of the "we" sections) as potential evidence (unless confirmed by Saul's letters) is not debilitating, or even much of a hindrance. We do not lose much, because it is overwhelmingly in reports of his words that we can learn what Saul thought about Yeshua's life. However, the author-editor of the Acts of the Apostles writes monologues and dialogues the same way that most ancient writers did: not as reportage of what actually was said, but as set-pieces of what the person involved should have said. So, in Acts we do not have the words of Saul, but the dramatic reconstruction of Saul. Secondly, the words that Saul speaks in Acts are not derived from his own theology, but from that of the author-editor of the Book of Acts. In fact, whoever wrote the Acts of the Apostles was both a skilled dramatist and a smart theologian and Saul as a character in his narrative is a convincing dramatic figure. But he is not a Saul who is compatible with the Saul who wrote the epistles.[30] And, thirdly, the lines given to Saul in

Acts have little to do with the historical Yeshua. Mostly they involve the Apostle's missionary activities and his conflicts with the world around him.

Therefore: as intriguing, and ultimately frustrating, as is the search for a convincing chronology that runs through Saul's entire life as a member of the Yeshua-faith, it is a side-issue. The indeterminacy of the evidence provided by the historical sources should not distract our attention from the central point: in the letters we have the actual words of Saul to investigate. Their meanings as they reflect his knowledge and beliefs about the historical Yeshua are not conditional upon anything but the most general time frame; nor is knowledge of the precise order in which the epistles were written a pre-requisite for determining the meaning of any given statement. Certainly a probable chronology and a reasonable order-of-composition can be an aid to establishing context but, at the heart of the matter, it is Saul's words we have to deal with.

5

Within the critical literature, the order of the seven authentic letters is a scramble: there is no general agreement and each specialist has his or her own order. The points that most would agree on are that among the seven letters in question: (a) I Thessalonians is the earliest; (b) I Corinthians is the most-likely second epistle; (c) 2 Corinthians comes soon thereafter, and in its original form probably was two separate missives, I Corinthians 1–9 and 10–13; (d) Romans comes near the end of the Apostle's career and close to the end of the skein of his writings. Greater agreement than that one cannot assert without bending the available opinions to suit an external template. That the leading scholars in the field cannot come any closer to agreement about the ordinal arrangements of Saul's letters is vexing in one sense (one wants to know as much as possible about this massive and angular personality), but it does not materially affect our own search – for we are looking for the historical Yeshua, and the historical Saul is simply a mode of access. The interpretation of the meaning of Saul's opinions and information about both Yeshua of Nazareth and Jesus-the-Christ contained in, say, Galatians is not much changed whether one follows those scholars who believe Galatians to have been just prior to the composition of Romans, or those who believe it was produced at the same time as 2 Corinthians. Each of Saul's letters is almost (almost, but not quite) an independent literary-historical unit and, as far as I can see, no great impairment to our understanding of his views of Yeshua results from our having to be somewhat tentative about the positioning of some of the letters.

As I have explained, for a chronology of Saul's life the only efforts that work within the rules of the historical profession are those that take their information from Saul's own writings and that use the Book of Acts only as a source of amplification of those words, not as a source of information reliable on its own. The pioneer in proceeding this way, John Knox, summarized the life, as inferred from the epistles, as follows, beginning immediately after Saul's conversion:

> He remained in the neighborhood of Damascus for three years or more. Afer a visit to Jerusalem to become acquainted with Cephas, he returned to Syria (probably to Antioch), then went on (probably soon afterward) to Cilicia. In the course of the next fourteen years he lived and worked in Galatia, Macedonia, Greece and Asia, and possibly elsewhere. He ran into increasing difficulty with conservative Jewish Christians, probably from Judea, and finally went to Jerusalem to talk with the leaders there about the growing rift. This conference ended, as we have seen, with their giving him the right hand of fellowship, but with the stipulation of aid for the poor. This aid Paul set about raising. In Romans, we see him, the collection completed, ready to embark for Jerusalem to deliver it, but apprehensive as to what will happen there.[31]

I would prefer to leave it like that – a verbal statement of what we can say with assurance occurred in Saul's life between, roughly the year 30 CE and roughly the early 60s. However, I realize that most people want dates, so here is one version of the most rigorous date-specific chronology I have yet seen, that derived by Gerd Luedemann from the epistles. Two dates are given, reflecting the two competing dates that dominate in the literature for the date of the crucifixion, the later date being the more commonly accepted:[32]

Crucifixion	27 or 30 CE
Saul's conversion	30 or 33
Period in Arabia	31–34 or 34–37
First visit to Jerusalem	33 or 36
Syria and Cilicia	34 or 37
European mission	36ff or 39ff
Corinth	41 (date disputed)[33]
Intra-faith furore at Antioch and Jerusalem Conference[34]	47 or 50 CE } sequence disputed
Second visit to Jerusalem	47 or 50
Saul collects money for Jerusalem "tribute"	47ff or 50ff
Galatia	48 or 51
Ephesus	49 or 52
Corinth	49 or 52
Macedonia	50–51 or 53–54
Corinth	51–52 or 54–55
Jerusalem to deliver collection	52 or 55

And there the information from Saul's own hand ends, with Saul alive and delivering an apparently large purse of money to the elders of the Yeshua-faith in Jerusalem, a body headed by Yacov, brother of the late Yeshua. After that, the traditional lore of the Acts of the Apostles and of the early church fathers becomes vivid, but not entirely convincing. What can be safely inferred from Acts 27:1–28:16 (one of the so-called "we" sections of Acts which implies, probably, a more direct source of evidence than the rest of the book) and by an avid follower of Saul, Clement of Rome, writing c. 95 CE (1 Clement 5:4–7), is that at some time after delivering the collection, Saul got into trouble in Jerusalem and was sent for trial in Rome, a process than was anything but speedy. There he was eventually executed. When these events took place and what Saul may have done in the mission field before the weight of the state collapsed upon him is open to the widest speculation. (Jerome Murphy-O'Connor, for example, presents an intriguing, and not-impossible, suggestion that Saul actually succeeded in his long-time dream of conducting a mission to Spain.)[35] But, unfortunately, after the year 55 (or 52 if one prefers the earlier base-date for the crucifixion), we are in the land of guess-work. The only thing that is certain is that sometime before the beginning of the Roman-Jewish War of 66–73 CE, Saint Saul met his death.

Naturally, it would be nice to tie what we seem to know about Saul's life to the composition date of some of his letters. Recall here that four of the seven authentic letters have elicited very strong consensus on their order-of-composition: 1 Thessalonians is first, then 1 Corinthians and 2 Corinthians (probably in two parts), and, considerably later, Romans. Marrying this consensus to the chronology presented earlier, one has the following suggestions:

1 Thessalonians[36]	46 or 49 CE
1 Corinthians	49 or 52
2 Corinthians 1–9 and 2 Corinthians 10–13 (priority uncertain)	50 or 53
Romans	51–52 or 54–55

Where one inserts Philippians, Philemon, Galatians is a matter of complete indeterminacy. Most scholars have placed them between 2 Corinthians and Romans, but there is a good deal of flexibility as to what order is to be preferred. For our purposes it is not terribly important, for, when dealing with Jesus-the-Christ and with Yeshua of Nazareth, Saul does not write a set of connected narratives, but provides a body of epistles that are not quite stand-alone items, but close.

· 7 ·

Missionary in a Swirling Universe

I

BECAUSE SAUL WAS SUCH AN EXCEPTIONAL PERSONALITY, IT IS EASY to forget that much of what he did was ordinary; and when he was doing something unusual, often it was making more explicit, or taking to logical limits, beliefs and practices that were the common currency of his own times. Much of what he did was simply to act as a Judahist of his own times, for there was plenty of variation in the Yahweh-faith, as we have demonstrated earlier, enough to encompass easily most of his apparent eccentricities. His missionary activity is a case in point.

Now, in approaching his missionary work – and many of his related activities – we have to free ourselves from the dual set of prejudices that keep us from recognizing his essential Judahism. These stem from two sets of attitudes, each of which wishes to retrofit the post-70 CE context into Saul's life and, indeed, to project values of the middle ages into his story. Put bluntly, many Christians and many Jews have a big investment in separating Saul from pre-70 Judahism. On the part of Christians, this begins with the post-70 Gospel writings which become increasingly anti-Jewish (a trajectory of increasing anti-Jewish feelings that can be traced from Mark through John)[1] and which, in the high-middle ages turn into anti-Semitism. Within that value system, Saul, being defined as a great Christian, has to be characterized as being às non-Jewish as possible in his basic mission. Simultaneously, Jewish commentators, responding both to the anti-Semitism which characterized Christianity from the fourth century onwards (when Christianity and state power came to a complicitous arrangement) have, for the most part, wanted nothing at all to do with Saul. Modern Jewish scholars, for instance, will accept Yeshua as one of their own forefathers, but Saul, for most of them, is unthinkable. In part, this stems from a misreading (in my view) of Saul's thought, but mostly it comes from the way Saul's thought was later misapplied by Christians as a chapbook for anti-Jewish arguments. Throughout our examination of Saul as a source for information on, first, the early Yeshua-faith and then, the historical Yeshua, the underlying theme will be that he – like his master, Yeshua – was operating within the rubrics of the multiple Judahisms that prevailed until the destruction of Jerusalem in 70 CE. These two men have to be seen on their own terms, not ours, to the extent that this is humanly possible.

In the matter of Saul's missionary activities, for example, we should abandon the Guinness Book of Records mindset that Paul-was-the-first-Missionary and notice that he was engaged in an animated and ambulatory form of what was a commonplace activity among keen Judahists of his time. To put an anachronistic, but understandable, label on the situation: every branch of Judaism was engaged in some way in what modern evangelicals, Jewish revivalists, and charismatic Catholics call "outreach." Late Second Temple Judahists continually reached out, trying to touch others, to bring them to the right path. Sometimes this touching became a bit literal, as with the Sicarri practice of sticking needles or stilettos into their opponent's bodies. Those were exceptional practices: what was pervasive was the effort that we observed in the rich texts of the period from the Maccabeans to the Temple's destruction. Scores of Judahist parties (of which we have texts of only a tiny minority: but very convincing documents they are), worked hard at defining their own unique beliefs and at presenting them in a fashion that would convince Judahists of other stripes to join their set. All that, one might argue, took place within the world of the Yahweh-faith, but that hardly vitiates the point that Saul was of that world: he emphasizes his "Hebrew" and his Pharisaic heritage, and his entire theological adventure is a tortured attempt to get ever-deeper into the covenant with Yahweh.

Crucially, even when trying to attract Gentiles (which was his primary task, but not his sole one, for he preached in synagogues as his entry point into new communities), he was only acting out in a conscious and particularly animated fashion a set of behaviours that were common among Second Temple Judahists. To wit: although a major historiographical argument exists today about the extent of early Common Era "missionary" movements by Judahists directed at the Gentiles, it is undeniable that the Judahist faith in the first century (and, later, Rabbinic Judaism as it was articulated in the second through sixth centuries) was attractive to many Gentiles and that various branches of Judaism in Saul's time made openings for non-Jews to become associated with the worship of Yahweh. The range of relationships was considerable. The most visible in the time of Saul and Yeshua was the granting of various privileges of association with Temple worship. For instance, Gentiles were permitted to give gifts to the Temple. Money was accepted from Roman rulers (who were following their tradition of keeping provincial religious groups happy) for the adornment of the holy edifice. Semi-admission of Gentiles was part of Herod's fundamental Temple architecture: a Courtyard-of-the-Gentiles permitted them to mix with Juda-hist worshippers in a defined area. The Temple authorities allowed Gentiles to purchase sacrifices to be offered in the Temple. Also, from at least the year 6 CE onwards (and perhaps from Herod the Great's time), daily sacri-fices for the Roman emperor, in the form of two lambs and a bull, were offered.[2]

It is easy to understand how Gentiles would be awed by the Temple, since it was probably the most impressive religious structure then in existence, and one can easily recognize how that awe could be converted into genuine rever-ence for the Hebrew deity. That, of course, was in Jerusalem; outside the holy city, a second, formidable instrument of religious suasion operated, namely the Septuagint. Although still in progress in Saul and Yeshua's time, this Greek translation of the Hebrew scriptures served as a marvellous conduit of religious energy. It allowed Greek-speakers easy access to the content of the Hebrew scriptures. Though intended as a device for keeping diaspora Juda-hists within the ambit of the Yahweh-faith, it simultaneously permitted the penetration of Judahist ideas into non-Yahwist cultures. This could occur any place Greek was read, which was in most of the then-known world. If there was a Jewish missionary movement in the late Second Temple era (and it seems there was; only the size of it is in question), that movement was made possible by there being a convenient Greek translation of the Torah and Prophets. And when Saul preached to Gentiles, it was made considerably easier not only by his having a Greek text to quote to them, but by some of his congregation already being acquainted with the Hebrew scriptures, by way of the Septuagint.

In both Eretz Israel and in the diaspora lands, many Gentiles came to imi-tate and attend Judahist religious ceremonies. Josephus reported that in Anti-och "multitudes of Greeks" attended certain ceremonies.[3] Saul preached to both Gentiles and his own co-religionists in synagogues according to Acts, and this is one of the places where we can trust that document, because it has wide circumstantial verification in third-party sources.

In the time of Saul and of Yeshua, a continuum had emerged of Gentiles who were attracted by Judaism and who were in some manner welcomed. Some offered sacrifices at the Temple in Jerusalem, while others attended synagogues. In neither case does it appear that halachic demands were made on them: they were not expected to keep the rules of the children of Israel, merely to show respect.[4] Other Gentiles, however, moved closer and volun-tarily kept many of the 613 commandments. At some point they entered the category of "God-fearers," Gentiles who assumed most of the beliefs and practices of one branch or another of the Judahist faith, without formally con-verting. This continuum of Gentile adhesion of course was most striking in the diaspora, where Judahists were in a minority and where a mélange of cultural and ethnic groups surrounded them. The result is that in a synagogue in one of the provincial hubs of the Roman empire, one would not only find Judahists of varying stripes, but Gentiles whose beliefs ranged from traditional pantheism (they worshipped Yahweh as only one of several gods), to henotheism (the allegiance to a single god, without subscribing to the belief that he was the only god), to those who adopted philosophic monotheism and saw Yahweh as the most convincing form of that belief, to those who were devoted to Yahweh and his rules, not on a philosophic level, but as a day-to-day commitment.[5] All this made for an immensely complicated situation, the socio-religious constitution of each synagogue being unique. As far as an understanding of Saul's work is concerned, this complexity had two implications: that when he was preaching in the first instance to his Judahist co-religionists, he frequently was being heard by Gentiles as well; and when he preached to Gentiles, in the usual case he was probably dealing with individuals who already had a knowledge of some of the practices and beliefs of the Yahweh-faith and were favourably disposed to it.

Some Gentiles moved beyond being "God-fearers" and became full fledged proselytes. The specific ritual requirements for conversion to Judahism in the late Second Temple era are unknown[6] but circumcision was required in almost all cases. (Exceptions will be noted later.) It is not clear how strongly the Judahists of the Second Temple era sought converts (as distinct from welcoming Gentiles as associates, "God-fearers," and as financial supporters of the faith). Because, since the Middle Ages, the Rabbinic Jewish faith has not been a proselytising religion (whatever impulses it may have had along that line were stifled by anti-Semitism), it has seemed natural to accept that this was always the case. However, there is very strong evidence that there was indeed what can be legitimately called a "missionary consciousness" in late Second Temple Judahism and in the early years of the Rabbinic Jewish faith. This missionary consciousness is most profitably thought of as being localized in each case (in Antioch, for example, it was very strong) and as representing a fighting back in the widest sense against Hellenization. Diaspora Judahism, in its self-assertion and the protection of its heritage, unconsciously but pervasively adopted a missionary consciousness. Saul, though undeniably a unique individual, worked within that idiom.[7] As Samuel Sandmel noted, Matthew 23:15, a denunciation of proselytism by the Pharisees should "persuade us that at least the Pharisees maintained or countenanced something of a missionary movement."[8] And Saul, of course, was a Pharisee.

2

Not only was Saul as a missionary acting within the behavioural boundaries of late Second Temple Judahism, but the world that his letters reveal is consonant with the picture of multiple Judahisms, continually in flux, mutating quickly, engaged in a harsh and continual competition for adherents with each other. Each of the seven authentic epistles of Saint Saul has a worried quality to it. Sometimes this involves a direct denunciation of a competitor; at other times an unspoken, but obvious awareness that there are in the neighbourhood other colporteurs of various forms of Judahism (and, indeed, other forms of the Yeshua-faith). Saul is ever aware that his disciples must be guided away from all of these competitors. Saul is very hard on poachers on his territory. Apparently, in this matter he believed that forgiveness is a divine quality, so he did not practice it himself.[9]

The fortuitous by-product of his vindictive possessiveness of his several flocks was that his letters contain indications of the beliefs of some of the competing forms of the Yeshua-faith among the first and second generations of believers, before the Temple's destruction. Of course the letters have to be read carefully, for one has the equivalent in Saul's vilipending of his rivals of the denunciations of capitalism in the speeches of Fidel Castro, albeit blessedly shorter: one can learn some accurate facts about the opposition, as long as one does not proceed literally or conclude that one knows the full story. Still, one catches some fascinating glimpses of the competition.

Take the letter to the Philippians as an instance.[10] Written from imprisonment, the place of incarceration is not given. The fascinating part of the letter for our present purposes is that in the third quarter of his text (chapter 3), Saul becomes a beserker. He tells his disciples at Philippi to "beware of dogs" (3:2). These are "evil workers" (3:2), who "are the enemies of the cross of Christ" (3:18), and "whose end is destruction, whose God is their belly, and whose glory is in their shame, who mind earthly things" (3:19). That is the holy Billingsgate of the wholly enraged. Saul reserves his most memorable line for the practice that is to him the symbol of perfectionist praxis. He says, "Watch out for the cutters." A perfect word: cutters (the Jerusalem Bible, 3:2; the New International Version has the less acute "mutilators of the flesh"). Somebody whom Saul fears is making inroads in his community. It is a group of outsiders, not an internal infection in the community. (This is clear from the absence of any denunciation of locals and, specifically, by 1:28).[11] And whatever they are preaching is attractive to a well-informed body of Yeshua-followers (otherwise why would Saul become so animated in his warning?)

What views can we infer the seducers offer? First, that all Yeshua-followers, being by definition Judahists, must enter the covenant with Yahweh by being circumcised. (Circumcision is a metonym for Saul, certainly, but one doesn't warn an audience "beware of the cutters" unless there was serious snipping proposed.) Secondly, the outsiders are apparently legal perfectionists, or at least very rigorous. Verse 19, "whose God is their belly" probably refers to strict dietary rules and perhaps to the extreme concern with table purity that characterized the Pharisees. This is made more likely by Saul's emphasis that he was himself at one time a Pharisee (3:5), and by his making it clear that, although as a Pharisee he had been halachically "blameless," he nevertheless had persecuted the followers of Yeshua (3:6). Thirdly, the outsiders clearly did not accept the idea of Yeshua as a sacrifice for human sins (cf 3:18 and 3:20), and this means that they did not understand Yeshua as Messiah the same way Saul did (and probably not at all). And, fourthly, they were not very impressed with Saul's apocalyptic views involving the return of Jesus-the-Christ and the transformation of all believers, living and dead, into cosmic entities (3:10–11, 21).

Here, in assessing the historical implications of these outsiders' views, it matters not at all whether they were Yeshua-followers who were keen on traditional Judahist beliefs and practices or whether they were Judahists (most likely some branch of the Pharisees) who were not themselves followers of Yeshua but who hoped that the Yeshua-followers could be convinced to come into line with their own beliefs. What is evidentiarily telling is that their views were attractive to a significant number of Saul's flock and that these disciples did not see such beliefs as incompatible with being followers of Yeshua (that's why Saul has to warn them: they are about to buy the package). This says that in the period shortly before the great Destruction, it probably was acceptable to some serious members of the Yeshua-faith to contemplate embracing a form of the faith that required full adhesion to standard Judahist practice (which means, essentially, that all Gentiles had to convert fully to Judaism), which saw Yeshua not as a saviour, but at best as a valuable teacher, and that did not have faith in the doctrine of the Second Coming of Jesus. This was enough to fill Saul's heart with terror.

The existence of plural Yeshua-faiths within the solar system of multiple Judahisms in the late Second Temple era is confirmed by an earlier case in Saul's career: that covered in Second Corinthians. And here again, Saul is very worried about poachers and the highly competitive nature of the Judahisms of the late Second Temple period again is exemplified. The present Second Corinthians breaks sharply at the beginning of chapter ten and it is in chapters 10–13 that we learn most about yet-another form of the Yeshua-faith.[12]

This time it is certain the alternate form of belief is formulated by individuals who are Judahists (11:22) who are also followers of Yeshua. Saul denounces them as "pseudo-apostles" or "false apostles" (2 Cor 11:13) which means that they are coming to Corinth as senior members of the band of Yeshua-followers. They were definitely outsiders (11:4) and, although their origin is not specified, there was only one home base for the apostles, namely Eretz Israel. Whether or not they actually were from Jerusalem is impossible to say. In responding to their challenge, Saul asserts that he is "not a whit behind the very chiefest apostles" (11:5, repeated 12:11), which means that his reference group is the leaders of the Jerusalem set, headed by Yacov, with Peter (Cephas) and John the son of Zebedee the other primary figures. But, significantly, Saul does not name these Jerusalem "pillars" and the omission seems deliberate. (He was capable of rebuking Peter directly, as we shall see below, but here he only uses irony.) His problem was not with the Jerusalem "pillars" but with some senior followers of Yeshua who came from Eretz Israel, but not necessarily from Jerusalem, and who claimed to be apostles and to have a superior form of knowledge of Yeshua to that Saul possessed. Their message is of "another Jesus, whom we have not preached ..." (11:4). Saul is in trouble here, because, if one accepts Acts' definition of an apostle as having been with Yeshua when he was on earth (Acts 1:21–22) these outside apostles, on the surface at least, had a greater right than Saul to declare what the faith was all about. It is entirely plausible that they may have had a more accurate knowledge of the historical Yeshua than did Saul.[13]

The sarcasm of calling them "pseudo-apostles" was not going to carry the day, nor would Saul's literally demonizing them. (He compares the outsiders to Satan – 11:13–14). Yet Saul desperately wants to win: he is very possessive, and deeply wrapped up in the intense religious competition of the late Second Temple era. His detailed response is to brag in a way that combines the ritual boasting of the warrior (he approaches some of the classical forms in his boasts), with the braggadocio of the adolescent. He also has some emotionally hard-hitting points, aimed at the hearts of the Corinthians, rather than their minds. He ranks himself with the chief apostles; he puts forward his claims as one of the seed of Abraham; he recalls his beatings – lashed with thirty-nine stripes five times, with rods three times, once stoned, three times shipwrecked, robbed, hungry, thirsty, and more. I think John Knox is right, concerning 2 Corinthians 10–13, that "only a blind reader of Paul's epistles could miss the signs of the egoism and pride that are behind this indignation."[14]

Yet, simultaneously, he is genuinely worried about the Corinthians being seduced by beliefs that will be their spiritual destruction: so indirectly he tells us something of what this alternative version of the Yeshua-faith is. Crucially, there is his silence: even though we are dealing with Judahists from Eretz Israel he does not warn about legal perfectionism. "Circumcision" – which is clearly the code word for (to him) excessive halachic rigour – is not mentioned. Instead, he is worried about the preaching of "another Jesus, whom we have not preached ..." and about his own disciples receiving "another spirit, which ye have not received, or another gospel, which ye have not accepted ..." (11:4): in other words, a whole alternative view of Yeshua and an alternative way of experiencing Christ. I suspect that the term "spirit" here is diagnostic. The fear that the Corinthians' "minds should be corrupted from the simplicity that is in Christ" (11:3), is most likely a fear that they will take up something we do not really have a word for: "spirithood," "pneumatic-visions," might be close. Saul is worried about the locals' possible seduction because, manifestly, the competing apostles were spiritualists of some sort. That explains the extraordinary vision that Saul relates to his Corinthian Christian disciples: that a "man" (Saul himself) fourteen years previously was taken up into the third heaven and was caught up into paradise itself where he heard words that were so sacred that it was not lawful for a human to utter them (12:2–4). Now, given that Saul's entire method of refuting the outsiders was to equal or, if possible, to upstage them on every item of their agenda – he is as good a Hebrew as they, he has undergone more hardship on missions, he was one of the top rank of apostles – he is raising the bidding on the spirit-vision matter because that is one of the points the outsiders preach. So, Saul's boasting has its uses: it defines the dimensions and shape of a single coin, of which the obscured obverse is the outside apostles' beliefs, the clearly articulated reverse, Saul's own words.

Thus far, then, we have seen Saul indicate the existence of two separate forms of the Yeshua-faith (that denounced in Philippians and that in Second Corinthians) in addition to his own. Another form had appeared earlier, and is documented in First Corinthians. This can be termed a "self-generated local mutation" and though we have First Corinthians as the chief example, local variants must have been a possibility everywhere, for there was in the first and second generation no coercive regulatory power, no authority for standardization; save, as we shall see in a moment, the prestige of the Jerusalem church which was headed by Yacov, the brother of Yeshua; and his power was limited to those who paid him fealty.

First Corinthians is a rich source, because two nettles in Saul's sandals make him very communicative: things are happening in Corinth that divide the Corinthian Yeshua-followers from each other, and things are occurring that divide them from him, especially syncretistic relations with "pagans." Written from Ephesus (see 1 Cor. 16:8), First Corinthians is a single letter,[15] part of a correspondence with the Corinthians of which (as always) we have a record only of Saul's side. Saul feels very proprietorial of the Yeshua-followers in Corinth, and a fevered pastiche of metaphor expresses this. Agricultural: "I have planted, Apollos [a missionary colleague] watered" (3:6); maternal: "I have fed you with milk" (3:2); paternal: "as my beloved sons I warn you" (4:14). There is nothing coy in his desire for their allegiance. "Wherefore I beseech you, be ye followers of me" (4:16). He needs these people and they, he asserts, in turn need him, for his is the conduit that takes them to the Christ: "... for the seal of mine apostleship are ye in the Lord" (9:2).

Part of what has agitated Saul is that he has learned that his Corinthian disciples are fractioning themselves into separate camps. This was natural social evolution and he should not have been so surprised. The course of development was logical. Saul (if Acts 18:4 can be trusted) began his missionary work in Corinth exactly in the location anyone would: in a synagogue. Synagogues, it should be remembered, were not temples, but were, originally, houses where the Judahist community met, and if in a place like Corinth the synagogue was no longer a domestic house, it still was a vernacular building. There, "he reasoned" Sabbath after Sabbath for a year and a half and persuaded many Judahist and Greek listeners to become followers of Yeshua (Acts 18:4–11).[16] Now, three or four years later (estimates vary), the Yeshua followers have evolved their own synagogues, or "house-churches" and the several congregations are not getting along with each other. They bear different banners: "I am of Paul; and I of Apollos; and I of Cephas; and I of Christ" "(1 Cor.1:12) and there may have been more.[17] There are no direct signs, or even strong indirect ones, that outsiders were involved.[18] Religious differentiation was taking place within the Yeshua-followers and though we might today point to literally hundreds of parallel cases, this natural social evolution bothered Saul greatly.

It is impossible to align any specific set of beliefs and practices with any specific outside group, but the bundle of things that make Saul unhappy is large and contains a variety of items that worry and to some degree bewilder him. For example, the Corinthians are embracing various forms of "pneuma-tika" (9:11) which here are spiritual gifts: uttering profound words of wisdom that come from the spiritual realm; passing on knowledge received directly by spiritual means; speaking in tongues, interpreting words spoken in tongues, healing of the body by spiritual means, the working of various miracles, prophesying, evincing the ability to recognize invisible spirits (12:8–10). These diverse spirit-gifts have produced splits within the Yeshua-followers because the believers who had one such gift privileged it and implicitly downgraded their co-religionists who had other gifts. Effectively, differentiation of religious experience (which inevitably implied differentiation of religious belief) was occurring. Saul's first response is to remind everybody that "by one Spirit are we all baptized into one body ... and have been all made to drink into one Spirit" (12:13). He works out an extended metaphor about the way parts of the human body specialize, but are all equally necessary (12:12–31), and then delivers one of his most compelling exhortations, the "love chapter," 1 Corinthians 13, a tiny masterpiece.

But he is still fundamentally uneasy with these spiritual gifts, even though he has given them his tacit approval: the individuals are parts of the body of Christ. So, one encounters a continuing lecture, one that sounds like that of present-day parents talking to their teenage children about alcohol and soft drugs: we'd rather you didn't, but if you do, do so only in moderation, and take a sober friend along. In Saul's world this translates to: I'd rather that you keep order and dignity in your worship of Christ, but if you have to prophesy or have to speak in tongues, do so in a way that will enhance the worship of your fellow-believers, not distract them; and if you are seized by a spirit-message, keep silent about it unless there is someone with you who can interpret it to your fellow worshippers. (See 1 Cor. chapter 14.) Do things that bring you all together, not that separate you, and above all, "let all things be done decently and in order" (14:40).

This Corinthian situation, one can safely infer, is a simulacrum of what must have occurred in the pre-70 CE years, the pre-textual era, in scores of towns and cities as the Yeshua-faith expanded: it became differentiated into groups that were distinguished from each other by the nature of their spiritual experience, their mode of worship and, ultimately, by what they believed about all things religious and, especially, about Jesus-the-Christ. What Saul gives us in 1 Corinthians is a case study in a general phenomenon. Specialization within the churches was a process that split Yeshua-follower from Yeshua-follower. I was not being outré when I suggested (in chapter six) that the early, pre-written Yeshua-faith was like the John Prum movement: fluid, inventive, open to wide divergencies of narrative and interpretation and to fighting. Once segmentation and differentiation (call it "heresy" if you will) begins, it is very hard to stop. Witness Clement of Rome's writing to the Corinthians in the mid 90s, reminding the faithful of Corinth of what Saul had told them in First Corinthians and upbraiding them for continuing to be fractious and refusing to accept what were now becoming standard-issue Christian beliefs (1 Clement 47:1–7).

What is equally valuable as historical evidence is a secondary set of issues in First Corinthians, and these threatened to split Saul from some of his Corinthian disciples. The fault-line that is defined in Chapters 10–12 (and referred to elsewhere in the epistle) is remarkably revealing because it indicates clearly (1) that among the several forms of Yeshua-faith that were emerging in Corinth, one tendency was to make syncretistic alliances with "pagan" religions and (2) that Saul himself, while working hard at sounding like the cool, controlled advisor of his flock, was, when pushed, reflexively and instinctively devoted to some basic aspects of Judahist praxis. In his spine, if not in his head, he remained a diaspora Pharisee.[19]

Saul likes to paint himself as a protean figure, a spiritual Scarlet Pimpernel: "… Unto the Jews I became as a Jew, that I might gain the Jews; to them that are under the law, as under the law … To the weak became I as weak, that I might gain the weak: I am made all things to all men, that I might by all means save some" (9:20–22). He presents himself as being balanced and open-minded on matters of Halachah, that is, Judahist law and its interpretation: "All things are lawful unto me, but all things are not expedient" (6:12);

and, concerning dietary rules: "meat commendeth us not to God: for neither, if we eat, are we the better; neither, if we eat not, are we the worse" (8:8). It all seems so flexible, so, well, liberal.

But consider the related specific injunctions that run against this theoretical flexibility. First, Saul is absolutely opposed to the local practice of Yeshua-followers suing each other in civil courts (6:1–8). Why should that bother him? Because it is a public scandal, to be sure. One suspects that the deeper reason is that he has in his mind a judicial model of proper conduct that comes from late Second Temple Judahism: the *Beth Din*. This was a local law court (literally "house of judgement") composed of three or more wise men acting as a court of law. Exactly how it acted on a local level is unknown (certainly procedures varied by locale) but even a passing glance at the Mishnah, the great law code which was completed c. 200 CE, but which quotes precedents dating back into the early Common Era, makes one thing clear: that virtually every aspect of everyday life and of conflict within the community was to be taken care of inside the community of faith.[20] Saul, manifestly, accepts this basic Judahist position, and advises his people to stay away from Roman public law.

Secondly, he responds to Corinthian practices concerning women and worship with some prohibitions that are often misread: he seems to be personally misogynistic. In this case, he is not, for he is merely being a good Judahist. Thus, he repeats standard Pharisaic decrees that women keep silence during worship (14:34) and that they should not appear in public with their own hair showing (11:6). Long hair, Saul realizes, is a great glory to a woman (11:15), but in most branches of late Second Temple Judaism, it was a glory reserved only for her husband to behold. Saul is simply being rigorous, a good Pharisee, when he says that if in public, a woman should cover her head; if not, let her head be shorn (11:6). (This rule, which comes down to us in the Rabbinic Jewish faith, still holds for Orthodox Jews in our own time.) Notice that while Saul is reflexively, instinctively and thoroughly a Judahist rigorist on the issues of women's hair and of the *Beth Din*, he keeps talking as if he is not nearly as halachically-bound as he actually is: "Circumcision is nothing, and uncircumcision is nothing," he says (7:19). Then, he adds a very difficult phrase which literally reads "... nothing, but the keeping of the commandments of God" and which is rewritten in various translations as "what does matter is to keep the commandments of God," or close words thereto.[21] This makes the specific verse more understandable, but it leaves his readers in Corinth (and in the present) on the same cleft stick that the syntactically difficult original statement did: namely, how can circumcision or uncircumcision be "nothing," when, as a commandment, women are to be covered in public and silent in worship? Are the halachic imperatives of circumcision less binding than those against public display on the part of females? Saul's whole presentation here is in deep trouble, for he is a man caught in a scissors of his own device: he is pinched between his ideational commitment to the spirit, rather than the letter of Halachah, and his instinctive personal attachment to orthopraxy. Saul can never stop being a devout Judahist, nor would he wish to: it is the marrow of his being.

This is the background to his response to an issue that seems most to disturb him: the eating of foods offered to idols. Despite the surface appearance, and despite Saul's once-again trying to play very cool, very distanced on this matter, he is very upset and his response is based on Judahist halachic principles of the most basic sort. It appears that a significant number of Yeshua-followers were working out a syncretic relationship with the local deities in Corinth, probably those honoured in the cult of Demeter and Kore and those of the cult of Asklepios. This occurred because the behavioural licence-fee for admission to full participation in the Corinthian polity was that one showed up at social events conducted in or near "pagan" temples and had a meal as part of the celebration. These could be occasions as simple as weddings, or weightier events such as the commemoration of the founding of the city or some heroic battle. By their very nature, such occasions were also religious celebrations. If one refused to eat the food on these occasions, one renounced full membership in the local polity, so the motivation to work out some kind of relationship was strong on the part of the Yeshua-followers.

Clearly many had worked out their own concordat. That the food served on these occasions had been ritually slaughtered according to cult practice and "offered to idols," whatever that may have meant, was something they could live with. But that the cult food of the Demeter and Kore cult was the pig[22] makes it clear that more than just a bit of a meal was in question, for no one of Judahist-background among the Yeshua-faith could eat pork without having made a conscious decision to work out a compromise with the local pagan faith. But even if meat was not consumed, foods offered previously to idols implied a rejection of the table purity doctrine that characterized Pharisaic Judaism and this was something Saul could not deal with. Yet, he does not wish to say "no," for he understands that agreement gained by consent is better than agreement through coercion. So he puts matters this way: since some of the religiously weak among you are injured by this practice, you should all consider stopping it, even though we all know that there is nothing in those idols, really, and that we could eat the food without spiritual harm if we really wanted to do so. That is his manifesto, and it is effective rhetoric, for who can argue with the idea that, in our faith, the strong should protect the weak? However, I think he is genuinely repulsed with the idea of taking table-fellowship so far as to include eating together with "pagan" Gentiles at their own religious celebrations (even if pork was not involved), for that is to meld together with them and their beliefs in some way that he cannot quite articulate. He makes this underlying fear clear when he says "that the things which the [pagan] Gentiles sacrifice, they sacrifice to devils, and not to God" (10:20). Now the word that the KJB translates as "devils" and most other translations call "demons" has no modern counterpart and the meaning is neither devils nor demons, which in modern usage have strong negative connotations. The "pagans" are sacrificing to unseen spirits that have positive characteristics, such as assuring bountiful harvests and family fecundity. For Saul, the problem with these "demons" is not that they are rebarbarative entities, but rather that they are attractive and so too are the faiths to which they are attached. Saul rightly recognizes that if one eats food offered to these amiable spirits, one joins them: "and I would not that ye should have fellowship with devils" (10:20). Here we see that in some primordial way, Saul believes in the reality of these spirits, and his antidote is the classic Pharisaic one: keep table separate at table.

The same point comes through in his very confusing suggestion that everyone abstain from food offered to idols out of respect for the "weak." He precedes this point with an assertion that has the ring of a scared schoolboy, "that an idol is nothing in the world, and that there is none other God but one" (8:4). And, then, buried in his let's-be-careful-for-the-weak pitch, is the espousal of a fascinating bit of spiritualism. He says that if someone eats idol food in the belief that it has been sacrificed to a spirit, then their conscience, being weak by virtue of their believing this, is defiled (8:8). And, therefore they "perish," despite Christ's having died for them (8:11). None of this is surprising within the context of late Second Temple Judahism (recall all those spirits in the Book of Enoch). Spirits filled the world of Second Temple Judahism and could lead to loss of soul. Thus, in the food-before-idols matter, Saul is not really as calm, as above the fray, as he appears. He has learned of local syncretism, and is manifestly afraid of his people losing Christ's salvation through table fellowship with the followers of other-world spirits. Saul lives in very fraught worlds, both visible and invisible.

3

The reader probably has noticed that thus far, in arguing: that Saul's missionary activity was not alien to Second Temple Judahism; that he was engaged in a very competitive activity; that the multiplicity of Judahisms and, within those Judahisms the multiple, competing versions of the Yeshua-faith worried Saul deeply; and that many of his most basic reflexes were strictly from within Judahism and reflected his pharisaic background – in making those arguments I have been proceeding backwards in time, using the youngest source (Philippians) first, then Second Corinthians, then First Corinthians. This is not an eccentric proceeding, but instead is an attempt to break the perceptual-set that so often surrounds Saul (his being wrongly presented as an anti-Judahist or non-Judahist) and to overcome the excessive inter-textuality that usually besets the reading of his epistles: especially the misdirection that occurs when his entire set of letters, except for those to the Thessalonians, is read as a footnote to the so-called "Jerusalem Council" of approximately 50 CE. It is now clear, I hope, that a whole data-set on multiple-Yeshua-faiths and their interaction with the rest of Second Temple Judahisms and with "pagan" religions, demonstrably exist and do not have to be read through the historically smeared window of the Jerusalem meeting.

So, we can now follow another backward-bending graph of events found in Saul's letter to the Galatians.[23] This is a late letter (perhaps the middle 50s), but it contains three datum points that turn it into an historical narrative (albeit a sketchy one): conflicts in the Galatian church, earlier related difficulties between Saul and Peter (Cephas), and a still-earlier dust-up in Jerusalem which had resulted in a covenant of behaviour between Saul and the Jerusalem leadership, headed by Yeshua's brother, Yacov.

The situation in Galatia to which Saul is responding has a distant resonance with the "demon" problem in First Corinthians. Here Saul cries out to his disciples, "Oh foolish Galatians, who hath bewitched you ...?" (Galatians 3:1). This is not a figure of speech.[24] Saul lives in a world of swirling spirits, good and bad, these inhabit people, cry out from within them, and produce aberrant behaviour. They can be cast out by spiritual means. Whereas in Philippians he uses a canine metaphor to vilify those who try to steal his people, here he borders on a belief in lycanthropy. His former flock has been led astray by wolves in apostles' guise and they "bite and devour one another ..." (5:15). Now the Galatians are following the Judahist liturgical calendar (4:10) and other forms of ritual bondage (4:9). The whole issue of circumcision has again arisen, both in its literal aspect and as a symbol of the entire Judahist halachic system. In Saul's purity system, forced circumcision of Gentiles is unnecessary, unhalachic, and, most telling rhetorically, unseemly. He accuses those who want the Gentiles of the Yeshua-faith to be circumcised as doing so "that they may glory in your flesh" (6:13). In modern English he would have said, "the bastards are only counting scalps."

Over the years, a lot of time has been wasted in asking who the wolves at the door of the Galatians actually were. Saul tells us clearly by revealing how his memory path works. All of the trouble in Galatians is discussed in the context of two problems that he recalls with barely-controlled anger: (1) being summoned to Jerusalem for a rough negotiating session some years previously, and (2) having to bash Peter (Cephas) forcefully in Antioch, when that apostle helped to sow dissension (2:1–14).[25] Saul's connecting these Antioch incidents with those in Galatia is a function of their being in some way a continuation of the negotiations that had occurred previously in Jerusalem. Any other explanation is just too clever.

So, we walk back with Saul along his memory path to the problem he had with Peter.[26] This occurred in Antioch on-the-Orontes in Syria.[27] There, he and Barnabas (who, if the Acts of the Apostles is accurate, was senior to Saul in the mission field)[28] have a successful mixed congregation of Yeshua-followers. And those Yeshua-followers of Judahist birth and Yeshua-followers of "pagan" birth joined in meals together. (We are not talking here about the Eucharist, but about fellowship with each other while taking substantial nourishment.) How they did this is unknown: did each group bring and prepare its own food? did the Judahists abrogate kashrut for these bonding meals? did the Gentiles for this occasion eat only food that was ritually prepared to suit the conscience of the Judahists? We simply do not know. Clearly, though, they ate together as one body of believers and to Saul – to whom the image of one-body-in-Christ was ever present – this unity was what counted.

While on a visit to Antioch, this unity was endorsed and participated in by Barnabas (a Judahist, originally from Eretz Israel) and, more importantly, by Peter, one of the three "pillars" of the Jerusalem community when he visited Antioch (2:11). And then the unity was sundered. Emissaries were sent from Yacov in Jerusalem. So great was the authority of these agents of Yacov (who, as we shall see in a moment, was the most powerful figure in the world of Yeshua-followers), that both Peter and Barnabas stopped eating with the Gentile-born followers of Yeshua and withdrew to the separate table-fellowship, and so did the other Judahist-born members of the Antioch congregation (2:12–13).[29] Whether or not Yacov had sent these men as emissaries to enforce ritual separation in the Antioch community between Gentile-born and Judahist-born is not clear and does not matter: they were enforcing what they knew he wanted. Saul does not go further into details of what these Jerusalem-sent emissaries demanded, but most likely it was enforcement of the belief that to become a full member of the Yeshua-community one had to become a full member of the Judahist community: to be circumcised and to honour the food taboos of the faith. In any case, Saul lit into Peter with a vengeance. "I withstood him to the face, because he was to be blamed," is his own summary (2:11). He essentially called Peter a fraud, for Peter himself did not fully honour the Judahist rules, yet here he was trying to compel the Yeshua-followers of Gentile-birth that they had to live like strict Judahists (2:14).

There the matter rests. We do not know who won, but I suspect that battle was drawn. Had Saul swept the day, he would have told us, for he is never loath to retail his achievements; and had the Gentile-born followers of Yeshua lost – that is, been successfully led to convert fully to Judahist praxis as defined by Yacov and the Jerusalem brethren – then Saul would never have brought up the case. The Antioch story is told in the context of the big compromise in the early Yeshua-community – the so-called "Jerusalem conference" – so we take it to be in Saul's mind a parallel episode to events in Antioch, a sequence that is neither a complete disaster nor a satisfying victory.

The "Jerusalem conference," of roughly 50 CE, is one of the biggest misnomers in all the chronicle of late Second Temple Judahism and here we are about to abandon it. It is also called, equally misleadingly, "the Apostolic council." Both of these terms provide a false continuity with the later era, when Christianity was no longer one of the many variant Judahisms. Church apologists tie this Jerusalem, or Apostolic council, into the litany of the unfolding *magisterium*, as marked, for example, by the councils of Nicaea, Chalcedon, Trent and Vatican II.

There was none of the flowing robes of later Christian dignitaries about this meeting. It was a negotiation between a bunch of crabbit middle-aged men whose bones ached. Barnabas, Saul's senior partner, a man who had been on the road for the best part of two decades; Saul who had been battered and beaten so often for the faith that he must have hurt even when he slept; Peter (Cephas) who had logged long tours as a missionary; John the son of Zebedee, one of the original disciples, a man whose brother had been the church's second recorded martyr (Acts 12:2); and Yacov, the brother of Yeshua, an ascetic, reserved, devoutly rigorous Judahist, who was the head of the Jerusalem Yeshua-community and, at mid first century, the authoritative figure in the Yeshua-faith. Other individuals were on the periphery of this group – Saul's disciple Titus, an uncircumcised and therefore highly vulnerable Greek, and several elders of the Jerusalem congregation, unnamed. But the real negotiation was between the three "pillars" of the Jerusalem community on the one side and Saul and Barnabas on the other. It was a tough room.

Here is Saul's version of events as found in Galatians 2:2–10: (a) Saul – who makes himself the centre of the story and Barnabas an outrider – had been on his missionary tours for nigh on two decades and had not been to Jerusalem in this period, save on one occasion, fourteen years previously. So although they had heard of him in Jerusalem, he was not known in person to most of the Yeshua-believers in Eretz Israel, although they praised Yahweh for his labours; (b) Saul received a revelation from the Almighty to go to Jerusalem and this he did of his own volition, taking Barnabas and Titus with him; (c) there he discreetly let the several leaders of the Jerusalem community know the character of the Gospel that he preached; (d) some of them – a vulpine group of "false brethren" – spied on him and tried to force him to have Titus circumcised. This was a real issue (especially, one suspects, to Titus), but also a symbol of a demand that all Yeshua-followers must also be fully-fledged Judahists, which is to say proselytes to Judaism; (e) Saul fought hard and (f) eventually the three power-brokers – the "pillars" Jacov, Peter and John – agreed to a saw-off: Saul and Barnabas could go to the Gentiles and convert them to the Yeshua-faith without requiring them to convert fully to Judaism and the Jerusalem people would continue on their own mission to their fellow Judahists. On the surface, this resembles the division of the then-known world between the monarchs of Spain and Portugal in 1493. As Saul depicts these arrangements, he was a spiritual prince of equal standing with Jacov, and the mission to the Gentiles was as central a portion of the Yeshua-faith as was the mission to the Judahists. However, (g) Saul agreed to collect money for "the poor" of the Jerusalem community.

We are viewing here Saul's later summation of what should be called the "Jerusalem Deal." That is not flippant. The Hebrew word with which all concerned (except, perhaps Titus) were well acquainted was *BRT* – "covenant" – which means a deal and, indeed, in the Hebrew scriptures to "cut a covenant" is used in the same sense we would today say "cut a deal." Nothing high-flown was taking place here. The Yeshua-faith had come within a hair's-breadth of exploding, but in the end a barely-workable deal was cut. How long it would have lasted, had not the Destruction of Jerusalem and of the Temple in 70 CE occurred can be only speculative: given continuing friction on the issue of halachic requirements for those of Gentile-origin that arose during the later 50s, I suspect that it would not have held once the generation that had negotiated it – the generation of Yacov and Saul – had passed away.

Now, the proceedings of the negotiations and the final contents of the Jerusalem Deal as told by Saul are a touch unconvincing by virtue of the account's being so obviously self-serving. First, Saul most probably did not go up to Jerusalem voluntarily, but he was sent for by someone or some group of individuals to whom he granted authority or, at minimum, whom he did not want to offend unless absolutely necessary.[30]

Secondly, I think a more realistic reading of the physics of the situation is not Saul's suggestion in Galatians that there were three parties (his, Yacov's, and the third party of false-brethren) but rather that there were two parties (his and the Jerusalem community) and that he managed during negotiations to bring around the power figures (the three "pillars") to a deal, one that a rump (the "false brethren") of the Jerusalem community found objectionable, but had to accept in deference to the "pillars."

Thirdly, I believe that Yacov, Peter and John were extremely shrewd and remarkably generous in finding a small bubble of negotiating room that permitted them to make a deal with Saul rather than split permanently asunder the Yeshua-faith. This small space of opportunity opened up the seemingly-intractable stalemate on circumcision. There is no doubt that the rigorists in the Jerusalem congregation (the ones Saul calls false-brethren) demanded the mark of full conversion to Judahism on the part of all Gentiles that adhered to Yeshua. Now, among the things that we all think we know for certain is that a male proselyte to Judahism in this period absolutely had to have his penis ritually reduced. For most converts this was indeed the case; however, a small, but halachically sophisticated opposition to this view existed. The contra-view held that although of course all males born Judahist had to be circumcised, for proselytes it was enough for them to undergo a ritual bath (the relationship between mikveh and baptism-by-immersion is too obvious to require comment). There is evidence for this contra-view in the argument of one of the Tannaim of the late first or early second century, Rabbi Joshua ben Hananiah, who held that a man was a "proper proselyte" even if he had not been circumcised, but had performed the necessary ritual ablutions.[31] This opinion, that circumcision was not absolutely necessary for an adult male proselyte was argued in the mid-first century of the Common Era in the case of Izates, king of the minor satrapy of Adiabene who, following his mother's converson to Judahism, wished to be circumcised. One set of his halachic counsel advised against this, and held that "worship of God was of a superior nature to circumcision."[32] These words, which could have been uttered by Saul as a summary of his own position, indicate, as does the opinion of Rabbi Joshua, the existence of a minority tradition opinion that the Jerusalem "pillars" could fall back on. It was halachically respectable, if not generally accepted. It permitted them to let Saul go his own way and convert Gentiles to the Yeshua-faith, without requiring the Gentiles to become full proselytes to Judahism. And it allowed Yacov, Peter and John to tell their disgruntled allies in Jerusalem that, like it or not, this was a legitimate interpretation of Torah. Had they not had such a bubble of halachic tradition, one doubts that they would have been able to compromise at all with Saul and with the growing body of Gentile-based Yeshua-followers. (I insert here a merely personal judgement: not only were the three "pillars" being imaginative and prudent in finding a way to accommodate Saul, they were being generous. If one considers that the Jerusalem church encompassed some of the original disciples, a goodly number of believers who had known Yeshua when he was on earth, and also the members of Yeshua's own family, the heads of that church must have found it very tempting to tell Saul to go away, that he was not of the real Yeshua-faith. Yet they resisted that temptation. Instead, they allowed a man who never directly heard a word that Yeshua had said, had never laid eyes on him, and who had the vexing habit of telling them how to interpret not only Torah in general but Yeshua in particular, to be embraced. Yes, as I shall show in a minute, they drove a hard bargain, but the real miracle is that they did not stone Saul. Perhaps this was the first real ecumenical moment.)

Fourthly, and most importantly, Saul did not walk away with anything like a 50–50 split. This was not a case of a division of the world between equals, as in 1493, but the humbling of an arriviste by the aristocracy of the Yeshua-faith.[33]

The key to this conclusion is the so-called "Jerusalem collection" which Saul agrees to take up. He says it is for the poor of Jerusalem (Galatians 2:10) and he must have used that explanation as he tirelessly begged from community to community, but that was a face-saving formula. No one was starving among the faithful in Jerusalem, nor were a significant number even seriously poor: if they were, Saul would not have taken a decade to collect the money for them and to schlepp it to Jerusalem. No, something else was involved. Jerome Murphy-O'Connor puts it well in his summary of the Jerusalem Deal: "a financial contribution from Gentile believers seemed like a reasonable *quid pro quo* for Jerusalem's concession on circumcision, and no doubt would have been proclaimed as such to the church by the three Pillars."[34] That sounds venal, but it is not. A reasonable analogy (admittedly anachronistic) would be that of early European feudalism, wherein a vassal paid tangible homage to the crown, in return for being allowed entry into his own demesne. Saul acknowledged the superiority of his masters in Jerusalem and in turn they allowed him to run his own spiritual fiefdom. There is no question who was who in this relationship. To the end of his days, Saul recognized the superiority of Jerusalem. One of the more acute observations, seemingly a throw-away line, about the situation, comes from Raymond Collins who notes that "in point of fact, all seven epistles in the canonical corpus which contemporary scholarship unanimously deems to be the genuine work of Paul somehow address themselves to financial considerations."[35] And chief among these is the worry of putting together the Jerusalem collection. To nearly the end of his life, Saul was collecting money and was desperately worried that the Jerusalem authorities would change their mind and not accept the funds that he collected as dues. In his letter to the Romans, he asks for prayers "that the aid I carry to Jerusalem may be accepted by the saints" (Jer. Bible, Romans 15:31). This is not a fund-raiser's gimmick. He understands that if his lords do not accept his homage, he is no longer their liege: he fears that his mission thereby will be declared illegitimate.

Here let us introduce two more parallels (the scriptures work in analogies and parallels and we get closer to their heart by adopting the methods of their author-editors than by attempting the historiographic equivalent of laser surgery). The first of these stems from simply noting that as far back as pre-exilic times, it was a duty of all Judahist males twenty years of age and upward to contribute annually to the Temple in Jerusalem. (See Exodus 30:13–14 and, for post-exilic continuation, Nehemiah 10:32). In the late Second Temple era, the Roman authorities continued to grant them the privilege of remitting the funds, which is to say, they protected the Judahists as they brought money from the diaspora and from the distant areas of Eretz Israel to

Jerusalem. This annual collection can be termed the "Temple tax," and it continued at least into the fourth century of the Common Era.[36] Hence, the question becomes, was the Jerusalem collection an analogy to the Temple tax? or was it, in fact, the Temple tax itself, which Saul was collecting on behalf of the Gentile-born Yeshua-followers and was passing on to the leaders of the Jerusalem church who, in turn, were paying it to the Temple authorities? There is no answer, but the ratio is clear:

> Saul's collection: Jerusalem "church" authorities =
> Diaspora Jewry's Temple tax: Temple authorities.

Take the even, take the odd: in either case, Saul was being required to raise money from Gentile-born believers in Yeshua to pay as some sort of tax to the "church" in Jerusalem.

And here another, potentially unsettling analogy: in promising to raise funds from his Gentile mission to turn over to the Jerusalem "saints," Saul can be seen to have been paying what we would today call a "franchise fee." Pay, or you can't play, seems to have been the situation, and he accepted it. This grossly anachronistic suggestion has some value because it leads us to recognize that in dealing with the Jerusalem community of Yeshua-believers, he was negotiating with the most powerful group in the development of Christianity between the death of Yeshua and the destruction of Jerusalem. It is the one group whose influence the shapers of the canonical New Testament did everything they could to minimize in the historical record: the Family Firm.

Oh dear: "Family Firm." Irony? No: one is dead serious. Yeshua's mother and his brothers and sisters may not have been too impressed with him when he was on earth, but they seem to have come around after his death, especially Yacov. As presented in the New Testament, the reactions of Yeshua's family to his earthly ministry are very difficult to decipher. This is because the Four Gospels each systematically derogates Yeshua's family. Naturally his mother Miriam gets special attention in Matthew and Luke as the Blessed Virgin but, curiously, after giving birth to him she becomes a slightly doubting, slightly-perplexed figure. Of course she raised him, but when he was twelve years old and the family visited the Temple, she was totally surprised by his arguing Torah with the professional scholars (Luke 2:41–52). This is curious, considering that the same author-editor (Luke) has her being aware of her son's allegedly divine origin; one thinks he might have let her draw some conclusions from that origin. Miriam is reported as being present along with Yeshua's brothers at his first miracle, the turning of water into wine at Cana in Galilee (John 2:1–11). There she apparently frets at him about the shortage of wine and he snaps back at her, "Woman, what have I to do with thee?" (2:4). Later, Miriam is present at the crucifixion (John 19:25 and probably Matthew 27:56 and Mark 15:40). In John's version, she is addressed from the cross by Yeshua: "Woman, behold thy son!" (John 19:26), a cruelly ambiguous phrase at best. Something historically significant, but not immediately obvious, is being communicated here by the Gospel writer.

Interestingly, whenever Miriam is mentioned in the company of Yeshua's siblings – Yosef, Shimon, Yudah, and Yacov, and the unnamed sisters – she is diminished and this almost seems to occur because she is in their presence. We have already noted the scene at Cana of Galilee. In another episode, his mother and his brothers came to see Yeshua. They stood outside where he was speaking, for there was a crowd around them. When word was taken to Yeshua that they were there, he declared "Who is my mother, or my brethren?" And then he added that whoever does the will of God – he said this indicating his disciples – "the same is my brother, and my sister, and mother" (Mark 3:31–35; cf Matthew 12:46–50 and Luke 8:19–21). The rejection by Yeshua of his family has an unspoken Newtonian moral physics behind it: he rejects them because they do not embrace him. Luke's way of putting this is to have Yeshua declare "my mother and my brethren are these which hear the word of God, and do it" (Luke 8:21), a phrase that implied clearly that his own family was neither hearing Yahweh's word nor following His will – at least not as Yeshua defined it.

The apparent rejection of Yeshua by his own family (and his consequent distancing of himself from them) is a pattern the Four Gospel writers develop as a side-bar, but it is a matter of some significance to them – and of significance to us, because it relates to events in Saul's lifetime that we need to have confirmed. Thus, Mark carefully tells his readers that the family of Yeshua early in his career (just after he had named the twelve disciples), tried to forcibly restrain him, because they thought he was out of his mind (Mark 3:21).[37] The Gospel of John declares outright that his brothers did not believe in him (John 7:5). And one of the most-quoted phrases from the Synoptics is Yeshua's saying that "a prophet is not without honour, but in his own country, *and among his own kin, and in his own house*" (Mark 6:4; cf Matthew 13:57; emphasis added.)

What are we seeing here? Nothing less than a clear derogation of Yeshua's earthly family (including his mother) in a pattern that runs like a scarlet thread through each of the Four Gospels. Why do the Gospel writers do this? The events and the situations they report may or may not be accurate, but fact has no bearing on the question I have just posed. Why, if the disbelief by his own family is true, do they bother telling us? (The Gospel writers are highly selective, and one explicitly tells us that he has left out a great number of things about Yeshua of which he has knowledge [see John 21:25]). And, why (to take the opposite case), if the situations here described are fictional, do they all go to the trouble to engage in the spiritual equivalent of malicious delation? Clearly, these stories count, and I think they can best be understood in the following context: (a)They all are written after the great reorganization of the world of the Yeshua-followers (and, indeed, of the entire world that once was Second Temple Judahism) that occurred after the nuclear-explosion of 70 CE. (b) After 70 CE entire new strands of the Yeshua-belief appeared and, more importantly, forms of the belief that had been pushed to the periphery now became important – for the centre no longer held and each little satellite had an opportunity to become its own sun. (c) Therefore, it was important to those newly-important forms of post-70 Christianity to free themselves of the previously dominant leadership, which was (I will argue) the Jerusalem "church" which had been run by Yeshua's family from soon after the crucifixion until the Destruction of the Temple. And (d) in order to effect that emancipation from the remnants of the Family Firm, the brothers and sisters of Yeshua had to be derogated and Miriam as a living-and-breathing maternal figure (as distinct from the mysterious Virgin vessel that Matthew and Luke wish her to be) had to be limited. All this was especially important if any of the Family Firm survived, and they seemed to have done so. (Tradition has Miriam being taken by John, son of Zebedee, to Ephesus, and living her life out near there. Yacov had been martyred c. 62, but tradition has three relatives of Yeshua of the next generation surviving, two of them being poor farmers and the third martyred in the reign of Trajan.)[38]

Crucially, when read like a palimpsest, this evidence from the Four Gospels confirms and expands upon what Saul has told us in his letters. This is, first, that Yacov, who is in charge of the congregation of Yeshua-followers in Jerusalem, is Yeshua's brother, and that other brothers are also involved in running things. In his first visit to Jerusalem, about three years after his conversion, Saul spent time with Yacov, "the Lord's brother" (Galatians 1:19). This forms a solid evidentiary link between the Yacov who is Yeshua's brother in the Gospels and the Yacov who is a continual nemesis to Saul. It is this Yacov who participated with Saul in negotiating the Jerusalem Deal, and who Saul is desperate to have accept the Jerusalem collection, when it is completed.[39] The brothers of Yeshua are identified as being active in the Yeshua-faith in the First Letter to the Corinthians (1 Cor 9:5). Incidentally, in neither of these references to the family of Yeshua is there any hint of the later casuistry by which some of the early Church Fathers, such as Tertullian and Jerome of the third and fourth centuries argued, that these were Yeshua's cousins or, at most half-brothers; Saul knew these people and he knew how they were identified by those with whom they had grown up: they were Yeshua's family, bred in the bone.

Secondly, the necessity that each of the author-editors of the Four Gospels feels to hack away at the family of Yeshua confirms what Saul's own behaviour tells us (particularly his willingness to pay the equivalent of feudal dues to Jerusalem): that the centre of the Yeshua-faith between roughly, the mid-30s CE and 70 CE was in Jerusalem; that the central congregation of the Jerusalem faithful was the authoritative body within the world of Yeshua-followers (there could be other versions, but this was the stem); that, like all Judahisms, the Jerusalem "church" centred its cosmology around the Temple (a fact that almost got Saul killed, according to a colourful story in Acts 21:18–32); that the Jerusalem "church" was rigorously Judahist in its convictions, but was willing to make partial exceptions for foreign Gentiles, who were not required to become full proselytes to Judahism; and, that the Jerusalem "church" was run as a family enterprise.

That the Gospels may indeed be balefully correct in suggesting that the family of Yeshua did not follow him while he was on earth is indicated by Saul's own testimony which, being decades earlier than the material in the Gospels, is untainted by their ideological imperatives. The revealing case here is that of Yacov. In First Corinthians, Saul recounts his own experiences with the Risen Christ. Crucially, Saul never suggests that he had seen Yeshua in the flesh before the crucifixion and he does not now claim to have seen a physically resurrected Yeshua, but instead a glorified Christ. (When this occurred for him is indeterminate; it was the apparently not the time he was taken up into paradise, as related in Second Corinthians 12:2–4, as the chronology does not fit; the dating is not here critical.) The significant thing is that Saul reports that the Risen Christ was first seen by Cephas (Peter) and then by the twelve disciples (1 Cor. 15:5). The arithmetic is a bit off here, but the crucial point, as subsequent verses make clear, is that Yacov, the brother of Yeshua, was not one of the original disciples. Next, the Risen Christ is seen by 500 brethren. Only then is he seen by Yacov, and after him by "all of the apostles." (Notice that it is not all of the *remainder* of the apostles; Yacov is not included [15:7].) And only last does the Risen Christ appear to Saul (15:8). At minimum this sequence implies that, to Saul's personal knowledge, Yacov was not one of the inner circle of his brother's disciples and, if Saul's syntax is indeed clearly interpreted (the phrase is one of the few on which there are virtually no variant translations), Yacov was not an apostle at all until after the resurrection experience. Without strain, one can see Saul's experience of the Risen Christ as being presented as parallel to that of Yacov – a supernatural vision that occurred after the crucifixion – and which (here is the speculative leap) brought the rigorous Judahist (and, probably-Jerusalem Pharisee) Yacov to the Yeshua-faith the same way it brought Saul, the diaspora Pharisee. In a sense, Saul is paying a very big compliment to Yacov, because he is saying that, whatever his original disposition towards Yeshua may have been, he has experienced the Risen Christ as directly as I myself have.

Yacov rose quickly to power within the Jerusalem congregation. When, approximately three years after the crucifixion, Saul makes his way secretly to Jerusalem to receive instruction from the authorities there (he does so secretly because, as a former-persecutor of Yeshua-followers, he was in danger of his life), the two people who vet and instruct him are Peter and Yacov (Galatians 1:18–19). Their permission and instruction received, Saul slips out of Jerusalem not to return for another fourteen years.

Yacov's rivals for power in Jerusalem were, in theory, three of Yeshua's original disciples: James and John, brothers, the sons of Zebedee, and Peter (Cephas). James, the more assertive of the two brothers, was martyred by Herod Agrippa in c. 44 CE (Acts 12:1–2).[40] For reasons that are not reported, John did not come to the fore after his brother's death, and Peter acted as an emissary to various communities outside of Jerusalem and, at times, as a virtual errand boy for Yacov. (Certainly that is the way Saul viewed him in the Antiochian affray.)

Yacov's power can hardly be underestimated. Jaroslav Pelikan, a measured and reserved scholar, reminds us that Irenaeus in the second century had called Jerusalem "the church from which every church took its start, the capital city of the citizens of the new covenant." And Pelikan adds his own note that, in the centre community of emerging Christianity, Yacov, the brother of Yeshua, "was a kind of caliph,"[41] a judgement we can readily accept as long as "caliph" implies princely power, but not necessarily the right to pass on his kingdom by hereditary succession.[42]

Saul certainly gave him fealty as such. Although Saul clearly resented having to truckle to Yacov, he did so. Saul, though having plenty of opportunity to do so in his letters, resists the temptation to bad-mouth Yacov openly. The closest he comes is in oblique comment in writing to the Corinthians: he complains that unlike Peter and the "brothers of the Lord," he does not take a wife along with him for comfort on his travels, even though he has as much right to do so as do they (1 Cor. 9:5).

One does not have to become enmeshed in all the intertwined details of Yeshua's family and the Jerusalem church – indeed it is best not to do so[43] – to accept the basic point that here in Jerusalem, before the Destruction of 70 CE, was the primary sector of the Yeshua-faith in the late Second Temple era; and that of this phenomenon we know just enough to know that we do not know enough. Yet, for what Saint Saul gives us in the form of direct evidence produced before the destruction of the Temple and of Jerusalem we must be deeply grateful. Saul's epistles are never easy to read, but they do not require the almost-archaeological skills needed to decipher the pre-70 CE situation from texts that were written after the great Destruction.

Saul confirms for us directly and unambiguously that the characteristics which I discussed concerning late Second Temple Judahism in general – a pluralism of forms, a centring on Jerusalem, a wide variety of beliefs; variegated relationships with "pagan" groups, ranging from proselytizing them on the one hand to syncretism on the other – all hold for the critical sub-set of late Second Temple Judahism, the Yeshua-faith. The fundamental structural and ideational characteristics of the Yeshua-faith are the same as those of Second Temple Judahism in general, because the Yeshua faith was one of the Judahisms of the late Second Temple era. And so we expect pluralistic forms of the Yeshua-faith and a wide variety of beliefs concerning the human life of Yeshua of Nazareth and the cosmic character of Jesus-the-Christ; Saul confirms that there was no such thing as "the primitive church," but rather many communities, all operating within the broad tramlines of Second Temple Judahism; we expect the Yeshua-faith to have a variety of relationships with Gentile groups and with various Judahist groups. And we expect Jerusalem to be the centre point of the Yeshua-faith, Mount Zion unmoveable.

All those things concerning the early Yeshua-faith Saul confirms with strong, direct, positive evidence. Without his letters we would always have to view the first four decades of the Yeshua-faith through the harmonization provided by the Acts of the Apostles. Yet, so much is still unseen. If only we had other pre-70 witnesses. How many versions of the Yeshua-faith were flickering about? How many sets whose names we do not even know had their own traditions, both historical and theological, now forever lost?

· 8 ·

Saul and Four Basic "Facts" About the Historical Yeshua

I

WHEN WE LISTEN CAREFULLY TO SAUL, WE HAVE STRONG AND direct evidence for one set – *and only one of many sets* – of beliefs concerning the historical Yeshua that were held by his devout followers in the thirty years after his crucifixion. Ultimately, one hopes that what Saul believed character-ized Yeshua's earthly existence has some relationship to what we limply think of as "historical reality." That, though, is as much a matter of faith as of epis-temology. While one can live with the forever-sophomoric objection that we can never really know any historical event (not fully, not 100 percent, we grant and then get back to work), there lingers the more unsettling question that is apt to be raised by anyone who has lived for a while and has paid atten-tion to humanity's bent behaviour: can we trust Saul? And, really, even if we had been left memoirs about Yeshua by other well-informed persons of Saul's generation – say Yeshua's brother Yacov and his mother Miriam, and Peter, and John the son of Zebedee – would we trust them? Not completely, for even the most innocent eye sees things through the parallax of personal conviction. Well, all we have prior to the destruction of the Temple and the re-ordering of the world of the Yeshua-faith is Saul, so we should be grateful that he tells us a fair amount and that perhaps this information is actually reflective of the "real" earthly history of Yeshua of Nazareth.

In doing so, we are flying in the face of the conventional wisdom. James D.G. Dunn has summarized the present-day scholarly situation. "The largest consensus still maintains that Paul knew or cared little about the ministry of Jesus apart from his death and resurrection …"[1] These are two separate asser-tions: (a) that Saul did not know much and (b) that he did not care much and they are independent of each other. I wish to concentrate here on "a," the view that Saul had an empty head as far as the historical Yeshua was concerned.[2] It is preposterous.

Recall what we already know from the chronology of Saul's religious career. He was a persecutor of the Yeshua-faith. Whatever else that may have entailed, he certainly was in position to learn a lot about Yeshua. How he assimilated that information is another matter, but recall that three years after his conversion he secretly went up to Jerusalem and spent fifteen days living with Peter (Cephas) and, also, he met Yacov (Galatians 1:18–19). Now, in more than a fortnight of intensive discussion with Peter he must have been tutored in all the basic actions and sayings of Yeshua as Peter knew them. Further, Saul obviously was being examined not only on his own character, but on his knowledge and ideology. The one-time audience with Yacov, direct heir to the headship of the Yeshua-faith, has the appearance of a *viva voce* examination of a doctoral candidate by a stern External Examiner. Saul passes, manifestly: he knows his Yeshua and his interpretations are within the acceptable boundaries of the plasticities of the time.

And recall that fourteen years later, Saul went up again to Jerusalem and this time went through a complex negotiation with the Jerusalem believers, headed by Yacov, Peter and John, the son of Zebedee. Whatever else occurred there, each side clearly expressed its knowledge and interpretation of the life of Yeshua of Nazareth and, again, Saul's work received the imprimatur (Gal 2:1–9). Saul may not have enjoyed his relations with Jerusalem, but he certainly was informed about the life of Yeshua.

Further, he continued to have interactions – sometimes unpleasant ones – with representatives of the Jerusalem church and probably with other Yeshua-groups from outside of Jerusalem (Philippians, Galatians, Second Corinthians, all stem from such occurrences). He knew not just the life story of Yeshua, but was directly acquainted with at least one, and probably all, of the brothers of Yeshua. His third visit to Jerusalem, which resulted in his imprisonment, certainly gave him a chance to become closely reacquainted with the Jerusalem church. And Saul was knowledgeable about (and mostly horrified by) other traditions of the Yeshua-faith, especially those that were strongly spiritualist (see Second Corinthians). Each version of the faith of course implied not only a different complex of immediate religious experiences on the part of the specific community of believers, but also variant traditions of what characterized Yeshua while still on earth. Thus, Saul, being as knowledgeable as anyone among the Yeshua-followers about the varieties of the faith, was inevitably highly knowledgeable of the traditions concerning the historical Yeshua.

These inferences derive from direct evidence in the epistles of Saul. They should not even slightly surprise us, given our background knowledge of late Second Temple Judaism. For the religiously alert – and the Yeshua-followers were nothing if not hyperattentive – the world was one great spider web, the hub of which was Jerusalem, and any motion any place on the web was transmitted through the entire reactive lattice. Even if we had not the compelling evidence of Saul's ties to the centre, we still would assume he was picking up, almost tactilely, every variant of Yeshua's life story and the vibratory signals of each significant variation of interpretation. Saul himself was constantly sending and receiving letters, detailing messengers and instructing emissaries; communication was his business.

So, Saul knew his Yeshua. Most scholars find this hard to accept, because it leads to a maddening sequence of investigation which begins in earnest with this query: if Saul did indeed acquire a full folk-knowledge of the historical Yeshua, why, why did he not tell it to us, why did he make us depend on material that is post-70 CE in its origin?

A facile and familiar answer is that he taught the historical story of the earthly Yeshua to his own disciples in person and that in writing his letters Saul took for granted that they had assimilated the basic facts and, perhaps, sayings. That he taught the Yeshua-history while he was in each community is not merely plausible, but has *prima facie* validity. However, it lacks explanatory robustness in relation to the matter at hand. When dealing with the specific communal or personal situations that occasioned each of his letters, one would think that Saul would remind them of some aspect of Yeshua's life or words. One expects him to recall to an erring congregation the teachings of Yeshua that Saul had given to them and for him to urge that they relearn their lessons. He doesn't.

What this leads to is a possibility (I think it is a probability) that most biblical scholars abhor: that Saul did indeed know his life of the historical Yeshua; that he had a full awareness of the miracle stories, sayings, and of various folk-beliefs about Yeshua, most of which are now forever lost; that he taught the most important stories and sayings to his own followers – but that, when moments of spiritual crisis loomed, all the stories, all the sayings, and, indeed the entire earthly life of the historical Yeshua did not count. Only the post-earthly Christ did.

This distancing of his version of Christianity from the historical Yeshua has three aspects. First, Saul has such an intense and high regard for the Risen Jesus that his enthusiasm inevitably puts the earthly Yeshua in the penumbra, barely visible. Secondly, Saul is openly contemptuous of certain beliefs about the historical Yeshua that he knows are circulating throughout the web of Yeshua-followers. Thirdly, Saul at times consciously diminishes the figure of the historical Yeshua, pointing out where he was wrong on a given halachic issue. And, fourthly, running through all three of the preceding facets is a casual attitude towards the mundane facts about the historical Yeshua, an attitude that these are of secondary moment because, actually, they were mundane.

No wonder Questors for the historical Yeshua dislike Saul. Yet, Saul actually tells us a lot about the historical Yeshua; however, he does so almost unintentionally and he does so by writing non-narrative history. That is hard history to read, but we have to be careful of privileging the Synoptic Gospels and thus becoming the investigative equivalent of the drunk-and-the-car-keys. It's an old story. Consider it a mashal. A man, with drink taken, revolves slowly around a mercury vapour lamp in a near-empty parking lot. In the orange light he searches for something on the ground. "Lost your keys?"

"Yes."

"Where's your car?"

"Over there." He gestures towards a vehicle forty metres away.

"Why look here?"

"The light's better."

2

One of the splendid things about Saul is that he made judgements: all sorts, including historical judgements. The epistles are the most opinionated portions of the New Testament and they are full of Saul's spikey, aggressive, tortured, loving personality. After time spent, for example, with the Acts of the Apostles, which has all the cutting edge of a speech to a downtown Rotary club, one encounters Saul with relief. Here is a real person, a real mind, someone who knows he is put on earth to make decisions, and he makes them. The letters of Saul can be considered to be (among many other things) a set of opinions about the historical Yeshua, both directly and indirectly expressed. The move to watch with Saul on historical issues is the way that he uses the back of his hand. He contemptuously slaps away folk-history of Yeshua that he finds rebarbarative. That inside-move is something we have observed already in his letters concerning rival forms of the Yeshua-faith: usually he refutes a view of which he disapproves by carrying on a discussion that does not include any direct indication of his opponents' position. He rarely dignifies the opposing theological arguments, and this holds for his historical judgements as well. His caesurae are lethal, his silences scalding.

What were the big things Saul believed about Yeshua of Nazareth? Most importantly, that he was Moshiah. He uses the Greek version, "Christos." He never says "Yeshua is the Messiah," but that was hardly necessary. Homer did not need to say "Odysseus was big and handsome," he simply said "goodly Odysseus."[3] Exegetes have shaken to pieces the question of what, if any, difference there may be when Saul says "Christ Jesus," "Jesus Christ," or simply "the Christ," and the most compelling conclusion is that there is no conclusion: Saul uses the various names interchangeably and without subtle shadings of meaning. What counts is that he makes the messiahship of Jesus the fulcrum of his thinking and experience and in so doing makes it central to the Christian scriptures. The New Testament contains about 531 references to Christ (that is to Messiah) and 270 are in the letters of Saul.[4] One says "about," because there are variant texts and the numbers could be up or down a little bit; the main point is clear, however; namely, that it is Saul who first introduces the concept of Messiah into what is now the canon of Christian scripture and it is he who makes it central to the exposition of the meaning of the life of Yeshua of Nazareth.

This is a very big deal. Recall here the discussion in chapter two, section 2: Messiah was only a peripheral concept in late Second Temple Judahism. In the Hebrew scriptures the term referred to a king, prophet, or high priest, always a human figure, and never was there any reference to Moshiah as a redeemer or saviour either of individual souls or of a collective group of the righteous. The mentions of Moshiah in the Dead Sea Scrolls and the Pseudepigrapha of the late Second Temple period are minimal and they are never as a figure of redemption (as distinct from victory). Saul, in his writings and preaching has moved the Judahist concept of Moshiah from the periphery to the centre of his belief-system and has changed the character of Moshiah. "Christos" is an accurate translation of "Moshiah" (it comes from the pre-Christian portions of the Septuagint) but when Saul (and subsequent post-70 CE Christian writers) used "Christos," they had this radical re-invention of the concept of Moshiah in mind.

The originality of this re-invention of the older concept was that Moshiah (1) now was not a victorious figure, but one who lost, temporarily via the Cross;[5] (2) the Messiah now was a sacrificial figure, one through whom redemption occurred for those who affiliated with him;[6] (3) And Moshiah became a figure outside of time. He was a cosmic figure, one who would soon return and bring final order to the world.[7] Paul awaited him impatiently.

This centring of the figure of Moshiah and his redefinition eventually becomes one of the definitive differences between Rabbinic Judaism and Christianity.[8] And it was one of the reasons that the Yeshua-faith was able to adapt so swiftly to the new world that emerged after the destruction of the Temple. Saul's vision of Moshiah as a sacrificial and redemptive figure meant that even before the great Destruction, the foundation for a religion of sacrifice that could operate independently of the Jerusalem Temple had been laid.

Entire lifetimes have been worthily spent parsing the theological implications of Saul's concept of Messiah. Since we are here interested only in narrow matters of historical narrative, we can limit our comments to two central observations, each of which relates to sequence. The first of these is that, to Saul, Jesus is not the Messiah by virtue of the earthly career of Yeshua of Nazareth,[9] but by virtue of something that occurs after it was completed: the resurrection. For Saul, Yeshua of Nazareth becomes the Messiah – becomes Jesus-the-Christ – only with the resurrection. If there is no resurrection there is no Moshiah. (That is the gravamen of l Corinthians 15:12–17, and it is also the celestial mechanics that run throughout all of Saul's letters.)

The second matter of sequence is to note a major matter of indeterminancy: we do not know when or where Saul acquired the pivotal notion of Jesus being the Christ, nor when or where the post-70 CE writers did so. Conceivably, the idea that Jesus and the Messiah were one and the same person, and that this was a redemptive, sacrificed, and ultimately apocalyptic figure, grew up in several places and was mutually reinforcing.

However, the verifiable sequence is the following and is based on the extant texts: (a) the Messiahship of Jesus Christ was first introduced into the texts of the eventual New Testament by the Apostle Saul. (b) He either created the concept himself or heard it from others. (c) If he acquired it from others, this was not from Yeshua whom he never met.

And here is where Saul becomes skilfully oblique. He at no point suggests that Yeshua of Nazareth ever declared himself to be Moshiah, the Christ. He at no point says that Yeshua of Nazareth did anything during his earthly ministry that certified his Christship. He at no point says that anyone has ever heard or seen anything that he considers creditable that was done by Yeshua of Nazareth to claim Messiahship. He at no point refers to having heard anyone who knew Yeshua report that Yeshua claimed to be Moshiah. If Yeshua of Nazareth ever thought of himself as Moshiah or conducted himself in such a way, Saul is giving that idea no credence whatsoever. Yet, the resurrected Jesus is the Christ.

Saul, I think, has a truly brilliant (if often very fractured) mind, and brilliant as he is, he is even better at communicating hard arguments to his audience without losing them. Granted, he could be brutally direct when necessary, but he knows where the major arteries are, and he avoids damaging them. Part of his high rhetorical artistry is that on matters of belief he usually expresses negation of an idea he does not approve of, or believe in, not by outright attack on that idea, but by presenting an alternative affirmation. We observed this method several times in our earlier discussion of his disagreements with segments of the Yeshua-faith with whom he was competing. Here, on the matter of Moshiah, he is affirming the post-resurrection Christship of Jesus, while simultaneously displacing the idea that Yeshua of Nazareth acted or claimed Moshiahship while on earth.

That is a big idea to conjure with, so let it sit as merely a possibility, while we take the next logical step. If the Christship of Jesus was dependent on his resurrection from the dead, what did that mean to Saul? It was a real event to him, certainly. He has no doubt that the physically-dead Yeshua was buried (Romans 6:4 and 1 Cor. 15:4), or that "he rose again the third day according to the scriptures" (1 Cor. 15:4).[10] The question is, what did Saul believe rising-again entailed? Certainly it was a miraculous event of epic significance, since it is this event that produces the Christship of Jesus.

In First Corinthians, chapter fifteen, Saul provides what is probably his (and, therefore, Christianity's) earliest written account of the resurrection. This account affirms that Jesus died for "our sins," that he was buried and rose again on the third day. He was seen by Cephas and after that by 500 of his followers simultaneously. After that Jesus was seen by Yacov (his brother) and then by all of the apostles. "... and last of all he was seen of me also, as of one born out of due time" (1 Cor. 15:8).

Saul's story in 1 Corinthians 15:1–8 is remarkable in many ways. Its matter-of-fact tone is singular. There are none of the histrionics that characterize the Gospels' reports of the resurrection. It happened, Saul says, and then he ties it into his entire theological system. The spiritual implications, not the details of the resurrection, are where Saul wants to focus his readers' attention. And, secondly, note what is not included in Saul's account: any indication of the nature of the resurrection, physical, or in some sense, spiritual. All of those people Saul refers to saw something, but was it Jesus in the flesh or a vision of Jesus as a risen spirit? Saul does not say directly.

But remember that Saul had been a serious enemy of Christianity and, further, at the time of the death of Yeshua of Nazareth, Saul was not one of the company of believers. Yet, Saul draws no distinction between his seeing Jesus and the experience of the others. All had seen the same figure. Saul, in his own writings, does not provide any direct information about his own experience of encountering the resurrected Moshiah. However, the author of the Book of Acts narrates that, within a year or two of Jesus' death, when Saul, as part of his anti-Christian crusade, is on a journey to Damascus, he has a vision of Jesus, sheathed in light from heaven. Saul and the risen Jesus converse briefly, and thereafter Saul becomes a Christian and an enthusiastic proselytizer (Acts 9:1–11). The textual bridging here is obvious enough: Saul's own account in First Corinthians makes no distinction between his own experience of the resurrected Jesus and that of the other disciples, and in Acts it is clear that he encounters a visual embodiment of the spiritually resurrected Jesus, but not a physically resurrected human being. If one accepts this textual bridge, then it implies that Saul's own view was that he and the other disciples had encountered a spiritually-raised Christ, but not a physically resurrected Yeshua.

If that bridging between biblical books makes one nervous (I am not myself comfortable with it), it can be laid to the side: for even without using the material from Acts, a minimal point of interpretative certitude emerges: nowhere in his writings does Saul indicate a belief in the physical resurrection of Jesus. That is beyond argument. Moreover, within Saul's writings, there is a distinct implication that he accepted the resurrection only as a spiritual event. For example, when he writes on the general resurrection of the body, he says that "It is sown a natural body; it is raised a spiritual body. There is a natural body, and there is a spiritual body" (1 Cor. 15:44). If this holds for all the righteous, so much more does it hold for Jesus. "And so it is written, The first man Adam was made a living soul; the last Adam [Jesus Christ] was made a quickening spirit" (1 Cor. 15:45). And, "the first man is of the earth, earthy: the second man is the Lord from heaven" (1 Cor. 15:47). He concludes his argument by asserting the incompatibility of a physical resurrection with the triumph of righteousness. "Now this I say, brethren, that flesh and blood cannot inherit the kingdom of God; neither does corruption inherit incorruption" (1 Cor. 15:50).

This latter dictum is Saul's conclusion of a discussion of the difference between the natural body and the spiritual body. It says that flesh and blood, as in a physical resurrection of anyone, Jesus included, cannot be part of the Almighty's heavenly kingdom. Therefore, since, in Saul's view, Christ certainly is part of God's heavenly kingdom, and since present-world corporeality is incompatible with the sublime post-death heavenly state, it follows that Saul viewed the resurrection as a cosmic, not a corporeal event.[11]

The resurrection is not physical, not even in Romans 10:9, where Saul declares that if you affirm verbally "the Lord Jesus, and shalt believe in thine heart that God hath raised him from the dead, thou shalt be saved." Jerome Murphy-O'Connor has put it succinctly. After encountering the resurrected Lord, "he knew that Jesus now existed on another plane."[12]

One of the most attractive aspects of Saul's interpretation of the resurrection of Jesus is that it resonates nicely with ancient Hebrew texts. There are primary figures in the Tanakh who pass from the corruptibility of the physical body to the incorruptibility of the spiritual body. "Enoch walked with God; then he was no more, for God took him" (Gen. 5:24, JPS). And the prophet Elijah was taken up into heaven, by combined forces of a chariot and horses of fire, and of a great whirlwind (2 Kings 2:1–11). Both of these accounts resonate clearly with Saul's version of the resurrection of Jesus. The Elijah story is especially nice because Elijah's mantle is left behind after his ascent to heaven, just as Jesus' cloak is left at his crucifixion. As for the story of Enoch's rising from earthly and bodily imperfection to a heavenly and spiritual state, it invokes an entire orchestra of meaning, since the Book of Enoch was one of the richest of late Second Temple religious writings. The tale of Enoch in the Book of Genesis from the ancient writings, the Book of Enoch from the late Second Temple era, and the story of the spiritually-resurrected Jesus found in Saul's writings all work together. Saul's writing on the resurrection is biblical orchestration at its fullest.

It is also argumentative communication at its most skilful. Saul is working not simply with his own view of spiritual reality as based on the cosmic resurrection of Jesus Christ, but he is carefully eliciting the associations he wants in his readers (and listeners). He knows that his readers understand that Yeshua was killed and that they believe Jesus-the-Christ is a continuing reality, one that illuminates the daily life of each believer. And they have heard various views of the resurrection, including literal interpretations. Saul is here calling to the fore those associations and then addressing them; and, here again without saying that he is doing so. Fundamentally, Saul is presenting an argument against what he would see as the vulgarization, the literalization, and thence the corruption of the resurrection. His spoken words say that it is a spiritual event of the most sublime sort. His unspoken words are: don't sully it with tales of shrouds and revivified corpses.

The point where Saul's supernal rhetorical ability is seen in sharpest relief relates to the incarnation, the entry into a mortal person of a divine essence. Saul has no doubt that in some way Yeshua of Nazareth was the son of Yahweh. (For example, see Romans 1:4; 8:3; 1 Thess. 1:10). Significantly, Saul uses this idea – "Son of God" – rather than "Son of Man" (a term he never employs) to explain the eternal nature of Yeshua. The explanation for this choice of terms is, I think, fairly simple: despite "Son of Man" being a better-known concept in the Hebrew scriptures and in the extra-biblical literature of Saul's own time, Son of God is a lot stronger, and it permits a whole variety of sharper metaphors than the muddier Son of Man (which in the Hebrew scriptures usually meant simply "a human being") provides.

If Yeshua is the son of Yahweh, how does that come about? In Romans, Saul says that God sent his son "in the likeness of sinful flesh" (8:3). In Philippians, Christ Jesus is said to have been "in the form of God," and yet he "took upon him[self] the form of a servant and was made in the likeness of men" (Philip. 2:6–7). When Saul's personal eschatology is conjoined with the spinning dualisms of late Hellenism – form vs. substance, appearance vs. reality, the transcendent world vs. the world-of-the-senses, and on and on – these explanations of Yeshua's sonship of Yahweh flicker and move in a mind-splitting myriad of possibilities. Saul knows that Yeshua was God's son, but he cannot go farther in putting this faith into precise words.

Yet he can protect this precious belief against besmirching. He is fully aware of the character of the Roman cults that deified several of the emperors, frequently during their own lifetimes: one could scarcely travel or do commerce in the empire in Saul's time without running into votive monuments to Augustus and coins that declared Tiberius son of God. Caligula was particularly assertive of his own divinity and planned to set up a bronze statue of himself in the Jerusalem Temple.[13]

Anything that smacked of those cults, with their concretizing of false incarnations, repelled him. And we have to assume that he had heard of the various pagan myths of the divine impregnation, such as the particularly popular one concerning the birth of Perseus: his father was Zeus who, taking the form of a shower of gold, had impregnated his mother, Danae, a human being. From his encounters with the syncretizing parties in Corinth, we know that Saul was very leery of associations with "paganism." Any literalization of the mode of the incarnation of the Son of God would fall into those rebarbarative patterns.

Here, in a marvellous rhetorical arabesque, Saul engages with his audience in what is best thought as the intentional and explicit discarding of information. If we make the reasonable assumption that both Saul and many of his readers and listeners are aware that there are in circulation various explanations of Yeshua's being the Son of Yahweh, what is really fascinatingly effective is Saul's decision to discard that fact. He knows it is still a fact, and so does his audience, but his discussion runs on the basis of his having received their assent to make this material, which was once information, become what Tor Norretranders calls "exformation" – material that is known to both parties but which is now, by mutual consent, not discussed directly or referred to explicitly.[14]

Thus, Saul can talk compellingly about the concept of the Virgin Birth of Yeshua without ever having to use the term, and his readers fully comprehend. Saul produces two statements that are directly opposed to the idea of a Virgin Birth as the explanation for Yeshua's being in the form of man, whilst maintaining the substance of God. In his Letter to the Galatians, he says, "but when the fulness of the time was come, God sent forth his Son, made of a woman, made under the law" (Gal. 4:4). Given that Saul habitually uses "the law" in association with the corruptibility of the flesh, he is clearly saying that Jesus was conceived in the normal fleshly fashion. That this is Saul's view is confirmed in his Epistle to the Romans, where he writes:

> Concerning his Son Jesus Christ our Lord, which was made of the seed of David according to the flesh;
> And declared to be the Son of God with power, according to the spirit of holiness, by the resurrection from the dead. (Rom. 1:3–4)

Yeshua, Saul declares, was born of the flesh, not by divine impregnation; he was made the Son of God by the Almighty's gift of holiness. This, Saul says, is warranted by Yeshua's resurrection, which (as we have just observed) Saul interpreted in a spiritual, not in a physical sense. Hence, it follows that in Saul's view there was nothing special about the physical birth of Yeshua of Nazareth. Saul's phrasing is just too pointed to be random. He has, I think, picked something up in the air: not yet a fully-fledged, completely articulated version of the Virgin Birth, but something that is running through the margins of Christianity in the 50s and early 60s; it is not yet important enough or sufficiently widespread to demand a full refutation. Saul, in passing, flicks it away, like an impatient high court judge dismissing a solipsistic argument by junior counsel. Saul knows what he is doing; his readers understand. He is refuting a doctrine too lurid in his view to grant a name.

3

Saul, then, well may be telling us obliquely about some central judgements he has made concerning the historical Yeshua:

1 that Jesus was the Messiah (a category for Saul that begins with the resurrection; a concept that implies an apocalyptic return of Jesus and that involves a redemptive sacrifice of the Messiah). But that, special as Yeshua was, he did not see himself as Moshiah: had he done so, his Messiahship would have had to have started long before the resurrection.

2 that Yeshua's transformation into Jesus-the-Christ was a product of the resurrection. The resurrection for Saul is a cosmic, not a physical event. To put it bluntly, he does not evince any belief in the physical resurrection and, in fact, phrases his affirmation of the cosmic resurrection of Jesus so that his interpretation is a displacement – and thus a tactful rejection – of the notion of the physical event.

3 Saul judges that the only satisfactory way to understand Yeshua's life on earth is to see him as the Son of Yahweh. Yet, while formulating his particular form of incarnation-belief, Saul makes explicit statements which are incompatible with a belief in the Virgin Birth of Yeshua. He will not have it.

Here, we must reemphasize that these statements of belief about the historical Yeshua, which we infer from Saul's very cagey and complex interactions with his readers, represent the historical judgement of the leader of only one of many branches of the Yeshua-faith. Still, it is not a small or unimportant body of believers. Moreover, Saul's beliefs should not be seen as markedly eccentric. Despite his troubles with rigorists from Eretz Israel, Saul's teachings at least met the grudging approval of the head of the Jerusalem community, Yacov, brother of Yeshua, and of Peter and John, both of whom were among the original disciples. They may not have agreed fully with Saul, but they permitted him to keep preaching. And we should not forget that Saul, though he had never encountered Yeshua, knew some of the original disciples and almost certainly the members of Yeshua's family, in addition to Yacov. (Remember that Saul had noted petulantly that the brothers of Yeshua were travelling around with their wives.) Were there ever an encounter between Miriam and Saul (and that is not unlikely), it is one of history's great lost moments; oh, to hear them try to straighten each other out about Miriam's dear lost son.

These domestic reflections are apposite because the historical Yeshua existed in the everyday world. So it is revealing of that world, that Saul, despite perceiving the cosmic Jesus as Moshiah and the essence of Yeshua as nothing less than the incarnate Son of Yahweh, nevertheless is not entirely impressed with Yeshua as a rabbi (to use a term that is slightly anachronistic, but which is also frequently applied to Hillel and Shammai, the other great Judahist teachers of the same era as Yeshua and Saul). Specifically, Saul thinks Yeshua got things wrong on the pivotal halachic issue of divorce and he has no hesitation in overruling his spiritual master.

Saul knows a halachah of Yeshua, namely that, despite the relative permissiveness of the Mosaic law, divorce is not acceptable for a man unless his wife has committed adultery. No man was to marry a woman who was divorced, and if he does so, Yeshua says, he commits adultery himself (Matt. 5:31–32, doubled in Matt 19:9). And (in a detail that Saul knows but that the later Synoptic Gospel writers do not), Yeshua also prohibited women from getting what today would be called a "legal separation" from her husband – an actual divorce under late Second Temple interpretations of Mosaic law being obtainable only by the male (See 1 Cor.7:10–11). Saul reports that these three rules are commandments from "the Lord," a term he frequently uses for Yeshua (7:10), and then, he proceeds to subvert them by adding some refinements that he explicitly announces come not from the Lord but from himself. These are instances of fining-down a legal ruling to meet specific cases not covered justly by the general rule, and Saul's correction of Yeshua would fit perfectly as a mishnah by one of the Tannaim of the pre-Destruction era. Saul makes a special halachic envelope for those of the Yeshua-faith (who are covered in this social instance by the rules of Judahism, since the Yeshua-faith is one of the many Judahisms of the time), and who have what today is termed a "mixed marriage." A skilled legal interpreter, Saul fans out three variations of this basic situation, none of which Yeshua had thought to deal with. These are the cases in which a mixed-couple is living together happily (they should stay together, Saul says); those in which if the unbelieving partner desires to leave, either via a formal divorce or a legal separation (that partner should be allowed to go). And what about the third logical possibility, wherein the Yeshua-follower might want the separation or divorce, but the non-believer might not? Saul decides that case not by saying "stay married" – which is his direct meaning – but by a long discussion that adumbrates the principle that every Yeshua-follower should retain the place in life that Yahweh has assigned to him or her. (For the entire ruling, see 1 Corinthians 7:10–24.)[15]

We will return to the matter of divorce later, when discussing the Synoptic Gospels, because it provides an arresting instance of the intertwining of the two major sources of information on Yeshua, the Synoptic Gospels and the writings of Saul. Here the point is that Saul is totally confident in correcting the halachic teachings of the earthly Yeshua. He feels that on legal matters he is himself a more skilled teacher of the written and oral Torah than is

Yeshua – and in this instance, the only tight comparative case that exists, he is correct.

The idea that Yeshua of Nazareth was not an extremely profound student of Torah, that he was not a particularly original interpreter of the Law in its technical sense, is not one that Christian apologists have usually wanted to entertain. But Saul is close to telling us this directly. Close, but we now know our Saul: we are expected to draw our own conclusion, to take the final step ourselves.

Now, the four basic "facts" about the historical Yeshua with which Saul provides us (or, to keep the table level, seems to provide us), on the surface appear to diminish the historical Yeshua. Actually, they do not. They diminish mythological or legendary, or projective, or fanciful, or poetic – take your choice – ways of understanding the being that for Saul is Christ, the Son of God, the sacrifice for human sin, the soon-to-return judge of all humanity, living and dead. Saul has his own way of understanding the life of the historical Yeshua, but it does not involve mythologising its earthly character. All his glorification of the Lord Jesus takes place on a heavenly plane.

Saul, in refusing endorsement of the then just-emerging mythologies about the historical Yeshua lays bare the fundamental question of all later Christian propaganda. How does one explain to an unbelieving world the inner nature of a man who was externally not much out of the ordinary? Saul, with his emphasis upon the cosmic greatness of Jesus Christ, faces the issue much more squarely than do those believers who keep multiplying this-worldly characteristics that are supposed to be the datum-points of Yeshua's otherworldly greatness.

If Saul has it right, Yeshua of Nazareth was an ordinary religious man of the later Second Temple era: one who had only one truly distinguishing characteristic, but that one so intense as forever to defy direct description: an incandescent holiness that burned beyond his burial.[16]

Melding Saul and the Gospels:
A Beginning

1

THE AUTHOR-EDITORS OF THE FOUR GOSPELS HAD THE SAME PROBLEM that Saul had: how to explain the power of a man who was beyond-words holy. They took a totally different path than did Saul in his letters; they used the narrative form that in the Yahweh-faith found its primary example in the unified narrative that is Genesis-Kings in the Tanakh. They told stories about the earthly Yeshua which they believed proved that he was the Christ.

All Four Gospels were composed in response to the disaster that was the Jewish-Roman War of 66–73 CE. They were a way of preserving the faith and, simultaneously, of re-inventing it. The message at the heart of each of them is that it is possible to be true to God even though the Temple disappears. Each propounds a temple religion without a physical Temple and employs Yeshua of Nazareth as the once-for-all Passover lamb. This was a position – the Messiah as sacrifice – that Saul had advanced, in its basic elements, well before the massive disaster. Even if Saul's letters were not known directly to the author-editors of the Gospels, his ideas had certainly been communicated to Yeshua-followers in the Judahist Diaspora and to the leaders of the Jerusalem "church." Perhaps other leaders had come to the same insights independently. All that we know for certain is that Saul is documented as holding them first. The vector of Moshiah-Cross-Cosmic Resurrection-Second Coming later made possible Christianity's quick adaptation to the destruction of Jerusalem and the Temple, and the scattering of the Jerusalem "church." The narrative tapestry that each Gospel weaves, using the actions and sayings of Yeshua of Nazareth, fits within the template of which Saul was the first recorded draughtsman.

And there is one of the big problems for the historian: things fit a bit too well.

2

Here we must backtrack and reflect on yet-another aspect of the Quest for the historical Yeshua. I have indicated in earlier chapters (especially in chapters four and five) why we would do well to use a long spoon when we approach the spumescent products of two sets of scholars: those who are dead keen on redefining items from the Apocrypha and Pseudepigrapha and other non-canonical Christian literature as authentic ancient gospels, and those who are energetically constructing their own ancient gospels by sawing apart the existing canon of the New Testament. So far, the results are not impressive. Here we must turn to the third group of Yeshua-questors, the ones who use the existing canon (and especially the Synoptic Gospels) as their primary source of evidence. They try to place the Gospels in their various social, literary and cultural contexts, and they compare and contrast the way each Gospel deals with events reported in common. The best scholars in this group listen to silences as well as to plangencies. These are the biblical scholars who operate most in consonance with the evidentiary standards and probative methods of the professional historians in the secular world. In the work of individuals such as John P. Meier and E.P. Sanders, one sees first-rate scholars at work, and no sleight of hand in their methods.

At heart, the quest for the historical Yeshua has only two tasks: to place Yeshua in his own world and to get him out. In interrogative form: what were the contours of his religious world, and in what ways did he conform, and in what ways did he differ from them? Easily posed: but in the scholarly quest for the "historical Jesus," the two tasks usually clash, for the more one knows about the world of Second Temple Judahism, the less unusual Yeshua seems to be and, therefore, the less one seems to know about him as a specific individual.

The one point on which virtually all of the present generation of Questors for the historical Yeshua agree is that he was a Judahist. Arnold Wolf has expressed this well:

> There is a consensus among the new searchers for the historical Jesus. They differ on many issues: How much of the gospel records Jesus's own words and deeds? How much of what Judaism did he know and practice? Which brand of the many varieties of Judaism did he prefer? But no one thinks of him as anything but a Jew, a "marginal Jew" as Meier claims perhaps, but a Jew nonetheless. A "Mediterranean Jewish peasant" maybe if Crossan is right, a charismatic, a magician according to Morton Smith, or God-knows-what-kind of Jew – but a Jew for sure. A Jew and nothing but a Jew. A Jew totally within his Jewish faith and his Jewish roots. A loyal, perhaps even a revolutionary Jew, but a Jew and not an Aryan, a Jew and not a Christian, a Jew and not a cipher or an enigma which can never be understood.[1]

How then, Wolf asks, does one sort out what words (and actions) as reported in the Gospels reflect the historical Yeshua? The answer is that most biblical scholars provide a menu of "criteria" against which they then measure the given Gospel passages. There is a sort of unofficial competition as to who can draw up the longest or the toughest set of criteria. As John P. Meier has wryly observed, "so many criteria surely guarantee the results of our quest!"[2]

Since I think that only two or three of the many "criteria" for testing the Gospels are of even limited value, we should here understand what the central problem is.[3] It is that *there is no diagnostic provenance for any of the central motifs that are associated with the Jesus of the New Testament*. With three exceptions (which I will mention in a moment), every motif that is attached to Yeshua of Nazareth by the writers of the Four Gospels (and the Book of Acts and the Book of Revelation) comes from the shop floor of later Second Temple Judaism. None of them is a bespoke item crafted specifically for the Yeshua-faith and therefore capable of being defined either in terms of its origin or its date of creation. In chapter two I alluded to those concepts which are either found in the Old Testament, or in the rich literature of later Second Temple Judaism, as adumbrated in the Qumran Library and the rest of the Dead Sea Scrolls and in the scores of documents in the Pseudepigrapha and Apocrypha. The bank of concepts in the late Second Temple era was rich indeed: new theories of the origin of evil were coming to the fore; the nature of Yahweh was being transformed from an anthropomorphic tribal god to a just and sole god over the universe; new figures, angels and demons, were being introduced into Judahist life; the genre of apocalypse emerged; the conception of the individual resurrection of the dead became, if not dominant, at least well-known; Son of Man and Son of God, undefined, but vaguely powerful ideas, came into minority usage in the religious literature of Judah; the idea of the judgement of the individual dead at the End of Time was being articulated, although still not generally accepted. And there was more, the richest imaginable swirl of old and new religious ideas, all circulating around the Temple of Yahweh, just before or just after the birth of Yeshua, of Saul, of Yacov, of John-the Baptizer. (I cannot expect the reader to take all this on simple faith. For details and documentation, see my *Surpassing Wonder*, pp. 109–207.)

The historian's problems are obvious, but no less formidable for being so. First, because the various concepts (think of them as free-floating pieces of theology) that gyrred through later Second Temple Judaism were so numerous and so easy for any group to grab and use, there really is very little that makes any of them "Christian" (for want of a better term) when applied to Yeshua of Nazareth. In its collective arrangement of these components – in its re-invention of later Second Temple Judaism – Christianity is indeed unique as a totality, but none of its major parts bears a date stamp or stamp of origin. So, when one listens to, say, the Gospel of Matthew's presentation of Yeshua of Nazareth, one is really only hearing one very intelligent rearrangement of the generic components of later Second Temple Judaism and, by definition, the generic cannot define the specific.

Secondly, there is nothing whatsoever in the Second Temple motifs and concepts that the New Testament assigned to Yeshua of Nazareth that could not have been applied equally well to a score of late Second Temple figures without any change in meaning. Would the story have been significantly different if the motifs were attached to, say, John-the-Baptizer? No. Therefore, if the motifs arc not items that are specifically created to fit Yeshua of Nazareth, they probably should be used only very tentatively to make positive assertions (however indirectly derived) about the nature of his life, unless that material is backed up by third party independent attestation. At the lowest operational level this means that there is no easy and direct way to sort out whether Yeshua ever referred to himself as Son of Man or Son of God (much less, what he might have meant by those phrases), or whether those terms were simply picked up from the storeroom of Judahist concepts of the time and applied to him. This evidentiary uncertainty, which stems directly from there being no diagnostic provenance for any of the central motifs that the New Testament attaches to Yeshua, is extremely vexing but cannot be avoided. Only by facing it straight-on is there any chance of making much progress.

(A moment ago I mentioned that there were three motifs which are attached to Yeshua that are not straight out of the stockroom of later Second Temple Judahism. These are (1) the Virgin Birth, which fits badly with the various Judaism concepts, being drawn from pagan cults, most probably those of the Roman emperors; (2) the physical resurrection of Moshiah, and the cosmic resurrection of the Moshiah, neither of which has parallels in Judahist writings that I can discover. The cosmic version of the resurrection belief may be Saul's most original contribution to Christian cosmology; and (3) the Moshiah as a figure who redeems his people through his own individual suffering. This has very faint fore-runners in Isaiah 53 – the famous "Suffering Servant" passages – which Christian rewriters changed from a passage that refers in the Tanakh to the collective suffering of Israel, into a New Testament version, involving the foretelling of individual redemptive suffering.)[4]

It is the non-diagnostic provenance of the great bulk of the motifs attached to Yeshua that makes it necessary for the Questors for the historical Yeshua to employ all the "criteria" they do. The criteria are of very limited use (which is why I do not take up the reader's time with a tiresome list of the whole menu). Because: *with a single exception, all of the criteria employed by biblical scholars operate by defining the "authentic" or "confirmed" material of the historical Yeshua as being that which deviates in some way from the baseline of the Four Gospels' story of Jesus-the-Christ.* This means that the New Testament story is taken as being a norm – but as a negative norm – and the "authentic" sayings or behaviours of Yeshua (meaning those that are historically probable) are taken to be those that do not fit with the norm.

Here is an example. It is a method that is usually called the "criterion of discontinuity." This has several incompatible operational definitions within the Quest community, but we will take first an extreme one, one that requires direct dispatch because it still rears its head, especially in some branches of German-derived scholarship. This criterion derives from the clear fact that the Gospels are collections of Judahist sayings and motifs, and from the useful notion that those deeds or words of Yeshua which are reported in the Gospels, but which are incompatible with late Second Temple Judahism, are authentically those of Yeshua. That is not quite so crazy as it seems, because it is reasonable to argue that if the early followers of Yeshua – individuals whose background was within late Second Temple Judahism – treasured and maintained historical behaviours on Yeshua's part that did not fit with their own religious predispositions and their Judahist heritage, then they did so for a very strong reason: and this reason was that the act or words came directly from their master, the historical Yeshua, and that they had to be preserved no matter how awkwardly these facts might stick out in the entire narrative. That makes sense. However, consider how this exercise in historical arithmetic works in practice. Essentially, it is a formula. Let us assume for the moment that we know a great deal more about the Judahisms of the time of Jesus than we actually do. Even so, we would have a formula for assaying the words and actions of the historical Yeshua, as follows:

Words and actions of Jesus-the-Christ as found in the Christian scriptures
minus
all elements from late Second Temple Judahism
equals
the words and actions of the historical Yeshua.

That is truly amazing, for it suggests that if one gets rid of all the "Jewish" elements from the Christian record of Jesus, one will find the real Yeshua. This turns Yeshua from the one thing both external sources and the New Testament agree on concerning his religious background – that he was unmistakably a Judahist – and transforms him into the one thing that even the New Testament never asserts: that he was a Christian.

The "criterion of discontinuity" can be used in a different way, however, and it is marginally productive. Instead of subtracting all the "Jewish" elements from Jesus-the-Christ in the Christian narratives (a prescription for an historical disaster for reasons I have just detailed), one can start the other way. Accept as a basis one of the few things that we know about the historical Yeshua: that his life, values and outlook were those of a serious late Second Temple worshipper of Yahweh. He was a sort of Judahist whose precise label we know not (I suspect that he was one of the many forms of Pharisee), but that is not here important. If we constantly remind ourselves that Yeshua was a fervid member of the Yahweh-faith, then the criterion of discontinuity can help a little bit. Specifically, if we look for instances where his utterances and acts clash with known Judahist practices *as defined in non-New Testament sources*, then we may have a few of his authentic words and behaviours. Obviously we would need to be on our guard against bits of anti-Jewish propaganda put into his mouth by the author-editors of the Gospels. And we would need to work very hard on sorting out the entry-layers of the Mishnah, for those are the chief places where we obtain in-depth, non-Christian evidence of Pharisaic practices (Josephus and Philo are marginally helpful as well). So we assume that we will find Yeshua to be a Second Temple Judahist, but with a bit of distinctive colouration.

Good, so long as we do not overreach ourselves. With no impiety intended, let us briefly observe how this evidentiary principle would work with a modern figure, in this case the oracle of wisdom, and performer of miracles, Charles Dillon (Casey) Stengel. Casey is a good parallel because he operated within one of the tightest halachic regimes in the United States of America, namely professional baseball. The rules are highly codified, are enforced by priestly arbiters (called umpires), a Sanhedrin (the owners) and, in cases of serious disputes, a high priest (the Commissioner of Baseball). Nevertheless the rules are open to oral argument and re-interpretation (rhubarbs). Stengel was a sage who frequently spoke in paradoxes and parables, and there are authentic multiply-attested versions of many of his utterances. These include:

- The way our luck has been lately, our fellows have been getting hurt on their days off.
- I love signing autographs. I'll sign anything but veal cutlets. My ball-point pen slips on veal cutlets.
- It's like I used to tell my barber. Shave and a haircut but don't cut my throat. I may want to do that myself.
- I was such a dangerous hitter I even got intentional walks in batting practice.
- There comes a time in every man's life and I've had plenty of them.
- When I played in Brooklyn, I could go to the ballpark for a nickel and carfare. But now I live in Pasadena, and it costs me fifteen or sixteen dollars to take a cab to Glendale. If I was a young man, I'd study to become a cabdriver.[5]

These are all quotations taken from a written version of Stengel's words, contained in an "oral history" of the New York Yankees. That is, his statements, like those of many a Master, passed through an oral stage, treasured by his admirers, before being collected by a scribe and put in permanent form. If these sayings and parables, plus the odd memory of a few of Stengel's symbolic behaviour acts – the time he saluted a hostile crowd, for example, by doffing his cap: a sparrow flew out – were all that was left to us, we would be in the position which the "discontinuity criterion" places us concerning Jesus. We would have Casey Stengel with the everyday baseball left out, just as the discontinuity-method attempts to give us Yeshua, by taking Jesus-the-Christ and showing his deviances from Second Temple Judahism.

With Casey, we would miss the fact that, mostly, he did not say memorable things or engage in symbolic acts. He was an excellent player, and a better manager, one of the all-time greats: he respected the Halachah of baseball, even if he occasionally pushed at its edges. Mostly, he said things that were simple and conventional: "don't hit into a double play"; "use your fastball pitcher on a cloudy day"; and "don't try a drag bunt on a hard infield." Fortunately, we do not just have Casey's sayings and the records of his symbolic acts. We also have the baseball volume of *The Sports Encyclopedia*, which gives his managing record, year-by-year, and *The New York Times Book of Baseball History*, which provides newspaper reports of his actions, put together within twenty-four hours of their occurrence. These sources document that, though Casey had his memorable sayings and eccentric behaviours, he basically was a straight-ahead player and manager, just better at it than most, especially the managing. He spent most of his time saying and doing things that were almost exactly the same as other players and managers. Though he is now quoted as a prophet and miracle worker, in fact, his words, actions, beliefs and behaviour were only slightly different from those of his colleagues in the business. Fortunately, with Casey, we know how his life worked – its common moments and its quotidian behaviours. For Jesus-the-Christ we do not.

Nevertheless, as with Casey, we must treasure his odd moments – his moments of deviation from standard halachic norms – while keeping in the forefront of our consciousness that they were his odd times. Had we adequate knowledge of everyday life in Eretz Israel at the beginning of the Common Era – and adequate sources concerning Yeshua – we would probably find that he shared most of the beliefs about the way the physical world operated that prevailed among his compatriots. We would discover that he believed the sun revolved around the earth; that ships which sailed out of the mouth of the Mediterranean Sea fell off the edge of the earth, unless they were first eaten by sea monsters; that most diseases were caused by evil spirits; that women were inferior beings; that menstrual blood was among the most defiling of effluents; that heaven was up, Sheol down; that angels and demons affected everyday life; that some holy men could fly, in the extreme cases, all the way to heaven: and on and on: the everyday beliefs of a perhaps-literate

Palestinian artisan of his time. But one with a difference, and his odd moments are the fluorescent indicators that tell us that there was more to Yeshua than ever will meet our eyes.

The "criterion of discontinuity," then, works, although in quite a limited way. A second criterion that is of some use is labelled "the criterion of embarrassment." It too has several contradictory definitions. One of these is that a saying or practice of Yeshua is apt to be historically accurate if it is embarrassingly dissonant with the early Christian church's beliefs and practices. Again, this is on the principle that something Yeshua believed in strongly could not be easily swept away, even if the church later developed in other directions. To take a parodic case, had Yeshua been reported as saying "There shall be no hierarchy among you, and that includes you, especially, Peter," then those scholars employing this criterion would judge that the statement had a high degree of probability of being a real item. However, the whole procedure is a non-starter: our best knowledge of the early church comes solely from the Christian scriptures, so one is really asking if, in regard to church practices as found in the New Testament, there are therein words or actions of Yeshua which conflict with these basic texts. That is a good question, but it has nothing to do with historical discontinuity with the church, since, for the earliest period there is no history of the church outside of the basic texts. One can, therefore, remove the middle term – the church – as being redundant.

A second definition of the "criterion of embarrassment" is that it is operational when there are lumps within the Gospel narratives which embarrass the accomplishment of the narrators' main purpose – the transformation of Yeshua of Nazareth into Jesus-the-Christ. This would perhaps indicate something that was so well known about the historical Yeshua that it could not be erased from the story, even though it might raise problems for the Jesus-the-Christ story. Since the author-editors of the New Testament were so skilful at providing interlocking and integrated documents, this is a potentially very powerful tool: any embarrassing awkwardness that they dared not smooth over must have been very well known and very strongly maintained by those who kept alive the memory of Yeshua after his death. Moreover, this indicator is especially useful because (unlike most of the alleged indicators of the historical Yeshua), it points to Yeshua's actions. According to John Meier, there are four major occurrences of embarrassing events: the crucifixion of Yeshua by the Romans, his denial by Peter, the betrayal by Judas, and the baptism of Jesus by John the Baptist.[6] Of these, I can see only the fourth as a true embarrassment and thus an indicator of an authentic historical event involving Yeshua. (1) The crucifixion is hardly an embarrassment to the New Testament and its author-editors; they brilliantly integrate it into a religious system wherein the sacrifice of Jesus-the-Christ replaces the sacrificial system of the Second Temple. (2) Peter's denial of Christ, though embarrassing to one of the political factions within post-70 Christianity, is not an awkward moment in the narrative; it can best be considered as propaganda in the later factional battle for control of the church.

(3) As for the betrayal by Judas, it works splendidly within the Passion narrative. The incarnation of evil was one of the modes of understanding the world that was increasingly common in Second Temple Judahism, and Judas is appropriate both within that idiom and within the actual narrative flow. Judas fits perfectly with the post-70 CE invention of the bulk of the Jesus-the-Christ narrative. And it is of a piece with the low-level anti-Semitism (or at least anti-Pharisaism) that is woven into the Christian scriptures, as the Christian branch of Judahism drives to take over the heritage of the now-destroyed Second Temple religious system. That Judas – Judah, of course – was the active incarnation of the evil principle (he can be considered most accurately as one of the demon-figures that became so popular in late Second Temple Judahism), makes him fit smoothly with the ideology of the Christian scriptures. It is not an embarrassment, in the methodological sense. Indeed, if the Yeshua faith was to be presented as the replacement of the old religion of Judah (the replacement by virtue of being the Covenant's "true" form), then it was a fine piece of narrative construction to introduce a personality who represented late Second Temple Judahism – "Judas" – and who was antithetical both morally and behaviourally to Yeshua. Within the story, Judas operates in opposition to Jesus-the-Christ, the way that Satan in late Second Temple mythology acts towards the Almighty. Did Judas exist or was he an introduction into the narrative of one of the hundreds of demons that floated through the cosmology of late Second Temple Judahist sects? There is no evidence outside the Gospels, so the question remains open. However, this secondary question is germane: even if one takes as a given that Yeshua was betrayed by someone, would the story have a very different meaning if the betrayer was named, say, Yosef? Indeed it would: at minimum, then, we should accept the strong possibility that "Judas" was a stage name, introduced in early narratives of the Jesus-faith, to fit the need to differentiate that faith from other derivatives of the Yahweh-faith and, simultaneously, to demean those other religious groups. It all fits.

However, the fourth matter, Jesus' submission to John-the-Baptizer, is different. (See Matt. 3:13–17; Mark 1:9–11; Luke 3:21–22; and, cf. John 1:29–34). The underlying story is clear: Yeshua started his ministry as a disciple of John-the-Baptizer, and Yeshua's ministry began when he was admitted into the ranks of the Baptizer's disciples. The Four Gospels do everything they can to subordinate this embarrassing report, but there it sits. As I mentioned in chapter four, John-the-Baptizer is one of the three religious figures in the Yeshua-narrative who made enough of a mark on the outside world to have his existence attested by truly independent third-party witnesses (the other two are Yeshua himself and his brother Yacov). John-the-Baptizer's initiating Yeshua into holiness is one of those moments that is truly embarrassing (in the meaning of this version of "criterion of embarrassment") because it makes Yeshua a junior acolyte of the Baptizer, at least for a time. Further, his being baptized implies that Yeshua felt himself to be sinful and needful of cleansing: something one would expect of a religiously-sensitive young man who was opening himself to Yahweh's will, but not something a self-conscious Messiah-from-conception would do. Still, John-the Baptizer was too well known to be disregarded and the story of his baptizing Yeshua too deeply embedded in the Yeshua-tradition to be discarded: the authentication of this set of events is an example of a useful tool being skilfully applied by biblical scholars.

Yet, I am not convinced that the "criterion of embarrassment" as defined above works for sorting out the words of Yeshua from those of Jesus-the-Christ nearly as well as it does (in this single instance) with his actions. It is almost impossible to conceive of any saying that the collective memory of Yeshua's early followers forced the four Evangelists to preserve against their will: Jesus would have to have been reported as saying the equivalent of "I am not the Son of God, I am not here to fulfill the Torah, but to tell you to get back to your duties and pay more attention to the priests, scribes, and Pharisees." It has been suggested that Mark 13:32 is such a case: there Jesus says that no one, the Son of God included, knows the hour and the day when heaven and earth would pass away; only the Father knows. That is taken to be an authentic saying[7] of Yeshua, for it implies – in contrast to the rest of the Gospel material – that he does not have a divinely-given foreknowledge of events affecting his own ministry, something Jesus-the-Christ definitely has. Perhaps. But the text can just as easily be read in a very different manner: Jesus is surrounded by people at Olivet who keep pestering him with questions and he finally tells them: go away, watch and wait and stop bothering me. That is the latent content of his denial of foreknowledge in this passage, and I do not see that it embarrasses the scriptural narrative enough to permit an inference that this was a statement of the historical Yeshua.

I think a slightly more useful definition of the "criterion of embarrassment" would be to expand it to include instances where the reported utterances of Yeshua are at variance *with themselves*. Such items will not necessarily be authentic, but they will have a higher probability than do most of the other sayings ascribed to Jesus Christ. Any place where Jesus-the-Christ is reported as saying something that is out of kilter with the overall gestalt of his reported message raises two opposing possibilities: (1) that the *logion* is a cack-handed interpolation by a later author-editor or (2) it was a saying of Yeshua that, although dissonant with his dominant message as Jesus-the-Christ, had to be retained because so many people knew of it that it could not be erased. So, "embarrassment" has some promise.

These two, of all the criteria the Yeshua-questors employ – the criteria of embarrassment and of discontinuity, as refined in each case – are the two implements that seem to me to have some limited validity in the search for the historical Yeshua. And "limited," as I emphasized, is the salient word, for notice how each of them operates: they identify "authentic" words or actions of Yeshua of Nazareth by distinguishing them as residuals, as deviations, from the main story. This is sound technique, but the *final product formed by these methods must always be recognized as being comprised of the idiosyncrasies, rather than the substance of the life of the historical Yeshua.*

Anyone who has spent much time reading the rich literature of the "Quest for the historical Jesus" will notice that I have not mentioned a criterion that usually is given most weight: "the criterion of multiple attestation."

It is a chimera, and I desperately wish it were not.

Cast back to chapter four where I indicated that the real-life existence of Yeshua, John-the-Baptizer and Yacov, brother of Yeshua, were confirmed by multiple independent sources. Note the word *independent* because it is almost universally either elided or defined-out-of-existence by Yeshua-questors. An *independent* source is not merely a *separate* source. The New Testament is made up of many separate texts, but they are not independent historical witnesses. An independent source is one that comes from a disinterested third party. It is better if there are multiple independent sources for any historical occurrence because that increases the probability of accuracy. Multiple independent witnesses do not guarantee accuracy – sometimes a single unconfirmed report actually turns out to be more accurate – but over a large number of cases, the statistical probability is that multiple independent attestation will produce fewer errors and more accurate hits.

In every book I have encountered concerning the historical Yeshua written within the last ten years, the "criterion of multiple attestation" is the one that has been asked to bear the greatest weight. On the surface this appears sensible – at least if the Questors could be convinced to remember (which they rarely do) that multiplicity of witnesses merely increases the possibility of accuracy and is not a guarantee of certainty. So why should we flinch when we find them pointing out that, say, Matthew and Mark agree on something Yeshua said or did, and implying that this is multiple attestation? Because *in the entire New Testament there is no independent confirmation of anything.* And to note this is not derogative of the New Testament, but just the opposite: a recognition that the New Testament cannot be cut into little pieces, but that it is a marvellous unity in construction, motif, articulation and ideology. *The New Testament is a single source* and by definition a single source cannot produce multiple independent attestations of anything. The New Testament is composed of many separate texts, but all of them have been filtered, homogenized, and censored in their construction and in the weeding-out process that finally permitted each of them to be included in the canon. Thus, as historical evidence, the New Testament must be treated as comprising multiple (and, usually, variant) repetitions of material from a single source. Multiple appearances of a saying or piece of action in several of the New Testament books will increase the probability that the given item was a widely read part of the tradition of the Yeshua-faith, but it does not in any way increase the probability that the tradition itself was historically accurate. Until the Questors for the historical Yeshua recognize that they are dealing with *a single source problem*, instead of one characterized by multiple independent sources, they will continue to do the wrong kind of historical detective work and to do so with the hubris that characterizes most of the present-day efforts.

What I am saying here may be hard to take in, both emotionally and intellectually: I am saying that the New Testament is a maddeningly difficult historical source to work with because it is such a totally successful literary, artistic, theological and narrative invention. One does not acquire pieces of multiple independent evidence by mechanically slicing up the unity that is the New Testament. There are instances where one can see how and where the author-editors of the Gospels shaped earlier stories to merge with later beliefs, and one can detect the odd rough-spot here and there. But this requires the sensibility of dealing with a single object. To declare Matthew, Mark, Luke, John, Q, Special-Luke, Special-Matthew, Q1, Q2, Q3 (to use only a few of the slicings in vogue) all to be separate sources and thus independent attestations of some event or saying is to equate vandalism with neurosurgery. Both frequently employ sharp instruments, but that is all they have in common.

Whether or not this argument is accepted will probably be determined by factors independent of its own virtues or vices. (The one thing that history teaches is that there is no such thing as value-free reflection or, for that matter, argumentation.) Seriously interested scholars should read *Surpassing Wonder*, pp. 211–69. In the present context, I would emphasize the following. First, that the New Testament is a massive work of suppression and censorship. In the form that we possess it, only a very tight range of ideas and behaviours are permitted preservation. More potential books of scripture have been destroyed than are preserved. Secondly, this suppression and censorship takes place within the context of a re-invention of Judaism, in what Christians have come to call a "new Covenant." Thirdly, the Christian re-invention of Judaism – the forming of a temple religion without the Temple – is almost entirely dependent upon components that were defined before the life of Yeshua: they are found in the Tanakh and in the later Second Temple extra-biblical writings. Most of the characteristics ascribed to Yeshua were articulated before his birth. Fourthly, the Christian scriptures are explicitly modelled on the Tanakh, that is, on the Hebrew scriptures. They take their architectural form from the Tanakh. The five narrative books of the New Testament are a carefully constructed parallel to the Genesis-Kings unity of the Old Testament. Fifthly, the individual books of the New Testament are merged together into a whole by extremely powerful literary techniques: the interdigitation of symbol, icon, and motif which runs from one book to another; and the employment of a vast harmonic system that uses the Old Testament as its resonating board. At a verse-by-verse level, the author-editors of each book of the New Testament shaped their individual phrases so that they resonate with those of the Hebrew scriptures. With a very few infelicitous exceptions, the phrases of the New Testament, like pipes in a vast harmonic device, vibrate at sympathetic frequencies with those of the Old Testament upon which they are based. Almost nothing is said about Jesus-the-Christ that does not have the Hebrew scriptures as its sub-text.

Therefore, the combination of *post hoc* censorship and suppression in the formation of the Christian canon and, more importantly, the anterior consilience in rhetorical methods among the several author-editors of the New Testament (in the form we have it) means that when we come to investigate the historical Yeshua we have a single source, not a bag of multiple sources. Emphatically, this does not mean that we should stop looking for the historical Yeshua. But one-source problems require a different sort of sensibilities, a different set of historical skills, than do multiple-source exercises. In a single-source problem, the historian is sensitive less to adjudicating the differences between two conflicting statements than in viewing them as in some way organically related and, therefore, in asking how each of them grew to be part of the larger whole.

We can continue to use *multiple datum points* as indications of both the direction and the range of the growth of the unity that is the New Testament; we only have to avoid confusing these datum points with instances of multiple independent attestation of the nature of the historical Yeshua. Our knowledge that there were a number of versions of the Yeshua-faith extant prior to the great destruction of 70 CE does not mean that we can pick up a doublet here, a contradiction there, and say that these are independent multiple attestations since they come from different communities within the faith. The final versions of the books included in the Christian canon permitted variations, but only within an agreed matrix. E.P. Sanders shrewdly noted that "a person who believes in God's providence is inclined to read history 'backwards.' He or she starts with the outcome; since God intended the outcome, what went before must have happened to lead up to it."[8] The New Testament, as we now possess it, starts with a belief in God's providence and thus is an outcome, and that leads to a narrative and a set of explanations (almost all of which originate in late Second Temple Judaism) of what must have led to that outcome. Occasionally, by observing how this single organic entity grew, we may obtain an idea of the human history beneath it.

3

This is not revolutionary. Treating the New Testament as a single source should lead to a slightly more gentle, slightly subtler reading of the basic text, to less argument about philology and more tuning in to the marvellous celestial music of the scriptures. Maybe that is naive, but it is a small hope and perhaps could be indulged.

Certainly, if biblical scholars in search of the historical Yeshua were to treat the New Testament as a unity, they would pay more attention to the letters of Saul and assess them conjointly with the Synoptic Gospels. As a minor exercise in that direction, let us revisit the historical observations we inferred in chapter eight from Saul's letters.

The first matter is Yeshua's own self-concept. In reflecting on this, we encounter once again one of the inherently difficult situations faced by those who wish to discover the historical Yeshua: here it is that, ultimately, they would like to know what Yeshua thought and claimed himself to be; and this has to be done in the face of texts that seem almost intentionally designed to thwart that discovery. From a rhetorical point of view, the organic formation of layer after layer of pious patina in this single source (the narrative of Jesus-the Christ) means that getting to Yeshua's own self-awareness becomes very nearly impossible. In the narrative books of the New Testament, an exponential magnification of the claims of Jesus-the-Christ occurs and, simultaneously, a collapse of definition and of meaning takes place, so that concepts and terms of late Second Temple Judaism that once were separate are bonded together, as if welded, into one single entity.

Saul, it will be remembered, was absolutely convinced that Yeshua was Moshiah. Saul redefined Moshiah so as to be a suffering and humiliated figure, one whose effectiveness was dependent upon that humiliation and suffering. Crucially, Saul did not at any point assert that Yeshua of Nazareth ever claimed to be the Messiah. His Messiahship comes into existence only after his resurrection. One possible (indeed, the most reasonable) inference from this is that Yeshua had made no self-conscious claim to be Moshiah, and certainly not the way that Saul had re-invented the concept. This conjoins nicely with the fact that in the earliest Gospel, Mark, Yeshua never claims the title of Messiah directly for himself.[9] In Matthew and John, he is reported to claim the title overtly.[10]

Much more frequently in the books of narrative history in the New Testament, Jesus-the-Christ (the Messianic title is an automatic attachment to his name, but not a name he claims for himself), refers to himself as "Son of God," and "Son of Man." Saul, it will be recalled, had not used the term "Son of Man," but "Son of God" was frequently on the tip of his pen. Now, in the post-70 CE period the author-editors of the narrative of Yeshua of Nazareth are using very effectively devices that were part of the vocabulary of late Second Temple Judahism (the idea bank by which they themselves had been formed), to explain the nature of Jesus-the-Christ. They do this with great skill, so that the older units of thought are tied together in a brand new entity. The mode they use is simplicity itself: they effect the blurring of definitions so that equations of identity and the implosion of meaning occur. In tying together ideational units that previously had not been united in Second Temple Judahist thought (for instance, Son of God, Son of Man, and Messiah) the author-editors of the various New Testament writings did not follow the Greek pattern of thought, requiring hard proof. The classic Greek proofs with which most modern readers are familiar are those involved in plane geometry, where things-equal-to-the-same-thing-are-equal-to-each-other is a paradigmatic way of proving identity. The Christian writers, operating by thought processes that were derived from late Second Temple thought, instead produced equations of identity not by hard proof, but by association, repetition, and by altering and alternating nomenclature. Thus the reader eventually concludes, without its having been logically demonstrated, that the entities described are one and the same. This technique, though the bane of theologians (who, quite properly, spend much of their time drawing distinctions rather than obscuring them), works nicely within each given book of the New Testament. It works even better between books, because the fuzziness of definition and the use of multiple-nomenclature permits intertextual joinings of ideas and images. Things that are not exactly the same blur together. This technique should not be treated dismissively: blurring in the conceptual world is similar to welding in the physical world. It joins separate elements that would not otherwise lock together. And, if done properly, the strength of the weld is actually greater than that of the separate entities which it conjoins.

The character most sharply outlined is the Son of Man, who nevertheless blurs into the Son of God, who blurs into the Messiah. The attachment of each of these terms to Yeshua of Nazareth is the primary way that the New Testament employs to transform him into Jesus-the-Christ. "Son of Man," it will be recalled (see chapter two) was barely present in the Hebrew scriptures, except as a general term for human being: as in, "Lord, what is man, that thou takest knowledge of him! or the son of man, that thou makest account of him!" (Ps. 144:3). It was, however, found in the latter portions of the Book of Enoch, namely the Book of Similitudes, and there the figure is one of force and power and therefore carries quite a different meaning from that associated with the concept in the Tanakh. (See Enoch, chapters 37–71.)

It is this very late Second Temple "Son of Man" that Christianity takes over from Judahism. The Gospels have Jesus refer to himself as Son of Man about eighty times. The self-reference is both to himself in the immediate physical sense and to himself as an apocalyptic figure.

The most effective use of "Son of Man" by someone other than Jesus is found in Revelation (14:14) where the apocalyptic visionary who takes the name "John" sees someone, sitting on a cloud, with a crown on his head and a sharp sickle in his hand. This figure is "like unto the Son of Man ..." That is a phrase we have heard before, in the Book of Daniel (7:13) where it carried the Tanakh's meaning: it referred to a figure who resembled a human being. But now, when we read the phrase in Revelation, the meaning has changed entirely. The indeterminate usage of "Son of Man" in the Hebrew scriptures has, by virtue of its being a self-description ascribed to Jesus, been tied to him, both in his physical and his future forms. So, one "like" the Son of Man in the Revelation of John means one like Jesus, and clearly it refers directly to him. This is as forceful an end to the narrative of Jesus as one could imagine: his coming back to earth to precipitate the end-times. It is also a re-writing of the Book of Daniel that is so strong that it precludes most Christians ever reading that portion of the Hebrew scriptures without projecting into the Tanakh the figure of Jesus Christ.

Although arguments from silence are always dicey, I think it is worth repeating that in none of the letters that are incontestably by Paul, is the concept of Son of Man employed. Given that the Pauline letters are the only Christian documents that we possess which, in their present form, certainly were written before the destruction of the Temple, this may clarify a matter of chronology. The absence of Son of Man in Paul's writing seems to confirm the inference one draws from the Book of Enoch, where the Son of Man as an ideational unit is included only in the latest portions of the volume, namely chapters 37–71; the "Book of Similitudes." The inference is that the concept of the Son of Man as an individual, forceful figure developed extremely late in Second Temple Judahism and that it was not widely known until just before the Temple was destroyed. A reasonable suggestion is that Paul did not employ the Son of Man concept because it was not part of the vocabulary of the branches of Judahist thought with which he was familiar. In contrast, the Gospels, the Catholic epistles, and Revelation, all being completed considerably later than were Paul's letters, were formed in an era when the idea apparently had become a much more familiar and much more comfortable concept.

The construction "Son of God" in the Hebrew scriptures was not an apocalyptic notion nor one that was attached to a specific person (see chapter two). And even less than Son of Man was it found in an apocalyptic and personalized context in the literature of later Second Temple Judahism: it is found unambiguously only in a single text of which we are aware today (the "Aramaic Apocalypse," of which only a few more than 200 words are clearly decipherable). Nevertheless (in contrast to Son of Man), the idea of Son of God was sufficiently well known within the forms of Judahism that Paul was familiar with to permit him to be comfortable with it as part of his religious vocabulary. Paul employed it with great effect:

> For what the law could not do, in that it was weak through the flesh, God sending his own Son in the likeness of sinful flesh, and for sin, condemned sin in the flesh.
>
> (Romans 8:3)

The motif of Son of God runs from one book of the Christian scriptures to the next. Mark, the earliest writer of the Jesus narrative, starts with a bold assertion: "The beginning of the gospel of Jesus Christ, the Son of God" (Mark 1:1).

In the Four Gospels, Jesus is seen to be much more at ease in calling himself Son of God, than he is in using Son of Man. In part, this is a technical matter: the Gospel writers have the luxury of giving him an alternative to self-reference in the third person, for when he is discussing himself as Son of God, he can talk about "my Father," the sonship being implied and thus first person dialogue being made easier. Further, the concept of Son of God is easier for the Gospel writers to present comfortably than is Son of Man. The model of father-son relationships is simple to work with and easy for most readers and listeners to comprehend. It is a comfortable idiom, unlike Son of Man (who is the father of the Son of Man? – a natural answer is not readily to hand). The personalization – the attachment of the construct Son of God – to Jesus is entirely successful.

The way this personalized concept is employed varies from book to book, and that is no failing: blurring, not definitional sharpness, is the way the New Testament achieves its interdigitation of major motifs. Thus, in the Synoptic Gospels, Jesus is presented as the Son of God, but it is never stated that he *is* God.[11] In contrast, the author of the Gospel of John presents Jesus as a divine figure: see, for example, John 1:9, where Jesus is the "true Light," which, for John, is the divine principle. In the Letter to the Hebrews, Jesus, as Son of God, becomes a divine being who has existed from before the creation of the world: the reverberations of "the Before-Time" of Enoch 48:2–7 are obvious. And in Revelation, the Son of God returns to help judge the earth.

That both Son of God and Son of Man are attached to Jesus means that these concepts become, if not synonyms, names for different facets of a phenomenon that the writers of the Christian scriptures find too large to denominate by a single name, too compelling to ignore. The author of Mark comes close to making an overt equation when he has Jesus say that the Son of Man would come again to earth "in the glory of his Father with the holy angels" (Mark 8:38). Since "Father" here refers to the Almighty, the Son of Man and the Son of God are, therefore, one. Wisely, Mark leaves the reader to draw this inference, for the employment of a full-fledged Greek-style syllogism would have been intrusive and disruptive of the narrative. In a similar fashion, the author of Revelation makes the equation, but expresses it only by implication. Early in the first vision that is ascribed to John, the author presents the Son of Man as having eyes "as a flame of fire," and feet "like unto fine brass" (Rev. 1:14 and 15). In a subsequent action, the Son of God has "eyes like unto a flame of fire, and his feet are like fine brass" (Rev. 2:18). The motifs meld together.

The terms "Jesus," "Messiah," "Son of Man" and "Son of God" all collapse into one iconic point, the historical person who was Yeshua of Nazareth. Theologians and biblical exegetes spend a great deal of time and effort trying to distinguish the possible differences between these terms. They delineate the contexts in which each phrase is most apt to be used and they attempt to draw out sub-texts that are not found in a narrative reading of the Christian scriptures. These are legitimate exercises, but they are valid only if one honours a prior understanding: that the writers of the Christian scriptures intended to implode these meanings, rather than to differentiate them. And the canon is constructed so that these individual meanings collapse in upon each other.

The conversion of the historical figure of Yeshua of Nazareth into the theological figure of Jesus Christ occurs through the attachment to him of the three motifs of Son of God, Son of Man and Messiah. But why bother? Could these ideas not remain on their own, operating as abstract entities, as they had done in the late Second Temple texts? Perhaps: but it is clear that the religious communities for which the Christian texts were prepared desperately desired personification of religious ideas. One infers from Saul's letters that the presentation of Jesus-the-Messiah which Saul made to his own disciples underplayed (and, indeed, seems to have distrusted) the narrative aspects of the life of Yeshua of Nazareth. To Saul, everything that really counted about Yeshua happened at the crucifixion and thereafter.

One of the commonplace, yet shrewd, observations about the development of the Yahweh-faith is that it started out with a God who was convincingly anthropomorphic in many of his postures and reactions; and that, in the centuries running up to the Common Era, Yahweh became increasingly transcendent and true monotheism emerged. That trend is undeniable (compare the God of Genesis with that of the Wisdom literature) but as Yahweh came more and more to resemble an overarching and abstract principle, he simultaneously became much less satisfying to many (probably most) of the faithful. Thus, we observe in the para-biblical literature of the later Second Temple period, the invention of numerous active figures – angels, demons, and so on

– who do many of the things that Yahweh used to do, including dealing with humankind. Collectively, they personify an otherwise abstract God. Jesus, in the Christian scriptures, is the counterpart of Yahweh in the Genesis-Kings portion of the Hebrew scriptures. He is a figure around whom one can build a great historical narrative. The justification for such historical (and perforce anthropomorphic) narrative is that its inventors believe that any reader, any listener, will be able to understand that the light of something divine, usually gently suffusing, sometimes intensely irradiating, shines in the story.

That narrative, however, does not necessarily have a great deal to do with the historical Yeshua. The transformation of Yeshua of Nazareth into Jesus-the-Christ occurred organically. It was a natural development and an immensely strong one. In gauging this process of narrative expansion and ideational amplification, Saul is our only baseline, the earliest scripture, the first recorded observer of the Yeshua faith, and the only writer of New Testament material whose identity we actually know. He is therefore the core of the unity that is the New Testament, but that does not mean that later elaborations of the Christ figure follow contours he would have endorsed.

4

The Passion story is a case in point. As we have noted, Saul had no doubts about the earthly nature of Yeshua's crucifixion, nor about the world-changing consequences of his cosmic resurrection and, thereby, the establishing of his Moshiahship. None: and he awaited the return of his cosmic lord, the resurrection of the dead and the moral straightening of the bent world with an impatience that is palpable in his writings. Hurry, please Lord, is the punctuation in all his sentences.

Significantly, although he believes that Moshiah will, through his humiliation on the cross, redeem mankind, he holds one small historical point that differs from the later versions of the Passion of Christ developed by the Gospel writers. (The larger point, that he does not endorse the physical resurrection of Jesus Christ already has been discussed in detail in chapter eight.) One of the most pivotal texts in the entire Christian liturgy comes from Saul. It is his description of the Eucharist or Lord's Supper, and thus an historical pericope set in liturgic form. He says he has received it from "the Lord," a term that he usually employs to refer to Jesus Christ. Since he did not do this literally (Saul most definitely was not present at the original Last Supper), what I think he is doing here is saying that this is an historical event for which he gives the highest warrant of authenticity: it is as true as if Jesus Christ were telling it himself. Here is the great passage:

> For I have received of the Lord that which also I delivered unto you, That the
> Lord Jesus the same night in which he was betrayed took bread:

> And when he had given thanks, he brake it, and said, Take, eat: this is my body which is broken for you: this do in remembrance of me.
>
> After the same manner also he took the cup, when he had supped, saying, This cup is the new testament in my blood: this do ye, as oft as ye drink it, in remembrance of me. (1 Cor. 11:24–25)

Saul is presenting this piece of tradition as historically authentic but, crucially, he is recommending it to his followers as a performance-metaphor. "For as often as ye eat this bread, and drink this cup, ye do shew the Lord's death till he come" (1 Cor. 11:26).

We note carefully this iconic, or performative, aspect of the Eucharist, because one misses Saul's interpretation of it unless one understands it as part of a complex of metaphors. For example, the sacrificial aspect of the death and resurrection of Jesus Christ – the extreme innovation of the idea of a Moshiah who succeeds in cosmically redeeming his people through his earthly failure – is indicated in a complex metaphor that makes the death of Jesus Christ part of the chain of rituals that were held at Pessah:

> Purge out therefore the old leaven, that ye may be a new lump, as ye are unleavened. For even Christ our passover is sacrificed for us:
>
> Therefore let us keep the feast, not with old leaven, neither with the leaven of malice and wickedness; but with the unleavened bread of sincerity and truth.
>
> (1 Cor. 5:7–8)

Notice what Saul suggests and what he does not. Without using these precise words, he says, Jesus Christ is for us our Passover lamb. It is a figure of speech and, simultaneously a liturgic image: one that is embedded in a whole range of Pessah imagery and associations. Most emphatically, it is *not* a statement that the historical Yeshua of Nazareth was crucified at the time of Passover. Saul has every opportunity here and in his definition of the Eucharist (1 Cor. 11:23–25) to say that this was the case and he does not. Saul is a skilful, if sometimes free-swinging, rhetorician and he knows the difference between saying that Yeshua was put to death at Passover and that his death was iconically similar to the events of Pessah. He endorses the latter and implicitly rejects the former.

In sharp contrast, the Four Gospels take the metaphor of Jesus-the-Christ as a Paschal lamb and they literalize it, employing it simultaneously as a theological construct and as an historical datum. The author-editor of the Gospel of John reports seeing Jesus and says this of him "Behold the Lamb of God, which taketh away the sin of the world."[12] That theological figure of speech becomes in all the Four Gospels a literal dating-point. The writers of the New Testament's historical narrative report that the Last Supper occurred at the time of Pessah. That there are incompatibilities between John and the Synoptics over which days of Passover events occurred on is worth noting in passing but chiefly to confirm that each of the four texts required a Passover framework for its narrative to work.

Why was this necessarily the case? Because the minor festivals of later Second Temple Judahism were not sufficiently consequential to bear the weight of a world-tilting occurrence. Neither the new (post-164 BCE) Feast of Dedication (Hanukkah) nor Purim, which were apparently just becoming established in Jesus' time, would have been appropriate for the New Testament message, since neither harkens back to the Law of Moses, and rhetorical contact with Moses' Torah is part of the narrative strategy of all the Christian writers. The longer-established minor holidays were indeed consequential, but they memorialized occurrences that were not of primary importance in the Tanakh and therefore would not fit well with the most important liturgical moment in the Christian story. These secondary feasts included: the first fruits of barley; the second passover (to be observed by those who had been on journeys at the original passover); the first fruits of wheat; the feast of the new wine; the festival of oil; the festival of booths (or tabernacles, referring to the generations spent living in tents in the desert); and there were others. The one major festival that had sin, death and redemption as its theme, the Day of Atonement, was a bad metaphorical fit: it involved two sacrificial animals (both of them being goats, which are not common figures in the literary iconography of Judahism) and because one goat was slaughtered, the other set free and this according to the random drawing of lots. The whole point of the Yeshua-faith was that the death of its leader was anything but random.[13]

Alone of all the Judahist festivals, Passover (Pessah) marries with the Christian story. Although, as Gillian Feeley-Harnik notes, "there is no detailed evidence for the organization of the Passover in Jesus' time,"[14] it is highly probable that the week of Pessah was a collapsing together of two separate feasts, that of Unleavened Bread, and Passover proper. The combined feasts commemorated Israel's time of wilderness wandering, the Exodus from Egypt, and Yahweh's sparing of the first-born (the passing-over of the angel of death) just before the Exodus. The rituals of the time involved the breaking of bread, the sacrifice of a lamb, the sprinkling of blood, the solemn sharing of wine, but in precisely what context and in what order of events is unknown. Nor is it clear, in Jesus' time, the degree to which the rituals were conducted as collective and public events (we know from Josephus's reports of Jerusalem at the time of Pessah, when thousands of pilgrims converged on the Temple, that there certainly was a public aspect) and to what degree the rituals were based in the individual home (as indicated in Passover's origins as described in Exodus chapters 12 and 13). The practices of public and private liturgy of course were not incompatible with each other: the unknown element is the balance between the two.

Passover was the one Yahwist-derived festival that melded with the motifs and beliefs adopted by the writers of the New Testament. Only it, of the several holy celebrations declared in the Tanakh, permitted a deep resonance to occur between the Hebrew scriptures and the Christian narrative. If the Christian writers were to be successful in transforming Yeshua of Nazareth into Jesus-the-Christ, then it was irrelevant when Yeshua died. Jesus, however, had to have shed his blood at a moment in the liturgical calendar determined by the day of Passover. In the Synoptic Gospels the crucifixion takes place on the first day of Pessah; in John it occurs on the eve of Passover. The Last Supper becomes a superior version of the Passover meal, and this holds, whether it was what a century-and-a-half later the Mishnah defines as a seder (the Synoptic pattern), or whether it took place in a casual setting on Passover eve (the Gospel of John's view). In either case, the meaning is that all subsequent Passovers are redundant.[15]

Here, the trade-off is clear: in return for the resonance and the amplification which the Christian writers achieve by their appropriation of the Hebrew texts, they surrender their right to be independent chroniclers. If Yeshua is indeed to be identified as Jesus Christ, he has to die at Passover. So: he did. And, as twenty centuries of the celebration of the Christian eucharist indicate, this re-invention of the Passover meal was indeed wondrously successful.

All this leaves Yeshua of Nazareth out of the picture, a virtual irrelevance. That is just the point. Given the icons and metaphors that the post-70 CE Christian church had adopted and adapted from late Second Temple Judaism, the narrative of the Passion does not work unless the Last Supper, crucifixion, and resurrection occur in, or on the eve of, Pessah. When Yeshua of Nazareth actually was crucified is irrelevant.

Now, as observers of this process we have two major alternatives. (1) We can infer that, most likely, Yeshua was put to death during the term of Pessah. Statistically, there is roughly a one-in-fifty chance of this, so it is not an implausible suggestion. (2) Or, we can accept that Saul's First Letter to the Corinthians implies that Yeshua was not put to death at the time of Passover, but that his death was *like* the sacrifice of a Passover lamb, and that this tradition (from whatever source) was later literalized when the life of Yeshua was put into narrative form.

5

Finally, as a further indication as to how paying attention to Saint Saul's letters can open some possibilities about the historical Yeshua that otherwise lack direct evidence are the (perhaps) intertwined matters of Yeshua's views on divorce and the establishment of the concept of the Virgin Birth. Saul, it will be recalled, thought Yeshua's teaching on divorce unimpressive and rigid and he therefore amended it. Also, he not only ignored the construct of the Virgin Birth, but seems to have actively disdained it. In his refusal to endorse the Virgin Birth, Saul was joined by the author-editor of the Gospel of Mark and, later, by the author-editor of the Gospel of John. (In neither case can one accept as of any probative weight the point that both Mark and John start their story considerably after Yeshua's birth; both are good at retrofitting into their narrative flashback-concepts, -sayings, or -actions concerning Jesus that they feel are apposite and accurate; either one could easily have inserted a half-sentence reference if he had affirmed the concept.) The author-editors of Matthew and Luke, however, adopt the Virgin Birth as a way of making the sums add up for literalist audiences: if Jesus was the Son of God, well, then, the literalists wanted to know, how did he get to be that? The Virgin Birth was far outside the tradition of the Hebrew scriptures and of late Second Temple Judahism (see chapter two's discussion of *ALMH*) but was conveniently to hand in the Gentile religions. The best inference is that Matthew and, especially Luke, are adaptations of "pagan" myths, and in the case of Luke, probably a direct assimilation of the imperial cult of Augustus.[16]

But maybe there was more to it than merely an expedient interpolation of material from the Gentile cults. Does the inclusion of the story serve any other purpose than keeping literal-minded contemporaries satisfied?

One side-function of the Virgin Birth story is to raise Jesus above John-the-Baptizer. This is a matter that was very important to the early church: witness the heavily-patterned subordination of the Baptizer in the Gospel of John (1:15–36). Manifestly, some of the people to whom the early scriptures were addressed remembered, or had heard of, John-the-Baptizer as a figure larger than Jesus (this was inevitable, given that, as the Gospels indicate, John was a voice in the land before Jesus began his own ministry) and this had to be addressed. So, in Luke, John-the-Baptizer is reported to be a relative of Jesus and crucially, while still in the womb of his mother Elisabeth, he recognizes Yeshua, who at that time was in the womb of his mother Miriam (Luke 1:39–41, and 44). This recognition is indicated by John's leaping for joy in the womb; the subordination of the Baptizer to Jesus is shown, when this inter-womb salute occurred, by Elisabeth's saying to Mary "and whence is this to me, that the mother of my Lord should come to me?" (Luke 1:43). Clearly, putting John-the-Baptizer in his place was a considered goal of the Lucan narrative, and it is successful. The question arises, however: could not this have been achieved just as effectively without the invention of the Virgin Birth? The story of the embryo's salute would carry the same meaning, whatever the method of Jesus' own conception.

The cost to narrative integrity of the introduction of the Virgin Birth is so great – it isolates Jesus' origins from all ancient Hebrew and subsequent Judahist traditions, which is something the rest of the New Testament strives mightily *not* to do – that one still wonders, why was it included? Was it merely a lapse into literalism concerning the Son of God; or is it something more than an infelicity? One obvious possibility is that the Virgin Birth refers to some aspect of the life of Yeshua of Nazareth that either had to be remembered silently, or (as in Matthew and Luke) had to be painted over.

That this might be the case is indicated by three seemingly unrelated items in the Gospels. In Mark 6:3, there is a fascinating identification of Jesus. "Is this not the carpenter, the son of Mary, the brother of James, and Joses, and of Judah, and Simon? and are not his sisters here with us?" This identification of Jesus is not ambiguous either in the original or in any major translation: two sets of figures are present, Jesus ("the carpenter") and his siblings. Jesus is identified solely by his maternal ancestry ("Mary's boy" is how the Living Bible puts it), with no reference to his father. In a society that was highly patriarchal (in the modern sense of the word), not identifying Joseph as Jesus' father was tantamount to saying that he was not indeed the father. In either the Gospels of Matthew or of Luke that might be taken as an endorsement of the concept of the Virgin Birth, but the text is found in Mark, the author-editor of which indicates no apparent knowledge of, and certainly no enthusiasm for, the Virgin Birth.

That Mark's version (within the context of that Gospel) implies physical illegitimacy on the part of Jesus is indicated by the way that Matthew (whose author is very keen on the Virgin Birth) amends Mark's text so that this interpretation is quickly by-passed. "Is not this the carpenter's son?" the Matthean passage begins (Matt. 13:55) and quickly, efficiently, Jesus "the carpenter" is changed to Jesus, "the carpenter's son." Matthew's move is clever, but it leaves behind the dull luminescence of Mark's text, the eerie glow one gets when decaying wood emits foxfire.

The second diagnostic marker is found in Mark 3:21 and occurs when Jesus' brothers and sisters try to have him taken away for being out of his head: "beside himself," in the King James Bible. It was his family who saw him as a lunatic, and since neither his father nor mother is mentioned – as would have been the normal notation in an historical narrative such as Mark – one infers that it was solely his brothers and sisters who were involved. At minimum, one observes here a significant intra-family split, with Jesus on one side, his siblings on the other. Recall here that none of his siblings affirmed him until after his death.

It is no accident that Mark's material on the intra-family fight between Jesus and his siblings is not picked up either in Matthew or Luke, despite these books employing in other places a good deal of Mark's material. The reasons for this are (one suspects) the same as the amendment by the author-editor of Matthew of the identification of Jesus as "Mary's boy." Mark's material calls into question the idea of Jesus' legitimacy not only by (a) identifying Jesus only by maternal origin but also (b) by indicating an intra-family fissure between Jesus and the other children: a fault line that a contemporary reader or hearer (someone, for example, encountering Mark's words in the last thirty years of the first century of the Common Era) could easily interpret as perhaps stemming from Jesus and his siblings having quite separate earthly fathers. Thus, it was necessary for the author-editors of Matthew and Luke to paint over this baleful phosphorescence. They did so with bright colours, using the methods of ancient encaustic portrait painters: vivid wax colours, fixed permanently with heat, forever bright, forever distracting.

That brings us to the third diagnostic point, a strange tic in the Synoptic Gospel's reports of Jesus' teachings. It occurs in his discussion of the practice of divorce which, in the context of the law of Moses, usually meant men getting shut of their wives: the divorce of a man by his wife is not covered in the Torah. Jesus' views are reported in Mark (10:2–12) and are slightly expanded, but not significantly amended in Matthew (19:3–12, with a partial doubling in 5:31–32), and briefly noted in Luke (16:18). (Here an important point of evidence must be made explicit. My discussion of these texts does not hinge on the reader accepting that the Synoptics report the words, or even the general views,[17] of Jesus. One can believe [a] that these are his historical words, or [b] that they are his general views, or [c] that the texts reflect what the early church believed his views to have been, or [d] that the texts reflect what the authors of these three Gospels think his views *should* have been, given their knowledge of Christian tradition to the point of their writing. My point below is belief-neutral as far as those matters are concerned: it holds in any of those four cases.) Now, the signal characteristics of most of Jesus' reported teaching concerning the Torah are, first, that he was very respectful of it (much more so than later Christian commentators have tended to recognize) but, secondly, that in general he emphasized maintaining the spirit of the Torah more than the letter.

The texts on divorce – the fracturing of families – stand out sharply against that trend. Here Jesus is reported as being more rigorous, and more rigorist, more demanding in the letter of Torah, than are the Hebrew scriptures, and certainly more demanding than were the prevailing standards of the late Second Temple era. The Synoptics give us three distinct magnifications of the letter of Torah, all of them being a response to the question, "Is it lawful for a man to put away his wife?" (as Mark 10:2 and slightly amended in Matthew 19:3). One of these magnifications is that Jesus is reported as taking the Book of Genesis' fundamental definition of marriage:

> Therefore shall a man leave his father and his mother, and shall cleave unto his wife: and they shall be one flesh. (Gen. 2:24)

and adding, after paraphrasing that definition:

> What therefore God hath joined together, let not man put asunder.
> (Mark 10:9; Matt. 19:6)

This precludes divorce, and is the logical foundation for Jesus' second intensification of the letter of the Law. He admits that Moses permitted divorce (see Deuteronomy 24:1–4 for the divorce law that is ascribed to Moses; the grounds for divorce are "some uncleanness in her," as the KJB has it, or "something obnoxious about her," in the Jewish Publication Society translation; however, though not mentioned in the Law of Moses, it had become possible by the later Second Temple period for women to divorce men: this is distinctly mentioned in Mark 10:12). Moses' permissiveness on this issue occurred, in Jesus' reported view, because of the "hardness" – the imperfection and corruption – of the human heart (Mark 10:5; Matt. 19:8). Jesus sets himself as more rigorous than Moses: in Mark's version he will have no divorce whatsoever, and in Matthew's, he will permit divorce only for a woman's having committed adultery (Matt. 19:9; doublet in Matt. 5:32). And, in a third intensification of the letter of the Law, Jesus specifically rejects Moses' permitting a woman to be remarried after having been divorced, and Moses' permitting a man to marry a divorced woman. (Deut. 24:1–4 presents different instances of permitted remarriage and of the marriage of men to divorced women.) Jesus finds Moses too soft, however, and in Mark is reported as decreeing that any man who divorces a wife and himself remarries, or any woman who divorces a husband and herself remarries, commits adultery (Mark 10:11–12). In Matthew and Luke the prohibitions are entirely male-oriented (no female-initiated case of divorce is hypothesized), but it is added that any man who marries a divorced woman commits adultery (Matt. 19:9; 5:31–32; Luke 16:18). In sum, the point that cannot be denied is that however one parses the halachic details of Jesus' views of what is today termed "family breakdown," he was either extremely sensitive to deviations from the normal family pattern or, alternately, the collectors and compilers – the author-editors – of Christian traditions, believed that he had cause to have been highly sensitive on this issue and, hence, they configured their narratives in conformity with that conviction.

Were we dealing with any historical figure other than Yeshua of Nazareth, one of the most obvious hypotheses that one would derive from the three diagnostic markers that I have discussed, when combined with even Matthew and Luke's admitting that from a purely biological point of view Miriam's pregnancy was beyond explanation, is: that Yeshua was the product of a woman who, while betrothed to a man named Joseph, became pregnant by another man. Yet, Joseph stayed with her: loyal, though mortally humiliated by this cuckolding, and later his union with Miriam was fruitful, producing several brothers and sisters of Yeshua. That is hardly a complex, or original, explanation, but it fits with the Gospels and with what we must take as the limits of human biological possibility. It is, I suspect, the tradition of the origins of Yeshua of Nazareth shared by Saul and by the author-editors of Mark and of John.

But even if this is the case, it is merely a now-inert historical artifact. The story of Miriam, as Virgin, kept growing, right into the twentieth century, in an amazingly and dizzying supernal spiral.[18]

6

Spiral: the word applies to all Christianity, but most especially to the first sixty or seventy years of the faith. The history of the Yeshua-faith as it turned into Christianity, a religion separate from the simultaneously-evolving Rabbinic Jewish faith, is not one of linearities ("trajectories" in the phrase of some recent biblical scholars) nor of simple synchronicities (the multiple-attestation fallacy). The closest I can come to catching visually the nature of the faith's history in the first century is to suggest that the lines of historical development resembled the entity whose discovery is now part of twentieth-century folklore: the genetic code – DNA – as disentangled by Francis Crick, James D. Watson and Maurice Wilkins. It is formed as a double helix, which is a tough arrangement to figure out from the outside. The history of the Yeshua-faith is much more complicated even than that. Conceive of a multiple-helix (how many strands? make your own guess) composed of several very flexible ribbands, each in spiral shape, forming part of an immensely complicated unity.

In dealing with this dizzying entity, we recognize certain fundamental realities, that: (a) the basic structure (shape, twist, and torsion) were determined by the multiple Judahisms of the late Second Temple era; (b) within the framework set by these multiple Judahisms, several versions of the Yeshua-faith emerged. (We observed evidence of these in chapter seven.) All this characterized the era before history took a sharp bend, the destruction of Jerusalem and its Temple in 70 CE. (c) Thereafter, the Yeshua-faith mutated into Christianity and ultimately (in a 300-year process), a *single* text emerged, one that permits variants only within a narrow range and therefore does not permit independent historical verification of issues related to the historical Yeshua, simply on the basis of there being more than one report of the same incident.

Hence, if one wishes to get somewhat closer to the historical Yeshua, one must proceed indirectly, focussing attention upon the process by which the unity that is the Yeshua-narrative emerges, and always remembering that the character of the narrative does not depend upon the historical Yeshua, but that the Yeshua whom we can, to some small degree, come to know historically, depends upon the narrative. So we should spend our time trying to sort out the different bits of this Christian genetic code. Always we must remember that even at the earliest moment – at the moment individuals listened to Yeshua – there was a multiplicity of ideas of what he had just said and done.

Saul gives us entry into only one portion of this complex code. But one can scarcely deny that he was there very early indeed and that he had strong views about the nature and consequence of the historical Yeshua. There is a certain common sense in using the earliest known source of information from within the Yeshua-faith as the initial entry point into this amazingly complex multiple helix.

· IO ·

Words from the Master's Table

I

THE POSSIBLE RELATIONSHIP OF THE EPISTLES OF SAINT SAUL AND
the Four Gospels (but especially the Synoptics) has long been a topic of in-
decisive debate. Here we will be concerned chiefly with *sayings* (as distinct
from biographical and behavioural material) that may relate to the historical
Yeshua and with a few items concerning early church traditions that may
reflect on that issue. We will not engage in the kind of textual truffle hunting
that results in random occurrences or common folk sayings being taken as
instances of meaningful inter-textual joinings. To take an example, the parallel between Saul's advising the Thessalonians "... be at peace among
yourselves" (1 Thess 5:13) and Yeshua's reportedly saying to his disciples,
"... have peace one with another" (Mark 9:50), has no value whatsoever as
an indication of any relationship between the Synoptic Gospels and Saul's
epistles, and would have none even if the wording were exactly the same:
most leaders, whether of religions, armies, or just heads of large families
often have to tell their broods to calm down and keep quiet. Lists have been
made of over 900 alleged parallels in the Synoptic Gospels, a credulity that
threatens to discredit the entire enterprise.[1]

The big question is: given the crucial characteristics of the New Testament
– that it is one single document, the product jointly of synergetic collective
invention and of heavy canonical suppression – do the multiple data points in
Saul's letters and in the Synoptics relate at all to each other when they touch
on the words of the historical Yeshua? If they do, then the evolution of the
multi-strand helix that is first-century Christianity may become a bit more
comprehensible. This is easy enough to state as an issue, but it is an immensely difficult relationship to document and to analyse in the actual cases
that come to hand.[2]

Things have not been made any easier by the conventional wisdom in the
field. (1) Almost everyone uses the Synoptics as a validating device for

checking Saul's observations about the historical Yeshua. To do this without enquiring into the appropriateness of the procedure is *louche*. It is an unusual situation wherein the first circumstantial witness to a set of events is automatically judged according to the continuity of his views with those of the second, third, and fourth circumstantial witnesses. Why writers a generation after Saul should automatically be privileged is not immediately apparent, especially given the historical chasm that was opened in 70 CE. (2) Most Questors for either the historical Yeshua or for the early historical documents of the Yeshua-faith assume a regular development of the tradition of Jesus-the-Christ, something that gets larger and larger as it comes towards us, and does so at a predetermined speed. Thus, the words of Yeshua are thought to flow regularly into oral tradition and then into "pericopes" (related memory-units), and then into "proto-gospels" comprised of several pericopes and then into a full Gospel (Mark) and then into the full four canonical Gospels.[3] So, this means that Saul's authentic letters, which are usually bracketed in the period 49–62 CE, are compared with material in the Synoptics which has its focal date set by the earliest Gospel, Mark, which is usually dated just after the Destruction of the Temple in 70 CE. In any case, what this does is provide a false scale of dating and thus a false relationship: Saul's letters are held up alongside the Synoptics, with the implication that the Synoptics were almost completed when Saul was writing, so the two can be considered equally mature parts of the emerging Christian story. No, this does not work, because the nice, calm, even schematic by which the Synoptics are described as evolving (and all this is presented without any probative evidence) is unreal. It is much more realistic to suggest that the narrative's emergence was an extremely uneven process: long periods of snail-like development alternating with short periods of furious activity when, effectively, time was compressed and a decade or two's worth of activity was accomplished in the twinkling of an eye. The most significant of those moments occurred during the emergency-era in Christian history, the response to the trauma of 66–73 CE which, had the Yeshua-followers not been in equal parts fortunate and immensely and quickly creative, the faith well might have died. As far as the present exercise is concerned, this dictates that we do *not* treat Saul's letters and the Synoptics as emerging from the same era, but as datum points from very distinct generations of Yeshua-followers. The Synoptic Gospels are much, much later, far more than their merely being chronologically second would indicate. They are the product of the survivors of a war, and just as a twenty-two-year-old who has seen combat is decades older than an eighteen-year-old who is just about to graduate from high school, so the Gospels are the product of grizzled veterans, whose view of the future is far from naive. In this regard, despite his own personal trials, Saul's letters have the still-innocent enthusiasm of someone who does not foresee the hard ground that has to be traversed before he gets safely home. He has no clue, whatsoever, that Jerusalem the Golden will soon be a dusty swirl.

I suspect that one reason the Gospels are wrongly placed as chronologically coincident with Saul's letters in many analyses and, in many cases are actually treated as if they were *prior* to the epistles, is the pervasiveness of a fallacy that unconsciously runs through so much biblical history: the tendency to treat something that speaks of an early set of historical events as if it is an early historical document; and, when doing comparative work, to deal first with the documents that deal with earlier events, and thus, without consciously intending to do so, skewing the actual textual chronology. Saul came first.

This is not to say that the Synoptic Gospels are not important as diagnostic tools for adjudging Saul's letters, as well as providers of material about the historical Yeshua on their own account. Anyone using Saul as a source has a ticklish historical problem: although his letters exist as witness to information about the historical Yeshua, some of his references to the sayings of the historical Yeshua can be recognized in our own era only because they are duplicated in the Synoptic Gospels and are there ascribed to Yeshua. This probably was not the case in his own time, when his audience recognized toss-off phrases of Yeshua without citations, the way today's pop or country music fans recognise riffs and quotations from songs that are encapsulated in other pieces.

Now, when noting in the discussion which follows, certain non-random resemblances between what Saul says in the epistles and what is later said in the Synoptics about the historical Yeshua, I am presenting no overall theory of relationship whatsoever, merely indicating possibilities. Fundamentally, the potential relationships are simple and limited: (a) Saul was imitated by the Synoptics, perhaps at third or fourth hand; (b) Saul picked up material that was in the earliest form of oral tradition among followers of the crucified Yeshua, and used it. This same material was later employed in the Synoptic Gospels; or (c) that the similar material in the epistles and the Synoptics came from totally diverse sources and its near-identical nature is explained not by commonality of origin but by the commonality of purpose the source material serves in each set of final texts. No single pattern has to dominate. Each instance could be one of those three alternatives and, given the complexity of the multi-helix of Christian development, one suspects that all three were in play.

The potential complications that we can control for are the instances in which Saul and the other New Testament writers each base their own words on the same text in the Tanakh. This occurs thirteen times.[4] These instances are not included in the passages that are discussed below. Thus, in the material that I shall be discussing, when there are significant relationships between things Saul writes concerning Yeshua of Nazareth and things that the Gospel writers set down, it is either because they are both repeating a non-biblical saying or motif that floated through late Second Temple Judahism or they are in some manner using material that was peculiar to the early Yeshua-faith. Since we do not possess anything approaching a full inventory of the ideas, motifs, clichés and folk-sayings of late Second Temple Judahism, it is always possible that some item that seems original and freshly minted for the Yeshua-faith may in fact be a borrowing. I know of no way to control for this possibility.

2

As an indication of how sayings-material about the historical Yeshua might lie buried in Saul's text, it is helpful to note the way Saul smoothly integrated – smoothly to the point of virtual concealment – sayings-material from early church history. Several places in the epistles, Saul incorporates in his own rhetorical flow material that many scholars identify as being pre-Saul formulas of early Yeshua-followers:[5]

> For all have sinned,
>> and come short of the glory of God;
> Being [=Yet, we are] justified freely by his grace
>> through the redemption that is in Christ Jesus:
> Whom God hath set forth to be a propitation
>> through faith in his blood,
> to declare his righteousness
>> for the remission of sins that are past,
>> through the forbearance of God.

(Rom. 3:23–25)

The actual dimensions of the original creed are impossible to determine, but the stylistic and substantive shift within the epistle is noticeable. Romans is Saul's most self-consciously literary letter, so such jumps are not the product of personal mood-shifts, as occur in some of the other epistles, but are substantive. A little later, Saul seems to add two lines of the creed which he previously had omitted, a distich that fits very nicely between the third and fourth verses above:

> Who was delivered for our offences,
>> and was raised again for our justification.

(Rom. 4:25)

The line in the ancient church between a creed and a hymn probably was blurred, since each was probably sung in the same way the metrical Psalms were, and in Philippians 2:5–11 Saul introduces into an otherwise collo-quial text one of those hymn-creed compositions. It is a complete entity in itself and clearly is not his own creation, for otherwise the joining to his domestic advice to the Philippians would have been smoother.[6] Were the hymn-creed to be placed in early medieval liturgical form it could be sung as follows:

[Proper]   Let this mind be in you,
                  which was also in Christ Jesus:
[Antiphon] Who, being in the form of God,
                  thought it not robbery to be equal
                  with God:
             But made himself of no reputation,
                  and took upon him the form of a servant,
                  and was made in the likeness of men:
             And being found in fashion as a man,
                  he humbled himself,
                  and became obedient unto death,
                  even the death of the cross.
[Gloria]   Wherefore God also hath highly exalted him,
                  and given him a name
                  which is above every name:
             That at the name of Jesus
                  every knee should bow,
                  of things in heaven,
                  and things in earth,
                  and things under the earth;
             And that every tongue should confess
                  that Jesus Christ is Lord,
                  to the glory of God the Father.
                  [Amen]   (Phil. 2:5–11)

Other examples of possible hymns or Christological creeds are not quite so clear. For instance, Galatians 3:28 and 1 Corinthians 8:6, concerning the oneness in Jesus Christ of all believers may be creedal or may simply be an example of Saul's repeating an idea that is important to him. However, for our purposes concerning the sayings of the historical Yeshua, we infer from this material that Saul knew a good deal about the traditions held by early Yeshua-followers, but he did not feel a need to put tags on these pieces of knowledge. He just used them.

3

Because I wish to keep us sharply aware of the danger of assuming that the material in Saul's letters is later in origin than the material that went into the Synoptic Gospels or, worse, that Saul's information necessarily was dependent upon early versions of the material that went into the Synoptics, notice the following. Saul, writing in roughly 48–51 CE states that he was called by God even while in his mother's womb (Gal. 1:15). This can be taken as a personal form of what later became the doctrine of predestination, but equally it could be understood by Saul's disciples as a literal statement, that God spoke to Saul, called him to a mission, even while he was in his mother's body. Literalised, this assertion by Saul has its parallel in earlier Judahist writings – Isaiah 49:1, "The Lord hath called me from the womb." – and in later, post-70 CE Christian texts. The author-editor of the Gospel of Luke, composing twenty to thirty years after Saul, has the embryo of John-the-Baptizer become energized by his election for divine service when Miriam, the mother of Yeshua, visits John's mother (Luke 1:39–45). Thus, John-the-Baptizer also is called for a divine mission while still in the womb. Since John-the-Baptizer never appears in Saul's epistles, the motif of being-called-from-the-womb was free for usage. One could argue that it passed from Saul's letters into the general folklore of the Yeshua-followers and thence into Luke's composition. However: migrate it did.

To take another case that concerns biographical fact, but which by analogy indicates how sayings-material was potentially transportable as between texts: one finds that Saul seems to make a direct genealogical statement about Yeshua of Nazareth, that he was a descendant of Jesse, the father of King David (Rom 15:12). This is a trope of Isaiah 11:1 and 11:10. It is also a precedent for the genealogies of Yeshua that are found in Matthew (1:1–25) and Luke (3:23–38) which, though not in complete agreement with each other, pass through the common nodal point, Jesse, father of David. Here, instead of suggesting either that Saul was the source of the genealogical tradition in the Synoptics (one point does not a genealogy make), or that Saul derived his reference primarily from early beliefs that Yeshua was of the Davidic line, note: there is a source, Isaiah, that served Saul's purposes very well by predicting that a scion of Jesse would be the spiritual or secular monarch over the Gentiles, and this source Saul cites. Thus, we would do well to see the commonality as a case of separate authors reaching the same conclusion from different directions and for quite different reasons. The Synoptics care about origin (cause), Saul cares about reigning over the Gentiles (effect). Neither, it appears, borrowed from the other.

So when we encounter Saul's reporting that Yeshua was crucified (1 Cor. 2:2; Gal. 3:1), died (1 Cor 15:3), and was buried (1 Cor. 15:4), it would be a mistake to make any assumptions about the origin of that material. This is important, because when one gets to the resurrection of Yeshua (which, as argued in chapter eight was for Saul a spiritual or cosmic, not a physical resurrection), Saul's report of those who shared in this vision differs from those reported later in the Gospels. Compare the material in First Corinthians (15:5–8), with Matthew (28:1–20), Luke (24:13–53), Mark (16:9–20) and John (20:11–25). Among the several differences, the most important are: (1) most obviously, Saul himself, though included in his own list of those who encountered the Risen Christ, is not reported in any other. (2) Cephas (Peter) is the first to see the Risen Christ in Saul's version, not in any others; (3) Saul has no resurrection appearances being granted to women; (4) only in Saul's version is there reference to 500 disciples seeing the resurrected Christ simultaneously; (5) and only in Saul's report is an appearance to Yacov, brother of Yeshua, specified. Given that we are here dealing with defining the perimeter of what was a collective vision of the paranormal (to use a neutral phrase, instead of, say, "mass hallucination"), there is no determining which, if any of the five conflicting accounts – the Four Gospels' and Saul's – is right. Each of the five accounts is the equivalent of a set of validation stamps, for whoever shared this paranormal experience became part of the core of the post-crucifixion Yeshua-faith, and, by spiritual genealogy, those who followed in their train also acquired greater legitimacy than those who did not have such lustrous mentors. Thus, no one should be surprised that Yacov, the head of the Jerusalem church from, roughly the mid-30s to the mid-60s, was written out of post-70 CE resurrection accounts. Jerusalem no longer had any power. Or, conversely, one could state the situation as follows: in any account written before 70 CE one would expect Yacov to be included as a witness to the resurrection, for in that period he had great power within the "church." Manifestly, to adjudicate whether Saul's account is in error, and therefore inferior to the Gospels or, alternately, that it was accurate and therefore superior to the Gospels, is a fool's errand. Each account of the resurrection served the social needs of those to whom it was being read.

Where I think Saul is demonstrably superior in accuracy concerning the combination of Yeshua's words and behaviour is in his definition of the Eucharist, which becomes the central liturgical exercise of the Christian church. The Eucharist involved a formula but, unlike the creedal formulae, it is embedded in an event that is reported as being specific to Yeshua's life story. And, very unusually for Saul, he warrants the historic authenticity of this occurrence – he has "received of the Lord" (1 Cor. 11:23) the facts and words he passes on to his disciples. That is his equivalent of saying, "what I give to you is God's Truth."

Saul makes one assumption and two central assertions about the Lord's Supper (1 Cor. 11:23–26). First, he assumes that it was usual for Yeshua to eat with his disciples. Frequent table fellowship is taken as the ordinary background for the extraordinary event. Secondly, he asserts that at this extraordinary event, Yeshua articulated and commanded maintenance of a formal ritual. And, thirdly, Yeshua did this at a time when he knew he was in mortal danger. These three attributes of the historical Last Supper hang together convincingly, because Saul does not overreach himself, nor is he at all confused about what he is asserting. Everything is clear.

In contrast, the Gospels try to add another assertion to the mix: that the Last Supper occurred at the time of Passover. This is too much weight for the story to support, and as a result they all make a tangled knot of the Eucharistic event. The author-editor of the Gospel of John has a very long Last Supper on the eve of Passover (chapters 13–14) and does not have Jesus engage in a Seder or institute any ritual meal. John introduces such a body-and-blood ritual, but the words of institution are uttered in a discourse in a synagogue in Capernaum (6:53–59). The result is very messy textually, for one has to chainsaw the Capernaum material out of its apparent context and move it to Jerusalem. In Mark (14:17–25) and the derivative Matthew (26:26–29), the time is Passover, and in this instance, Jesus defines the cup and the bread, the body and blood, but the author-editor neglects to have him instruct his disciples to repeat the ritual after he is gone. And in Luke (22:15–20), the context is Passover, and the manuscript tradition indeterminate: one manuscript tradition omits both the body and blood references and Yeshua's instruction to do this in remembrance of him; the other inserts material from Saul's version in very close quotation.[7]

On the matters of the Last Supper and institution of the Eucharist, Saul focussed on what counted, and his account is simple, clear, direct, in contrast to the Gospels'. Therefore he should be our primary entry point into this central part of Yeshua of Nazareth's life story.

4

In point of fact, as Victor Furnish points out,[8] there are only three clearly-labelled places where Saul and the Gospels agree even roughly about words Yeshua used (as distinct from biographical information about his genealogy, birth, life and death). These are instances in which "the Lord" (who, in the contexts here relevant, means Yeshua) is directly reported by Saul as uttering certain words. These are the Eucharistic words (1 Cor. 11:23–25) which has its approximate counterparts in the Gospels, as discussed above; the hard words of Yeshua on divorce (1 Cor. 7:10), discussed in chapter seven; and Yeshua's statement that those who preach the gospel should "live by the Gospel," meaning not have to do secular labour to support themselves (1 Cor. 9:14; with very rough parallels in Matt. 10:9 and Luke 10:7).[9]

That is not much. So, the question becomes, can one use as an interpretive analogy the situation we viewed earlier: Saul's including in his letters creedal and liturgical material from the early church, which he integrated into his own exposition but did not label as historical material? If so, there should be instances in his writings where he uses Yeshua's words without citing them as such. These will be recognisable in the present discussion by their having parallels in the Synoptic Gospels. An easy case serves as an example. In I Thessalonians (4:15–5:3), Saul introduces a set of apocalyptic predictions by saying they are being pronounced "by the word of the Lord" (4:15). He then depicts the Lord (meaning Jesus Christ) as coming down from heaven and subsuming into heaven those of the Yeshua-followers who are alive, presumably in Saul's own lifetime. They shall be forever in the clouds with Jesus. That day, though, was unpredictable; it would come "as a thief in the night" (5:2). Now, Saul here effectively asserts that he was quoting Yeshua of Nazareth, but reporting in the mode of indirect discourse. The material is reported as being uttered directly by Jesus Christ in Matthew (24:30–31, 24:39, and 24:43, interspersed with the Parable of the Fig Tree).[10] If (and of course it is a big "if") the material in Matthew is probatively relevant, then Saul's indirect quotation is the earliest document we have indicating that the early folklore of Yeshua's followers maintained that Yeshua of Nazareth did indeed have an eschatological message of some sort. Even so, "early" here means roughly twenty years after Yeshua's death; and there is always the possibility that Matthew employed an oral version of Saul's writings as his own source. (He clearly did not have a written epistle to copy.) Even so, the configuration of the data seems to leave the most probable interpretation that (at minimum) the eschatological-apocalyptic aspect of Yeshua found in the Synoptics was not an add-on that was inserted after the semi-apocalypse of the Temple's destruction in 70 CE; evidently, the Yeshua-followers believed by the mid-first century that Yeshua had borne an eschatological message concerning the end of time. This leaves aside the question of whether or not Yeshua himself had preached such a proclamation, but it makes it clear, at least, that Saul was not likely to have been the founder of that tradition: other Yeshua-followers held it too, as the Synoptics indicate.

Most other ties of Saul's unlabeled words of Yeshua to the versions later encapsulated in the Synoptic Gospels are harder to identify. I cannot see that in the present state of scholarship there are as many as ten that are sufficiently close textually to be adjudged solid.

One of the most obvious is Saul's advice (is it cynical, despairing, or merely prudent?):

> Render therefore to all their dues: tribute to whom tribute is due; custom to whom custom; fear to whom fear; honour to whom honour.   (Rom. 13:7)

This same wisdom is employed in the Synoptic Gospels as a response to a trick question put to Yeshua: was it halachically lawful to give financial tribute to the Roman emperor? This was put to him by malicious Pharisees (Matt. 22:15–22), or by a combination of Pharisees and lickspittle Judahist outriders of Herod Antipas (Mark: 12:13–17) or by the chief priest and the scribes (Luke 20:19–26). In each version the trap is the same: either Yeshua replies treasonously (such as "do not pay tribute to Caesar") or he says in reply, "yes, pay tribute to Caesar" and he can then be accused of not being true to the religion of Yahweh, for he will have recognized a pagan vizier over Israel. Yeshua however, outwits his seducers by a technique that later we see, in the Mishnah, the Yerushalmi and the Bavli, as standard Rabbinical technique: he answers a question with a question. He has his interlocutors show him a bit of money (a paltry this-worldly object) and he asks them, whose image and whose name is on it? They reply "Caesar's." The minute they do so, Yeshua has escaped the trap: whatever he says next necessarily is predicated upon his opponents' answer to Yeshua's question, and therefore the resultant answer is their moral weight to carry, not his. It is at that point that Yeshua utters the wonderfully ambiguous phrase, "Render therefore unto Caesar the things which are Caesar's; and unto God the things that are God's." Was this phrase a cultural cliché of the time? (It does sound like the first-century equivalent of a motor-car bumper-sticker.) Did Saul distill it from the folk tradition concerning Yeshua and put it to his own use? Did the author-editor of Mark pick it up from one of Saul's disciples and turn it into such a sharp set-piece that it was unhesitatingly taken over by the composers of Matthew and Luke?

Similar indeterminancy surrounds another splendid phrase. In the "love chapter," in 1 Corinthians Saul says, "and though I have all faith, so that I could [re]move mountains, and have not charity, I am nothing" (1 Cor. 13:2). Faith that could move mountains is a concept of charismatic force all on its own. It surfaces in Mark (11:23) when Yeshua says that whoever has complete faith would be able to move a mountain and throw it into the sea. Later, Matthew probably (but not certainly; the matter is problematic)[11] incorporates Yeshua's words that if a person has even as much faith as a grain of mustard seed, that person can move a mountain (17:20). And the author-editor of Luke (17:6) reports Yeshua as saying that if one has the amount of faith of a mustard seed (thus following Matthew), that person can will a sycamore tree (Luke's own touch) to be moved into the sea (the Markan sea-motif.)

Another obvious commonality – and a wonderfully memorable image – has already been referred to: the concept in Saul that Jesus Christ ("the Lord") shall return to earth "as a thief in the night" (1 Thess. 5:2). This is an exhibit in the argument that Saul had access to some of the same material that later evolved into the Synoptic Gospels.[12] (This is an argument which does not cancel out the possibility that on some matters the exact opposite process occurred: that the transmitters of the Synoptic strand of the tradition acquired access to material that was uniquely preserved in Saul's letters; a multiple helix is a complicated entity indeed.) Saul seems to have made a meaning-changing pun on a parable of Yeshua that found its final form in Matthew and Luke. The Lucan version (12:35–41) has Yeshua comparing the future appearance of the Son of Man to the situation in which a thief would break into a house. The tale is a bit unfortunate, because the analogy between the Son of Man and a nocturnal thief backfires: thieves, after all, are up to no good. Matthew's version (24:42–44) works slightly better because the Son of Man is moved slightly out of the centre of the frame, by Matthew's referring to the master over the household servants as "Lord," in the admonition "Watch therefore: for ye know not what hour your Lord doth come" (24:42). This is a blur of meaning, for "Lord" refers both to the head of the household and to the Son of Man. Saul, in his version, has no reference to the householder and to the Son of Man. He employs "Lord" in his characteristic way, to mean Jesus-the-Christ, and, simultaneously, avoids any messy analogies. It is not the Lord who shall come as a thief in the night, but rather "the day of the Lord." No backsplash: single authorial control here is much superior to the Synoptics writing by committee.

Some scholars see a similarity based on common origins of Saul's statement that "… All things indeed are pure …" (Rom. 14:20) and the author-editor of Mark ascribing to Yeshua "There is nothing from without a man, that entering into him can defile him …" (Mark 7:15, repeated in a weakened form in Matt 15:11). Perhaps this is actually the case, but the phrasing and, indeed, the substantive content are sufficiently different to leave me unconvinced: separate responses to separate situations, with no interaction between Saul and the folk tradition underlying the Synoptic Gospels.

To my mind, the most intriguing intersection of Saul and the Synoptic Gospels occurs with the irenic admonition "Bless them which persecute you: bless, and curse not" (Rom. 12:14). This appears in Yeshua's utterance in the Gospel of Luke's Sermon on the Plain: "But I say unto you which hear, Love your enemies, do good to them which hate you, Bless them that curse you, and pray for them which despitefully use you" (Luke 6:27–28). In Matthew, in the Sermon on the Mount, Yeshua's words are "But I say unto you, Love your enemies, bless them that curse you, do good to them that hate you, and pray for them which despitefully use you, and persecute you" (Matt. 5:44). Initially this is intriguing because it shows an identity of precept between material that Saul presents in his own voice and material that Luke and Matthew report as being a specific teaching of Yeshua.

Moreover, this intersection of Saul's material and Matthew's and Luke's occurs in conjunction with the only material in any of the Four Gospels that is structured truly mnemonically. In the Sermon on the Plain and the Sermon on the Mount one has the Beatitudes ("Blessed are …"), a formula that in each case (four in Luke 6:20–22 and nine in Matthew 5:3–11) is very easy to remember. As I mentioned earlier, the one thing that historians' studies of oral sources in scores of cultures has made certain is this: that which is remembered easiest is remembered longest. Which is to say: of the "sayings" materials (as distinct from biographical facts about Yeshua) that underlie the Synoptic Gospels, the Beatitudes are the least apt to have been corrupted by the corrosive passage of oral transmission. Now, emphatically, this does not mean necessarily either that they were melded into the folklore concerning Yeshua early in its development (being highly memorable relates to transmission, not to origin) nor that, if they were actually said by Yeshua of Nazareth, he thought them up himself (there is nothing in them that does not fit with sayings the later Rabbinic sources ascribe to various Rabbis). All that granted, if one were forced to plunk for a single set of utterances in the New Testament that most likely represents the authentic teachings of Yeshua of Nazareth, this is where I would place my bet.

This is significant in relation to Saul, because by virtue of its incorporation of the Beatitudes, the Sermon on the Plain and the Sermon on the Mount assume a curatorial function concerning other tightly-treasured sayings of Yeshua. Consider first the structure of Luke's Sermon on the Plain and then Saul's verbal architecture in his parallel passage. In the Gospel of Luke's version, Yeshua first articulates the Beatitudes (6:20–22, with a codicil in 20:23) and then balances them with a series of four Woes ("Woe unto you" 6:24–26) which are manifestly derivative from the Beatitudes and are presented in mirror-fashion. (They are not included in Matthew's Sermon on the Mount.) Then comes the material about loving one's enemies (6:27–28) and this is the structural fulcrum between the Beatitudes and a catena of miscellaneous admonitions (6:29–38).

Here the salient point is that Saul presents a sermon very similar to Luke's both in structure and substance, a bipartite set of admonitions, whose balance point is the imperative "Bless them which persecute you" (Rom. 12:9–21). In fact, if – say in the year 75 CE, someone had taken Romans 12:9–21 and incorporated it into a gospel, affirming that "Jesus said ...," – we would have no difficulty accepting Saul's sermon as being the words of Yeshua of Nazareth. That certainly is not the case for most of Saul's writings.[13]

Now, if we can accept that counter-factual illustration as being enlightening, and if we accept the structural similarities of Saul's sermon in Romans to the Sermon on the Plain, then we have inferred the likelihood (not the certainty: likelihood) that Saul had access to material about the historical Yeshua that was of a degree of probable accuracy (or inaccuracy) equal to most of that upon which the Synoptic Gospels were based and, further, that he incorporated big slabs of that material into his writings, presenting them as his own words, rather than as the words of Yeshua.

Thus, I think the big job confronting the next generation of Yeshua-questors will be to disinter from Saul's words those that came from Yeshua of Nazareth. Saul was the most peripatetic of the early preachers of the Yeshua-faith and unless one assumes that he always talked and never listened (an assertion to which his own letters give the lie) he must not only have preached Yeshua, but also learned of him. Throughout his letters one encounters references to other missionaries, and some of these must have exchanged stories and sayings of Yeshua with him. Although he was the advance-guard of the Yeshua-followers in many areas into which he forayed, in others (clearly, and crucially, for example, Rome), the faith was established before his arrival. Therefore, he must have learned material about the historical Yeshua even in areas of the Diaspora. And one should not forget that Saul knew of the Yeshua-faith long before his call to be a follower of Yeshua; and, after his call, he visited Jerusalem at least three times and in each instance interacted intensely with members of the Jerusalem community of Yeshua-followers, led by Yeshua's brother Yacov. Saul knew a lot of facts and sayings of Yeshua and he uses the sayings in his writing, as I have just demonstrated.

Where matters become problematical and must, therefore, be left in more technically adept hands, is when Saul employs Yeshua's sayings, but does so in instances where the Gospels do not have any record of such sayings being ascribed to Yeshua. At that point, the scholarly safety net disappears. The historian is on his own. In the odd case – I Thess. 4:15–17 – Saul evidently cites a saying of Yeshua for which there is no other record; but in this case he labels it.[14] Since we know (a) that Saul sometimes employs the same material as is found in the Synoptic Gospels, but without labelling the sayings as being Yeshua's words, and because (b) we also know from his repeating of early church liturgic and creedal material that he habitually repeats earlier items without indicating that they are not, in fact, his own words, then (c) in all probability, there will be a goodly number of items in Saul's letters that are words which at least one strand of the multiple helix that was the early Yeshua-tradition ascribed to Yeshua, but which were not picked up by the author-editors of the Gospels.

The delicacy of touch required for disinterring such buried treasures is not common in the community of Yeshua-questors. And it is not the kind of thing that can be done by committee. With items of this fragility, many hands make shattered shards.

Saul and the Imitation of Christn

I

GIVEN THAT SAUL NEVER MANAGED TO COME WITHIN A STONE'S throw of Yeshua of Nazareth, it undoubtedly will take a generation or two before historians of the earthly Jesus come to use Saul's letters as the prime entry point into their subject.[1] Big ships can turn only slowly and by small degrees, and there are few historians' vessels larger than the Quest for the historical Yeshua. And even if the existing enterprise did not have the massive momentum of habit to drive it, the character of Saul's epistles – so dauntingly prickly and allusive in places, so crackling with electricity in others as to almost preclude handling – would turn many Questors away. Henry Chadwick in his Wood Lecture was both kindly and correct when he said: "We are reminded of the warning and regretful words in 2 Peter 3:16 that in Paul's letters there are 'certain things hard to be understood which the unlearned and unstable wrest to their destruction.' "[2] Yet, one must quickly add to this warning the portion of the scriptural verse that Chadwick left out: "... the unlearned and unstable wrest, *as they do also the other scriptures*, unto their own destruction." Chadwick was right – "I suppose that the apostle Paul has always been something of a problem"[3] – but the author of the pseudepigraphic Second Peter was even more on: *all* the texts that make up the Old and New Testament are difficult. The seemingly excessive difficulty of Saul's letters as an historical source is just that – seeming. They are not an easy read, granted, but I don't think that they are any harder to deal with than are the narrative Gospels. Crucially, their apparent difficulty dictates that no one can approach them as an historical source with the same reckless naiveté that is virtually invited by the Gospels. Because each of the Gospels is constructed in the form of an historical narrative, each has an inveigling quality, a seductiveness that lulls one into playing on its terms. In contrast, the letters of Saul, being proclaimed on their surface as non- or even anti-historical, force one to be continually alert, to go against the letters' surface grain, and thus to be constantly open to matters of proof and disproof.

The surface situation in Saul's letters is as follows: as far as I can see, there exist only six references in the seven authentic letters of Saint Saul that one could term "direct," or "pointed" references to the biography and behaviour (as distinct from the sayings) of the historical Yeshua:

1 Yeshua was born by normal human process (Rom. 1:3; see chapters eight and nine for a discussion of this point).
2 He was particularly worried by the matter of divorce (1 Cor. 7:10–11; again, see chapters eight and nine).
3 Yeshua had a last meal with his disciples (1 Cor. 11:24–25) which was not set at the time of Passover.
4 He was crucified and buried (Gal. 3:1; 1 Cor. 15:4).
5 Yeshua's mission was to those of the Judahist faith (Romans 15:8), not to the Gentiles.
6 And, Yeshua believed that holy men (preachers of Yahweh's truth) should be supported by their followers, rather than work for a living in the ordinary way (1 Cor. 9:14).

In addition, one finds four "sidebar references" to the behavioural aspects of the historical Yeshua: that is, contexts in which a factual assertion about the historical Yeshua is made in a discussion that is primarily about some other topic:

1 Yeshua had brothers (1 Cor. 9:5). Some of them eventually married (they are reported as taking wives with them on missionary journeys) but whether or not these marriages happened while Yeshua still was alive, or later, is not stated. Yeshua's sisters are not mentioned by Saul.
2 Yacov was the name of one of these brothers of Yeshua (Gal. 1:19.) The names of the others are not given. Yacov, clearly, was the dominant brother after Yeshua's death, but this has no necessary implications concerning birth order amongst Yeshua's siblings or Yacov's position in the family pecking-order while Yeshua was alive.
3 Yeshua had twelve special followers (1 Cor. 15:5).
4 Yeshua's death occurred because he was betrayed or, at minimum, "handed over" to the Roman authorities (1 Cor. 11:23).

And, one encounters three allusive references which, though not in strict logic leading to a tight historical inference, nevertheless can be seen as implying certain facts – and these solely on the basis of Saul's letters, without interpolations from other sources:

1 Cephas (Peter) was a specially important member of the community of Yeshua-followers after the master's death. However, based solely on Saul's

references, one cannot with absolute certainty infer (a) that he was one of "the Twelve" while Yeshua was alive or (b) that he had a spiritual leadership position while Yeshua was on earth (1 Cor. 15:5; Gal. 2:7–8). Those, though, are the meanings one would plunk for even if one did not know of the Four Gospels or the Acts of the Apostles.

2 Another person of special worth was John who, along with Yacov and Cephas, was one of the "pillars" of the post-crucifixion Yeshua-followers in Jerusalem (Gal. 2:9). Although from other biblical references, it is clear that this is John, son of Zebedee, one of "the Twelve," these facts go undeclared in Saul's epistles. However, by virtue of the name being tied in Saul's writings with two men who definitely had been well-acquainted with Yeshua either as followers or as family, one would have guessed that John was either an important original disciple or one of Yeshua's brothers.

3 It is a minority possibility – small, but nevertheless real – that Saul communicates a fact about Yeshua's ancestry. This perhaps occurs when (in Romans 15:8) he quotes First Isaiah's prediction that David's monarchical line would be re-established and that the Gentiles would recognize its suzerainty (Isaiah 11: 1, and 11:10):

> … There shall be a root of Jesse, and he that shall rise to reign over the Gentiles; in him shall the Gentiles trust (Romans 15:12).

This can be taken as being an allusive reference to Yeshua's putative father, Yosef, being of Jesse's line, Jesse of Bethlehem being the father of King David (1 Sam. 16:1). However, we would not make this connection on our own, without prompting from the genealogies of Yeshua found in Matthew (1:1–17) and Luke (3:23–38). In Romans, the quotation is part of a cascade of references to the Tanakh (Rom. 15:4–13), items that justify Saul's own mission to the Gentiles. This is accomplished by Saul's placing Yeshua's life amongst scriptural references that show the Gentiles coming under Yahweh's providence. Still, there is just the possibility that here we have a murky allusion to Yeshua's father being of Davidic ancestry and being associated with Bethlehem.

That is all. Whatever other references to the historical Yeshua's biography and behaviour exist in Saul's letters are either untagged or deeply encoded. However, before giving up on Saul and marching back to the Synoptic Gospels and the Gospel of John, we must consider two possibilities, which are *not* mutually exclusive: either one or both could be true. First, we really should entertain the possibility – distasteful both to believers and to those whose livelihood is based on hunting the historical Yeshua – that the material in Saul's seven authentic letters represents a responsible assertion of almost everything that can be said about the historical Yeshua with more than a 50 percent chance of accuracy (that is the point where the possible becomes the probable). Granted, there are a few fugitive items in the Gospels (names and places mostly, a few sayings) and a few less-than-even possibilities that might turn out to be the actual case: but maybe Saul gives us the best-defined and most trustworthy platform of probabilities concerning what we can know about the earthly Yeshua. We take his factual assertions as accurate, for they are hardly fantastical; they have the pedestrian droop of the truth. We yearn to hear Saul tell us more, but he refuses: a few historical references and the rest, he seems to tell us, is in the realm of faith.

Now, am I not confusing a minimum (the bundles of facts, very probably accurate assertions, Saul grants to us) with a maximum, the total body of historically–probable statements about Yeshua of Nazareth one can infer from the entire Christian canon? No: Saul is a platform, not a ceiling. However, given (a) that he is the earliest writer among Yeshua's followers and that he alone wrote before the almost apocalyptic destruction of Jerusalem and the Temple and (b) given that he completely refuses to mythologize the historical Yeshua, the factual information we garner from Saul is much more trustworthy than anything that comes in a narrative that glorifies the earthly life of Yeshua, as do the Four Gospels. A useful rule of New Testament evidence can be derived from this situation: that any name, place, or event relating to the historical Yeshua that is found in Saul's writing can, when also found in the Gospels or the Acts of the Apostles, be taken as being factually accurate.[4]

Here is the second possibility: that without stretching beyond our balance-point, we may be able to touch in Saul's writings facts conveyed about the historical Yeshua that are unlabelled as such, or which are enhulled within arguments that have rich theological implications, but in which Saul makes no manifest historical assertions about the behaviour of Yeshua of Nazareth. To do this, I think we should grant to Saul the claim that he frequently makes: that his life was given up to the service of the Almighty through his preaching of the gospel of Jesus-the-Christ. Saul's life was similar to that of a present-day performance artist. He shaped himself as a continually-evolving offering-in-progress to his God and his letters are the record of that performance. We are justified in reading the record of Saul's life as the first recorded instance of a life given over to the Imitation of Christ.

At times, Saul is breathtakingly immodest in his Imitation.[5] For example, in Romans (15:8) he points out that Yeshua "was a minister of the circumcision for the truth of God ..." That is, a Judahist whose mission on earth was to preach to his fellow Judahists. Then, slightly later, Saul affirms that he himself is "the minister of Jesus Christ to the Gentiles, ministering the gospel of God, that the offering up of the Gentiles might be acceptable, being sanctified by the Holy Ghost" (Rom. 15:16). There one has Saul's life in a compressed moment: (1) he is in subordination to Jesus Christ as far as his faith and message is concerned, but (2) his own mission to the Gentiles is a simulacrum of Yeshua's mission to the children of Israel. Yeshua never preached to Gentiles, Saul did. Thus, there is throughout Saul's life a sense of equilibration – not equality, but equilibration – with the mission of his Lord. His mission follows the contours of Yeshua's, but in another province.

In discussing his own call to the Yeshua-faith, Saul provides a narrative and implicit references that imply a predetermined destiny for himself. He posits that Yahweh had "separated me from my mother's womb, and called me by his grace" (Gal. 1:15). When that divine election was actualized, he continues, it was so that he could "preach him among the heathen" (Gal. 1:16). Certainly Saul knew of the claim of the prophet Isaiah that "The Lord hath called me from the womb ..."(Is. 49:1). And more to the point, Saul was adapting the assertion of the prophet Jeremiah, who hears Yahweh saying "Before I formed thee in the belly, I knew thee ... and I ordained thee a prophet unto the nations" (Jer 1:5) – more to the point because "unto the nations" included the Gentiles.[6]

Sometimes, Saul's identification with Jesus Christ can be so close as to be unsettling: "I am crucified with Christ," he tells the Galatians. "Nevertheless I live; yet not I, but Christ liveth in me ..."(Gal. 2:20). He can demand of his own disciples, "Be ye followers of me, even as I also am of Christ" (1 Cor. 11:1). And after a congregation has become bonded to him, Saul can command, as he does of the Thessalonians: "and you became imitators of us," he notes, using the plural to refer to himself, "and of the Lord ...," his term for Jesus Christ (1 Thess 1:6, RSV). Whatever else this may be, it is not evidence of low self-esteem.

On certain matters, Saul is confident in reversing a precept or concept of the historical Yeshua. We discussed one of these instances – the matter of divorce – in chapter eight. That was a relatively small matter. A much bigger one is the meaning of mission within the unfolding divine narrative. Yeshua of Nazareth preached to his fellow Judahists and not to Gentiles. This behaviour – this practice of mission – implies either that Yeshua did not see the redemption of the Gentiles as part of the divine plan or that it was the first stage in a two-phase sequence: Judahists first, then, in some way, Gentiles. Now, as E.P. Sanders makes clear, Saul interpreted the divine plan in just the opposite way: Israel would be brought to salvation after the Gentile mission and, indeed, because of it.[7] Thus, Saul can tell the Romans that Israel is "blind" (Rom. 11: 25, KJB), or "hardened" (most other translations), and only after the full cohort of Gentiles have "come in" will Israel be saved (v. 25–26).

Here we require a formulation of the way that Saul's own Imitation of Christ functions as a key to certain aspects of the historical Yeshua, and an apposite one comes from the field of topology. As a conceptual aid, we can consider the lives of the historical Yeshua and the historical Saul to have been what topologists term "contiguous similar figures." Such figures can be simple (as, say, a triangle) or extremely complex (such as a figure whose perimeter includes both curvilinear segments and straight portions). The key point is that if they are truly similar, and if they hold in common a single segment of a straight line, then each portion of one figure has a corresponding segment on the other figure. Moreover, if one were informed that the two figures meet these conditions, but that one of the figures has been partially erased, it would be possible (with a bit of hard calculation) to reconstruct it by using data from the figure that was intact.

Don't bolt. When taken into the historical realm, this metaphor does not imply a mechanical formula, but rather a mode of thinking. Here the crucial point is that sometimes one needs to pull away from the particularistic details of an historical problem and try for a moment to see the pattern of the whole: *gestalt*. Thus (1) given that Saul and Yeshua had a number of points in common (at minimum the religio-cultural matrix of late Second Temple Judahism), and (2) also given that Saul defined his own life as an Imitation of Christ (that is, he tried to pattern his ministry on the contours of his Lord's), but (3) noting also that Saul carved out his mission in very different turf from that of Yeshua, then (4) we would expect that the pattern of Saul's life might tell us something about the pattern of Yeshua's, provided compensations are made for the obvious differences in time and of place of their respective ministries.

2

The first pattern-question that arises is one that the Questors for the historical Yeshua have wrestled with, like Laocoon and the serpents, for generation after generation: is it realistic to conceive of someone who was completely immersed in later Second Temple Judaism, such as Yeshua presumably was, as having propounded a religiously-revolutionary view of reality, while employing only the icons, symbols, constructs, and praxis of Judaism? Of course that is theoretically possible, but the best evidence of this being a practical possibility would be if anyone had done just that, and at a high level of historical documentability, in roughly the era of Yeshua of Nazareth. Which is where Saul comes in.

In my reading of the twentieth century's hundreds of Questors for the historical Yeshua, it seems that a rough pattern emerges. Two responses to this fundamental pattern-question have prevailed. One of them holds that Yeshua was a thorough-going Judahist, but that he was not really revolutionary in his message, merely a wisdom teacher who fit into his own times quite smoothly. The other is a formulation based on centuries of Christian badmouthing of

Jews, but tarted up as critical history: that yes, Yeshua had been a religious revolutionary, but the revolutionary parts of his message had nothing positive to do with his Judahism, and were in fact a direct rejection of it. So, a kind of *cul de sac* was reached: either Jesus was a good Jew and he was not a religious revolutionary, or he was a religious revolutionary and he was not a good Jew.

Several ingenious attempts out of this dead-end have been proposed. One of these is to present Yeshua as a political or nationalistic revolutionary of some form. This is an historical possibility (though I think a very small one), but it makes the basic question go away by declaring it moot: that Yeshua was not a religious leader *pur laine* and that is that. The problem here is that the Christian scriptures insist that Yeshua was a religious leader and, in any case, there (as yet) is no compelling evidence of his being a political revolutionary: blessing the poor and leading them to the barricades are two quite different activities. The other way out of the conundrum has been to declare Yeshua an apocalypticist and, at the same time, a continuing Second Temple follower of Yahweh. That is all right as far as it goes, but it does not go very far because unless Yeshua's sole message was a vacant and violent cry that the-sky-will-fall, the real question remains: underneath the superstructure of the apocalyptic did he have a message that reordered the religious universe and did he articulate that message while still employing the concepts of Second Temple Judahism?

The so-called "Third Quest" and the "New Quest" for the historical Yeshua of the last one-third of the twentieth century have held in common an increasing commitment to understanding Yeshua as a solid, devout Judahist. But most of the Questors have shied away from defining him as a religious revolutionary. He can be a Judahist with a difference – a Cynic, and marginal-Jew, a magician – but he rarely is credited with the historical agency of being the founder of a radically new form of the Yahweh-faith. Not a Christian, certainly: but is this flaccidity historically fitting? The Gospels, being post-70 CE, tell us vexingly little on this matter, for the energy impelling them is the then-endangered Christian church and its desperate fight for survival: not the fierce message (if such it is) of Yeshua of Nazareth.

Here Saul helps immensely. One of the splendid things about Saul is that, unlike Yeshua, we actually possess his own words. We do not need to accept indirect reportage, at second-third- . . *nth* hand, as with Yeshua. What we undeniably find in Saul is a genuinely revolutionary religious thinker (always, of course, defined within the terms of what was revolutionary in his own time, not ours). We are able to document how a fervent adherent of the Yahweh-faith, working almost entirely with the symbols, icons, and constructs of late Second Temple Judahism, was able to build an apparatus of religious apperception that was brand new, not in its components, but in the way it operated and the purposes towards which it worked. Remember, we are not here talking a particularistic congruence between Saul and Yeshua, but rather the topological relationship of contiguous similarity; and at a certain level of generalization it is possible that Saul's Imitation of Christ provides information on the parameters and possibilities of the earthly mission of Yeshua of Nazareth.

If this is to be a plausible suggestion, we must first clear the road of one or two conceptual roadblocks. One of these is that Saul was a Diaspora Greek Judahist and Yeshua a Galilean and therefore the two lived in such different intellectual environments that they are not comparable figures in any sense. Saul spoke Greek as his first language and Yeshua spoke Aramaic, in all probability. Whether either one of them had biblical Hebrew as a language is uncertain (although probable in both cases, as they both worshipped in the Second Temple), and whether the two of them would have had a lingua franca (most likely demotic Greek or possibly Aramaic), is not demonstrable. However, this misses the point that the interactions between the religious metropole, Jerusalem, and the Diaspora was continual. Moreover, it is noteworthy that, if his letters are an accurate indication, Saul had nothing approaching a classical education. His knowledge of Gentile literature "does not involve anything more than the possession of a small stock of conventional quotations useful for a Jewish preacher addressing a Gentile audience in the synagogue."[8] Moreover, Yeshua did not come from as far in the back-of-beyond as is usually presented. He grew up only a few miles from Sepphoris (on the road from Nazareth to Cana-of-Galilee) which recent excavations reveal to have been an up-to-the-minute Roman provincial city, with the physical and cultural amenities that implies. Yeshua undoubtedly saw this world long before he encountered that of distant Jerusalem.

A more broadly based argument against considering Saul and Yeshua to have had at least one strong contiguous line in common – knowledge of the character and power of the wide variety of motifs, icons and beliefs that ran through the multiple Judahisms of their time – is that "Palestinian Judahism" and "Hellenistic Judahism" were not comparable. This view – which I hope I disposed of in chapter two's discussion of the nature of the multiple Judahisms of the late Second Temple era – is no longer in fashion among biblical scholars. This has obvious implications for the long-sweep history of both the Jewish and the Christian faiths; Craig C. Hill's summary encapsulates the present consensus: "the diversity of first-century Judaism challenges the notion that the earliest church was divided into ideological groups called Hellenists and Hebrews."[9] But there remains a significant concern – namely, how to build into any understanding of later Second Temple Judaism, both in Eretz Israel and the Diaspora, the background-influence of Roman and, especially, Greek-derived culture?

The basic problem is that Greek cultural influence upon the followers of Yahweh is immensely complicated. It varied greatly by geographic location, social class, and according to the cultural and religious commitments of those who encountered it. Further, although the impact of Greek culture on the followers of Yahweh has been discussed frequently by scholars from the late Renaissance onwards, inevitably it has been in terms of analyses that reflect as much about their own "modern" concerns as about the ancient world.

The most immediately revealing symptom of just how fraught the matter is, is found in there being no agreed scholarly vocabulary concerning even the most basic definitions of the question of the degree of Greek cultural influence on Palestine and upon Diaspora followers of Yahweh. Scholars use the same words, but without shared meaning, and thus they talk past each other. The fundamental terms are "Hellenism" and "Hellenization" (or "Hellenisation"). In using either of these terms, the foundation stones of any rational discussion of the matter, one needs to know in each piece of scholarship (a) if these words are taken as having separate meanings or if they act as synonyms; (b) does either term refer to forced cultural change engendered by Greek authorities? (c) does either one refer to the assimilation of Greek ideas and institutions being enforced by the elite of the Judahist religion? and (d) does either term refer, instead, to a voluntary assumption of certain Greek-derived attitudes, beliefs and practices by the Judahist masses, occurring in roughly the way that the citizens of the former Soviet Union took up blue jeans and rock and roll?[10]

Rather than parse the arguments concerning terminology, I am here issuing a simple fiat for the purpose of the present discussion: (1) since, in the period we are here considering, Palestine was not under Greek control, nor was Egypt, home of the most important Diaspora communities, the possibility of enforced Hellenization is of minor import; (2) "Hellenization" therefore will be used to refer to the energetic and purposive attempts of some Judahist leaders to introduce cultural, religious, and social practices that had their origin in Greek culture, broadly defined. (3) "Hellenism" is employed to describe the osmotic process whereby, without compulsion, programmatic or moral suasion, Greek-derived beliefs and practices seeped into the Judahist culture and religion. (4) The adjective form "Hellenistic" refers to things that are in some significant way influenced by Greek substrata. I do not use the terms "Hellenistic Judaism" as an antipole to "Palestinian Judaism" for, as Shaye Cohen presciently observes, all forms of the Yahwist religion were influenced to some degree in this period by Greek cultural constructs;[11] and (5) "Hellenic" is used as an adjective referring to items directly associated with Greece.

The blurring of our understanding, which is caused by a lack of an agreed vocabulary for talking about Greek influence, points to something fundamental about the nature of the scholarly enterprise on this question: it is ensnared in non-rational, non-scholarly attitudes, and hampered by ideological and religious commitments. There is a split between classicists and Semiticists. On the surface this looks like a simple industrial dispute, the kind that characterizes so much of academic life. However, there is much, much more to it. Until recently, classicists and "ancient historians" (usually a code name for historians of Greece and Rome) were in charge. They held the endowed chairs and these were among the most prestigious posts in the older universities of Europe, the British Isles and North America. Anyone who sat at the classicists' table dined by their rules. It is only in the last decade or two, with the rise of non-western history as a major sector of study in most universities, that the assumptions the classicists and ancient historians introduced into historical scholarship in the nineteenth and early twentieth centuries have been questioned and largely abandoned. Yet, "for any historian whose education was influenced by the European classical tradition, there was an inclination to see the spread of Greek culture as the central historical phenomenon of the era of Alexander and his successors ..."[12] So Tessa Rajak notes. Thus arose a set of alleged polarities between Semitic and Greek cultures.[13] As recently as the mid-1990s, one of the world's leading classical historians, Fergus Millar, could write a history of the Roman Near East wherein the discussion took as a fundamental assumption that "in each period it will not be inappropriate to start from the model, or hypothesis, of a sharp contrast between Greek city (and later Roman *colonia*) on the one hand and Jewish community on the other."[14] Although modern scholars (such as Millar) have been innocent both of the snobbery and of the latent anti-Semitism that such polarized thinking engendered in early times, there is no question that such a distinction implicitly privileges the Greek.

One method of escape from the artificial polarization of Semitic and Hellenic simply declares victory for the Greeks. The modern keystone of this approach is the work of Martin Hengel, who in his 1966 doctorate in the Faculty of Protestant Theology in the University of Tübingen, concluded that the Yahwist religion and its accompanying culture had become so Hellenistic by the time of the Maccabean revolt (or perhaps even earlier) that the Semitic-Hellenic polarity is conceptually redundant.[15] This position, though extreme, has the appeal of making the dichotomous mindset disappear; but, like most psychosurgery, is a cure worse than the disease it wipes out. It results in the suppression of a whole body of historical data on Judahist practices that were not Hellenistic and which remained clear of Hellenism and Hellenization right up to the end of the Second Temple period. Moreover, if the traditional Hellenic-Semitic polarity, when employed by classical historians, implicitly makes the Hellenic the dominant form, this viewpoint goes even further and makes it essentially the only one.[16]

Such a line of argument is especially attractive to some Christian scholars, because it provides the ideational equivalent of a biblical slingshot, one which allows early Christianity to shoot past the stage of being part of the Semitic mindset of the followers of Yahweh. The (to some) embarrassing fact of

Christianity's having been founded upon Judahist foundations is nicely elided by an argument that effectively removes the Semitic from the historical process at a very early stage. Christianity, which later becomes strongly influenced by classical cultural forms, is thereby perceived as having been a classical form from its very beginning. Just how strong the demand was for an argument such as Hengel's is indicated by the statements of the great Protestant theological biblicist Rudolf Bultmann, made a full two generations before Hengel's work was even begun. Bultmann contrasted Greek thinking about God with Judahist thought: "For the Greek it is in the first place axiomatic that God, like other objects of the world, can be examined by the thinking observer; that there can be a theology in the exact, immediate sense. That Judaism has no such theology is due not to any incapacity or lack of development in its thought, but to the fact that Judaism has from the beginning a different conception of God; He does not in any sense belong to the world of objects about which man orients himself through thought."[17] That is virtually a cry for help: Christianity is a Greek form – will no one rid me of its pestilent Semitic heritage? In denying, as David Flusser puts it, that "ancient Christianity is constructed primarily upon Jewish premises,"[18] the history of Christianity is damaged. Equally, the alleged Hellenic displacement of the Semitic obscures almost totally the kaleidoscopic historical development within the Judahist religion in its most fertile period, the last two and a half centuries of the Second Temple era.

One response among Semitic scholars (Jewish for the most part, but not entirely) has been to accept the idea that there was a natural and unavoidable polarity between Hellenistic and Yahwistic thought, culture, and society, but to argue that in fact the Greek cultural invasion was almost entirely unsuccessful. The clearest articulation of this view, that Greek-derived culture was almost entirely ectopic to the Judahist religion in the last two and a half centuries of the Second Temple, is that of Louis H. Feldman of Yeshiva University in New York. He argues that the Greek language was little used in Palestine, however much it may have been employed in the Diaspora; that the characteristic forms of Hellenic culture (epic drama, the gymnasium, and rationalist philosophies) were resisted in Palestine and especially strongly in Jerusalem. He suggests that it was not until the middle of the second century of the Common Era that one finds evidence of a Hellenistic cultural invasion in any depth. (The evidence for it at that time is found in the letter of the Jewish rebel chief Bar Kochba, who wrote to his subordinates in Greek.) Feldman concludes: "the question is not so much how greatly Jews and Judaism of the Land of Israel were Hellenized, as how strongly they resisted Hellenization."[19]

Certainly Feldman and those who hold his viewpoint, have some striking moments to refer to, indicating that, yes, there was a war between Hellenistic and Judahistic forms, but that there is a potential case for arguing that within the Promised Land, the followers of Yahweh were the victors.[20] The show-case exhibit in their argument is the heroic and undeniably successful revolt, and revolution, of the Maccabees. According to 1 and 2 Maccabees, two forms of force or programmatic Hellenization set off the successful revolution of 167ff BCE. The first of these was persecution from outside the country, directed by one of the last outriders of the etiolated Greek empire, the Seleucid King Antiochus IV Epiphanes. The revolt thus engendered and the governmental forms that emerged out of the successful rebellion are well documented in third-party sources, ranging from artifacts (coins, etc.) to Roman governmental documents.

It seems best to focus on Hellenism, by which is meant the voluntary assimilation of ideas and social practice that originated in Greece, but which may have arrived in Palestine after being mediated by other cultures. This removes the cartoon-like quality of much of the debate, for one cannot set up simple dichotomies, such as domination versus resistance; imperialism versus localism; the Greek and Roman city versus Jerusalem. And it removes the implication that Hellenistic ideas and practices, when adopted by Judahists, were the product of some volitional, programmatic and anti-Yahwist campaign. No, they were adopted because it made sense to the people to do so.

Here, a comparison may help. (If I am using a plethora of metaphors, it is because the era, the richest in world religious history, cannot be captured directly; its wondrous complexity often is beyond words that are merely denotative.) One is a comparison to "Americanization," a phenomenon that many European and Asian cultural leaders worried about in the first thirty or forty years after the Second World War. Seemingly, American culture was taking over large chunks of the earth, and many national governments reacted to protect their local cultures from this contamination. American culture was the Hellenistic culture of a later age, in the sense that it – like the Hellenistic – became ubiquitous, was seductive to most members of contact societies, while distrusted by traditionalists and some local cultural elites; and, in common with the Hellenistic, it was misnamed. "Americanization" for the most part was just something that happened to America first. It had some unique features determined by America's heritage as a republic and as a sometime New World, but mostly it was merely what happened to the USA first, a stage of modernization. Understandably, this stage of modernization was misnamed, and therefore misunderstood, as constituting Americanization. Presently, at the start of the twenty-first century, it has become clear that several other societies are farther along this path of social-cultural evolution than is America, so the optical illusion, that the world is being Americanized, has disappeared. Hellenism was like that. It had a few features that were unique to Greece, but mostly it was a stage of social-cultural development common to the ancient Near East and fast-emerging southern Europe. Hellenism was something that happened to Greece first, so we have the optical illusion that developments in ancient Greece were a mammoth causal engine, driving change throughout the then-known world.

It follows that Hellenism (defined as a stage of social-cultural development) should have become pervasive in a country like Palestine once that region had passed certain economic and social thresholds – the recovery from the depopulation of the wars of the sixth century BCE, the reforging of thick economic ties with surrounding regions, and the maintenance of a reasonable degree of civil order – and once the region engaged in frequent cultural contacts with surrounding nations. The robustness of these extra-Palestine cultural contacts was guaranteed by the nature of the Judahist Diaspora, which implied a set of two-way cultural exchanges: the metropole, Jerusalem, provided religious standards and stability for the several Diaspora communities, and in turn, the Diaspora served as a conduit of new, foreign ideas back to Jerusalem. Therefore, "all of the Judaisms of the Hellenistic period, of both the Diaspora and the land of Israel," were Hellenistic: "that is, were integral parts of the culture of the ancient world." Some were more prone to Hellenism than were others. "But none was an island unto itself."[21] How could it be any other way?

Yet, is this not to accept the argument of Martin Hengel about the domineering pervasiveness of Hellenistic culture? No: although Hellenism was pervasive, this does not mean that there necessarily was an opposition between Hellenistic culture and that of Judaism. One must honour the insight of Samuel Sandmel who held that the Yahwist faith could become Hellenistic, but without loss of its own identity and without the destruction of any of its own essential characteristics.[22] Of course Hellenistic influences affected the several variants of Judaism that were flowering in Palestine and beyond, but this was a synergistic situation. As Eric M. Meyers has observed, the Hellenism we find, for example, in the architecture of Eretz Israel and in linguistic contacts, should not be considered "so much an invasion of indigenous culture from the outside, but rather a new means of expressing local culture in alternative and often exciting ways. The appearance of some forms of Greco-Roman culture in a Jewish context need not signify compromise or traumatic change."[23] Thus, the ubiquity of Hellenistic influence, delineated as a stage of the society, economy, and culture of the entire Ancient Near East can be granted without presenting it as an external hegemonic force that pressed hard upon Judaism. Both Saul and Yeshua operated in similar conceptual worlds wherein the substance of religious thought was traditional to the core. Stylistics elements and modes of expressing substantive concepts, however, were open to Hellenistic influences and the impact of these influences varied according to geographic region, social class, and a whole bevy of local factors. Thus, while Saul and Yeshua operated in a single conceptual world, they inhabited different provinces of that world.

Crucially, despite Hellenic influence, the centre point of both of their conceptual worlds was Jerusalem, not Athens or Alexandria. The intellectual storehouse from which each drew all of his identifiable substantive material was that of later Second Temple Judahism.[24] Thus, Joseph Klausner, one of the pioneers among Jewish scholars of the texts related to late Second Temple Judahism and to early Christianity concluded that "*there is nothing in all the teachings of Paul as there is nothing in the teaching of Jesus, which is not grounded in the Old Testament, or in the Apocryphal, Pseudepigraphical, and Tannaitic literature of his time*" (emphasis his).[25] David Flusser, after spending a lifetime studying the Tanakh and later Second Temple texts wrote, indicating how deeply embedded the Jesus of the Gospels is in traditional Second Temple lore, that "we could easily construct a whole gospel without using a single word that originated with Jesus."[26] And, indeed the entire Christian scriptures is remarkably Semitic in its conceptual structure. As A.N. Wilson notes, "The New Testament posits a quite different way of viewing the *kosmos*, a way which we find in the pages of the Old Testament and in the Dead Sea Scrolls, but not among the Greeks."[27] This does not deny Hellenistic influence, as previously discussed, but it keeps it in perspective.

As an illustration of how Saul and Yeshua were part of a tradition that ran from the writers of the Pentateuch to the Tannaim (the earliest level of Rabbinic thinkers), let us take the apophtegm that is known as "the Golden Rule." Accept for the sake of argument that Yeshua actually said what is reported of him in the Gospel according to Matthew (7:12) and Luke (6:31), the phrase which is most familiar in the form "Do unto others as you would have them do unto you." Saul, in summarizing the human relationship dictated by Torah, did so as follows: "Thou shalt love thy neighbour as thyself… Love worketh no ill to his neighbour" (Rom. 13:9–10). These two forms of the Golden Rule, Saul's and Yeshua's harken ultimately to Yahweh's voice as recorded in Leviticus (19:18):

> Thou shalt not avenge, nor bear any grudge against the children of thy people, but thou shalt love they neighbour as thyself: I am the Lord.

In the Book of Tobit, a popular Judahist novella from the Maccabean era, the injunction takes this form:

> And what you hate, do not do to anyone, do not drink wine to excess or let drunkenness go with you on your way. Give some of your food to the hungry, and some of your clothing to the naked. Give all your surplus as alms, and do not let your eye begrudge your giving of alms. (Tobit 4:15–16)

In another Judahist text from the first or second century BCE, a monarch is told by a wise man that if he wishes to avoid personal misfortune and be bountifully blessed, he should rule his people mercifully. This was part of a reciprocal transaction, "for God guides all men in mercy" (Letter of Aristeas, v. 207). Much closer in form to Saul and Yeshua's version of the Golden Rule, although stated in negative form, is that ascribed to their contemporary, Hillel:

> What is hateful to you, do not to your neighbour; that is the whole Torah, while the rest is the commentary thereof; go and learn it.
>
> (Bavli, Shabbath 31a [Soncino ed., p. 140])

The inference is obvious: in this matter neither Yeshua nor Saul was propounding many original insights; they were moulding their concepts from within a very rich tradition of Judahist thought.

3

We do not know directly anything about the mental kitbag with which Yeshua of Nazareth approached the world (we are privy only to its reconstruction, two generations later, by his post-70 followers), but we do know with some precision the tools that Saul used to analyse and, ultimately, reshape his own world. He possessed three major elements, all from later Second Temple Judaism. First (and least importantly), Saul possessed a very flexible interpretative instrument, namely a version of the Hellenic mode of analysis, allegorical thinking, that had been domesticated by Judahist thinkers so that this Gentile thought mode was made to serve, rather than to undercut, Judahist thought. The chief exemplar of Judahist allegorical thought was Philo of Alexandria (often called Philo Judaeus, or simply Philo), who, among his other achievements, rewrote the Pentateuch in such a way as to make Moses the ultimate source of Platonic truth![28]

Although Philo is the most important proponent of the tradition of Judahist allegory, the method dispersed throughout Judahist thought: that this did so is illustrated not only by the New Testament's ascribing several allegories to Jesus, but the Rabbinical literature ascribes allegories to its own intellectual progenitors, the Pharisees. The allegorical method, in Judahist hands, became an indigenous mode of self-expression, less architectonic and less given to driving to a logical (or, often, illogical) final conclusion than was the original Greek mode of thought. In Saul's work, allegory emerges both as a "half-way hermeneutic," a way of interpreting certain texts from the Books of Moses and the Prophets so as to give them contemporary relevance and, at other times, in typological thinking in which figures in the Old Testament are projected upon a cosmic screen and become "types" of Christ.[29] It would be surprising if Yeshua was as steeped in allegorical thinking as was Saul (it was, after all, a mode of thought whose geographical centrepoint was in the Diaspora lands), but it would have taken a strong act of the will for him not to have been influenced by it, given its utility as a way of interpreting texts in the Tanakh.

Secondly, Saul's mind was fitted out with almost the full range of concepts that had appeared in Second Temple Judahism from, roughly, 200 BCE onwards. (These were discussed in chapter two.) Their existence is directly evidenced by a rich set of texts, which range from the Dead Sea Scrolls to myriad items in the Pseudepigrapha and Apocrypha. Here one is not claiming that Saul had directly read any of these texts (although certainly it is possible) but, rather, that he had become acquainted with the complexes of ideas that run through several of these texts and that he used some of these constructs as tools for understanding his own world and for communicating with his followers. Thus, one finds in Saul's epistles most of the new modes of religious apperception and expression that came to the fore in the 200 years before the Common Era: the personification of good and evil, most particularly in figures that had agency, such as angels, demons and, of course, Satan; the resurrection of deceased human beings (in what form was never very clear) and the eternal judgement of the individual; apocalyptic conceptions of future time; and the figures of the Son of God and the newly-defined figure of Moshiah. All those items, in Saul's own combination, have been referred to already in the text. Saul was moving in what Wilfred Knox called "a common circle of ideas" from the later Second Temple era, ones which we are familiar with from written examples, but which must have circulated mostly by word of mouth.[30] If Saul indeed tells us what was in the intellectual kitbag of an informed Judahist missionary of the early Common Era, these same concepts should have been available as well to Yeshua of Nazareth.

Thirdly, and most importantly, Saul's mind was saturated in the great primal unity on which the Tanakh is based, Genesis-Kings, and in the Prophets. That is, he not only was well acquainted with the contemporary fashions of his era (as found in allegorical thinking and in the swirling visions, rewritten Torahs, and crimson apocalypses of the time), but he knew great chunks of the Old Testament by heart. That the version he memorized was the Septuagint has been well established, but that was no drawback: the Greek text was accepted as constituting scripture in the Diaspora and as being as authoritative – otherwise how could the separated brethren in the Judahist Diaspora worship? And Saul was also acquainted with the Hebrew original, for a few times he uses the Hebrew version of a citation to the Tanakh in Hebrew, rather than Greek.[31] It is almost impossible to grasp how deeply awash in the Judahist scriptures Saul was. In fact, they, and their late Second Temple re-inventions in what is called "extra-biblical literature" *were not something he thought about, but were instead, the way he thought.* One can recognize that almost his entire store of theological metaphors – the Judge, the Rock, the Root of Jesse, the Second Adam, the Seed of Abraham – was derived from the Tanakh; and one can point to the number of times that Saul demonstrably quotes part of the Old Testament: one hundred-plus instances, which comprise about one-third of the formal citations of material from the Tanakh in the Christian scriptures.[32] Yet, even noting these facts minimizes the degree of Saul's immersion in the scriptures, for his direct scriptural citations and his use of Old Testament pattern-figures are merely the visible portions of his much more pervasive subterranean consciousness of the richness of late Second Temple Judahist traditions and ideas. They were the air he breathed, his food, his water, his very substance.

This being the case, how could Saul (and by pattern-similarity, Yeshua of Nazareth) possess a consciousness that was, in religious terms, revolutionary? Is it not a contradiction to see someone as deeply immersed in late Second Temple Judahism and, simultaneously, the inventor of radically new forms? No. There was in his time both precedent for this phenomenon and a method for it. The precedents are simply the multiple forms of Judahism that existed at the time, most of which had arisen as attempts at radical reform or as an attempted conceptual *putsch*. Everyone from the Pharisees to the Essenes to the Awakeners to the unnamed minds that produced the hallucinogenic Book of Enoch and those who carved the ice-cold hatred of the War Scroll and those who defined the alternative Pentateuch of the Book of Jubilees and the designer of the heaven-sent architecture of the Temple Scroll testify to the potentiality of being both saturated in Judahist culture, motifs, practices and beliefs and being simultaneously religiously subversive and, indeed, revolutionary.

Crucially, the tradition that began with the writing down of the primary scriptures of the Yahweh-faith – Genesis through Kings – a tradition that runs right down to the present day in its myriad Jewish and Christian versions, provided a set of rules for thinking as a revolutionary, while still remaining within the respective fold. This was accomplished by the acceptance of an agreed "grammar of religious invention." That extraordinary governing phenomenon I have dealt with in great detail in *Surpassing Wonder*, and cannot rehearse it here with any degree of fullness. For our present purposes, the key point is that Saul acted within the paradigms of that grammar. He granted honour and respect to the major symbols of the Judahist tradition; he used almost entirely a vocabulary of exposition that came from the Tanakh and from later Second Temple extra-biblical traditions; he continually argued that all his new ideas were old ideas, that he was merely pointing out the correct interpretation of information that his Judahist co-religionists already possessed; whenever possible, he cited precedents found in the scriptures; and, by taking scripture out of context, by taking iconic figures (Abraham, Adam, etc.) from their original contexts and by placing them in new positions, by employing late Second Temple constructs (Messiah, Satan, Son of God) in new combinations with these older figures, he was able to reverse totally the meanings of many of the basic concepts held by most forms of Second Temple Judahism. Here, I emphasize, not only that Saul was not violating the implicit rules of his tradition, but that he was not even doing anything unusual. These same techniques (with appropriate adaptions for the time in which they were employed) were adopted by virtually everyone who wanted to effect religious reform or revolution within the pluralisms that worshipped Yahweh. One sees the same techniques in the author-editors of the Dead Sea Scrolls, in the Christian writers that succeed Saul, in the founders of the Rabbinic Jewish faith, and right down to the Protestant Reformation and, in our own day, in New Age Christianity and various forms of Jewish Renewal, such as the "Discovery Seminar," which rewrites the scriptures, in part employing skip-coded computer programs. The basic rule is simple: the more radically new the concept being introduced, the more the author has to claim it is found in ancient writings. And better yet, actually believe it.

At a low level, one sees Saul re-inventing old beliefs, giving them new and different meanings, in his employment of incidental texts. For example, at one point (Rom. 10:19) it suits his argumentative purposes to ascribe to Moses words that in the original text (Deut. 32:21) are uttered by Yahweh. And he feels free to change words. Thus, Psalm 14:3 – "there is none that doeth good, no, not one" – becomes theologized, "good" being replaced by a very different concept, righteousness: "As it is written, There is none righteous, no, not one" (Rom. 3:10). Most of the time these nickel-and-dime alterations in the original are undramatic and unobtrusive and their effect is gradual. (At their worst, they are slightly comic, and remind one of the child's reading of Psalm 23, as an admonition to good behaviour, lest "thy rod and thy staff they come for me.")

Where Saul really does his heavy lifting is his total redefinition of the character of the covenant of Yahweh with humankind. Since there exist several thousand books explaining Saul's belief system, the briefer we are here the better. Fundamentally, Saul redefined the covenant (the ground-base metaphor of all variants of the Yahweh-faith) by (1) including the Gentiles directly in it, not merely as a residual godly afterthought; (2) reduced sharply, but not entirely, the privileged status of the Chosen People; (3) redefined "Torah" as "Law," and downplayed the demands of Halachah; (4) introduced Jesus-the-Christ as an embodiment of true Torah; (5) sharply changed the figure of Moshiah, which was emerging in late Second Temple times, from an anointed rescuer of the Judahist polity into a crucified paschal victim; and (6) employed the fundamental figures of Adam and Abraham in contexts that virtually reversed their meanings in the Tanakh. They become pillars of Saul's new construction, which is nothing less than a completely new arrangement of the motifs and constructs that he found, piece by scattered piece, in the Judahisms of his own time. Saul may be inconsistent at some moments, illogical at others, but no one can accuse him of having been small-minded.[33]

That judgement holds unless one proposes that all the apparently-original ideas that Saul expressed were those that he has picked up (second- or third-hand) from the earthly Yeshua of Nazareth. If so, Saul is one of the most successful plagiarists of all time. Because we have not a single word that Yeshua himself set down (why, oh why, could he not have had some distant followers who needed counsel by epistle?), we cannot conclude with absolute certainty that Saul's radical re-invention of late Second Temple Judahism was not dependent upon Yeshua's. However, such dependency in matters of detail seems extremely unlikely: Saul's entire faith focuses upon Yeshua becoming the Moshiah through his crucifixion and subsequent cosmic resurrection. Saul's faith and the construction of his own belief system begin where the earthly Yeshua leaves off.

Am I not here leading us to the threadbare assertion that Saul created Christianity? No. The invention of Christianity was a cumulative process in which Saul was only one player among many. Most of the process of inventing Jesus-the-Christ took place after Saul's death (in the early 60s CE) and, largely, after Jerusalem and the Temple were destroyed in 70 CE. (It would be gratuitous to exclude from the historical process Yeshua of Nazareth himself and thus to make him a cipher.) The purpose of looking at the *gestalt* of Saul's life and mission is that in his Imitation of Christ he shows that a person could be totally immersed in late Second Temple Judahism – a "good Jew" in the vernacular – and still be a religious revolutionary. What holds true for Saul, then, holds possible for the historical Yeshua.

This long discussion is in effect an answer to the brilliantly illuminating and mordantly corrosive suggestion by Burton L. Mack that maybe Jesus died in a motorcar accident.[34] That, I take to be a salient way of saying that, according to the available records, it is just as possible that Yeshua was crucified for random reasons (being in the wrong place at the wrong time), than for his having a revolutionary religious message; and that we know so little of his belief system that this random-event model cannot be disproved. Now, it is true that Saul tells us little about the historical Yeshua in direct fashion. However, by the heuristic speculation we are here following, his own Imitation of Christ reflects the contours of his master, a deep immersion in the Judahist faith of his time, a revolutionary religious construction of that faith, and, for his reward, martyrdom. Saul tells us, I think, that Yeshua was crucified because he deserved it. Yeshua's thorns were, indeed, a crown.

Thus we escape from the infinite rescission that underlies much of the recent Quests for the historical Yeshua. Although it may be correct that, as the

"Q" industry claims, there are only seventy or so Gospel verses that go back to Yeshua; or that there are perhaps ninety, as the Jesus Seminar suggests,[35] such assertions (even if they are ultimately found to be accurate) are apt to lead to the implied and unexamined inference that because we at present know so little of the religious ideas of Yeshua of Nazareth that, therefore, Yeshua himself was so very little.

Saul knew otherwise.

4

The visual model that I have been here employing – that of contiguous similar figures – has one special condition laid on: that the two figures are joined for a portion of their respective perimeters by a brief straight line. This is appropriate because on certain issues – the worship of Yahweh as the one god of the universe being the most crucial – the axis of orientation is held jointly by Yeshua and Saul. I suspect that a second broad band of experience, while not identical, probably overlaps for each of these two figures: their experience of Pharisaism.

The topic of Pharisaism is perhaps the single most puzzling historical issue in the shared history of Christianity and of Rabbinic Judahism. The post-70 CE texts of the Rabbinic Jewish faith view the Pharisees as their progenitors; the post-70 texts of Christianity present the Pharisees as their original enemy. The scholarly literature, if anything, is more deeply confusing.[36] Only two individuals – Saul and Flavius Josephus – actually have left direct affirmations that they were Pharisees. Yet, the character of the Pharisees is fundamental to the religions we know today as the Christian and the Jewish faiths: the Pharisees were the progenitors of Rabbinic Judaism, which is the form that became dominant after 70 CE, and the Pharisees were the biggest competitors of the early Yeshua-followers. Therefore, the matter is a volatile one.

Instead of losing ourselves in the contentious secondary literature on this matter, it is better, as far as an understanding of Saul and of Yeshua is concerned, to deal with the contemporary texts. Operationally, that leaves us Saul's letters and, with reservations for their being post-70 CE, a bit of Josephus, the Four Gospels and the Acts of the Apostles. The chief Rabbinical text, the Mishnah, was not edited in its present form until approximately 200 CE and it requires considerable delicacy when interpreting its information on pre-70 CE Pharisaism; its anachronistic use, unfortunately, is endemic.

Perhaps the single most important point to realize about the Pharisees is that they were not the equivalent of a political cell in the days of the Cold War. This bears emphasis, because the Mishnah, which derives from one set of Pharisees who survived the destruction of 70 CE, gives that impression if read uncritically. Instead of a tightly-disciplined party, with central control and unified admission requirements throughout their domain, the Pharisees should be considered to have been a tendency, a constellation of small groups that held overlapping views, and which could be mobilized towards a common goal.

Undoubtedly, Jerusalem was the hub of Pharisaism, but we should not assume that Pharisaism, virtually alone among the multiple Judahisms of the late Second Temple period, was limited to the spiritual metropole. Certainly Pharisaic notions permeated the rest of Eretz Israel and were noised abroad in the Diaspora. And, once that happened, individual groups of Pharisees came to their own accommodations with the local Judahist congregations and with the larger society. Which is to say: the Pharisees of Alexandria, of Tarsus, of Galilee, would have had a great deal in common with most Pharisees in Jerusalem, but they would perforce have been slightly different.

That granted, Pharisaic groups shared primary characteristics. First, they were a lay group. Their leaders were learned men, often spending a lifetime in deep scholarship, but in the pre-70 period they were not set aside as professional holy men. The term "Rabbi" was sometimes used by contemporaries, but it did not carry the freight it later was to acquire when these scholars became the functional replacement of the priests who had served in the Temple before its Destruction. Secondly, unlike the formal religious establishment, the Pharisees accepted the relatively recent notion of the resurrection of the dead and of divine judgement of the individual. Probably they meant a spiritual, rather than a physical resurrection, but the documentation on this is very spongy, so one should keep an open mind. Thirdly, their chief intellectual interest was in Halachah, the interpretation of the 613 commandments found in the Pentateuch, and the case law that cascaded from those original precepts. Crucially, one should not see this legal interest as indicating a rigidity in religious outlook or practice. The Pharisees were remarkably flexible, because they were beginning to operate according to a theory that was later called that of the "Oral Torah." This was the belief that a parallel and equally valid set of religious laws existed side-by-side with the Written Torah. In practice, this belief, when combined with their interest in the evolution of case law, meant that they could introduce quite radical changes, all the while asserting that they were really only expressing the true meaning of Torah. And, fourthly, the Pharisees were distinguished by *praxis*. They were very attentive to ritual cleanliness, and most particularly to food cleanliness, in the sacral sense of the term. In everyday life this made them a bit difficult to deal with; their constant fear of various forms of spiritual contagion meant that they did not mix easily with those who did not accept the system of taboos, monitions, and commands their version of Judaism entailed.

Saul states unequivocally that he had been a Pharisee. He had been:

circumcised the eighth day, of the stock of Israel, of the tribe of Benjamin, an Hebrew of the Hebrews [a Hebrew born and bred, N.I.V.]; as touching the law, a Pharisee.   (Philippians 3:5)

This statement, like Saul's assertion of other aspects of his previous background (Rom. 9:3–5, Gal. 1:14) is part of a piece of rhetoric whose purpose, ultimately, was to subvert his own upbringing. But that does not mean it was not true when he said he had been a Pharisee. The fact fit with his argument, but it is stated very much in passing. He does not advert elsewhere to his own Pharisaism. Significantly, at no point in his letters does Saul badmouth the Pharisees. As we have seen, he was capable of Billingsgate on a fishmonger's scale, but he gave the Pharisees not just distant respect, but the respect of keeping his distance.

Until quite recently,[37] Jewish scholars have either shied away from dealing with Saul or have declared him to have been a liar. At times, conspiracy-theories of Saul's origins have been put forward.[38] Now, there are quite good reasons why anyone associated with Rabbinic Judaism (which dominates the modern Jewish faith) would not want Saul associated with the genealogy of the faith, even in a limited and collateral position. Saul, after all, was the apostle to the Gentiles and ultimately those who adopted his line of reasoning attempted to highjack the covenant with Yahweh. And, parts of Saul's letters can be read as accusing the Chosen People of deicide: Saul refers to the Jews "who both killed the Lord Jesus, and their own prophets, and have persecuted us …" (I Thess. 2:15). Never mind that this may be a later interpolation; and never mind that, if authentic, Saul here was constructing a trope of passages in the Tanakh where the Chosen People were denounced for denying the prophets (e.g Neh. 9:26 and 2 Chron. 36:15–16);[39] the concept of "Christ-killer" as part of the litany of Christian anti-Semitism was repeated century after century and cost thousands and thousands of Jewish lives. Granting that Saul's arguments were used by later Christians in a morally spavined, indeed evil manner, that does not mean one erases him from history. He existed and he very probably was a Pharisee and, if read on their own terms (not those of later miscreants), Saul's letters provide the only direct information we have on one important sub-set of late Second Temple Judahism: the Pharisees of the Diaspora. Rejecting him as a fake-Pharisee because he does not fit perfectly with the Jerusalem Pharisees as depicted in the Mishnah is volitionally obtuse. Samuel Sandmel rightly saw the opportunity that Saul presented: "As to Saul's being a Pharisee (Phil. 3:5), rather than challenge the authenticity either of the verse or of the purport, as some have done, I would contend that one needs to understand the label Pharisee from Paul's content, and not content from the label. We are completely in the dark respecting Pharisaism in the Greek Dispersion."[40]

So we grant Saul his self-declared Pharisaism. But we do *not* grant the Pharisaism ascribed to him in the Acts of the Apostles. There the basic fact is embroidered as a very skilled piece of propaganda which involves the core genealogy of Pharisaism and of early Rabbinic Judaism: namely the great

Hillel, his son or grandson (traditions vary), Rabban Gamaliel I and his grandson Rabban Gamaliel II (a leading figure in the last two decades of the first century of the Common Era). As context, recall that in the last thirty years of the century, the Yeshua-faith was mutating into Christianity and Pharisaism into Rabbinic Judaism, and that these two branches of the multiple Judahisms of the pre-70 CE era were beginning their centuries-long contest for the heritage of the covenant with Yahweh. Now note what the author-editor of Acts does. First, early in his chronicle of the apostles he introduces the figure of "Gamaliel," who, from the author-editor's viewpoint is best described as a righteous Pharisee. A master of Torah, a leading Pharisee, a respected figure among all branches of Judaism, Gamaliel on one occasion protects several of the apostles from a mob that, having been offended by their preaching, wishes to kill them. They get off with a beating (Acts 5:29–40). This figure, Gamaliel, having been established, is re-useable. When Saul is in a parallel position of danger, having been seized when he tried some act of worship in the Temple, and placed on trial, the author-editor of Acts places in Saul's mouth a claim that he himself never made – namely, that he had been trained in Jerusalem at the feet of Gamaliel (Acts 22:3). Thus, in the later first century, the author-editor of Acts is able to provide Christians with a defence against Rabbinic Judaism: since Saul learned all he could from Gamaliel I and, through his epistles, teaches us how morally insufficient that education was, we need not be impressed or unsettled by the derivative person of Gamaliel II. We already are victorious.

Fine propaganda, but questionable history: would Saul have left out of his own letter, wherein he boasts of the rigour of his own Pharisaic education, his having studied with Gamaliel I? The subtlety with which the author-editor of Acts manipulates the anti-Pharisaic sub-text goes farther. In Acts, Saul is made to claim something he does not state in his own letters: that he is the son of a Pharisee (Acts 23:6). This pushes the genealogical discrediting of Pharisaism back in time to its largest figure: for if Saul was taught by Gamaliel I, who was his father taught by? There is no direct answer, but the predecessor (either father or grandfather) of Gamaliel I was the great Hillel. So not only is an historical ratio buried in the sub-text of Acts that discredits post-70 CE Pharisees (Saul: Gamaliel I = post-70 Christians: Gamaliel II), but an implied derogation of the founding-genealogy of Pharisaism is implied (Saul: Gamaliel = Saul's father: Hillel). This material's brilliance as propaganda virtually guarantees that it is not creditable as history.

So one either has to reject Saul's claimed Pharisaic background (a viewpoint I find cavalier to the point of irresponsibility) or accept it and use his epistles as autochthonous evidence of one variant of Pharisaism. And we read those letters without reference to the material in the Acts of the Apostles.

Accepting, then, the probability that Saul actually had been a Diaspora Pharisee, there remains a curious side-issue. Why, if the Christian narrative of Jesus-the-Christ (the Four Gospels) appears to hold Pharisaism in obvious contempt, does Saul assert his Pharisaism without flinching? It is put forward in Philippians 3:5 as part of a set of personal characteristics that are just facts, nothing for which apology is due – his being circumcised, his being one of the Chosen People, his being of the tribe of Benjamin, his being born of "Hebrew" parents, and his being a Pharisee are all just biographical facts. These are segregated from the characteristics for which he does indeed have to apologize: "concerning zeal, persecuting the church" and, as a euphemism for his badly misplaced zeal, "touching the righteousness which is in the law, blameless" (Phil. 3:6).

Saul's factual, non-histrionic, reporting of his own Pharisaism is deeply in conflict with the anti-Pharisaic tone that runs through much of Gospels' material. In the Gospel of John, for example, the vices of all forms of Judahism are summed up in the Pharisees, and there is almost no civil interaction with them. Instead, there is demonization. The Gospel of John has the Pharisees occupying in the Judahist religious polity a position which was only obtained by their Rabbinic descendants in the years after the Temple's destruction: they are presented as part of the religious and civil establishment and as the spearhead of enforced religious conformity. The only Pharisee to receive a good press in John is Nicodemus, "a ruler of the Jews," (that is, probably, a member of the Sanhedrin) who comes to Jesus by night and asks for spiritual advice. He addresses Yeshua as "Rabbi" and treats him with respect (3:1–21). Later, when the Pharisees and the chief priests resolve to seize Yeshua (note the alliance), Nicodemus argues that it was a violation of Torah to seize anyone before his words were heard and his actions observed. For his courage, Nicodemus was accused of being a crypto-Galilean, that is, a follower of Jesus (7:32–53). Nicodemus is last heard of bringing a hundred weight of spices (a fortune) to the secret place where Yeshua's body was taken immediately after his crucifixion (19:38–39). Nicodemus stands out because the Pharisees as a group are painted as powerful, malicious, oppressive, and almost unrelievedly evil: in John's narrative, the figure of Nicodemus is brilliantly drawn, so as to make an ideological point: that the Pharisees' practice of evil was a matter of their own choice (they all could have acted like Nicodemus), and because their actions were volitional, they were fully responsible for them. The gravamen of the charge against them in the Gospel of John is that the Pharisees are the chief instigators of deicide. They watch Yeshua carefully and are the instigating element against Jesus. (In John, unlike the Synoptics, there is only one reference to "the scribes"; it is the Pharisees whom John sees as the active agent.) After a good deal of intelligence-gathering by the Pharisees, they and the chief priests convene a council, to discuss the danger Jesus presents to all of them: if he is allowed to teach, soon we will have no followers and the Romans will see this and take away the privileged position that they permit us to occupy. So, the Pharisees and the chief priests resolve to have him killed (11:47–53). Crucially, when Judas Iscariot strikes a deal to identify Jesus to his enemies, it is a malign covenant among Judas, the high priest, and the Pharisees (18:2–3). It is hard to conceive of a more bitter hate-cocktail than that: the Pharisees, the leaders of the Jerusalem Temple, and Judah generally ("Judas" being the perfect stage name for all the Judahisms of Jesus' time) are Christ-killers: the instigators, the primary agents are the Pharisees, the touchstones of the tradition of Rabbinic Judaism.

Luke and Matthew (particularly the former) are much softer on the Pharisees, but still hard. In Luke, Yeshua is reported three times to have had a meal in the home of a Pharisee (7:36–50, 11:37–54 and 14:1–35). On the first occasion, he gently explains to his host, Simon, the nature of the forgiveness of sins. In the second instance, he has an argument with the Pharisee about ritual cleanliness before meals and calls the Pharisees, "fools," and "hypocrites" for being so shallow in their devotional life. And in the third case, he visits the house of "one of the chief Pharisees" (14:1) on Shabbat and there has a debate about what it is lawful to do on the Sabbath. Not surprisingly, Yeshua wins the debate. In these stories there is clearly a disapproval of the Pharisees and, in the second instance (11:54), the story concludes with the Pharisees committing themselves to catching Yeshua out in some grievous error, so that they can bring him before the authorities. However, the tone of the three tales is not acrid and Yeshua's having a meal with various Pharisees is an indication that the Pharisees and Yeshua-followers were not – in the view of the author-editor(s) of Luke – beyond the civilities of being able to break bread together.

The Gospel of Matthew permits each of these three meetings to take place, but for the author-editor(s) of that book, they are not occasions of comity, but of tense incivility. The meal in the house of Simon the Pharisee (Luke 7:36–50) becomes in Matthew a visit to the home (but not a bread-breaking) of "Simon the Leper"! (Matt. 26:6–13). The third meal (Luke 14:1–35), the Shabbat meal and discussion with one of the chief Pharisees, has portions retold in Matthew (Matt. 22:1–14 and 10:37–39), but in completely different contexts and with no reference to any Pharisee, let alone any indication that Yeshua shared Shabbat with one of their leaders. These two instances are revealing, but the discussion in the Gospel of Matthew at the second meal (cf. Luke 11:37–54) is the most revealing. Whereas Luke had gentled Jesus' indictment of the Pharisees' alleged vanity, pettifogging, and spiritual barrenness, by setting it within the confines of a Pharisaic house, wherein Yeshua accepts food and hospitality, Matthew (23:1–39) presents it as a long public

address. The "scribes and Pharisees" (but primarily the Pharisees) are denounced for mere show-acting in wearing tefillin and prayer shawls. They
grab the best rooms at feasts and the best seats in houses of worship; they
make long public prayers, yet toss destitute widows out of their lodgings.
And on and on: the Pharisees are called a generation of vipers and, in a rabid
pericope that borders on blood-libel (23:34–35, and 37), Matthew has Yeshua
state that the Pharisees and scribes will either scourge or kill the prophets and
wise men who will be sent to enlighten them, and thus will become responsible for "all the righteous blood shed upon the earth, from the blood of
righteous Abel unto the blood of Zacharias son of Barachias, whom ye slew
between the temple [sanctuary] and the altar" (23:35). That is formidable
guilt indeed, running from the first human murder (Gen. 4:8–10), to the murder of a priestly reformer in the reign of King Joash, whose death by stoning
(2 Chron. 24:20–22) Matthew turns into a parallel to the sacrifice of a lamb, a
strong Christian motif. All this guilt, Yeshua is supposed to have said, will
fall to the present generation of Pharisees and their accomplices, functionaries of Jerusalem's religious establishment. In the Gospel of Matthew, the alle-
gation of blood guilt on the Pharisees' part, stops just short of its logical
conclusion: that the Pharisees were largely responsible for deicide, the killing
of Jesus-the-Christ, for Matthew omits the Pharisees from the short litany of
villains who are central to the crucifixion.

The Gospel of Mark not only omits the Pharisees from the list of Christ-
killers, but makes them part of a civilized interaction with Yeshua. He
and the Pharisees argue points of Halachah, such as dietary rules (2:16–20),
table-cleanliness and cooking rules (7:1–23), matters that enhull big spiritual
principles in small, everyday practices, as both sides acknowledge. The argument is presented as being generally respectful on each side, if spirited. Only
rarely does Mark permit Yeshua to say something nasty about the Pharisees –
as, "beware of the leaven of the Pharisees, and of the leaven of Herod"
(8:15). And, on the rigour-of-the-law question, Mark does not permit a
simple dichotomy to emerge, with Yeshua embracing the spirit of the law, the
Pharisees the letter: when the matter of divorce comes up (10:1–12), Yeshua
asserts a position more rule-bound, less-flexible, less forgiving, than do the
Pharisees. Most significantly, the author-editor(s) of the Gospel of Mark
present the story of the crucifixion of Yeshua in a remarkable way: although
the Pharisees are mentioned early in Mark as plotting with the "Herodians"
to destroy Yeshua (3:6) and, later, as trying to catch him in seditious speech
(12:13), when one comes to the Passion story, they are absent. One has the
elders, the high priest, the chief priests, the scribes, all mentioned as participants, but no Pharisees. Perhaps this is sloppy narration on the author-
editor(s)' part, but I strongly doubt it: the Gospel of Mark is too tight a

composition, too spare in its words, too far from being frivolous in execution to drop a major set of characters carelessly. The exclusion of the Pharisees from the Passion story – and thus from direct blame for the death of Yeshua – should be taken as a conscious decision. That said, the Gospel of Mark indicates that, at the time of the Temple's Destruction or shortly thereafter: (a) the Pharisees were established as major rivals of the Christians, but that they were not a polar antithesis of Christianity, for in Mark's account, Yeshua debates with them in a common vocabulary and is on occasion more Pharisaic than they are; and (b) that the Pharisees were neither to be declared the sole Judahist faction that opposed Christianity, nor to be demonized as the killers of the Christ.

Seemingly, a trend-line exists: the earlier the stories of Yeshua the more he and the Pharisees are shown to have affinities for each other. Indeed, if it were not for the labels that distinguish Yeshua and the Pharisees, one could read the Gospel of Mark and not know which one was the Pharisee. Modern scholars of Jewish history have argued that the historical Yeshua of Nazareth was not at odds with the Pharisees on the basic matters: "In the whole of the New Testament," Paul Winter writes, "we are unable to find a single historically reliable instance of religious differences between Jesus and members of the Pharisaic guilds ..."[41] This may be a touch strong,[42] but the observation is fundamentally correct: the historical Yeshua of Nazareth was not in a root-and-branch war with the Pharisees. Whatever arguments he had with them were fought within a shared frame of reference and in modes of discourse that were mutually comprehensible.

And that, I think, hints at the reason Saul was not embarrassed, nor did he consider it particularly noteworthy that he himself had once been a Pharisee. His model, Yeshua of Nazareth, had been a Pharisee as well: like Saul, a Pharisee of a slightly off-brand sort. Neither Saul nor Yeshua was from the hub of Pharisaism, Jerusalem, and both were strongly influenced by local elements in their distal societies, the Diaspora and the north of Eretz Israel, respectively. Both had real difficulties when they tried to deal with the way the religious game was played in the first century's equivalent of the Big Casino. And, indeed, both were martyred after breaking Jerusalem Rules.

Saul's Imitation of Christ worked so well for him because the contours of his life could be made similar to those of Yeshua of Nazareth (particularly in his developing a mission to the Gentiles similar to that of Yeshua to the Judahists), and also because the two men shared common points of orientation: the fundamental devotion to Yahweh, and the predisposition to argue about religious matters in a common vocabulary, learned in their respective branches of Pharisaism. Thus, that strange argument between Yeshua and Saul about various divorce Halachot which we discussed in chapter eight,

makes more sense and is less disrespectful than it at first appears. Saul, arguing in the manner a trained Pharisee would argue, corrects Yeshua's views on
divorce. And in doing so, he is in part defending the juridical decisions on
family law of a standard late Second Temple *Beth Din* against Yeshua's interpretation, which is more restrictive than is contemporary practice, indeed,
more so than the Law of Moses. (Compare Deut. 24:1; Matt. 5:31–32 and
19:9; 1 Cor. 7:10–15.)

By virtue of Saul's having written his epistles, at minimum he gives us a
chance to see in full flow how a Pharisee would have argued case law and
how a forceful late Second Temple Judahist would have delivered his views
in the form of public rhetoric. That is very valuable, because the earliest document that reflects Pharisaic halachic argument – the Mishnah – reports its
debates only in sketchy, telegraphic form; so much was going on, but so little
could be remembered and recorded. And, as far as public rhetoric was concerned, Saul is valuable because, apart from Philo of Alexandria (whose writings certainly were not meant to assume a speaking voice), there is no record
of how a serious Judahist controversialist would have spoken to an audience
of real people. Saul, dictating madly, gives us that at times. And here is the
bonus: if Saul can be taken as being a Diaspora analogue of his master,
Yeshua, then perhaps Saul's directly-dictated texts can give us an indication
of the character (not the content, the character) of the Galilean preacher
whom we glimpse so unclearly in the strongly propagandistic biographies of
him written after the year 70 CE.

Saul expected those of his converts who were Judahists to continue to
practice Judaism and to respect its laws (1 Cor. 7:19) and he expected the
same of himself. Anything else would have been hypocritical: it was only
the Gentile followers of Yeshua to whom the finite rules of Torah did not
apply, at least not fully. Crucially, the letters of Saul that we possess indicate that whether trying to persuade Judahists (as his preaching in synagogues inevitably implies) or Gentiles, he assumed a common culture with
his audience. Whether Judahist or Gentile, this audience was talked to in
the vocabulary of the Tanakh, of popular late Second Temple motifs, and in
Judahized forms of allegory. "The foundations of his theology are so thoroughly Jewish that it is doubtful whether he would have found it easy to
commend it to those who did not already regard Judaism with some measure of veneration. It may be presumed that he would have employed the
methods generally in use among the Jews in dealing with their Gentile
adherents ..."[43] That is, he preached mostly to Gentile "God-fearers," to
proselytes, to the sympathetic, with the same rich set of allusions that he
would have used for an audience composed solely of members of the
Diaspora. His Gentile audience was pre-selected and wherever Saul found a

Diaspora synagogue, he found Gentile adherents. Because of the missionary aspect of late Second Temple Judahism as it existed in the Diaspora
(see chapter seven), Saul did not have to change his message in order to
attract Gentiles. (That his having attracted Gentiles led to problems that
thereupon forced his own further theological development, especially as
regards the definition and boundaries of Torah, is another matter entirely
and is quite a way farther along in the chain of events.) One emphasizes this
point, because early in the twentieth century, it was common to suggest that
because of the appearance of certain terms in Saul's writing – "mysterion"
being the central one – Saul's entry to Gentile circles was facilitated by
his having adopted several concepts from Hellenistic "mystery religions."
In counterpoint, Arthur Darby Nock, Martin Hengel, Raymond Brown and
Devon Wiens all contributed to a demonstration that, in fact, Saul's ideas
and concepts, even those that appear most outré, have a sourcepoint in
late Second Temple Judahism.[44] That Saul's ideas may have sold particularly well to Gentiles because of their apparently-Hellenistic characteristics
does not mean that they were anything but Judahist in origin. Sometimes
independently-derived ideas coincide.

As far as we know, Yeshua of Nazareth never engaged a Gentile audience
in discussion (one excludes Pontius Pilate and the functionaries involved in
the Passion story, for that was a legal proceeding, apparently). Indeed, if
Mark (chapter seven) is to be believed, Yeshua compared the Gentiles to
dogs under the table. Eventually they are fed the crumbs (Mark 7:24–30), but
they are not partakers of the full banquet. Yet, despite his preaching only to
his co-religionists, I doubt if Yeshua's message would on that account have
been much different from Saul's. Probably Yeshua would have dealt in detail
with some technical matters of Halachah that Saul ignores, but otherwise he
would have pulled the same things out of his kitbag: a virtual calliope of Old
Testament references and his own choice of merry-go-round figures, icons
and symbols from the steaming mists of late Second Temple Judahism. How
he put these parts together we have little idea, but it must have been fully as
religiously revolutionary in nature as Saul's inventions, for it resulted in his
execution.[45]

5

The two men in the first century of the Common Era whom I most wish I
could have heard give a religious oration, uninterrupted by the heckling of
louts, unhampered by the pettifogging of small-minded lawyerly pedants, are
Yeshua of Nazareth and Hillel, the fountainheads of today's Christian and
Jewish faiths.

Instead, we have to settle for Saul, but that is no hardship.

Saul at his best was capable of celestial music. Take chapter thirteen of First Corinthians.

> *Though I speak with the tongues of men and of angels, and have not love, I am become as sounding brass, or a tinkling cymbal.*

This has all the marks of a polished speech that Saul has memorized for frequent recital.

> *And though I have the gift of prophecy, and understand all mysteries, and all knowledge; and though I have all faith, so that I could remove mountains, and have not love, I am nothing.*
>
> *And though I bestow all my goods to feed the poor, and though I give my body to be burned, and have not love, it profiteth me nothing.*

The medieval scholars who broke the Christian scriptures into chapters did a sensitive job of defining this piece as a distinct entity: Saul in his first letter to the Corinthians has effected a smooth job of construction in tying it to other material concerning the spiritual body of Christ and concerning various spiritual gifts; but this remains a separate item, a crown jewel, in a setting that is merely workmanlike.

> *Love suffereth long, and is kind; love envieth not; love vaunteth not itself, is not puffed up;*
>
> *Doth not behave itself unseemly, seeketh not her own, is not easily provoked, thinketh no evil;*
>
> *Rejoiceth not in iniquity, but rejoiceth in the truth;*
>
> *Beareth all things, believeth all things, hopeth all things, endureth all things.*

This is the only oration in all the scriptures, Hebrew and Christian, that is given to us in the speaker's own words. Elsewhere, noble sentiments are put in speakers' mouths, in the mode of the time. These may catch the general tone of the original, but there is no substitute for authenticity.

> *Love never faileth: but whether there be prophecies, they shall fail; whether there be tongues, they shall cease; whether there be knowledge, it shall vanish away.*

What is most compelling is the mixture of high faith with genuine modesty in the face of the *mysterium tremendum*:

> *For now we know in part, and we prophesy in part.*

> *But when that which is perfect is come, then that which is in part shall be done away.*

Only someone who held the Almighty's hand, like an infant in his parent's grasp, could confess:

> *When I was a child, I spake as a child, I understood as a child, I thought as a child: but when I became a man, I put away childish things.*
> *For now we see through a glass, darkly; but then face to face: now I know in part; but then shall I know even as also I am known.*

And only someone with immense faith, wisdom, and love could conclude:

> *And now abideth faith, hope, love, these three; but the greatest of these is love.*

There: that is Saul's Imitation of Christ.

Epilogue

This is an open-ended study. It has to be, for it rests on a central paradox of the Christian canon and the way that it is employed by its readers: if they seek in the Four Gospels for the historical Yeshua, they find instead the meta-figure of Jesus-the-Christ, immortal, invisible, God's co-equal device; and when they study carefully the letters of Saint Saul, they do so with the clearly discernible figure of a real person, Yeshua of Nazareth, outlined in shadow on each page.

Saul is a key that can unlock a door. What is on the other side of the door is still to be determined. One hopes that some few biblical scholars will address the Quest for the Historical Jesus in the way that I have suggested. If they do so, they certainly will find intellectual joy and genuine adventure and perhaps a great deal more.

Notes

CHAPTER ONE

1 There exists no physical description of the apostle that has any degree of authenticity. The most common "description" is taken from a mid-second century hagiography called the *Acts of Paul*. The author is unknown and was judged a fraud by prominent church fathers (notably Tertullian). The work, which may have been the product of a female author, was circulated in a truncated version known as the *Acts of Paul and Thekla*, the latter being a woman who allegedly acts as a co-missionary with the apostle and who is associated with many miracles. It is from this source that the imaginary, but compelling, description of Saul stems: "Small in stature, baldheaded, bowlegged, of vigorous physique, with meeting eyebrows and a slightly hooked nose, full of grace." And "at times he seemed a man and at times he had the face of an angel." (See: Michael Grant, *Saint Paul* (New York: Charles Scribner's Sons, 1976), 3; Dennis R. MacDonald, "Acts of Thekla," *Anchor Bible Dictionary* [hereafter *ABD*], 6:443–4; Arthur Darby Nock, *St. Paul* (New York: Harper and Brothers, l937), 233; Philip Sellew, "Acts of Paul," *ABD*, 5: 202–3.)

    Fourth-century descriptions have him wearing a pointed beard, his body bent and slight. And some fourth-century likenesses show him with a pointed beard and little hair, resembling an early version of Lenin. By the Byzantine era, a saintly nimbus is a standard feature (Grant, p. 3; Margaret M. Mitchell, "The Archetypal Image: John Chrysostom's Portraits of Paul," *Journal of Religion*, 75 (Jan. 1995), 15–43.

2 Dieter Georgi, "The Early Church: Internal Jewish Migration or New Religion," *Harvard Theological Review*, 88 (Jan. 1995), 42.

3 Joseph Klausner, *From Jesus to Paul* (tr. from Hebrew, William F. Stinespring) (New York: MacMillan, 1943), 270.

4 For a classic discussion of Wrede on this matter, see Johannes Weiss, *Paul and Jesus* (tr. from German by H.J. Chaytor) (London and New York: Harper and Brothers, 1909), esp. 1–35.

5 Hans Dieter Betz, "The Birth of Christianity as a Hellenistic Religion: Three Theories of Origin," *Journal of Religion*, 74 (Jan. 1994), 15–24.

6 Victor P. Furnish, "On Putting Paul in his Place," *Journal of Biblical Literature* (1994), 7.

7 Samuel Sandmel, *The Genius of Paul* (New York: Farrar, Strauss and Cudahy, 1958), 213.

8 This view is well summarized in Wolfgang Stegemann, "Paul and the Sexual Mentality of His World," *Biblical Theology Bulletin*, 23 (winter 1993), 162–7.

9 *Guardian*, 11 Sept. 1997.

10 Cullen Murphy, "What If? History's 'Parallel Universe,'" *Atlantic Monthly*, Aug. 1995, 16.

CHAPTER TWO

1 The discussion which follows is developed in considerably greater detail in my *Surpassing Wonder: The Invention of the Bible and the Talmuds*, chapters five through seven and the associated citations (430–51). Details of ancient texts cited are provided there as well as reference to the modern discussion which I have found most useful. In the present chapter, I will add a few more useful references and, of course, I will document direct quotations.

2 Sanhedrin, 10.6.29C (Neusner edition).

3 The classic statement of the relationship of Greek mystery religions to the Yahweh-faith was put forward by Erwin Goodenough. In some of his later formulations, he overstated his case, but in his great *By Light, Light. The Mystic Gospel of Hellenistic Judaism* (New Haven: Yale University Press, 1935), he put forward a carefully qualified view: "that the thesis of this book is that Judaism in the Greek Diaspora did, for at least an important minority, become primarily such a mystery" (5). One can hardly deny that in their pure forms the Greek mystery religions and Judahism were so different as to be from incompatible realms of religious experience; but in marginal areas where the two met, some followers of Judahism clearly adopted Greek practice: use of representational symbols, highly allegorical modes of thought, and the presentation of the divine mysteries in highly encoded forms. See Gary Lease, "Jewish Mystery Cults since Goodenough," *Aufstieg und Niedergang der Romischen Welt*, II, *Principat*, 20.2, 858–80.

The influence of the Septuagint – the Greek translation of the Hebrew scriptures, carried out largely by Judahist authorities in pre-Christian times – is a vexed matter. Although, after 70 CE Jewish authorities came to reject the Septuagint, before that time, it was accepted in Diaspora places of worship as being an authoritative text, just as was the Hebrew original. Significantly, some of the Pauline letters contain quotations from the Septuagint, not the Hebrew version. For a valuable popular discussion, see Melvin K. Peters, "Why Study the Septuagint?" *Biblical Archaeologist*, vol. 49 (Sept. 1986), 174–81.

One reason for emphasizing the importance of Hellenized Judahists in the pre-Destruction era (that is, individuals whose primary language was Greek and who frequently had no Aramaic – the everyday language of Eretz Israel – and little Hebrew – the holy language) is that although they are under-recorded severely in the Judahist religious literature of the period, Diaspora followers of Yahweh were, in all probability, the majority of the faith. A responsible (but by no means definitive) estimate is that in the time of Saul and Yeshua, there were as many as eight million Jewish persons in the world, three million of whom were within Eretz Israel, four million elsewhere within the Roman Empire, and another million in Babylon and other lands that were not subject to Roman rule (Alfredo M. Rabello, "The Legal condition of the Jews in the Roman Empire," *Aufstieg und Niedergang der Romischen Welt*, II, *Principat*, 13: 690–91).

As far as Saint Saul is concerned, the crucial point about the Diaspora-Eretz Israel dichotomy is to recognize its existence, but not to overemphasize it. The "Hellenic-Palestinian" split is easy to overread: it was just one of several lines of fissure in the highly complex tessellation of the Judahist faith in the first century of the Common Era. Saul cannot simply be dumped in the Diaspora and thus presumed to be uninformed or eccentric in his pre-conversion beliefs. See Victor P. Furnish, "On Putting Paul in his Place," *Journal of Biblical Literature*, (1994), 3–17.

Although I will not in this book make much of the point, it is worth recognizing that so long as one does not stereotype the Diaspora, Saul's writings give us not only our earliest view of the historical Yeshua, also the only direct witness "to a world of everyday Hellenistic Judaism now vanished." In other words, he is a major marker in the history of both the religions that grew out of the Yahweh-faith. See Alan F. Segal, *Paul the Convert. The Apostolate and Apostasy of Saul the Pharisee* (New Haven: Yale University Press, 1990), a fine study that has not received the recognition it deserves.

4 See *Surpassing Wonder*, chapter four and the associated notes on 429–30. Particularly useful is Jon D. Levenson, *Sinai and Zion. An Entry into the Jewish Bible* (San Francisco: Harper and Row, 1985).

5 A very important (and blessedly well-written) discussion is Mark S. Smith, *The Early History of God. Yahweh and the Other Deities in Ancient Israel* (San Francisco: Harper and Row, 1990).

6 Lease, 872. This follows a pattern that goes back to the earliest identifiable altar sites of the Yahweh-faith in Eretz Israel: the occurrence of female fertility figurines alongside the official altars of the Temple faith. Neil A. Silberman, "Land of the Bible," *Archaeology* (Sept-Oct 1998), 41.

7 Salo Baron, *A Social and Religious History of the Jews* (New York: Columbia University Press, 1937), vol. 2, 25, quoted by Lease, 872.

8 See the introduction and translation of 4 Maccabees by Hugh Anderson in James H. Charlesworth (ed.) *The Old Testament Pseudepigrapha* (New York: Doubleday, 1985) vol. 2: 531–64.

9 The Book of Jubilees, translated from Ethiopic by O.S. Wintermute, is found in Charlesworth, 2:35–142. Both the introduction and the text are models of scholarship. The text is especially useful because it is marginally annotated with references to the biblical texts the author of Jubilees employed, as well as cognate references to the Dead Sea Scrolls.

10 Norman Cohn sees the Book of Jubilees as "a true apocalypse." (Norman Cohn, *Cosmos, Chaos and the World to Come: The Ancient Roots of Apocalyptic Faith*, New Haven: Yale University Press, 1993, 177). This seems to me to expand beyond usefulness the term "apocalypse." Granted, there are prophetic elements in the work as there are in many parts of scripture. The overwhelming body of the text is a retelling (and a correction, from the author's viewpoint), of errors in the existing "Books of Moses."

11 J.C. Vanderkam, *Textual and Historical Studies in the Book of Jubilees*, vi, cited in Wintermute in Charlesworth, 2:41.

12 Florentino Garcia Martinez, *The Dead Sea Scrolls Translated* (Leiden: Brill, 1994), 468, 471, 472, 488–9, and 512.

13 Compare the fragments in Martinez, 238–45 with the full text in Charlesworth, 2:52–141.

14 See the listing of the contents of each cave in Martinez, 467–513.

15 R.H. Charles, *The Book of Jubilees, or The Little Genesis, translated from the Editor's Ethiopic Text* (London: Adam and Charles Black, 1902), in his "Introduction," lxxxiii-vi discusses the influence of Jubilees on the New Testament. In the letters of Saul that are usually called "authentic," he shows parallels between portions of Jubilees and the following: Rom. 4:15; 2 Cor. 5:17 and 6:18; Gal. 2:15, 3:17, and 5:12. These correspondences are real enough, but the individual sequences are so short that any of them could be the function of random convergences, rather than direct influence of Jubilees upon Saul. That said, one has to grant two points: (a) that it is statistically unlikely that all of the parallels are random and (b) more importantly, that Saul is quite at home with the really radical aspect of Jubilees, the willingness to improve upon the Torah of Moses.

16 Wintermute in Charlesworth, 2:43.

17 For a succinct summary of the mechanics of these two calendar systems, see John C. Kirby, *Ephesians. Baptism and Pentecost* (Montreal: McGill–Queen's University Press, 1968), 66–7.

18 For a discussion of the scattered type of demons, and scripture references thereto, see Joanne Kuemmerlin-McLean, "Demons: Old Testament," *ABD* 2:138–40.

19 Despite later efforts to retro-edit the third chapter of Genesis to turn the "serpent" into "Satan," this is unsuccessful. "Satan" in the primary unity, Genesis-Kings, is used as a term of insult to persons on earth, or as a verb indicating the leading of someone astray, or as a reference to a celestial being who, as Elaine Pagels notes, "appears in the Book of Numbers and in Job as one of God's obedient servants." Elaine Pagels, *The Origin of Satan* (New York: Random House, 1995), 39.

20 One assumes that, like any good inventor, the author of the Book of Jubilees here was using something that was conveniently to hand, a concept that must have been developing in Judahist culture since the return from the Babylonian exile. For differing views of whence this idea arose in post-exilic Judaism, compare Pagels, 35–62 and Cohn, 129–93.

21 Cohn, 182.

22 The Book of Enoch, translated, with an introduction by E. Isaac is found in Charlesworth, vol. 1: 5–89.

23 The usual dating of the Book of Similitudes is in the period 105–64 BCE (Charlesworth 1:7. See also Charlesworth, "The Concept of the Messiah in the Pseudepigrapha," in *Aufstieg und Niedergang der Romischen Welt*, II, *Principat*, 19.1, 206–07), but I suspect it is somewhat later, between 40 BCE and 70 CE. This is because it apparently contains a reference to the Parthian invasion of 40 BCE. The latest date is 70 CE, for there is no reference, direct or indirect, to the destruction of the Second Temple, and that was an event that no writer of apocalyptic literature could have ignored.

24 For an admirable survey of the Tanakh's usage of Moshiah, see Franz Hesse, "Chrio etc.," in Geoffrey W. Bromiley (ed. and trans.), *Theological Dictionary of the New Testament* [hereafter *TDNT*], 9 (1974), 497–509.

25 See the *Oxford English Dictionary*.

26 Richard A. Horsley, in "Popular Prophetic Movements at the Time of Jesus. Their Principal Features and Social Origins," *Journal for the Study of the New Testament*, 26 (Feb. 1986), 3–27, and in "Messianic Movements in Judaism," in *ABD* 4:791–7 argues that the term "Messianic," insofar as it is attached to a social movement, should refer only to those headed by a popularly-declared king, or "Messiah." This seems to me to run sharply counter to the usage of the term Moshiah in the Tanakh where it also refers to priests and prophets.

27 William Scott Green, "Messiah in Judaism: Rethinking the Question," in Neusner, Green, and Frerichs (eds.), *Judaisms and Their Messiahs at the Turn of the Christian Era* (Cambridge: Cambridge University Press, 1987), 6. The article (1–13) is a major *tour de force*.

28 I am here following James H. Charlesworth, "Introduction," James H. Charlesworth, *The Old Testament Pseudepigrapha*, 2:xxxii–iii.

In addition to the items here mentioned in the period between the Maccabean revolt and the destruction of the Temple, one should add the pre-Maccabean text, the Wisdom of Ben Sira, which, in 45:15, 46:13, and 48:8, speaks of anointing. In the first case it deals with Moses anointing Aaron, in the second of the anointing by the prophet Samuel of various princes, and in the third, the prophet Elijah is said to anoint prophets and kings. None of these is a Messianic reference.

29 The standard abbreviation for this text – CD – stems from its having been found in Cairo, and to the document's making reference to Damascus.

30 "Messianic Apocalypse," (4Q521) in Florentino Garcia Martinez (ed.), *The Dead Sea Scrolls Translated* (Leiden: E.J. Brill, 1994), 394. Unless otherwise noted, all Qumran quotations are from this edition.

31 A clear and brief statement of this interpretation is found in James C. Vanderkam, *The Dead Sea Scrolls Today* (Grand Rapids: William B. Eerdmans, 1994), 117–18.

32 Marinus de Jonge provides two further potential (albeit ambiguous) references to a Messiah in the Dead Sea fragments. ("Messiah," *ABD*, 4:783). For his earlier thinking on this matter, see his article, in Bromiley, *TDNT* 9:517–21.

33 Helmut Koester, "The Memory of Jesus' Death and the Worship of the Risen Lord," *Harvard Theological Review*, 91 (Oct. 1998), 338.

34 Geza Vermes, *Jesus the Jew. A Historian's Reading of the Gospels* (London: Fontana/Collins, 1976, origin ed., 1973), 222.

35 Ulrich Luz, *The Theology of the Gospel of Matthew*, translated by J. Bradford Robinson (Cambridge: Cambridge University Press, 1995, orig. German ed., 1993), 30.

36 The one significant exception to this is the New International Version (1973–87), a Protestant evangelical production. Recent Christian versions that accurately translate the Hebrew text include the New English Bible, the New Revised Standard Version, the Good News Bible, and the Revised English Bible.

37 The one possible exception is the "Aramaic Apocalypse" (4Q246) which talks of one who "will be called son of God, and they will call him son of the Most High" (col. 2:1, found in Martinez, 138). Some scholars believe that the lost fragments of the text contain the designation "Messiah." (Norman Golb, *Who Wrote the Dead Sea Scrolls? The Search for the Secret of Qumran*, London: Michael O'Mara Books, 1995, 379). This would mean that the equation of Son of God and of Messiah occurred, in at least one Judahist text, before the Christian scriptures merged the concepts. However, one must point out that until there is actual evidence for this imaginative interpolation into the Qumran fragment, one would do well to stay aloof: it would not take great imagination to claim that Messiah was missing from most of the Qumran fragments and could plausibly be added. Strange, though, that the references biblical scholars most wish to find are those that are least apt to be found, and thus must be interpolated.

38 In this discussion I am led by the excellent article, "Kingdom of God, Kingdom of Heaven," by Dennis C. Duling, *ABD*, 4:49–57.

39 Martinez (ed.), 138. Its numbering in the Qumran sequence is 4Q246. This is the same fragment into which some scholars interpolate the idea of Messiah. See note 36 above.

40 E.P. Sanders, *Paul and Palestinian Judaism. A Comparison of Patterns of Religion* (Philadelphia: Fortress Press, 1977), 423.

41 Ibid., 423.

42 Bruce Chilton and Jacob Neusner, *Judaism in the New Testament. Practices and Beliefs* (London: Routledge, 1995), 23.

43 Because some present-day Jewish groups believe that a "third temple" will be reconstructed on the Temple Mount, and on the same dimensions as earlier temples (which earlier one is a matter of dispute), a good deal of research has been done on the earlier structures and much of it now is augmented by leading-edge computer graphics. For a selection of such graphics, see the special issue of *Eretz* (May-June 1996). As is usual in such exercises, the messy details are not included: the killing rooms, incineration structures, and blood drainage facilities.

44 I am avoiding entirely the questions of the distribution and functions of the synagogue or *proseuche*, because the evidence at present available can only lead to indeterminate conclusions. Indeed, the history of the development of the synagogue as an institution is one of the least documented aspects of the evolution of what we today call the Jewish faith. Certainly institutions that can be called "synagogues" without anachronism existed before the destruction of the Second Temple. Significantly, they are not mentioned in Ezra-Nehemiah which is the last of the Tanakh's post-exilic historical books to be written. Nor, in 1 and 2 Maccabees, wherein the persecution and epic vandalism of Antiochus Epiphanes in the second century before the Common Era is chronicled, do synagogues find mention. Yet, some sort of social gathering place must have existed, particularly in Diaspora communities, and it is hard to envision such a meeting place, even if merely a large private house, not having religious usage: where, after all, could Diaspora Jews, and those in Palestine who lived far from the Temple, read and pray together? Hence, the evidence is very confusing. By the beginning of the Common Era there certainly existed synagogues all over the Diaspora: the New Testament is an excellent witness (that most valued of sources, a third-party witness), for Saul and some of the other apostles preached frequently in synagogues in Diaspora lands. Within Palestine, synagogues certainly existed: one scholar has estimated that as many as 360 synagogues existed in Jerusalem itself, and this on the eve of the Temple's destruction. A more sceptical scholar points to reference to over fifty synagogues in literary sources. Yet, in sharp contrast, there are only four actual archaeological sites within Palestine that have been found that can clearly be identified as synagogues. The problem, it would appear, is simple, but very frustrating: if (as seems to be the case) synagogues were either private houses used on Shabbath and on festival days for religious observances, or if they were religious-cum-community centres built on the model of a private house, most of them will have left no physical evidence that distinguishes them from everyday vernacular structures. Whatever the historical problems, we should not lose sight of the central fact that synagogues were not mini-temples and did not in any way rival the Jerusalem ritual centre.

See: Rachel Hachlili, "Diaspora Synagogues," *ABD*, 6:260–3; Rachel Hachlili, "The Origin of the Synagogue: A Re-Assessment," *Journal for the Study of*

Judaism, vol. 28 (Feb. 1997), 34–47; Howard Clark Kee, "The Transformation of the Synagogue after 70 CE: Its Import for Early Christianity," *New Testament Studies*, 36 (1990), 1–24; Eric M. Meyers, "Synagogue," *ABD*, 6:251–8; Louis I. Rabinowitz, "Synagogue," *Encyclopaedia Judaica*, 15:579–83; "World's oldest synagogue unearthed near Jericho," *Jerusalem Post* (Int. ed.) 11 April 1998 (The proposed dating is 70–50 BCE).

45 In roughly 145 BCE the legitimate high priestly line set up a rival temple at Leontopolis (*Encyclopaedia Judaica*, 12:1402–04).

46 See the "Temple Scroll," translated in Martinez, 154–84.

47 Jonathan Kirsch. *Moses. A Life* (New York: Ballantine Books, 1998), 392n27.

48 Koester, "The Memory ...," 343.

49 Jacob Neusner (quoting a translation by Judah Goldin) in *First-Century Judaism in Crisis. Yohanan ben Zakkai and the Renaissance of Torah* (New York: Abingdon Press, 1975), 146–7.

50 See Craig Koester, "The Origin and Significance of the Flight to Pella Tradition," *Catholic Biblical Quarterly*, vol. 52 (Jan. 1989), 90–106.

51 The influence of Jerusalem on post-70 Christianity did not suddenly cease, but certainly it waned. For an important discussion of post-70 "Jewish Christianity," see Roy A. Pritz, *Nazarene Jewish Christianity from the end of the New Testament Period until its Disappearance in the Fourth Century* (Jerusalem: Magnes Press, 1988). See also: Craig C. Hill, *Hellenists and Hebrews. Reappraising Division within the Earliest Church* (Minneapolis: Fortress Press, 1992); Gerd Luedemann, *Heretics. The Other Side of Early Christianity* (Louisville: Westminster/John Knox Press, 1996), 52–60; Wayne A. Meeks and Robert L. Wilken, *Jews and Christians in Antioch in the First Four Centuries of the Common Era* (Missoula: Scholars Press, for the Society of Biblical Literature, 1978); Jacob Neusner, *Judaism in the Matrix of Christianity* (Philadelphia: Fortress Press, 1986); Jack T. Sanders, "The First Decades of Jewish-Christian Relations: The Evidence of the New Testament (Gospel and Acts)," *Aufstieg und Niedergang der Romischen Welt*, II, *Principat*, 26.3, 1938–78; M.D. Goulder, "The Jewish-Christian Mission, 30–130," ibid, 1979–2037; Joan E. Taylor, *Christians and the Holy Places. The Myth of Jewish-Christian Origins* (Oxford: Clarendon Press, 1993).

52 The literature on the Pharisees is immense. At present, in scholarly circles (as distinct from confessional ones), the reigning viewpoints are those of two opposing giants, Jacob Neusner and E.P. Sanders. Each has written a good deal and their work is best approached through a search-engine. However, as the most compelling historical work of each, I would recommend: Jacob Neusner, *The Rabbinic Traditions about the Pharisees before 70* (Leiden: E.J. Brill, 3 vols, 1971), and E.P. Sanders, *Jewish Law from Jesus to the Mishnah. Five Studies* (London: SCM Press, 1990). Neusner's post-1971 work, which is scrutinized in Sanders's 1990 volume, is a large corpus and cannot be easily captured. However, as far as his specific points of difference with Sanders are concerned, see Neusner's,

"Mr. Sanders's Pharisees and Mine," *Bulletin for Biblical Research*, 2 (1992), 143–69.

53 I can only apologetically refer the reader yet again to *Surpassing Wonder* where this process is placed in the context of a repetitive pattern in Jewish history, namely the animated engagement in creating "scriptures" at times of trauma. Fortunately, the most influential of these stimulus-response patterns involved a conjunction uncommon in biblical studies, namely a set of independently-attested primary causes that can be tightly related to text-creation. These instances are (a) the formation of the Genesis-Kings unity as a response to the destruction of Solomon's Temple, (b) the focussing and compression of Pharisaism into Rabbinic Judaism which begins in earnest after the Temple's destruction and (c) the creation of the Four Gospels in response to the same stimulus.

The chief reason that I hope the reader will find time to look at the larger argument in which the present Christian case is situated is that it brings us back to the basic point: that it is an historical mistake – and, I think, an invitation to cultural amnesia – to press to an ever-earlier date the separation of the faiths that we know today as Christianity and Rabbinic Judaism, and to minimize Christianity's Semitic foundation.

CHAPTER THREE

1 Herbert Butterfield. *The Whig Interpretation of History* (London: Bell, 1931).
2 David Flusser, *Jewish Sources in Early Christianity* (trans. from Hebrew, John Glucker) (Tel-Aviv: MOD Books, 1989), 15.
3 *Theos* is also used to refer to Yeshua (see John 20:28), which makes possible a melding of meaning on this term similar to that which occurs with "Lord."
4 George Howard, "Tetragrammaton in the New Testament," *ABD* 6:392. Howard speculates that the earliest versions of the New Testament documents contained "Yahweh" in quotations from the Hebrew scriptures and that these references were overwritten by later scribes, perhaps in the mid-second century.
5 T.J. Leary, "Paul's Improper Name," *New Testament Studies*, 38 (1992), 467–9.
6 Leary, 468–9.
7 This holds whatever one thinks the somatic or psychological problem may have been that the apostle refers to as his "thorn in the flesh, the messenger of Satan to buffet me" (2 Cor. 12:7). Paul's homophobia, when combined with this coded expression of his problem, has provided an opportunity for imaginative sub-Freudian analysis.
8 Arnold Jacob Wolf, "Jesus as an Historical Jew," *Judaism*, 46 (summer 1997), 377.
9 Donald A. Hagner, "Paul in Modern Jewish Thought," in Donald A. Hagner and Murray J. Harris (eds.), *Pauline Studies: Essays presented to Professor F.F. Bruce on his 70th Birthday* (Exeter: Paternoster Press, 1980), 143. For the most

impassioned argument against this emerging Jewish viewpoint, see Hyam Maccoby, *The Mythmaker. Paul and the Invention of Christianity* (London: Weidenfeld and Nicolson, 1986). Maccoby's view is that Jesus and his followers were Pharisees; that Jesus had no intention of founding a new religion; that Paul never was a "Pharisee rabbi," but a religious adventurer who founded Christianity by taking it away from "normal Judaism."

10 Pliny, *Epistles*, 10:96–97; Tacitus, *Annales*, 15:44.

Slightly before Tacitus, Suetonius (*Claudius*, 25:4) had referred historically to a group of the 60s CE, who were the followers of a certain charismatic, Chrestos. This may be a garbled reference to Christians, but the case is very unclear.

Tacitus, and several of the church fathers, later refer to Nero as having perse- cuted Christians in 64 CE, blaming them for the fire of Rome. It is not clear, however (a), if the name "Christian" was used in Nero's time or (b) whether Nero viewed them as a separate religion or rather as a particularly troublesome Jewish sect, or merely as a convenient (and very unlucky) scapegoat, among the many Judahist factions.

11 Dieter Georgi, "The Early Church: Internal Jewish Migration or New Religion?" *Harvard Theological Review*, 88 (Jan. 1995), 39–40; Michael J. Wilkins, "Christian," *ABD* 1:925–6.

12 Chapter 29 of Epiphanes's *Panarion* is translated in Ray A. Pritz, *Nazarene Jewish Christianity. From the end of the New Testament Period until its disappear- ance in the fourth century* (Jerusalem: Magnes Press, the Hebrew University, 1988), 30–5.

13 Ibid., 32–3.

14 Leland J. White, " 'Judaeans' or 'Jews?' – Does it make a difference to us?" *Biblical Theology Bulletin*, 25 (Summer 1995), 54.

CHAPTER FOUR

1 S.G.F. Brandon, *The Fall of Jerusalem and the Christian Church. A Study of the Effects of the Jewish Overthrow of AD 70 on Christianity* (London: SPCK, 1957), xix. See also 249–51.

2 An example of the kind of useful skepticism of "liberal" scholarship is Michael J. Wilkins and J.P. Moreland (eds.), *Jesus Under Fire* (Grand Rapids: Zondervan Publishing House, 1995).

3 An admirable summary is E.P. Sanders, *The Historical Figure of Jesus* (London: Penguin Books, 1993), 63–6.

4 Flavius Josephus, *Jewish War*, 7:7.

5 Aileen Goulding, *The Fourth Gospel and Jewish Worship. A study of the relation of St. John's gospel to the ancient Jewish lectionary system* (Oxford: Clarendon Press, 1960).

6 The reader may notice that I do not in this book attempt to apply directly to the life of Yeshua of Nazareth references in classical Rabbinic literature to him. This is not because I am unfamiliar with the sources nor because (with very strong compensation for their provenance and purpose) they are not valuable for recreating the mental world of the pre-70 CE Pharisees, the forebears of the Rabbis. However, the direct references to Yeshua of Nazareth in the Rabbinic literature are of no direct historical value whatsoever. They are late (200 CE in the form we have them at the earliest, but mostly two or three centuries later) and they are so *partis pris* as to be historically unindicative, save of the fact that the emerging Jewish faith was well aware of the emerging Christian faith.

   Within the Rabbinic literature, the Babylonian Talmud has the most extensive references to Christianity and to Yeshua of Nazareth. The instances in the Babylonian Talmud of references to Christianity that can be identified as such, with a high degree of probability, are as follows: Shabbath, 116a (Soncino Edition, 571, see *n*3); Sukkah, 48b (Sonc. 227); Ta'anith, 27b (Sonc. 145); Yebamoth, 16a (Sonc. 87, see *n*8); Sanhedrin, 58b (Sonc. 399), 61b (Sonc. 417, see *n*5), 90b (Sonc. 604–605), 97a (Sonc. 656), 99a (Sonc. 672); Abodah Zarah, 27b (Sonc. 137 and 85*n*3), 48a (Sonc.239).

   The references that seem with a high degree of probability to be to Jesus or to his immediate family are as follows: Hagigah, 4b (Sonc. 17, see *n*11); Sotah, 47a (Sonc. 246, see *n*3); Gittin, 57a (Sonc. 261, see *n*4); Sanhedrin, 43a (Sonc. 281, see *n*4–7), 106a (Sonc.725, see *n*5), 107b (Sonc. 735, see *n*4); Abodah Zarah, 16b-17a (Sonc. 84–85).

   I would emphasize that none of these references to Jesus is of any use in the so-called quest for the historical Jesus. They are, however, useful as an indication of what the religious leaders of the Babylonian Jewish community of the fourth-through-sixth centuries considered worth recording from amidst the welter of rumour about the founder of the Jesus-faith.

7 "Josephus" (Joseph ben Mattathias was his Hebrew name and Flavius Josephus his Roman name, but "Josephus" is the general and unambiguous usage) came of a Hasmonean family, was well educated in both Judahism and in Graeco-Roman culture. As a young man in his late twenties, he served as a general on the northern front in the 66–73 war against the Romans. Then, by a passage of diplomacy not well revealed in his writings, he found favour in the Roman imperial court and spent the rest of his life on a Roman pension, writing three significant books plus his own *Life*: (1) his history of the war that resulted in the crushing of the Second Temple religion; (2) his *Jewish Antiquities* which is a reprise of Jewish history from the Creation onwards; and (3) a strong reply against *Apion*, an anti-Semitic tract of his time. The key to understanding Josephus is that his works were written after 70 CE and therefore they have the knowledge that defeat was the seemingly-last page of Jewish history. Yet,

Josephus is spiritedly pro-Yahweh and believes there is something beyond defeat.

Josephus's writings are important in both Jewish and Christian history. In Jewish history they are the only continuous source running from the beginning of Greek rule until early Rabbinic times. They fill a crucial gap. Similarly, Josephus's writings provide a view of life in the period just before and after the birth of Jesus that is unrivalled. It is not perfect, but nothing approaches it in density and texture. Yet Josephus received very little attention from Jewish scholars until the later nineteenth and the twentieth centuries. For the most part, he was preserved through Christian scholarship. Why the Rabbis of the second through sixth centuries should have been so repelled by him is difficult to see. (Having said that, it is true that as a retired Jewish general, living on a Roman pension, he was not above reproach personally, nor, in his explication of controversial events was he apt to blame Rome directly: he usually found a convenient third party, neither main-line Jewish, nor Roman, to blame.)

In the present era we are blessed. The Loeb Library edition of his writings is conveniently available. The depth of twentieth-century scholarship on Josephus is extraordinary. Louis H. Feldman's volume of 1,055 pages, *Josephus and Modern Scholarship (1937–1980)* (Berlin: Walter de Gruyter, 1984) is not only comprehensive in its listings, but provides thumbnail sketches of most of the important scholarly articles.

That scholarly richness recognized, the curious thing about the majority of Josephus scholarship as practised by individuals who read him for religious information (as distinct from classicists who are using him as a secular source) is its overwhelmingly whiny tone. Josephus is constantly being treated as if he wrote an awkward midrash, or some primitive prolegomena to the rabbinical era, when, in fact, he was an historian, and one of a type with whom we are well acquainted: the retired general, well educated, who spends his retirement years trying to explain to himself why his own life, and the life of his own people, developed the way they did. His most obvious counterpart in our own century is Winston Churchill, whose five-volume history of World War II is very similar to Josephus's *The Jewish War*. Like Churchill, Josephus writes well, using borrowed documents and research assistants extensively. Generally, though, his standard of accuracy is higher than Churchill's, for Josephus, being on the losing side of his war, got the big picture with a sharper, if crueller, accuracy than did Churchill, whose vision was obscured by the cigar clouds of victory. Further, in his *Jewish Antiquities* Josephus tells us certain things with a richness of detail that is unprecedented: we know more about the court and doings of Herod the Great (hardly a minor figure for either Jews or Christians) than we do about any comparable Greek or Roman figure of antiquity; and through Josephus we know more about Palestine than about any other Roman province.

As long as we remember that Josephus was primarily an historian and judge him that way – instead of demanding that he be a theologian, exegete, or Jewish apologist – then he is of immense value. His work requires the same kind of fine-tuning any historian's work demands: he was, after all, in secure retirement, writing an average of ten or eleven lines of Greek prose a day, and enjoying life. Factual errors of course demand correction, and unconscious attitudes require delineation, but always with the knowledge that in Josephus's writings we have a tiny miracle. Without them most of what we see stretching from the conquest of Palestine by Alexander of Macedon to the levelling of Jerusalem would be unconnected swirls of dust, interrupted by mounds of out-of-context texts – the Qumran library, the Book of Daniel, the Synoptic Gospels – which are difficult enough of comprehension without their being relieved of context. For a sensible appreciation of Josephus, see P. Bilde, "The Causes of the Jewish War according to Josephus," *Journal for the Study of Judaism*, 10 (Dec. 1979), 179–202.

8 There is an immense literature on John-the-Baptizer. Items I have found particularly useful include: Paul W. Hollenbach, "The conversion of Jesus: From Jesus the Baptizer to Jesus the Healer," *Aufstieg und Niedergang der Romischen Welt*, II, *Principat*, 25.1, 196–219; Jerome Murphy-O'Connor, "John the Baptist and Jesus: History and Hypotheses," *New Testament Studies*, 36 (1990), 359–74; Charles H.H. Scobie, *John the Baptist* (London: SCM press, 1964); Ben Zion Wacholder, "The Timing of Messianic Movements and the Calendar of Sabbatical Cycles," *Hebrew Union College Annual*, 46 (1975), 201–18 (see esp. 213–15); Robert L. Webb, *John the Baptizer and Prophet. A Socio-Historical Study* (Sheffield: JSOT, 1991); Walter Wink, *John the Baptist in the Gospel Tradition* (Cambridge: Cambridge University Press, 1968).

9 The Slavonic versions of Josephus's *Jewish War* also have several obviously-interpolated references to Yeshua. See the third volume of the Loeb edition, 648–52, 655, 657–8.

10 A.D. Nock, *Conversion. The Old and the New in Religion from Alexander the Great to Augustine of Hippo* (Oxford:Clarendon Press, 1933), 7.

11 Although I am quite skeptical of the excessively enthusiastic effort to find James-the-Brother-of Jesus in every nook and cranny of the early Common Era, the reader should be aware of the on-going project of Robert Eisenman, the first massive volume of which is *James the Brother of Jesus. The Key to Unlocking the Secrets of Early Christianity and the Dead Sea Scrolls* (New York: Viking, 1996).

12 Jurgen Becker, *Paul. Apostle to the Gentiles* (trans. from German by O.C. Dean, Jr.) (Louisville: Westminster/John Knox Press, 1993), 7.

13 Readers who have been schooled in traditional Roman Catholic historiography, wherein Peter is made the great figure of the Gentile church, will note that I do not find him to be such in the historical record. His existence is not recorded in third-party contemporary sources; his position in Jerusalem is very much subordinate to Yacov's; much of what he is traditionally credited with by New Testament readers

depends on the accuracy of the identification of "Cephas" with Peter, an equation
that is not nearly as solid as is usually assumed; and, in any case, Saul has as
strong a claim to be the founder of the church in Rome (his missionaries having
been sent there) as does Peter. The New Testament does not affirm that Peter ever
resided in Rome, or was martyred or buried there. This is not to gainsay that, once
Jerusalem was levelled, the importance of whomever was in charge in Rome
would become critical for Christianity and, possibly, central. Thus, later bishops
of Rome projected into the post-70 era an apostolic founder. (For the papal case,
put forward with restraint, see Daniel Wm. O'Connor, *Peter in Rome. The
Literary, Liturgical, and Archeological Evidence* (New York: Columbia University Press, 1969). For late-first century evidence (c. 95) that Saint Saul was seen as
being equal, or exceeding Saint Peter in his authority as the founder of Roman
Christianity, see the Letter of St. Clement of Rome (usually called "First
Clement"), Clement being the third successor of St. Peter as bishop of Rome. In
that letter, "Pauline" texts and activities are frequently instanced, those of Peter
hardly at all. See the translation in *The Apostolic Fathers* (ed.) Francis X. Glimm,
et al. (Washington D.C.: Catholic University of America Press, 1946), I, 9–58.

14 Koester's career, his bibliography, and his most noteworthy ideas are easily
approached through Birger A. Pearson (ed.) *The Future of Early Christianity.
Essays in Honor of Helmut Koester* (Minneapolis: Fortress Press, 1991). The
reference to "the German armed forces" (apparently something different from the
Nazi army) is found on p. xi.

15 Koester's views on Secret Mark's authenticity are summarised in his *Ancient
Christian Gospels. Their History and Development* (Philadelphia: Trinity Press
International, 1990), 293–303.

16 John Dominic Crossan, *The Historical Jesus. The Life of a Mediterranean Jewish
Peasant* (San Francisco: Harper 1991), 328–33.

17 John Dominic Crossan, *The Birth of Christianity. Discovering what happened
in the years immediately after the execution of Jesus* (San Francisco: Harper,
1998), 115.

18 Robert W. Funk "and the Jesus Seminar," *The Acts of Jesus. The Search for the
Authentic Deeds of Jesus* (San Francisco: Harper, 1998), 116–17. The Jesus
Seminar was predisposed to be open-minded to the point of credulity about extra-
canonical texts, so one suspects that, by whatever route, the Fellows would have
endorsed Secret Mark. However, the apparent route of their coming to their affirmation of its authenticity is interesting. When the Seminar published its *The Complete Gospels. Annotated Scholars Version* (Sonoma: Polebridge Press, first ed.,
1992, second ed. 1994), edited by Robert J. Miller, the volume included a translation of the text of Secret Mark and a fulsome affirmation of the document's
authenticity: "… there is almost unanimous agreement among Clementine scholars that the letter is authentic." (1994: 408.) For some reason, the Seminar did not
by-line the names of the translators and editors of the various "complete gospels,"

nor include their names in the table of contents. However, a list of contributors makes it clear that the Seminar's work on Secret Mark was done by Helmut Koester (1994:xiii).

19 The comparison is not made flippantly. The obvious inauthenticity of the Hitler diaries and the pontificating authentication of them were remarkably similar to the case of Secret Mark. See Charles Hamilton, *The Hitler Diaries. Fakes that Fooled the World* (Kentucky: University of Kentucky Press, 1991). Despite the book's subtitle, the persons most fooled were the more professorially self-important, particularly the risible Professor Hugh Trevor-Roper (later Lord Dacre), a figure out of an Evelyn Waugh novel, and the hard-bitten editors of *Newsweek* who bought the package (see special issue of *Newsweek*, 2 May 1983).

20 *The Complete Gospels* (1994), 411.

21 See Crossan, *The Historical Jesus*, 412.

22 The scarcity of what would be appropriate scholarly skepticism should not obviate the fact that a few scholars had the good sense and spine to resist the tide. Among the skeptics, the most common (and least career-threatening) objection was to accept that the manuscript indeed was ancient, but to argue that it was an early fraud. Thus: Patrick W. Skehan in the *Catholic Historical Review*, 60 (1971), 451–3; and Eric Osborn, "Clement of Alexandria: A Review of Research, 1958–1982," *Second Century Journal*, 3 (1983), 223–5. The only scholar immediately to suss out the spurious nature of the entire enterprise was Quentin Quesnell, "The Mar Saba Clementine: A Question of Evidence," *Catholic Biblical Quarterly*, 37 (1975), 48–67. Amidst a variety of technical arguments, Quesnell kept hitting the key point: why is there no physical evidence that the alleged manuscript exists? Probably because of fear of litigation, Quesnell did not state the obvious inference: that the whole thing was a forgery. The editors of the *Catholic Biblical Quarterly* gave Smith a direct right of reply (38 [1976], 196–9), wherein he denied having invented the text and Quesnell in counter-reply skittered away from alleging fraud and was satisfied to suggest "that a person who introduces an exciting new manuscript find to the world had the basic responsibility to make the manuscript available for scientific examination" (200).

That Morton Smith had pretty well scared off his critics was made clear in 1982, when Helmut Koester, editor of the *Harvard Theological Review*, invited him to summarize the state of the debate on Secret Mark. He did so in "Clement of Alexandria and Secret Mark: The Score at the End of the First Decade," *Harvard Theological Review*, 75 (Oct. 1982), 449–62. Not surprisingly, Smith summarized the situation favourably. "In sum, most scholars would attribute the letter to Clement, though a substantial minority are in doubt" (451). The only alternative considered was that the letter was "Pseudo-Clementine," meaning that it was an ancient pseudepigraphical effort.

The comical effect (were these guys actually being paid by academic institutions?) of having Professor Morton Smith sit as judge on the case of the

Mysterious Missing Letter of Professor Morton Smith, was heightened by a "terminal note" to Smith's apologia which invoked the most powerful secular endorsement Smith could garner. Smith wrote "In correspondence [about an article he was writing on Secret Mark] Professor Koester made the following statement which he has given me permission to quote: 'If the letter is 'Pseudo-Clement,' – and I don't think it is – it must be ancient and the fragment *Secret Mark* that it quotes (as well as the reference to the Carpocratians etc.) must be genuine. The piece of *Secret Mark* fits the Markan trajectory so well that a forgery is inconceivable' " (459).

Thus, Secret Mark has of its own momentum cruised into most of the work on the Historical Jesus and upon early Christian texts conducted in the 1980s and 1990s. Most "liberal" scholars unreflectively accept it and the more rigorous scholars who see it as a chimera, simply ignore it as a distraction. The field of the Quest for the Historical Jesus would be considerably clarified if (a) someone would definitively drive a stake into the heart of this particular scholarly vampire and thereafter (b) those scholars who have affirmed the work would publicly recant and then examine how they might recalibrate their own scholarly standards so as to avoid being gulled in the future.

As a model of the sort of scholarly palinode that is required, see Jacob Neusner's "Foreword" to the reprint of Birger Gerhardsson's *Memory and Manuscript. Oral Tradition and Written Transmission in Rabbinic Judaism* ... (Grand Rapids: William B. Eerdmans, 1994). When Gerhardsson's study of transmission had appeared thirty years earlier, Neusner – then an acolyte of Morton Smith – had accepted and retailed a scathing review of Gerhardsson's work. Now, in his mature years, he made amends, writing a handsome, balanced introduction to the Swedish scholar's work, pointing out where he himself had erred. As a minor part of that exercise, he provided a fairly definitive description of his mentor.

> Smith made his career as a ferocious critic of others. Smith thereby surrounded himself with a protective wall of violent invective; what he wished to hide, and for a while succeeded in hiding, was the intellectual vacuum within.
> In all Smith wrote three important contributions to scholarship, one [*Palestinian Parties*] a model of argument and analysis though broadly ignored in the field to which it was devoted, another a pseudo-critical but in fact intellectually slovenly and exploitative monograph [*Jesus the Magician*] and the third an outright fraud.

Right: fraud.

23 Myriad surveys of the Quest are available. Useful discussions which reflect on the nature of the Quest include: William Baird, *History of New Testament Research* (Minneapolis: Fortress Press, 2 vols, 1992); Paula Fredriksen, *From Jesus to Christ. The Origins of the New Testament Images of Jesus* (New Haven: Yale

University Press, 1988); Clive Marsh, "Quests of the Historical Jesus in New Historicist Perspective," *Biblical Interpretation*, 5 (Oct. 1997), 403–37; Stephen D. Moore, "History after Theory? Biblical Studies and the New Historicism," *Biblical Interpretation*, 5 (Oct 1997), 289–99.

24 John Dominic Crossan sees the Epistle of Barnabas as prior to the Gospel of Mark, and, by implication, pre-Destruction (Crossan, *The Historical Jesus*, 376). This is hard to credit as the epistle (16:3) refers to the destruction of the Temple. David Curry Treat, "Epistle of Barnabas," *ABD*, 1:610–14.

25 Robert W. Funk, Roy W. Hoover, and the Jesus Seminar, *The Five Gospels. The Search for the Authentic Words of Jesus* (New York: MacMillan, 1993).

26 The Gospel of Thomas had previously (1992, rev. ed.1994) been published by the Seminar in *The Complete Gospels* with an introduction by Stephen J. Patterson. The relevant scholarly context on pre-70 dating is found in the writing of James M. Robinson, one of the Seminar's most influential members, who held that the Gospel of Thomas was at least as old as the hypothetical gospel "Q," which can be taken to mean that (except for Sauls's epistles) it is the oldest document in the Christian tradition. See James M. Robinson, "On Bridging the Gulf from Q to the Gospel of Thomas (or Vice Versa)," in C. Hedrick and R. Hodgson (eds), *Nag Hammadi, Gnosticism, and Early Christianity* (Peabody: Hendrickson, 1986), 162–3. Further, Helmet Koester, the unseen presence at all such debates, had declared that some of the material came from the middle of the first century. (See note 33 below.)

27 Ron Cameron, "Gospel of Thomas," in *ABD*, 6:535. "Didymus" is Greek for twin, and "Thomas" is a second-name. Therefore, Judas, or Jude, is the focal name.

28 I find the argument of Christopher Tuckett completely convincing. He demonstrates that, with the possible exception of the Gospel of Thomas, the Christian documents at Nag Hammadi are based on the Synoptic Gospels. Thus, they can have no value as independent attestations of the life of Yeshua. See Christopher Tuckett, *Nag Hammadi and the Gospel Tradition* (Edinburgh: Clark, 1986). Two points should be here made explicit. First, no judgement is implied about the spiritual or theological value of the Nag Hammadi material, merely that it has no applicability to the historical question at hand. Second, I am not engaged in ascribing-value-by-contrast. That is, merely because the Nag Hammadi texts are not here of historical value, that does not mean that the New Testament materials, on which they depend, necessarily are of historical value. That is an entirely separate issue.

29 The fragments, found at Oxyrhynchus in Egypt, are dated by their distinctive calligraphy.

30 Found in translation in *The Five Gospels* and in *The Complete Gospels*.

31 The scholarly literature which leads to this conclusion is summarized in Meier, 1:124–40.

32 *The Five Gospels*, 474.

33 Stephen J. Patterson, "Introduction" to the Gospel of Thomas in *The Complete Gospels*, 302–03.

34 *The Five Gospels*, 474. The major proponent of this idea has been Helmut Koester. See his *Ancient Christian Gospels. Their History and Development* (Philadelphia: Trinity Press International, 1990), 75–128.

35 Meier, 1:122–3.

36 Ibid., 1:123.

CHAPTER FIVE

1 The observation is that of Arthur J. Dewey, who provides an introduction and translation of the Gospel of Peter in Robert J. Miller (ed.), *The Complete Gospels. Annotated Scholars Version* (Sonoma: Polebridge Press, sec. ed., 1994), 399–407.

2 See John P. Meier, *A Marginal Jew. Rethinking the Historical Jesus* (New York: Doubleday, 1991), 1:116–18, and 146–7.

3 John Dominic Crossan, *The Cross that Spoke. The Origins of the Passion Narrative* (San Francisco: Harper and Row, 1988), passim. See also Crossan, *The Historical Jesus. The Life of a Mediterranean Jewish Peasant* (San Francisco: Harper and Row, 1991), 462–6. See also Crossan, *The Birth of Christianity. Discovering What Happened in the Years Immediately after the Execution of Jesus* (San Francisco: Harper and Row, 1998), 115–16 and 487–93.

4 Crossan in *The Birth of Christianity* (481–525) defends his views against some of his critics. The effort is most charitably described as being garrulous to the point of incontinence.

5 Found in *The Complete Gospels*, 180–93. See also Robert T. Fortna, *The Fourth Gospel and Its Predecessor* (Philadelphia: Fortress Press, 1988).

6 *The Complete Gospels*, 180n.

7 Fortna, "Introduction," in *The Complete Gospels*, 177.

8 L. Cope, cited in Robert T. Fortna, "Signs/Semeia Source," in *ABD*, 6:19. Incidentally, in this *ABD* article Fortna is much more controlled than in *The Complete Gospels*.

9 Robert Kysar, "The Gospel of John," in *ABD*, 3:918.

10 Reference to the semi-legendary "Council of Yavneh" whereby, it is alleged in c. 90, remnant Pharisees met and codified the rules for their scriptures and for membership in the emergent Jewish faith, seems to me of no value. The argument is that the "anti-Jewish" tone of John, and the need for a liturgical system that would be similar to the Jewish calendar, but which would replace it, point to the precipitating events for John's Gospel having been after Yavneh. The only drawbacks are (1) that the Council of Yavneh is now considered to be largely a fictive occasion (a projection onto Jewish events of the Christian conciliar model of decision-making) and therefore it could not have the causal impact that is suggested; and (2) it assumes a leisurely pace in the evolution of the Rabbinic Jewish

faith that is not historically verifiable, nor consonant with what is known about that faith's response to the great Destruction.

11 For the prevailing view, see E.P. Sanders, *Historical Figure of Jesus* (London: Penguin, 1993), 57. The minority viewpoint, that John is a superior historical source, is held by several scholars, some of them highly distinguished: for example, Fergus Millar ("Reflections on the Trial of Jesus," in Philip R. Davies and Richard I. White, *A Tribute to Geza Vermes*, Sheffield: JSOT, 1990, 363) and Elaine Pagels (*The Origin of Satan*, New York: Random House, 1995, 107).

12 The present state of opinion is summarized by Meier (1:46) and by Kysar (*ABD*, 3:919).

13 What I term the Synoptic Puzzle is usually termed in biblical circles the "Synoptic Problem." Not only does that unfortunate term make the issue seem as if it were some epidermal blemish that needed to be cleared up, but it misses the great pleasure, indeed joy, that many scholars obviously have found in trying to solve this, one of history's most important textual puzzles.

14 E.P. Sanders and Margaret Davies, *Studying the Synoptic Gospels* (London: SCM Press, 1989), 16–17.

15 Richard Heard, *An Introduction to the New Testament* (New York: Harper and Brothers, 1950), 54.

16 Joseph A. Fitzmyer, "The Priority of Mark and the 'Q' Source in Luke," in his *Jesus and Man's Hope* (Pittsburgh: Pittsburgh Theological Seminary, 1970), reproduced in Arthur J. Bellinzoni, Jr., *The Two-Source Hypothesis. A Critical Appraisal* (Macon, GA: Mercer University Press, 1985), 38.

17 William R. Farmer, *The Synoptic Problem. A Critical Analysis* (Macon, GA: Mercer University Press, 1976), esp. 199–232. For a multi-voiced expansion of Farmer's basic arguments, see William R. Farmer (ed.), *New Synoptic Studies. The Cambridge Gospel Conference and Beyond* (Macon, GA: Mercer University Press, 1983).

18 My usage: this term is less confusing than the several alternatives in scholarly usage: the "Two Gospel hypothesis," the "Griesbach hypothesis," the "neo-Griesbachian school," among others.

19 Augustine's view was that Matthew was first, Mark second, and Luke third, a different order from the present version based on Farmer's work, but a clear statement of Matthew's priority, nonetheless.

20 Frances E. Gigot, "Synoptics," *The Catholic Encyclopedia* (1912), 14:394, quoted in "Introduction," to Bellinzoni, 7, in Arthur J. Bellinzoni (ed.), *The Two Source Hypothesis. A Critical Approach* (Macon, GA: Mercer University Press, 1985).

21 This is clearly specified in David L. Dungan, "Two-Gospel Hypothesis," in *ABD*, 6:677–8.

22 J. Enoch Powell, "The Genesis of the Gospel," *Journal for the Study of the New Testament*, 42 (June 1991), 5–16.

23 I am not here asserting that there is no censorship or suppression in the Hebrew scriptures, the Christian scriptures, and in the tradition of Rabbinical Judaism. Certainly there is, and a lot of it. What I am suggesting is that the items that are preserved *within* the canonical textual traditions all operate according to a grammar of invention that is additive and transformative, not negative or reductive. That is, one text does not have the power to say that a previous text does not exist. The place where the suppression occurs, of course, is at the boundary walls: sometimes entire books are declared non-existent, and are suppressed, with no reference being made to most extra-canonical texts by those which are preserved within the canon. The chief exceptions are references in the Old Testament to lost books of narrative.

24 The term "Mark-hypothesis" is less confusing than the frequently used "two-source hypothesis" which is easily confused with the "Two Gospel hypothesis," that is, the Matthew-hypothesis.

25 Charlotte Allen, "The Search for a No-Frills Jesus," *Atlantic Monthly*, 278 (Dec. 1996), 58, and letter of correction, by John Updike (March 1997), 8. Whatever the problems with the Updike quotation, Allen's article is very perceptive.

26 The twentieth century's most influential statement of Mark's priority and of the relationship of this priority to "Q" is B.M. Streeter's *The Four Gospels: A Study of Origins* (London: MacMillan, 1924). This argument in its essentials still dominates the field, although Streeter's "two-source" argument has gradually splayed into a four-source argument and, today, into a multi-source explanation. (See the discussion in the text.)

27 It is a sign of both the bibliodensity and the querulousness of recent biblical scholarship that there is actually a literature on whether or not the siglum "Q" really originally meant "Quelle," or something else entirely. (See Meier, 1:50n9.) It simply does not matter.

28 For a general history of "Q" research, from the nineteenth century onwards, see: Arland D. Jacobson, *The First Gospel. An Introduction to Q* (Sonoma: Polebridge Press, 1992), 1–32; the journal *Semeia* has a special issue entitled *Early Christianity, Q and Jesus*, 55 (1991). Helmut Koester deals with "Q" in *Ancient Christian Gospels. Their History and Development* (Philadelphia: Trinity Press International, 1990), 128–71. The best substantive introduction, written with a clarity that is as rare in biblical studies as it is admirable, is John S. Kloppenborg, *The Formation of Q. Trajectories in Ancient Wisdom Collections* (Philadelphia: Fortress Press, 1987). For the implications of "Q" on the quest for the historical Yeshua, see John S. Kloppenborg, "The Sayings Gospel Q and the Quest for the Historical Jesus," *Harvard Theological Review*, 89 (Oct. 1996), 307–54 and, James M. Robinson, "The Q Trajectory: Between John and Matthew via Jesus," in Birger A. Pearson (ed.) *The Future of Early Christianity* (Minneapolis: Fortress

Press, 1991), 173–94. In surveying the above items, the reader should be aware that they are all written or edited by committed enthusiasts of "Q." For opposed viewpoints, refer to the material on the Matthew-hypothesis (section 2 in the text above) and on the alternate possibilities arising within the Mark-hypothesis (in the text, below), and also Appendix B.

29 For a discussion of this mode of reading the New Testament, see Robert Morgan, "Which was the Fourth Gospel? The Order of the Gospels and the Unity of Scripture," *Journal for the Study of the New Testament*, 54 (1994), 3–28.

30 Meier, 2:178.

31 Stanley D. Anderson (ed.), *Documenta Q: Q 11:2b–4* (Leuven: Peeters, 1996), v.

32 Allen, 54 and 56.

33 Crossan, *The Birth of Christianity*, 110.

34 Burton L. Mack, *Who Wrote the New Testament? The Making of the Christian Myth* (San Francisco: Harper, 1995), 47.

35 A.M. Farrer, "On Dispensing with Q," in D.E. Nineham (ed.), *Studies in the Gospels. Essays in memory of R.H. Lightfoot* (Oxford: Basil Blackwell, 1967), 55–88.

36 Michael D. Goulder, "Is Q a Juggernaut?" *Journal of Biblical Literature*, 115 (1996), 667–81.

37 Allen, 58.

38 Readers who are aware of the conventional wisdom in biblical studies will know that usually (but far from universally), the Gospel of Matthew is dated as being five to ten years later than the Gospel of Luke. That opinion does not come into play here, however, because (a) it is an opinion that is derived from stylistic, contextual, sociological and theological considerations and not from a consideration of the strict inter-textual relationship of the two Gospels and (b) indeed, in the conventional wisdom, it is held that the two Gospels were completely independent of each other. The view formulated by Farrar, Goulder and (less formally) by E.P. Sanders is that the two texts, Matthew and Luke, are not independent of each other. Therefore, one can replace the rather fuzzy extra-textual arguments with precise statements of textual relationships.

39 Michael D. Goulder, *Luke. A New Paradigm*. 2 vols (Sheffield: Journal for the Study of the New Testament, 1989).

40 Morton S. Enslin, "Luke and Matthew: Compilers or Authors?", *Aufstieg und Niedergang der Romischen Welt*, II. *Principat*, 25.3, 2357–87.

41 It is important to realize that even if those who are sceptical of "Q" have it backwards concerning the Minor Agreements – and, instead of Luke creatively rewriting Matthew, it was Matthew that re-did Luke – the result is the same: that "Q" is unnecessary, and that the visible texts are explained by visible texts, without any appeal to the Invisible Hand that is "Q." That said, both Goulder and Enslin make a compelling case for Luke's author-editor(s) having used Matthew.

CHAPTER SIX

1 For an extremely valuable entrance into the massive theological literature on Saul and his letters, see the frequently-updated American Theological Library Association's index, *Paul, the Apostle, and Pauline Literature. A bibliography.*

  Here it is important to note that in the English-speaking world the dominant work on the Apostle has been done by E.P. Sanders and familiarity with his main arguments is taken as a given in all of the significant studies conducted in recent years. See especially Sanders's *Paul and Palestinian Judaism. A Comparison of Patterns of Religion* (Philadelphia: Fortress Press, 1977); *Paul, the Law, and the Jewish People* (Philadelphia: Fortress Press, 1983); *Paul* (Oxford: Oxford University Press, 1991).

2 Paula Fredriksen, *From Jesus to Christ. The Origins of the New Testament Images of Jesus* (New Haven: Yale University Press, 1988), 52–3.

3 Will Bourne, "The Gospel according to Prum," *Harper's* (Jan. 1995), 60–2, 64, 66,67–70. The quotation is from p. 62. See also Edward Rice, *John Frum He Come* (Garden City: Doubleday, 1974).

4 This list is a direct paraphrase of Peter Richardson, "The Thunderbolt in Q and the Wise Man in Corinth," in Peter Richardson and John C. Hurd (eds.), *Jesus to Paul. Studies in Honour of Francis Wright Beare* (Waterloo: Wilfrid Laurier University Press, 1984), 108.

5 John S. Kloppenborg and Leif E. Vaage, "Early Christianity, Q and Jesus: The Sayings Gospel and Method in the Study of Christian Origins," *Semeia*, no. 55 (1991), 6.

6 Helmut Koester, *Ancient Christian Gospels. Their History and Development* (Philadelphia: Trinity Press International, 1990), 171.

7 Burton L. Mack, *Who Wrote the New Testament? The Making of the Christian Myth* (San Francisco: Harpers, 1995), 47.

8 Kloppenborg and Vaage, 7.

9 John P. Meier, *A Marginal Jew. Rethinking the Historical Jesus* (New York: Doubleday, 1991) 1:45.

10 *The Anchor Bible Dictionary* (ed.) David Noel Freedman, (New York: Doubleday, six vols, 1992).

11 Raymond F. Collins, *Letters that Paul Did Not Write. The Epistle to the Hebrews and the Pauline Pseudepigrapha* (Wilmington: Michael Glazier, 1988), 19.

12 Charles D. Myers, "Romans, Epistle to the," *ABD*, 5:819; Albert Pietersma, "Chester Beatty Papyri," *ABD*, 1:903.

13 Eldon Jay Epp, "Western Text," *ABD*, 6:909–12; Joel C. Slayton, "Codex Alexandrinus," *ABD*, 1:1089.

14 To qualify that statement: Clement cites individual documents that he believes are by Saint Saul, mostly 1 Corinthians and Hebrews, so it is not clear that he had before him an entire corpus. He may have possessed only individual letters, but he

also uses Romans, 2 Corinthians, and Philippians. See *The Letter of St. Clement of Rome to the Corinthians* (tr. Francis X. Glimm), in *The Apostolic Fathers* (Washington D.C.: Catholic University of America Press, 1947), 9–58.

15 The first two terms are those of Jerome Murphy-O'Connor, *Paul, the Letter-Writer. His World, His Options, His Skills* (Collegeville, Minn: The Liturgical Press, 1995), 114–30. For classic propositions, see E.J. Goodspeed, *New Solutions of New Testament Problems* (Chicago: University of Chicago Press, 1927); C. Leslie Mitton, *The Formation of the Pauline Corpus of Letters* (London: Epworth Press, 1955).

16 See Murphy-O'Connor (1995), 120–30.

17 Jurgen Becker, *Paul. Apostle to the Gentiles* (tr. O.C. Dean, Jr.), (Louisville: Westminster/John Knox Press, 1993, German orig., 1989), 8.

18 For useful discussion of these issues, see Raymond F. Collins, *Letters That Paul. Did Not Write. ...*, passim, and Robert M. Grant, *A Historical Introduction to the New Testament* (New York: Harper and Row, 1963), 60ff.

19 In practical terms, the greatest limit to the linguistic approach has been the training of those who use it. Too often, they know words, but not how to use quantitative data, and the resultant errors are prodigious. For a very shrewd discussion, see A. Dean Forbes, "Statistical Research on the Bible," *ABD*, 6:185–206. On the various epistles, see 187–93. The entire article is worth study.

20 Charles D. Myers Jr., however, makes this admirably clear. "Romans, Epistle to," *ABD* 5:816.

21 John Knox, "Fourteen Years Later – A Note on the Pauline Chronology," *Journal of Religion*, 16 (1936), 341–9; "The Pauline Chronology," *Journal of Biblical Literature*, 58 (1939) and *Chapters in a Life of Paul* (Nashville: Abingdon, 1950.) A revised edition with an introduction by Douglas R.A. Hare was published in 1989 (London: SCM Press).

22 Each of those scholars deserves great respect as exegete and commentator, and I view them as such: just not as rigorous historians.

23 John Hurd, *The Origin of 1 Corinthians* (London: SPCK, 1965); Robert Jewett, *A Chronology of Paul's Life* (Philadelphia: Fortress Press, 1979); Gerd Luedemann, *Paul, Apostle to the Gentiles. Studies in Chronology* (tr. from German by F. Stanley Jones) (Philadelphia: Fortress Press, 1984, orig ed. 1980); Jerome Murphy O'Connor, *Paul. A Critical Life* (Oxford: Clarendon Press, 1996).

24 Such as John Knox's vigorous argument in 1990, "On the Pauline Chronology: Buck-Taylor-Hurd Revisited," in Robert T. Fortna and Beverly R. Gaventa, *The Conversation Continues. Studies in Paul and John in Honour of J. Louis Martyn* (Nashville: Abingdon Press, 1990), 258–74. Other examples include: Paul J. Achtemeier, *The Quest for Unity in the New Testament Church. A Study in Paul and Acts* (Philadelphia: Fortress Press, 1987); Roger D. Aus, "Paul's Travel Plans to Spain and the 'Full Number of the Gentiles,'" *Novum Testamentum*, 21 (1979), 232–62; C.K. Barrett, *Essays on Paul* (London: SPCK, 1982); Jurgen Becker, *Paul, Apostle*

to the Gentiles (tr. O.C. Dean, Jr.) (Louisville: Westminster-John Knox Press, 1993, orig. ed. 1989); Gunther Bornkamm, *Paul* (tr. D.M.G. Stalker) (New York: Harper and Row, 1971, orig. ed. 1969); Daniel Boyarin, *A Radical Jew. Paul and the Politics of Identity* (Berkeley: University of California Press, 1994); Raymond E. Brown, *An Introduction to the New Testament* (New York: Doubleday, 1987); Raymond E. Brown, "Further Reflections on the Origins of the Church of Rome," in Fortna and *Gaventa*, 98–115; C.H. Buck, "The Collection for the Saints," *Harvard Theological Review*, 43 (1950), 1–29; C.H. Buck and Greer M. Taylor, *St. Paul: A Study in the Development of His Thought* (New York: Scribners, 1969); John K. Chow, *Patronage and Power. A Study of Social Networks in Corinth* (Sheffield: JSOT, 1992); J.M. Gilchrist, "The Historicity of Paul's Shipwreck," *Journal for the Study of the New Testament*, 61 (1996), 29–51; Dieter Georgi, *The Opponents of Paul in Second Corinthians* (Philadelphia: Fortress Press, 1986); Peter D. Gooch, *Dangerous Food. 1 Corinthians 8–10 in Its Context* (Waterloo: Wilfrid Laurier University Press, 1993); Michael Grant, *Saint Paul* (New York: Charles Scribner's Sons, 1976); Robert R. Hann, "Judaism and Jewish Christianity in Antioch: Charisma and Conflict in the First Century," *Journal of Religious History*, 14 (Dec. 1987), 341–60; Colin J. Hemer, "Observations on Pauline Chronology," in Donald A. Hagner and Murray J. Harris (eds.), *Pauline Studies. Essays Presented to Professor F.F. Bruce on his seventieth birthday* (Exeter: Paternoster Press, 1980), 3–18; Martin Hengel, *The Pre-Christian Paul* (London: SCM Press, 1991); Martin Hengel, *Between Jesus and Paul. Studies in the Earliest History of Christianity* (Philadelphia: Fortress Press, 1983); Martin Hengel and Anna Maria Schwemer, *Paul Between Damascus and Antioch. The Unknown Years* (Louisville: Westminster/ John Knox Press, 1997); Craig C. Hill, *Hellenists and Hebrews. Reappraising Division within the earliest Church* (Minneapolis: Fortress Press, 1992); John C. Lentz, *Luke's Portrait of Paul* (Cambridge: Cambridge University Press, 1993); Wayne A. Meeks, *The First Urban Christians. The Social World of the Apostle Paul* (New Haven: Yale University Press, 1983); Wayne A. Meeks and Robert L. Wilken, *Jews and Christians in Antioch in the First Four Centuries of the Common Era* (Missoula: Scholars Press, 1978); John P. Meier, "The Brothers and Sisters of Jesus in Ecumenical Perspective," *Catholic Biblical Quarterly*, 54 (Jan. 1992), 1–27; Jerome Murphy-O'Connor, "Paul in Arabia," *Catholic Biblical Quarterly*, 55 (Oct. 1993), 732–37); Jerome Murphy-O'Connor, *Paul the Letter Writer. His World, His Options, His Skills* (Collegeville, Minn: The Liturgical Press, 1995); Mark D. Nanos, *The Mystery of Romans. The Jewish Context of Paul's Letter* (Minneapolis: Fortress Press, 1996); Calvin J. Roetzel, *Paul. The Man and the Myth* (Columbia: University of South Carolina Press, 1998); Jack T. Sanders, "The First Decades of Jewish-Christian Relations: The Evidence of the New Testament (Gospels and Acts)," *Aufstieg und Niedergang der Romischen Welt, Principat.* 26.3, 1967–1978; James M. Scott, *Paul and the Nations. The Old Testament and Jewish Background of Paul's Mission to the Nations with special reference to the*

Destination of Galatians (Tübingen: J.C.B. Mohr, 1995); Dixon Slingerland, "Acts 18:1–18, The Gallio Inscription, and the Absolute Pauline Chronology," *Journal of Biblical Literature*, 110 (1991), 439–49; Krister Stendahl, *Paul Among Jews and Gentiles and other essays* (Philadelphia: Fortress Press, 1976); Pieter W. Van der Horst, "The Altar of the 'Unknown God' in Athens (Acts 17:23) and the Cult of 'Unknown Gods,' in the Hellenistic and Roman Periods," *Aufstieg und Niedergang der Romischen Welt, Principat*, 18.2, 1426–56; Ben Witherington, *The Paul Quest. The Renewed Search for the Jew of Tarsus* (New York: InterVersity Press, 1998).

25 Brevard S. Childs, *The New Testament as Canon: An Introduction* (London: SCM Press, 1984), 238.

26 On additional problems, such as the Christian manuscript tradition never having had Acts immediately follow Luke, see J. Dawsey, "The Literary Unity of Luke-Acts: Questions of Style – A Task for Literary Critics," *New Testament Studies* 35 (1989), 48–66.

27 This leads to the ironic point that some scholars find in the third Gospel traces of citation or indirect quotation of some of Saul's letters. See Anthony J. Blasi, *Making Charisma. The Social Construction of Paul's Public Image* (London: Transaction Publishers, 1991). If this is indeed the case (one reserves judgement), it is a fairly strong argument against the third Gospel and the Acts of the Apostles having been written continuously by the same hand, since the author-editor of the third Gospel would have known Saul's letters, but the author-editor of Luke would not have known them.

28 My formulation places a little more distance between Saul's epistles and probable historical accuracy than John Knox himself would have done. He tends almost automatically to take as a given the letters' accuracy and judges Acts by that standard. My acceptance of his method is based not on reflexive faith in Saul's accuracy, but simply on the praxis of Knox's method being based on its maximizing of the probability of accuracy.

29 The attachment to this Gallio date is quite amazing. Gerd Luedemann is the most hard-nosed of those who demand an epistles-only standard of evidence. He agrees that the grounds of presumption for any unconfirmed segment of Acts has to be negative and, further, concerning the Gallio material, he states: "We shall demonstrate that Luke's chronological references to world history are often incorrect and thereby deny the methodological right of developing a chronology of Paul on the basis of the reference to Gallio" (9). He accomplishes this task thoroughly. And then, so strong is the siren song of absolute dating, that Luedemann spends several tortured pages convincing himself that although Saul's trial before Gallio lacks historicity, that Saul could still have encountered the proconsul and that, really the argument for Saul's being in Corinth about the time of Gallio is strong enough in the letters for us to accept the years 49–52 as pegs on which to rest the dating of Saul's life (see 158–77).

I remain as unconvinced of the usefulness of the Gallio date as of every other unconfirmed portion of Acts. Readers who still are keen on the Gallio inscription should note Slingerland's demonstration (1991) that even if one takes the Gallio dating as one's peg, it is not at all precise: it covers a period from December 47 CE to February or March 54 CE. One can obtain more precise chronological readings than that by using the letters on their own.

30 Luedemann, 21–22 and 39n75–760, citing the work of P. Vielhauer.

31 Knox, (1950), 41–2.

32 Luedemann, 172 and 262–3.

33 This is the most controversial aspect of Luedemann's chronology. Most scholars opt for a later date, 49 CE being the most common. Here Luedemann departs from his epistle-based chronology. The 41 CE date is based on material in Acts and upon a fairly speculative attempt to date the edict of Claudius against certain Judahists. Thus far, in my judgement, neither side of the argument is decisive.

34 Most chronologists argue that the Jerusalem Conference preceded the imbroglio at Antioch. Luedemann makes a case for the local difficulties having preceded the conference and, perhaps, having been the cause of it. Saul, in Galatians 2:1–14 seems clearly to put the conference before the Antiochene problems.

35 Murphy-O'Connor, (1996), 31, 329–32.

36 The dating of the epistles is from Luedemann's chronology, with this exception: that for 1 Thessalonians which he places considerably earlier (c. 41 CE). Because Luedemann's work is so admirable – much the most rigorous in his use of historical sources and methods yet to be focussed on the chronology of Saint Saul's life – my rejection of his Thessalonians dating requires respectful explanation. His argument (210–61) for an early date (c. 41) in outline is as follows: (a) there are, he believes, important contrasts between 1 Thessalonians 4:13–18 and 1 Corinthians 15:51–52 and these rest on a quantum change in Saul's view of the character of the projected Second Coming of Jesus and the general resurrection of the dead; (b) that this is explicable by the operation of demographics, namely that between the writing of the two letters a lot of Yeshua-followers have died, and those remaining need an explanation that will join the living and the dead Christians when Jesus-the-Christ returns. Crucially, Luedemann believes that a few Yeshua-followers had died when 1 Thessalonians was written (and therefore this was the first time the problem of the dead-in-Christ had to be theologically dealt with) and that most of the first generation of Yeshua-followers had died by 50 CE when, approximately, 1 Corinthians was written (see Luedemann, 240 and 292). (c) Therefore one needs a period of time between the writing of the two texts that is sufficient to explain the demographic transition among the first generation of Christians to whom Paul is speaking in Thessalonians and (arguably) the second generation in Corinthians. This time period, Luedemann takes to be roughly a decade, using First Corinthians as his base-point, and inferring that First Thessalonians was written roughly ten years earlier.

In my view: (a) the dependent variable he is explaining is probably non-existent. The difference in the two texts as they stand is not determinative, for each explains that when Jesus-the-Christ returns, both the dead believers and the living ones shall meet him. Only by a very ingenious, but I think forced, search for a sub-text beneath the pericope in Thessalonians can one accept that this passage was the first time that Saul had said anything about the future resurrection of dead Christians (Luedemann, 212 specifies this), and that the Corinthians passage was written at a time when the doctrine was well known. Since the dependent variable does not seem to exist, the rest of the exercise is moot. (2) That said, even if the dependent variable were real, the independent variable – the demographics – still is wrong for the following reasons: (a) assuming Yeshua was executed in roughly 30 CE, it is unrealistic to propose that it was a decade later before it occurred to any of Saul's followers that the question of what would happen to dead Yeshua-followers when Jesus came back was worth worrying about. This issue would arise the minute any person died. Therefore the alleged sub-text implies nothing about dating, except that First Thessalonians was written after the death of Yeshua. (b) Assuming that by "first generation" scholars we mean any-one who was alive when Yeshua himself was – (biblical scholars are very muddy on this, but since Saul is always included in the first generation, and yet was not converted until after Yeshua's death, it follows that the definition of "first genera-tion" includes all who were alive during Yeshua's lifetime, and encompasses in that group those who believed after his death, rather than before) – then Luede-mann's admirably explicit statement of falsifiability comes into play. He states (292) that his thesis holds only if most of the first generation was dead by, roughly, 50 CE. (Anything less in his scheme of things would not be a sufficient change-over-time to account for the difference he believes exists between the demographic situation in the two texts.) This is an explicit statement of falsifiabil-ity, and the trouble is, it falsifies (disproves) his case. Although, given Middle Eastern health standards of the time, it probably seems intuitively obvious that most of the first-generation was dead in 50 CE, this is one of those things-everybody-knows that is far from certain, indeed, probably untrue.

It is undoubtedly true that life-expectancy in the Near East, Asia Minor and Mediterranean Europe (the homes of the first generation of believers) in Roman times was short. Let us say twenty-five years for the general population. Does this not mean that most (actually, almost all) first-generation believers would be dead by 50 CE? No. This for two reasons. First, the definition of first-generation includes all those alive while Yeshua was, so that – to take the extreme case – the age-cohort from which believers born in 29 CE was drawn would, on average, not die until the mid-50s. That is the extreme case, but the point is worth remember-ing: the first-generation of believers was younger than one is apt to assume. Second, and much more importantly, it is easy to miss the nature of life-expect-ancy data. In cultures such as those from which the first-generation came, life expectancy was notoriously short at birth. But, if a person survived the perils of the first year of life, life-expectancy shot up dramatically. And, once an individual made it to his or her twenties, the life expectancy for males was about the same as it was for males in western Europe at the time of the early Industrial Revolution. For women in their twenties, the life expectancy was shorter than their European counterparts in modern times, but once their child-bearing years were over (child-bearing being the big mortality risk for women), they lived as long as our own great-great-grandmothers. What this means is that among the people who comprised the first generation of Yeshua-followers, their life-expectancy was markedly longer than we would surmise by naively looking at the life-expectancy figures for the entire population: remember, people became members of the Yeshua-faith in the first generation only when they were able consciously to embrace the faith, which is to say that people became allegiant only after the worst demographic perils (various causes of infant and child mortality) were past. To take again the extreme case, those males born in 29 CE. Suppose (purely as a statistical exercise) a significant number of them joined the faith as young adults, say, twenty years old: their average death date would have been somewhere in the eighth decade of the Common Era.

Consider now another example: the most important generation in western history. Call it Generation Zero. That is, the people born at what we now call the beginning of the Common Era. Yeshua, Saul, John-the-Baptizer and Yacov were all part of that generation, so we will use them for illustration. Had they not all met death-by-misadventure, how long would they have lived? Since we know that John-the-Baptizer and Yeshua had survived to roughly age thirty in rude good health, a reasonable actuarial projection (see data references below) would be that they would have lived until the late 50s or early 60s of the Common Era. And, barring misadventure, Saul and Yacov, brother of Yeshua, having lived well into their fifties, and, perhaps, sixties, could have been expected (on purely demographic grounds) to have lived into the turbulent times of the Jewish-Roman War of 66–73 CE.

The point of the exercise is that even if Luedemann's analysis of textual differences between Thessalonians and Corinthians holds up, the demographic assumptions that lie behind his chronological conclusions are, at minimum, not proved, and, most likely, are widely inaccurate. The only escape from that conclusion would be to re-define "first generation" of believers to exclude those who, while alive while Yeshua was on earth, nevertheless did not become allegiant until after his death. This would exclude Saul and Yeshua's brother Yacov, so it is not a ploy worth attempting.

For relevant comparative material on mortality, see: Edward Rosset, *Aging Process of Population* (New York: MacMillan, 1964), 155 (which gives the third-century life-expectancy table derived by the Roman lawyer Ulpian), and G. Pison and A. Langaney, "The Level and Age Pattern of Mortality in Bandafessi (Eastern Senegal): Results from a Small-Scale and Intensive Multi-Round Survey,"

Population Studies, 39 (1985), (Table 2, 392–3 gives a year-by-year life expectancy table for a demographic group whose actuarial characteristics are very similar to those defined by Ulpian in his third-century study).

A final note: this exercise would not have been necessary had Luedemann taken 1 Corinthians 15:6 as an accurate demographic sample of first-generation mortality. Saul states categorically that most of those who saw Jesus immediately after the resurrection were still alive at the time he was writing First Corinthians.

CHAPTER SEVEN

1 See *Surpassing Wonder*, 284–7.

2 Josephus, *Jewish War*, 5:17 and 5:562–3; also 2:197, 409–17. See also the notes by E. Mary Smallwood to the Penguin edition of *The Jewish War* (London: revised ed., 1981).

3 Josephus, *Jewish War*, 7:45.

4 Paula Fredriksen, *From Jesus to Christ. The Origins of the New Testament Images of Jesus* (New Haven: Yale University Press, 1988), 149–51.

5 Shaye Cohen, "Crossing the Boundary and Becoming a Jew," *Harvard Theological Review*, 82 (Jan. 1989), 15–24. We have the least information on cases that were later considered heretical by both Jewish and Christian authorities and thus rarely recorded: the instances wherein Yahweh was incorporated into pantheism or some form of polytheism. See, for example, the case of the Theos Hypsistos (the god of healing) cult on Cyprus in the first through third centuries of the Common Era, which was predominantly Yahweh-based, but which eventually included in the later period, Jews, Christians and pagans. Terence B. Mitford, "The Cults of Roman Cyprus," *Aufstieg und Niedergang der Romischen Welt, Principat*, 18.3, 2205–07.

6 Philo Judaeus and Flavius Josephus both refer to conversion, but do not give much in the way of ritual detail. The Rabbinic literature is specific, but too late to be applied to this period (the Mishnah did not close until c. 200 CE), and, in any case, reflects only one of the several forms of praxis operative in the late Second Temple era.

7 The historiographic dispute on the intensity of the Jewish "missionary" movement divides fairly sharply between "minimalists," who essentially adopt the view that proselytes may have joined occasionally, but that the Jewish faith never actively sought proselytes or even allies from among the Gentiles, and "maximalists." The extreme maximalist position is that of scholars such as Dieter Georgi who hold that in Saul's time Judaism had "an enormous missionary impulse" (Dieter Georgi, *The Opponents of Paul in Second Corinthians*, Philadelphia: Fortress Press, 1986, 317). The strongest proponent of the maximalist view is Louis H. Feldman, *Jew and Gentile in the Ancient World. Attitudes and Interactions from Alexander to Justinian* (Princeton: Princeton University Press, 1993). Feldman produces so much evidence of assertive activity on the part of the

Yahweh-faith that in my judgment the case is proved. The only major weakness in Feldman's argument is that he uses estimates of Jewish population growth (292) to provide a *prima facie* case for large-scale proselytizing activities. The demographic estimates are too shaky to bear this much weight. (In this argument, incidentally, Feldman is following in the footsteps of pioneer Jewish scholar of the early Common Era, Joseph Klausner who, before World War II had developed the argument that "one could not explain the great number of Jews in the Diaspora near the time of the destruction of the Second Temple without bringing into account a considerable addition of male and female proselytes." Joseph Klausner, *From Jesus to Paul*, trans. by William F. Stinespring, New York: MacMillan 1943, orig. Hebrew ed., 1939, 32.) Feldman's case is strong enough without these quantitative data, and even if one concludes that the activities were not as productive of converts as Feldman asserts, the strength of the impulse still has been demonstrated. For a review of the literature, see James C. Paget, "Jewish Proselytism at the time of Christian Origins: Chimera or Reality? *Journal for the Study of the New Testament*, 62 (1996), 65–103.

One minor matter: much is sometimes made of there being no missionaries' names known in the late Second Temple period, except that of Saul. This is hardly demonstrative of there not having been any missionaries, for anonymity is the usual case in the period: we do not know the names of any Sadducees, nor any Essenes, and we have only two self-declared Pharisees in all the available literature. Moreover, if, as I have argued, Judahist self-assertion was mostly a matter of Diaspora cultures reacting to their local circumstances, then one would not expect there to be many peripatetic missionaries. And, within Eretz Israel, religious visionaries took on a variety of names: persons we call prophets, mystics, and messianic leaders could just as well have been denominated missionaries.

8 Samuel Sandmel, *The First Christian Century in Judaism and Christianity: Certainties and Uncertainties* (New York: Oxford University Press, 1969), 22.

9 The reader may notice that two terms which are very common in studies of the early Common Era are not employed in this study: "Jewish-Christians" and "Judaizers." In part this is because they are not employed in the scholarly literature with sufficient agreement on their meaning to give them utility as denotative units of speech. And their connotative elements are extremely misleading historically.

Take "Jewish-Christians." It is an historically useless concept for the late Second Temple period because the religions that we know today as Christianity and the Jewish Faith were not then in existence. (See my discussion of appropriate vocabulary in chapter three.) The term projects backwards into the era of multiple Judahisms the binary oppositions of the second century and thereafter. Secondly, "Jewish-Christian," if employed in the pre-70 CE period, is based on a cosmology that is inside-out. That is, it implies that "Jewish-Christians" were a subset of a larger phenomenon: "Christians." This diminishes Judahism in a way the post-

70 CE Christian propagandists would have approved, but it destroys reality. Christianity in the late Second Temple period (roughly, its first and second generations) was not an independent entity, an encompassing conceptual or social reality. The encompassing reality was late Second Temple Judaism, which, we have constantly emphasized, was a plural entity. The Yeshua-followers were a subset of this Yahweh-faith. Late Second Temple Judaism, not the Yeshua-faith, defined the universe within which various small sub-systems – Essenes, Pharisees, Zealots, Yeshua-followers – operated. The line between belonging to one of the Judahist groups and adhering to the Yeshua-faith was a permeable membrane, and one can conceive, for example, of Pharisees who, in their own way also adhered to Yeshua. (A plausible suggestion is that Yacov, brother of Yeshua, was such a person.) So, here we will keep to our extant vocabulary and speak of adherents of the Yahweh-faith, composed of multiple Judahisms, of which the Yeshua-followers were one group. There were no "Jewish-Christians," but instead worshippers of Yahweh who, as individuals, were Yeshua-followers. Potentially, they also adhered to one or more other forms of the Yahweh-faith.

As for "Judaizers," it is an unfortunate word, since from the Middle Ages onwards it played a small role in the articulation of Christian anti-Semitism; and, even without that carcinoma it still is a useless word, for it make us think we know more than we do. Saul uses the Greek verb "to Judaize" only once, and that is in Galatians 2:14 where he reports having rebuked Peter for, among other things, forcing Gentiles who had taken up the Yeshua-faith to live under the rules of Judahism. Note who is doing what to whom: Peter, born into the Yahweh-faith and continuing allegiant to it, and also a Yeshua-follower, has been beating on Gentile followers of Yeshua to act like good Pharisees (or something very close thereto) and to adopt not just the Judahistic beliefs implied in the Yeshua-faith, but other beliefs and praxis as well. Significantly, in the epistles wherein Saul denounces people whom later historians call "Judaizers," Saul does not use the term "Judaizer." It is an invention of the later church. Despite the absence of reliable evidence, most commentators and most present-day biblical scholars identify these "Judaizers" as being Gentiles who were followers of Yeshua but who also were deeply into one or more of the traditions of praxis that revolved through late Second Temple Judaism. It is confidently asserted that it was these Gentiles who were determined to make other Gentile adherents of Yeshua be severe Judahists: practitioners of ritual purification, circumcision, food taboos, the lot.

When Saul denounces unnamed persons for pushing Judahist praxis too strongly upon Gentiles, we should not assume that we know immediately who it was: it could have been lifelong Judahists who were allied to the Yeshua-faith; it could have been Gentiles who had become full proselytes to Judahism as well as followers of Yeshua; and it could even have been Judahists who themselves had no allegiance to Yeshua, but who recognized the Yeshua-faith as a branch of Judahism and therefore urged all of its members to carry out the full

613 commandments. Manifestly a term that is based on contradictory empirical foundations, it is neither descriptively nor analytically viable. It has to be abandoned and with it the overtones of the slur based on nearly two millennia of misreading of Saul: namely that anything smacking of "Jewish" practice was wrong and so said the first missionary of the faith. He didn't.

10 As with every epistle, one can find arguments that it was a single unit or that, in this case, the "Philippians," what we have is made up of material from two or three letters. The argument does not affect our present task, because the section we are here dealing with constitutes a single coherent unit. That said, I am most impressed with the single-text argument, primarily because the disjointed nature of the text fits with the emotional upset that Saul was here experiencing. Clearly, he has written something to them on the agitating subject previously (see 3:1, NIV).

11 Chris Mearns, "The Identity of Paul's Opponents at Philippi," *New Testament Studies*, 33 (1987), 194. The entire article (194–204) is a model of economical argument, and if I stray somewhat from Mearns's views, I am in his debt nonetheless.

12 Both Barrett *(Essays on Paul*, London: SPCK, 1982), and Georgi (1986) are convincing in arguing that, although two parts of the epistle (2 Cor. 2:14–7:4 and chapters 10–13) deal with an outside invasion, they are not from a single letter and that the situation had developed for the worse between the two missives. Chapters 10–13 are considerably more revealing about the outsiders than are early portions. For a careful attempt at constructing the chronology of the entire text in relation to Saul's activities, see Becker, p. 221. For a useful background piece, see Jerome Murphy-O'Connor, "The Corinth that Saint Paul Saw," *Biblical Archaeologist*, 47 (Sept 1984), 147–59.

13 Barrett, 60.

14 John Knox, *Chapters in a Life of Paul* (London: SCM Press, sec. ed. 1989; orig. ed. 1950), 83.

15 Jurgen Becker is convincing on this point. Jurgen Becker, *Paul. Apostle to the Gentiles* (tr. C Dean Jr) (Louisville: Westminster/John Knox Press, 1993; orig. German ed. 1989), 187–97.

16 Through 18:11 the Acts account seems circumstantial and is confirmed by portions of First Corinthians. Thereafter, in the "Gallio incident" it is not trustworthy, as Luedemann demonstrates (see above, chapter six, note 29).

17 It is unclear whether or not the "Christ" party was a real faction or just Saul's way of exasperatedly refusing to name all the parties, in effect saying, "and there are so many idiots around that they would even make Christ a factional totem." He was capable of such broad sarcasm. However, I suspect that there was a real group that effectively used such a slogan, for one of the few universals of sectarian propaganda is that it is very effective to deny being a sectarian by grabbing wholesale the name of the organisation or the identity of the founder. Thus in our own time we have religious denominations that say they are not denominations, but are

"Christians." I encountered a charming example of such a propaganda technique in Cookeville, Tennessee, where the Dairy Queen shop had a thirty-foot revolving sign with appropriate local messages on it. A convention was in town: "Welcome Disciples of Christ."

18 This does not stop Saul from giving an oblique elbow in the ribs to the two other missionaries who had visited the place previously, Apollos and Cephas (Peter). Apollos was an Alexandrian (a "fact" known only from Acts, so perhaps problematic) Judahist of considerable verbal abilities and probably a sophisticated education. He is put down by Saul's ostentatious modesty about his own limited gifts: "When I came to you, came not with excellency of speech or of wisdom ..." (1 Cor. 2:1). That is because such shiny baubles are misleading. "I determined not to know any thing among you, save Jesus Christ, and him crucified" (2:2).

In the case of Cephas/Peter, the elbow is sharper. In a discussion of the relationship of Yahweh's covenant with Israel, Saul says that the ancient Hebrews "drank of that spiritual Rock that followed them: and that Rock was Christ" (10:4). This identification of the "Rock" with Jesus-the-Christ directly robs Peter, and his disciples, of the right to use his own name as the Rock of the faith. This is a bit hard on Peter because his name was not a piece of argument, but probably a patronymic. Peter means "Rock" in Greek, and "Cephas" in all probability was its Aramaic equivalent.

19 Although I am here deviating sharply from large parts of his argument, attention should be called to a jewel of a piece of counter-conventional scholarship: Peter D. Gooch, *Dangerous Food. 1 Corinthians 8–10 in Its Context* (Waterloo: Wilfrid Laurier University Press, 1993).

20 There are two fine English language editions of the Mishnah, that of Herbert Danby (Oxford: Clarendon Press, 1933), written in virtually-classical English and that of Jacob Neusner (New Haven: Yale University Press, 1988), written in everyday American. Neusner's edition has a useful verse-reference system. Philip Blackman's bilingual edition runs to six volumes of text and apparatus: *Mishnayoth* (London: Mishna Press, 1951–1964). For a discussion of the nature of the Mishnah, see *Surpassing Wonder*, 295–327.

21 The quotation is from the Jerusalem Bible. Similar rewriting is found in the New International Version, in Today's English Version, the Living Bible, and the New English Bible.

22 Gooch, 7.

23 The historical-critical material on Galatians is some of the most interesting in the entire historiography of the New Testament. This is because the mission to the Galatians is the one documentable occasion where Saul may have dealt primarily with a culture that was totally-other as far as his experience was concerned. This, possibly, was the Celtic culture of the north of Galatia. (Of course, if Saul made it to Spain as John Murphy-O'Connor maintains, he would have encountered a sister culture, but the documentation is very weak. See Murphy-O'Connor, *Paul.*

A Critical Life (Oxford: Clarendon Press, 1996), 359–63.) The bedrock of the literature is Prof. Sir William M. Ramsay's classic *A Historical Commentary on St. Paul's Epistle to the Galatians* (New York: G.P. Putnams Sons, 1900). He argued against Saul's having dealt with the Celts and held that his mission centred on the Hellenized south. The argument between "south Galatian" and "north Galatian" proponents has surged back and forth over the century. At present, most chronologists of Saul favour the idea that he did indeed deal with the north and therefore with Celts, but there are still strong arguments being made against that view. See especially, James M. Scott, *Paul and the Nations. The Old Testament and Jewish Background of Paul's Mission to the Nations with Special Reference to the Destination of Galatians* (Tubingen: J.C.B. Mohr 1995).

For political and social background, see Robert K. Sherek, "Roman Galatia: The Governors from 25 BC to AD 114," *Aufstieg und Niedergang der Romischen Welt*, II. *Principat* 7.2, 954–1052, and Stephen Mitchell, "Population and the Land in Roman Galatia," ibid., 1053–81. For concise commentary, see Wayne A. Meeks (ed), *The Writings of St. Paul. A Norton Critical Edition* (New York: W.W. Norton, 1972), 10–12.

24 This is well argued in Jerome H. Neyrey, "Bewitched in Galatia: Paul and Cultural Anthropology," *Catholic Biblical Quarterly*, 50 (Jan. 1988), 72–100.

25 A balanced discussion is found in Gerd Luedemann, *Opposition to Paul in Jewish Christianity* (tr. M. Eugene Boring) (Minneapolis: Fortress Press, 1989; orig. German ed, 1983), 99–103.

26 As I indicated earlier (in chapter six), most chronologists of Saul have the Antioch event occurring after the Jerusalem "council." Luedemann (1984) has it preceding the "council" and being its possible cause. In the present discussion, I am accepting Saul's memory of events over the sensible, but circumstantial version Luedemann presents.

27 For social background, see Frederick W. Norris, "Antioch on-the-Orontes as a Religious Center: Paganism before Constantine," *Aufstieg und Niedergang der Romischen Welt, Principat*, 18.4, 2322–79.

28 See, Acts 9:27 where Barnabas accredits Saul to the Jerusalem brethren. See also several places (for example, 12:25) where the joint work of the two men is mentioned, Barnabas's name being given first. This is telling, since the author-editor of Acts is a fervid fan of Saul's.

29 It is unclear here whether or not the Jerusalem emissaries were prescribing the extreme table purity that distinguished the Pharisees. See E.P. Sanders concerning the possible characterization of the Pharisees as a "pure food club." E.P. Sanders, *Jewish Law from Jesus to the Mishnah. Five Studies* (London: SCM Press, 1990), 133. Sanders' entire book repays study. It should be read in conjunction with the seminal works of Jacob Neusner, with whom he has several disagreements. Taken together, these two scholars' work define the boundaries of recent discussion on the late Second Temple Pharisees.

It is possible that Saul's worries about food-before-idols may not have been Pharisaic in origin, but may have stemmed from realistic worries about the acquisition of foods (especially meats) in general. As Frederick Norris points out in his work on Antioch, the various temples were "both the butcher shops and the restaurants of the ancient world," and unless one had one's own animals or unless there was a "Kosher" butcher, idol-food was all that was available (Norris, 2376.) The main argument against this interpretation is that Saul, who was very wary of food-from-idols, was willing to eat with this particular group of Gentiles, thus suggesting the acquisition problem had been dealt with successfully.

30 Although the Book of Acts is a very dicey source on Saul's actions and (especially) his words, it probably is right on this matter (Acts 15:2), rather than Galatians (2:2). For an ingenious, but I think unconvincing attempt at melding the two views, see William O. Walker, Jr., "Why Paul Went to Jerusalem: The Interpretation of Galatians 2:1–5," *Catholic Biblical Quarterly*, 54 (July 1992), 503–10.

31 Bavli, Yebamoth 46a (Soncino ed., 303).

32 The king eventually decided to be circumcised. The story is in Josephus, *Antiquities* 20:17–48. I follow Klausner (1943), pp. 38–40 in these two references to circumcision not being necessary for all proselytes.

33 The reader may notice that I have made no reference to an item in the Book of Acts that is sometimes called the "Apostolic decree" and is supposed to have been part of the Jerusalem Deal. This is because I am fundamentally skeptical of the historicity of everything in Acts concerning Saul unless it is confirmed by, or consonant with, information in Saul's epistles (see chapter six on this matter). And in this case, the freight seems particularly badly mislabeled. It's a package for somewhere else.

The "Apostolic decree" – a label attached by later church figures, not by the author-editor of Acts – is said to be defined in three places. Presumably it was designed to apply to Gentile-born followers of the Yeshua-faith, since all the requirements were covered in Judahist law, and would have been redundant to anyone already a Judahist. In slightly variant versions (Acts 15:20, 15:29, and 21:25) it involves (a) abstaining from food offered to idols; (b) not eating strangled food; (c) not ingesting blood; and (d) not fornicating. None of these requirements are inimical to Saul's personal inclinations, for they are what any good Pharisee, even a former-one, would have done instinctively. Imposing them on Gentile-born believers was another matter, however. The historical problem is that if this were such a significant part of the Jerusalem Deal (Acts gives it to us three times), it should have been mentioned by Saul. My guess (it can only be that) is that the author-editor of Acts is here (a) either reporting a real deal made later, perhaps after Saul's death, between some members of the Jerusalem church and some leaders of mostly-Gentile churches outside Eretz Israel; or (b) the author-editor of Acts is inserting at what seems to him to be an appropriate point in his narrative a summary of the ancient material in Leviticus 17–18 which gives the rules for foreigners who are living in the midst of the children of Israel. On the latter view, see Terrance Callan, "The Background of the Apostolic Decree (Acts 15:20; 21:25)," *Catholic Biblical Quarterly*, 55 (April 1993), 284–97.

34 Murphy-O'Connor (1996), 349.

35 Collins, 183.

36 Alfredo M. Rabello, "The Legal Condition of the Jews in the Roman Empire," *Aufstieg und Niedergang der Romischen Welt, Principat*, 2.13, 711–12.

37 This is one of the places where the KJB is true to its time in using the word "friends." However, "friends" in the early seventeenth century usually carried the meaning "family," or "relatives," and those are the terms used by the Jerusalem Bible, the New International Version, the New English Bible, and the Revised Standard Version.

38 Hans von Campenhausen, "The Authority of Jesus' Relatives in the Early Church," in Hans von Campenhausen and Henry Chadwick, *Jerusalem and Rome. The Problem of Authority in the Early Church* (Philadelphia: Fortress Press, 1966), 5–6.

39 In the link between these two references, I am following John P. Meier, "The Brother and Sisters of Jesus in Ecumenical Perspective," *Catholic Biblical Quarterly*, 54 (Jan 1992), 15, n.26.

40 On the Jerusalem situation at that time, see Luedemann (1989), 44–52. See also Robert R Hann, "Judaism and Jewish Christianity in Antioch: Charisma and Conflict in the First Century," *Journal of Religious History*, 14 (Dec. 1987), 344–6.

41 Jaroslav Pelikan, *The Christian Tradition. A History of the Development of Doctrine*. vol. 1, *The Emergence of the Catholic Tradition* (Chicago: University of Chicago Press, 1971), 13.

42 For limitations on the applicability of the concept of caliph (which comes from Adolf von Harnack [1910]), see von Campenhausen, 10–19.

43 The way that enthusiasm on this issue can get out of hand is illustrated by the monumental (1074 pp) first volume of a projected two-volume study by Robert Eisenman, *James the Brother of Jesus. The Key to Unlocking the Secrets of Early Christianity and the Dead Sea Scrolls* (New York: Viking, 1997).

CHAPTER EIGHT

1 James D.G. Dunn, "Jesus Tradition in Paul," in Bruce Chilton and Craig A. Evans (eds.), *Studying the Historical Jesus. Evaluations of the State of Current Research* (Leiden: E.J. Brill, 1994), 155. The state of the debate has changed little since David L. Dungan's survey in *The Sayings of Jesus in the Churches of Paul. The Use of the Synoptic Tradition in the Regulation of Early Church Life* (Philadelphia: Fortress Press, 1971, xvii–xxix).

2 See discussion of the "Paul and Jesus Seminar," in Nikolaus Walter, "Paulus und die Urchristliche Jesustradition," *New Testament Studies*, 31 (1985), 498–522.

3 Here the reader should be made aware that many (perhaps most) scholars of the epistles do not see Saul's use of "Christos" as involving the connotations of Moshiah, but as being simply a proper name. Considering that the name comes from the Septuagint where it is a direct transliteration of "Moshiah," and considering that the word is used frequently by Saul in the context of a figure who will return (the parousia) to end time and to effect the resurrection of the dead, to see "Christos" as merely a bit of antiseptic nomenclature requires a remarkable act of the will. What is missed as well in this particular rejection of the messianic connotations of "Christos" is that not only is Saul using the concept constantly, but that he has radically re-defined it and this is one of his biggest influences on evolving Christianity. On the general misreading, see N.T. Wright, *The Climax of the Covenant. Christ and the Law in Pauline Theology* (Edinburgh: T. and T. Clark, 1991), 41ff.

4 Martin Hengel, *Between Jesus and Paul. Studies in the Earliest History of Christianity* (Philadelphia: Fortress Press, 1983), 65.

5 For example, 1 Cor. 1:23; Gal. 5:11.

6 For example, Romans 3:21–26; 1 Cor. 15:12–19; Gal. 3:26–27.

7 For example, 1 Cor. 15:23–28; Phil. 2:16; 1 Thess. 4:14–17.

8 Outside of the single instance of 4 Ezra (written late in the first century of the Common Era), there is no instance in the pre-medieval Jewish literature of the concept of a Messiah who dies. (James H. Charlesworth, "The Concept of the Messiah in the Pseudepigrapha," *Aufstieg und Niedergang der Romischen Welt*, II. *Principat* 19.1, 202n54.)

  Further, the fundamental text of Rabbinic Judaism, the Mishnah, virtually scrubs Moshiah from the conceptual grid. There are only two direct references to Moshiah in the Mishnah. One of these is in a section of Sotah (9:15) which is probably a post-200 addition and not part of the original composition. The other is in Berakoth (1:5) where it is ruled that a devout man must recite his evening prayers all his life, until the days of Moshiah.

  Significantly, in the commentaries on the Mishnah which culminate in the great Babylonian Talmud, Moshiah gradually reappears and acquires an eschatological dimension. The Christian idea of his being a sacrificial figure is not adopted, but the idea that Messiah shall somehow stop time and right the world, is developed. (See *Surpassing Wonder*, 386–92.) Thus, from roughly 200 CE onwards, Jewish and Christian concepts of Moshiah were converging, although never completely joining. Jacob Neusner summarizes the process as follows: "The Messiah-myth found no consequential place in the rabbinical canon at the outset, that is, in the Mishnah, but later on that same myth became the moving force, the principal mode of teleological thought in the Talmudic sector." (Jacob Neusner, "Mishnah and Messiah,"in *Judaisms and Their Messiahs at the Turn of the Christian Era*, ed., Jacob Neusner, William Scott Green and Ernest S. Frerichs (Cambridge: Cambridge University Press, 1987), 280–1. For a collection of classic articles, see Leo Landman (ed.), *Messianism in the Talmudic Age* (New York: KTAV Publishing House, 1979).

9 Romans 1:3 mentions that Yeshua was of the "seed of David," that is, of Davidic descent. This is the only real exception to the lack of interest in his earthly characteristics as related to his Messiahship and it is not put forward by Saul as a proof-text.

10 It is a mystery as to what scriptures Saul's statement refers. In the Hebrew scriptures and in those para-biblical writings known at present there is no reference to a Messiah being killed and being resurrected (in any sense) two or three days later. The closest parallel might be the story of Jonah spending three days and nights in the belly of a fish (Jonah 1:17) but the parallel is not there. Jonah was swallowed for disobedience to Yahweh's will, while Yeshua is crucified as a form of obedience. And the fish's vomiting out Jonah is such an indecorous event that to make that a parallel to the resurrection of Jesus the Christ would be inappropriate, indeed, a rhetorical disaster.

11 Similar conclusions are reached by E.P. Sanders and M.D. Goulder. Sanders states that Saul "regarded Jesus as 'first fruits' of the resurrection (1 Cor. 15:20) and thought that all Christians would become like him. He denied that the resurrected body would be a 'natural' body, but maintained that it would be a 'spiritual' body (1 Cor. 15:44–46)." E.P. Sanders, *Paul* (Oxford: Oxford University Press, 1991), 19.

   According to Michael Goulder, "most contemporary Jews believed in a life after death for the soul rather than the body ... and [the Jewish Christians], like Paul proclaimed that Jesus had been raised; so they held a 'spiritual' view of the resurrection, including Jesus' resurrection." M.D. Goulder, "The Jewish-Christian Mission, 30–130," *Aufstieg und Niedergang der Romischen Welt*, II, *Principat* 26.3, 2025–26.

12 Jerome Murphy-O'Connor, *Paul. A Critical Life* (Oxford: Clarendon Press, 1996), 78.

13 Donald L. Jones, "Roman Imperial Cult," *ABD*, 5:806–809. For background, see Duncan Fishwick, "The Development of Provincial Ruler Worship in the Western Roman Empire," *Aufstieg und Niedergang der Romischen Welt*, II. *Principat* 16.2, 1201–53.

14 For this, and for concepts on the uses of rhetoric to lead to correct association in a listener's head, see Tor Norretranders, *The Use of Illusion. Cutting Consciousness Down to Size* (Harmondsworth: Penguin Books Ltd., 1998).

15 For an ingenious detailed interpretation, see Dungan, 83–99.

16 Although one never draws too tight parallels in discussing religious phenomena, the reader may wish to observe the evolution of beliefs that have followed the

Lubavitcher Rebbe, Menacham M. Schneerson after his death in 1994. Although in his lifetime he refused to declare himself to be the Messiah, his followers talked of it frequently. After his death, a significant body of them declared him Moshiah, affirmed that he in some way had returned to his followers ("The Rebbe is among us. His presence is more profoundly felt than ever before"), and became convinced that the Rebbe would redeem mankind and would preside over the resurrection of the dead. See their full-page advertisement, *New York Times*, 8 July 1997. See also, Herb Keinon, "Messiah when?" *Jerusalem Post* (Int. Ed.), 29 August 1997.

CHAPTER NINE

1 Arnold J. Wolf, "Jesus as an Historical Jew," *Judaism*, 46 (Summer 1997), 376.
2 John P. Meier, *A Marginal Jew. Rethinking the Historical Jesus* (New York: Doubleday, 1991), 1:168. I will not here list all the criteria that recent Questors adduce. They are well described in Meier, 1:168–84.
3 Although the fundamental goal of the Quest is extremely simple – to find out what kind of late Second Temple Judahist Yeshua really was – anyone encountering for the first time the recent literature on the subject will find much of it confusing and (there is no avoiding this fact), confused. So, here some simple consumer-warnings might be helpful. Two fundamental fallacies are common and can be caught out easily enough once one is aware of them. First, it is very common to find that the distinction between the *probable* and the *possible* becomes blurred. Most Questors are believers (or lonesome former-believers) of one sort or another and the desire to come up with some affirmative statement about the historical Yeshua often leads them to talk about things that are historically possible in the same tone of voice as those things that are historically probable; soon the former becomes the latter. One should keep ever in mind the distinction that is used by professional historians in the secular world: the merely possible is unlikely to have happened. There is nothing wrong with discussing some historical long-shots, but they have to be clearly labelled.

Secondly, and closely related, the grounds of presumption are just the same as they are in secular history: an event is assumed not to have occurred, and a saying not to have been uttered, unless there is positive evidence of its having occurred. Although few good biblical scholars would take the position that an event defined in the Gospels occurred unless it is proved otherwise, the multiplicity of various "criteria" – things such as the existence of Aramaisms, the criterion of vividness of narration, the criterion of "coherence," whatever that may mean – frequently act like the smoke and mirrors of a skilled illusionist: often the Questors are self-mesmerized, and end up reversing the grounds of presumption upon which historical proof rests, and doing so quite unconsciously. A good rule: the more the second-storey neon flashes, the more frequently you should take a flashlight and check that the foundations are solid.

4 *Surpassing Wonder*, 245–51.

5 John Tullius, *I'd Rather Be a Yankee. An Oral History of America's Most Loved and Most Hated Baseball Team* (New York: MacMillan, 1986), 188–9.

6 Meier, 1: 603.

7 Meier, 1: 169.

8 E.P. Sanders, *Paul* (Oxford: Oxford University Press, 1991), 99.

9 In Mark 9:41, Jesus is reported as making a third-person reference to the Christ, but whether or not he refers to himself is indeterminate.

10 Matthew 16:13–23 and John 4:25–26.

11 This observation is A.N. Wilson's, *Jesus* (London: Sinclair-Stevenson, 1992), 110.

12 It is no accident that this phrase is used alongside Saul's words in Corinthians, as part of the Lord's Supper in several present-day Christian traditions.

13 See James C. Vanderkam, "Calendars: Ancient Israelite and Early Jewish," ABD 1:814–20. My assertions carry the ubiquitous warning phrase (so crucial when dealing with any aspects of later Second Temple Judahism), "within the present state of our knowledge." That is a requisite truth-in-advertising warning.

I am struck by how very little direct evidence there is concerning the occurrence and character of holy festivals in late Second Temple times. There is a fair amount of material in the Books of Moses on the various festivals and also in Second Chronicles. This brings the usage-pattern down to roughly 400 BCE. And there is a great deal of information on feast patterns in the Mishnah (late second century of the Common Era) and in the two Talmuds of the fourth through sixth centuries CE.

It is a mistake, however, (1) to project into the first century CE material from the Torah that is several centuries prior to that time, and even the material in Chronicles is separated by roughly four centuries from the practices of the late Second Temple. (2) Equally, it is fallacious to project back into the late Second Temple period descriptions from the Mishnah and the Talmuds. This cannot be done, because these depictions are part of the re-invention of one branch of Judaism, which turns into Rabbinic Jewish practice.

Therefore, when one seeks direct contemporary evidence of how the liturgical year actually was observed in, say, the fifty years before and after Jesus' death, one is left with the inferences one can draw from the Temple Scroll, the Book of Enoch, the Book of Jubilees, the New Testament, Philo, and Josephus, and they are not reportorial on these matters. (For an admirable summary, see ibid.)

I emphasize the paucity of direct data, first, to give the reader fair warning that my own suggestions are necessarily speculative; and, second, simultaneously to warn that much (indeed, most) of the scholarly literature that one encounters which discusses the Judahist liturgical calendars and practices at about the time of Jesus is misleadingly self-confident and assertive. This holds true for all stripes of scholarship. I can think of no area of scholarship on the Jewish and Christian faiths, and on their common antecedents, wherein the strength of scholarly assertion is so ill-correlated with the actual strength of the evidence.

14 Gillian Feeley-Harnik, *The Lord's Table. The Meaning of Food in Early Judaism and Christianity* (Washington, D.C.: Smithsonian Institution Press, 1994), 120.

15 The key Synoptic texts are Matt. 26:26–29; Mark 14:22–25; and Luke 22:17–20. Equally important historically is Paul's order of the commemoration of the Last Supper which he traces directly to Jesus (found in 1 Corinthians 11:23–34). This Pauline material is consequential, because it indicates that the belief in the specific order of Jesus' acts at the Last Supper had crystallized within the early church before the destruction of the Second Temple and therefore considerably before the Synoptics were written in their present form.

John, in making the Last Supper not a Passover seder, but a casual meal on the eve of Passover (John, chapters 13 and 14), followed by a post-prandial stroll, almost superciliously supplants the Passover. Instead of a ritual meal, he focuses upon the actions of Jesus after the meal had ended (Jesus washes his disciples' feet) and upon his long colloquy with them (John 13:2–16:33). John concludes this passage with a prayer by Jesus, in which he offers himself up to his Father, in what is very clearly a trope of the Passover ritual (John 17:1–26). John has the luxury of the discursive version because, as the accounts in the Synoptics and in Paul indicate, the actual ritual details of the Last Supper were well known among Christians. That the author of John intends his text to be read as a New Passover seder is indicated by the fact that early-on (John 1:29) he identifies Jesus and "The Lamb of God, which taketh away the sin of the world" and he is very careful to have the Roman soldiers pierce Jesus' side, rather than break his bones (John 19:31–37), so that the prohibition against breaking the bones of Passover lambs (Exodus 12:46; Numb. 9:12; and cf Ps. 34:20) is not abrogated.

One niggling detail remains, namely, that none of the Synoptics calls Jesus the Lamb of God. That makes no difference. Saul's statement that Jesus is the Passover victim was a given, antedating as it does the Synoptic writings: "For even Christ our passover is sacrificed for us" (1 Cor. 5:7). More importantly, the foundation-analogy of the Synoptics is this:

Isaac: Abraham = Jesus: Yahweh

And since Isaac was identified as a sacrificial lamb (Gen. 22:8–9), so too is Jesus, albeit one who, unlike Isaac, actually has his blood spilled. Finally, recall the figure of the Suffering Servant of Second Isaiah. The Servant suffuses the Synoptic Gospels, and (whatever one may think of this usage of the Old Testament texts), there is no question that the Servant was clearly identified as a lamb (Isaiah 53:7) and in the Christian re-invention of the text, this identification slides onto Jesus Christ. The idea of Jesus as the Passover lamb is not a textual anomaly, but the clear articulation at the end of the narration of Jesus' ministry of a pervasive presence that has been there all the time, a gift from the texts of the Old Testament to the writers of the New.

16 This is demonstrated by Allen Brent, "Luke-Acts and the Imperial Cult in Asia Minor," *Journal of Theological Studies*, 48 (Oct. 1997), 411–38.

17 As is the case in the otherwise-impressive, *The Sayings of Jesus in the Churches of Paul. The Use of the Synoptic Tradition in the Regulation of Early Church Life* by David L. Dungan (Philadelphia: Fortress Press, 1971), esp. pp. 139–50.

18 The "Infancy Gospel of Jesus," a second century text, has Miriam's mother Anna, who was childless, receiving word that she (Anna) would give birth, directly from an angel of the Lord. (The entire text of this gospel as translated and annotated by Ronald F. Hock is found in Robert J. Miller, ed., *The Complete Gospels. Annotated Scholars Version*, Sonoma, Cal.: Polebridge Press, 1991, 373–89.) Mary was given the title that is rendered in English, "Mother of God," by many sections of the church by the end of the fourth century. At approximately the same time, the idea that she was a "perpetual virgin" began to gain ascendancy. This means that she was a virgin not only before Jesus' birth, but afterwards as well, an inventive construct both biologically and linguistically. (For a summation of the importance of the Blessed Virgin to the church fathers and their early medieval heirs, see Thomas Aquinas, *Summa Theologiae*, bilingual ed., vol. 51 *Our Lady*, tr. and ed. Thomas R. Heath, London: Blackfriars Press, 1969.) During the high Middle Ages, a doctrine of her Immaculate Conception was formulated. This meant that she was free from all stain of Original Sin, unlike every other human being. This purity originated at the instant of her own conception and, being free of Original Sin, Mary was said to have led a totally sinless life. This doctrine was affirmed (although it was not then a binding doctrine) in church councils of the fifteenth century. It was promulgated as dogmatic and binding by Pius IX in 1854. (Few, if any, Protestants embraced the concept.) From the eighteenth century onwards, Mary was sometimes called a "mediatrix" of grace. This meant that she somehow stood in mediation between the Almighty and humankind. The relationship with Jesus Christ, therefore, was somewhat problematical, as the Catholic church did not wish to diminish Jesus' glory as primary mediator between God and humanity. Inevitably, however, making Mary the fourth (if subordinate) member of the Christian godhead diluted the power of the other three. Pope Benedict XV (1914–22) sanctioned this belief and approved a mass and office of "Our Lady, Mediatrix of All Grace." (Again, Protestants abstained from this belief.) The last stage in the translation of Miriam, the unfortunately-pregnant young woman from hard-scrapple Nazareth, into a demi-god (or, perhaps, more) was the articulation of the doctrine that Mary never died, but was instead taken bodily into heaven. Early church rites had memorialized Mary's death, but in the sixth century, one school of churchmen began to assert that she had never died and they began to preach the Assumption of the Blessed Virgin Mary into Heaven. After the declara-

tion of the Immaculate Conception in 1854, pressure upon the Vatican grew to declare as authoritative the Assumption of the BVM and finally, in 1950, Pius XII did so. (Once again, Protestants remained aloof.)

On these developments, see Jaroslav Pelikan, "Mary – Exemplar of the Development of Christian Doctrine," in *Mary. Images of the Mother of Jesus in Jewish and Christian Perspective*, 79–91; Jaroslav Pelikan, *Mary Through the Centuries: Her Place in the History of Culture* (New Haven: Yale University Press, 1996), and related articles in *The Oxford Dictionary of the Christian Church*.

CHAPTER TEN

1 A. Resch, *Der Paulinismus und die Logia Jesu in ihrem gegenseitigen Verhaltnis untersucht* (Leipzig: Hinrichs, 1904) cited in James D.G. Dunn, "Jesus Tradition in Paul" in Bruce Chilton and Craig A. Evans, *Studying the Historical Jesus. Evaluations of the State of Current Research* (Leiden: E.J. Brill, 1994), 159.

2 Here we will not be using the term "Jesus-Tradition" as within historical studies it obscures more than it illuminates. The "Jesus-tradition" usually refers to folk-lore and early aide-memoires concerning the sayings of Yeshua of Nazareth that eventually went into the Gospels (and usually it means the Synoptic Gospels). Thus, one has a misleading, and unjustified, contrast between the privileged "Jesus-tradition" and Saul's knowledge of early folklore and, perhaps, scraps of writing. They are not separate, non-interactive entities, and were the term Jesus-tradition to have historical utility it would have to include specifically both Saul's knowledge and that which went into the Synoptics, would have to eschew privileging either one as *prima facie* more valid and more valuable than the other, and would have to recognize the interrelatedness of the two. Further, room would have to be made for other variants of the Jesus-tradition, which manifestly was a multiple-strand helix.

3 Thus E.P. Sanders, *The Historical Figure of Jesus* (London: Penguin Books, 1993), 59–60. Sanders is here presented only as an exemplar of what is a general belief.

4 The instances are listed in E. Earle Ellis, *Paul's Use of the Old Testament* (Edinburgh: Oliver and Boyd, 1957), appendix IV, 187. For a subtle study of Saul's use of Old Testament material, see Richard B. Hays, *Echoes of Scripture in the Letters of Paul* (New Haven: Yale University Press, 1989). On the particularly tight line between Isaiah and the epistles, see Douglas A. Oss, "A Note on Paul's Use of Isaiah," *Bulletin for Biblical Research*, 2 (1992), 104–12.

5 Ben F. Meyer, *The Early Christians. Their World Mission and Self-Discovery* (Wilmington: Michael Glazier, 1986), esp. appendix I, 84–8.

6 For context, see Marinus de Jonge, *Christology in Context. The Earliest Christian Response to Jesus* (Philadelphia: Westminster Press, 1988), especially chapter 1. De Jonge identifies Philippians 2:6–11 as a hymn (134–5), but his arguments about the formula employed hold equally well if one considers the piece to be a creed.

7 On the two textual versions, see "Jerry A. Pattengale, "Last Supper," *ABD*,
4:234–41. One cannot accept (contra 238) that Saul and the author-editor of Luke
were writing as variants of a single traditional version of the institution of the
Eucharist. This follows even if the "Long Text" of Luke is indeed the authentic
one (as distinct from the "Short Text" which has no body and blood reference at
all). In the Long Text, it is obvious that the material about enacting a permanent
body-and-blood-of-Jesus ritual is an insert from an alien source, not an organic
part of a long-held tradition, because the resultant version has Jesus offering up
the cup twice, both before and after the bread. This solecism in the Gospel of
Luke occurs because Saul's material is inserted into an extant narrative that
included the Passover, a Last Supper consisting only of bread, but not wine as the
liturgical elements, and which did not include any indication of the need for future
remembrance of Jesus in this fashion. The result in Luke is a mess.

8 Victor P. Furnish, *Jesus According to Paul* (Cambridge: Cambridge University
Press, 1993), 40–65. This volume is a model of expository and historical
economy.

9 For a detailed discussion of the support issue, see David L. Dungan, *The Sayings
of Jesus in the Churches of Paul. The Use of the Synoptic Tradition in the
Regulation of Early Church Life* (Philadelphia: Fortress Press, 1971), 3–80.

10 On the identity of this and other parallels, see Nikolaus Walter, "Paulus und die
urchristliche Jesustradition," *New Testament Studies*, 31 (1985), 498–522.

11 Dunn, 163.

12 Dale C. Allison, Jr., "The Pauline Epistles and the Synoptic Gospels: The Pattern
of the Parallels," *New Testament Studies*, 28 (1982), 1–32.

13 I am focussing on the Sermon on the Plain, rather than the Sermon on the Mount,
on the basis of the argument explained by Allison, 11–12. This is because the
former is more apt to be the original order than is that found in the more discursive Sermon on the Mount; and Luke 6:27–38 clearly stands as its own structural
unit, the bond to the Beatitudes and the Woes being the love-your-enemies
sayings.

14 Jurgen Becker, *Paul. Apostle to the Gentiles* (trans. from German by O.C. Dean,
Jr.) (Louisville: Westminster/John Knox Press, 1993, orig. ed.1989), 116–17.

CHAPTER ELEVEN

1 Understandably, some enthusiasts are keen on inferring that Saul actually heard
Yeshua preach. They base this on a generous reading of Romans 15:3, 2 Corinthians 5:16 and 11:1, and Philippians 2:6–8, which can be taken to convey a
first-hand knowledge of Yeshua's ministry, and on credence in the assertion
(in Acts 22:3) that Saul studied under Rabban Gamaliel I, which would have required him to be in Jerusalem during Yeshua's lifetime. The interpretation of such
material in the epistles is shown to be a misreading in Victor P. Furnish, *Jesus*

According to Paul (Cambridge: Cambridge University Press, 1993), 14–18. The material in the Acts of the Apostles concerning Saul's having studied under Gamaliel I is almost certainly an historically misleading piece of later anti-Pharisaic propaganda, as is argued in the text, below (section 4).

2 Henry Chadwick, *The Enigma of St. Paul* (London: Athlone Press, 1969), 5.

3 Ibid, 3.

4 The reader should not infer that I am here falling into the trap of validating information by using the separate segments of the New Testament as multiple independent attestations. Remember the point made in chapter nine: separate texts within the canon of the New Testament are *not* independent historical witnesses. They have all been filtered, homogenized and censored in their construction and in their inclusion in the canon.

Thus, I am not arguing that a given event or saying is more apt to be historically accurate because it is found both in the Gospels and also in Saul's letters. Rather, I am suggesting something quite different: (a) that certain statements in the epistles are historically probable; (b) that when the same assertions are found in the Gospels, they are still probable in exactly the same degree they were probable when reported in Saul's letters; (c) that the incidents or sayings' probability of historicity does *not* increase merely because they are found in separate sources. However, the identity of material allows one to transport the same level-of-probability from Saul's letters to those historical moments in the Gospels on which the epistles and the Gospels make contact.

5 I am leaving aside a related matter: the degree to which Saul's boasting in arguments against opponents was a consciously ironic form. In the present text, we are dealing with fervent statements of selfhood. On his boasting, see Christopher Forbes, "Comparison, Self-Praise and Irony: Paul's Boasting and the Conventions of Hellenistic Rhetoric," *New Testament Studies,* 32 (1986), 1–30.

6 Krister Stendahl, *Paul among Jews and Gentiles and other Essays* (Philadelphia: Fortress Press, 1976), 8.

7 E.P. Sanders, *Paul* (Oxford: Oxford University Press, 1991), 3–4 and chapter eleven.

8 Wilfred L. Knox, *St. Paul and the Church of Jerusalem* (Cambridge: Cambridge University Press, 1925), 115*n*16.

9 Craig C. Hill, *Hellenists and Hebrews. Reappraising Division within the Earliest Church* (Minneapolis: Fortress Press, 1992), 3.

10 For examples of the conflicting definition of terms relating to the extent of Greek influence, see Shaye J.D. Cohen, *From the Maccabees to the Mishnah* (Philadelphia: Westminster Press, 1987), 35–38; G.W. Bowersock, *Hellenism in Late Antiquity* (Ann Arbor: University of Michigan Press, 1990), xi–xii; Louis H. Feldman, "How much Hellenism in Jewish Palestine?" *Hebrew Union College Annual,* 57 (1986), 83–111; Martin Hengel, *Judaism and Hellenism. Studies in their Encounter in Palestine during the Early Hellenistic Period* (London: SCM

Press, second ed. 1974, orig. pub. as *Judentum und Hellenismus* 1968), 2:1–5; Tessa Rajak, "The Hasmoneans and the Uses of Hellenism," in Philip R. Davies and Richard T. White (eds.), *A Tribute to Geza Vermes. Essays on Jewish and Christian Literature and History* (Sheffield: JSOT, 1990), 262–5.

    A standard, if already quite dated, discussion of the entire phenomenon is in W.D. Davies and Louis Finkelstein, *The Cambridge History of Judaism*, vol. II, *The Hellenistic Age* (Cambridge: Cambridge University Press, 1990).

11 Shaye Cohen, 36.

12 Rajak, 262.

13 Of course this was not universally the case. Among the most notable exceptions was Cyrus Gordon of Brandeis University whose work emphasized the commonality and interpenetration of Semitic and Hellenic cultures. See for example his *Before the Bible. The Common Background of the Greek and Hebrew Civilisations* (New York: Harper & Row, 1962).

14 Fergus Millar, *The Roman Near East, 31 BC – AD 337* (Cambridge: Harvard University Press, 1993), 352.

15 See Hengel, *Judaism and Hellenism* above, note 10, and also Martin Hengel, *The "Hellenization" of Judaea in the First Century after Christ* (London: SCM Press, 1989, original pub., 1989 as *Zum Problem der "Hellenisierung" Judaeas im 1. Jahrhundert nach Christus*). In this volume, Hengel backs off considerably from the more extreme position he took in his 1966 doctoral thesis.

16 It should be emphasized that Hengel is not patronizing or dismissive of non-Hellenic thought. He argues that "we must stop attaching either negative or positive connotations to the question of 'Hellenistic' influence" (1989:53). His point is simply that it was dominant.

    For useful commentaries, see Eric M. Meyers, "The Challenge of Hellenism for Early Judaism and Christianity," *Biblical Archaeologist*, 55 (June 1992), 84–91 and Robert Harrison, "Hellenization in Syria-Palestine: The case of Judaea in the third century BCE," *Biblical Archaeologist*, 57 (June 1994), 98–108.

17 Rudolf Bultmann, *Jesus and the Word* (New York: Charles Scribner's Sons, 1954, orig. German ed., 1926), 133.

18 David Flusser, *Judaism and the Origins of Christianity* (Jerusalem: Magnes Press, 1988), xvi.

19 Feldman (1986), 111.

20 One thing that the traditional classicists hold in common with scholars such as Feldman is that both groups unconsciously equate everything non-Jewish with the Hellenic. This leaves out the undeniable influence of Persian thought and, possibly, the influence of Zoroastrian notions. See Norman Cohn, *Cosmos, Chaos and the World to Come. The Ancient Roots of Apocalyptic Faith* (New Haven: Yale University Press, 1993).

21 Shaye Cohen, 37.

22 Samuel Sandmel, *Judaism and Christian Beginnings* (New York: Oxford University Press, 1978), 258.

23 Eric M. Meyers, "Galilee in the Time of Jesus," *Biblical Archaeologist* (Nov-Dec 1994), 41.

24 With Saul it is crucial to emphasize that Albert Schweitzer was right, that Saul was not the force that Hellenised Christianity. If his eschatological beliefs on the future return of Jesus Christ served as an ideological conduit for later Hellenizers, that was done neither by his intention nor with his foreknowledge. See Albert Schweitzer, *Die Mystik des Apostels Paulus* (Tubingen: J.C.B. Mohr, 1930), ix, and passim.

25 Joseph Klausner, *From Jesus to Paul* (tr. from Hebrew by William F. Stinespring), (New York: MacMillan, 1943, orig. ed. 1939), 482. The one exception, a major one I would argue, is Paul's idea of the Crucified Mosiah.

26 David Flusser, *Jesus* (trans. from German by Ronald Walls) (London: Herder and Herder, 1969, orig. ed., 1968), 72.

27 A.N. Wilson, *Jesus* (London: Sinclair-Stevenson, 1992), 64.

28 Philo's position in the history of Judahism, and of its heirs, the Christian and the Jewish faiths, is paradoxical. Philo left to posterity the largest body of religious writing set down by one person that exists prior to the destruction of the Second Temple. And Philo, in so doing, gave us the largest body of religious writings in the Jewish-Christian tradition that can accurately be ascribed to a single author, before the Middle Ages. Indeed, he is one of only two religious writers in the Yahwist-derived tradition who wrote before 70 CE whose works can be identified by author. The other is Saul. Both the range and the extent of Philo's writing is impressive to the point of being intimidating. In its modern form his work comprises twelve volumes (in the Loeb Classical Library) and this even though probably one-quarter of his works have been lost. Despite there being problems with some of Philo's writings (he is sometimes so discursive that one forgets by the end of an argument exactly what the topic is), he provides an unrivalled opportunity to observe the workings of a highly-devout Diaspora Judahist who is up-to-date on the writings of the Greek-derived philosophers of his own day. Philo's writing is a clear case of loyalty to Yahweh being prepotent over Hellenic-derived philosophy, and this even when Hellenistic forms of articulation are employed.

The writings of Philo Judaeus fall into three categories. One of these consists of his purely philosophical works. His mixture of Platonism and Stoicism is useful to the historian of philosophy who wishes to determine which philosophical notions were common currency in the great library-city of Alexandria at the beginning of the Common Era. These writings, a relatively small portion of Philo's entire output, do not directly shed light on religious matters. Secondly, and much more valuable for our present purposes, Philo wrote a small body of texts that detailed recent history. Yet, most valuable is the third component of Philo's writings, and these constitute the bulk of his work: the interpretation of the Books of Moses (especially Genesis) according to the vocabulary of Alexandrian philosophical thought. Philo created a parallel-text to the scriptures, one that simultaneously honours the older writings, and re-writes them. Crucially, in doing this, Philo was not acting heretically. In fact, he was a very strong adherent of the two beliefs that become central to Rabbinic Judaism as it develops after the destruction of the Second Temple: he was firmly convinced that Moses was the actual author of the Pentateuch and he believed there existed in oral traditions valid knowledge of events and beliefs concerning the Chosen People that went all the way back to the times of Moses. Philo's method of writing a parallel text was primarily through allegory, a method he sometimes took to extraordinary lengths. In the typical case, he would take a relatively small portion of the Pentateuch (the creation story, the story of Cain and Abel), or a specific issue that is referred to in the Pentateuch (drunkenness and sobriety, for example) and through a form of rhetoric remarkably discursive and confusedly allusive, he would continually reinterpret the basic events of the history of the Chosen People, emphasizing that they were mostly literally true, but, crucially, always true in some eternal sense. The major figures of early Judahist history are presented simultaneously as real people and also as Platonic types of various forms of truth; the Temple is transformed in allegory from being the sometime residence of Yahweh (in Tabernacle times he dwelt therein) into a cosmic representation of the unity of the one god that is Truth.

Philo accepts the Platonic worldview that undergirds his allegorical method of thinking, because that method is consonant with Mosaic history, not the other way around. That is, Judahism is anterior to Platonism and Platonism is not a foundation of Judahism's truth, a useful, but necessarily ancillary, validation of that truth.

The scholarly literature on Philo can be divided into two eras: that which precedes the work of Erwin Goodenough in the 1930s, and everything thereafter. Especially important among Goodenough's works were *The Politics of Philo Judaeus* (New Haven: Yale University Press, 1938) and *An Introduction to Philo Judaeus* (New Haven: Yale University Press, 1940). For a bibliography of the work done since Goodenough's era, see R. Radice and D.T. Runia, *Philo of Alexandria: An Annotated Bibliography, 1937–1986* (Leiden: Brill, 1988).

29 See E. Earle Ellis, *Paul's Use of the Old Testament* (Edinburgh: Oliver and Boyd, 1957), 51–6, and the classic, Leonhard Goppelt, *Typos. The Typological Interpretation of the Old Testament in the New* (tr. from German by Donald H. Madvig), (Grand Rapids: Eerdmans, 1982, orig. ed, 1939).

30 Knox 110n9. Although I think it would be pushing the evidence to claim that Saul was acquainted with any specific document among the many extra-biblical texts of the later Second Temple era (and especially wrong to claim he was familiar

with them in a form that has been preserved down to our own time), there are some intriguing proximities of thought. For example, given his emphasis upon movement between the earth and heaven, it is interesting that Judahist speculation of his era had fastened on the idea that Wisdom was an ascending and descending figure. (See Proverbs 8:27–31; Enoch 42:1-3; Wisdom of Solomon 7:24–30; Ecclesiasticus [the wisdom of Jesus Ben-Sirach] 24:1–7). Incidentally, if one is looking for the origin of the Christian notion of the Holy Spirit, instead of finding "pneumatic" elements in Greek sources, it would be more direct to examine continuities with Wisdom, as found in the Writings and the Apocrypha.

Another item related to ascension (a major motif for Saul) is the ascension of Enoch to heaven, found in vivid detail in Enoch 1:8–16:3, and in the more prosaic original in Genesis 5:21–24. See Alan F. Segal, *Paul the Convert. The Apostolate and Apostasy of Saul the Pharisee* (New Haven: Yale University Press, 1990), 46–8.

Knox noted some very close parallels between several lemma in Galatians, 1 Thess., 1 and 2 Corinthians and portions of the Testaments of the Twelve Patriarchs. He did not claim that Saul knew these documents, but suggested that either Saul and the writers of the Testaments worked similarly from the same Old Testament originals (and thus were part of a common circle of ideas) or that the resemblances were probably due to mere coincidence. (Knox, 108*n*9).

31 See Ellis, appendix 1:150–2, for a compendium of Old Testament references in Saul's letters and their relegation to the Septuagint and to the Hebrew texts of the Tanakh.

32 This is a modest, and I think, sensible estimate. In the last century, informal contests emerged as to who could count the most citations of the Old Testament in the New, and in 1900 one German scholar managed to scoop the field with a count of 4,105. For a survey of the various results from these citation-counts, see Walter C. Kaiser, Jr., *The Uses of the Old Testament in the New* (Chicago: Moody Press, 1985), 2–3. Ellis provides a tight list of 107 citations (150–1). Saul's use of the Pentateuch is particularly important. See James M. Scott, "Paul's use of Deuteronomic Tradition," *Journal of Biblical Literature*, 112 (1993), 645–65.

33 Entry into the literature on Saul's belief system is extremely difficult. A sensible recent theological discussion is James D.G. Dunn, *The Theology of Paul the Apostle* (Edinburgh: T. and T. Clark, 1998). For discussions that are fundamentally historical in outlook, the various works of E.P.Sanders are the best available. See (in addition to his *Paul*, 1991), *Paul, the Law, and the Jewish People* (Philadelphia: Fortress Press, 1983), and *Paul and Palestinian Judaism: A Comparison of Patterns of Religion* (Philadelphia: Fortress Press, 1977).

34 Charlotte Allen, "Q: The Search for a No-Frills Jesus," *Atlantic Monthly*, 278 (Dec. 1996), 54.

35 Charlotte Allen, *The Human Christ. The Search for the Historical Jesus* (New York: The Free Press, 1998), 272, 276.

36 In practical terms, the historically-oriented scholarly literature on Pharisaism comes from two sally-ports: Jacob Neusner and everyone else. Neusner is the most productive of workers in the field of Jewish history from, roughly, the beginning of the Common Era to the completion of the Babylonian Talmud, c. 600 CE. His lifework consists of nothing less than the reconfiguration of the world's understanding of the Pharisees and of Rabbinic Judaism. Among his many books on the Pharisees, the most useful in relationship to the historical Yeshua is *The Rabbinic Traditions about the Pharisees before 70* (Leiden: E.J. Brill, 1973), three vols.

   Because Neusner accepts the canons of evidence demanded in secular scholarship, his work is largely shunned by Jewish scholars who work in Yeshivot. However, among those who work by verifiable standards of proof and disproof, his one formidable opponent has been E.P. Sanders. See Sanders, *Jewish Law from Jesus to the Mishnah. Five Studies* (London: SCM Press, 1990), and *Judaism. 63 BC–66 CE. Practice and Belief* (Philadelphia: Trinity Press, 1991). For Neusner's response, see his *Judaic Law from Jesus to the Mishnah. A Systematic Reply to Professor E.P. Sanders* (Atlanta: Scholars Press, 1993).

37 The decisive breakthrough was effected by Samuel Sandmel in the 1960s.

38 The least lunatic of these is Hyam Maccoby's, *The Mythmaker. Paul and the Invention of Christianity* (London: Weidenfeld and Nicolson, 1986) and *Paul and Hellenism* (London: SCM Press, 1991). Maccoby is representative in his willingness to embrace Jesus as a true Pharisee, while seeing Saul as anti-Judahist and at heart anti-Semitic.

39 Thus Gerd Luedemann, *The Unholy in Holy Scripture. The Dark Side of the Bible* (tr. from German by John Bowden), (Louisville: Westminster/John Knox Press, 1997, orig ed. 1996), 81–5. One rejects as special pleading and evidentiarily weak the claim that the seemingly anti-Jewish passages in Saul's letter were directed against the House of Shammai and not against the House of Hillel, these being the two major branches of Pharisaism in Saul's time. Harvey Falk, *Jesus the Pharisee. A New Look at the Jewishness of Jesus* (New York: Paulist Press, 1985).

40 Samuel Sandmel, *The First Christian Century in Judaism and Christianity. Certainties and Uncertainties* (New York: Oxford University Press, 1969), 54n65. Alan Segal, who analyses Saul as a trained Pharisee, suggests an additional reason for employing Saul as an important Judahist exhibit: "If his discussion of transformation can be related to apocalyptic mysticism in Judaism, he also becomes the only Jewish mystic of this period to relate this experience confessionally." (Segal, 48)

41 Paul Winter, *On the Trial of Jesus* (Berlin: Walter de Gruyter, 1974), 186.

42 David Flusser (1969, 46–7) presents a persuasive case that in the argument reported in Mark (7:5–8), concerning the obligations of hand-washing and the perpetual worries about which bits of crockery were ritually clean and which were unclean, Yeshua was not directing his words specifically at the Pharisees. He was

really saying that "strict observation of ritual purity can itself encourage moral laxity" (Flusser, 47). Flusser argues that, though Yeshua may have criticized the Pharisees, he only once is recorded in the Gospels as doing anything that would have conflicted with the then-current interpretation of Halachah as accepted by many branches of Judahism, not just by the Pharisees. This was the incident of the plucking of handfuls of standing grain to eat on the Sabbath day (Luke 6:1–5).

43 Knox, 115–16n19.

44 These developments are summarized in Devon H. Wiens, "Mystery Concepts in Primitive Christianity and in its Environment," *Aufstieg und Niedergang der Romischen Welt*, II. *Principat.* 23.2, 1248–84.

45 I must re-emphasize that while Saul's mission was a topological simulacrum of Yeshua's, it happened in a very different province. Thus, I am not denying N.T. Wright's point that Yeshua and Saul, while coming from a single religious universe, nevertheless had to use the concepts of that universe in very different ways, for they faced quite different problems in their missionary activities. Saul had to deal with what can be called "Gentile issues." As Wright notes, "none of these issues, so vital to the work of Paul, was at stake in the ministry of Jesus. The evangelists [meaning, the Gospel writers] had plenty of opportunities to have Jesus meet Gentiles, and to discuss the question of the terms upon which they might obtain membership of the covenant people, but we find few such meetings, and no such discussions … *The key issue of Torah in Paul's churches was the question of Gentile admission, and thus of circumcision; and about that Jesus said not a word.*" N.T. Wright, *Jesus and the Victory of God* (Minneapolis: Fortress Press, 1996), 381, emphasis Wright's.

Appendices

Appendix A

Winnie-the-Pooh and the Jesus Seminar

IT IS NATURAL THAT MANY OF THE SCHOLARS WHO SPECIALIZE IN trying to find "the real historical Jesus" have become co-dependents. However much they differ from each other on matters of interpretation, evidence, and in their individual unconscious assumptions, they need each other and depend upon each other for confirmation that their quest for the historical Yeshua is a valid enterprise.

Here A.A. Milne enters the picture. He produced several brilliant examples of what, in early rabbinical times, would have been labelled a *mashal* or, in its earlier Christian form, a parable. One of these instructive stories is entitled "Pooh and Piglet Go Hunting and Nearly Catch a Woozle" and scholars who read it aloud to their children or grandchildren are likely to find that, while it puts the little darlings to sleep, it leaves reflective adults staring at the ceiling all night.

This mashal's *mise en scène* is a small copse on a fine winter day, snow on the ground, frost in the air. Winnie-the Pooh, a Bear of Very Little Brain, walks around reflectively, and to a casual observer, he seems to be thinking deep thoughts, rather like an abstracted Victorian clergyman collecting his ideas for a sermon. He walks round and round in a large circle. His friend Piglet, noticing this, joins him and asks him what he is doing. "Hunting," Pooh replies and adds mysteriously, "tracking something." Trouble is, Pooh doesn't know quite what he is tracking. "I shall have to wait until I catch up with it," he says. Ever helpful, Piglet suggests, "Oh, Pooh! Do you think it's a- a- Woozle?", Pooh admits that it may be, and the two of them follow the trail of this undefined animal. As they circle the spinney they find more and more woozle prints, as one woozle track is joined by another and then another, and another. Piglet decides that he really does not want to run into a whole herd of woozles, and is about to leave Winnie-the-Pooh to carry on the hunt alone, when a voice from the sky – in the guise of young Christopher

Robin who has been watching them from high in an old oak tree – explains to the two investigators that they have been going round and round the copse; and that they are going in circles and that the growing number of tracks has been produced by their own feet as they walked ever-forward.[1]

That is mashal, not an allegory. The quest for the historical Yeshua is not a search for a non-existent being: Yeshua the man certainly existed. Nor are New Testament historians Bears of Very Little Brain: quite the opposite; they represent some of the more supple intelligences of our time. However, the more one immerses oneself in the continually growing literature concerning the historical Yeshua, the more one realizes how dependent emotionally and cognitively the scholars are on each other, and how comforted they are by the ever-growing band of footprints that fill their path. Certainly their quarry must be just ahead. This co-dependence is exhibited by the richness of cross-citation found in the literature. The ratio of citation of primary sources to citation of secondary sources is very low. Of course, New Testament historians disagree with each other: scholars, like lawyers, are paid to joust. And just like lawyers who take opposing sides, and even do so with conviction, the various opponents are all part of the same evidentiary system.

With that as background, the case of the Jesus Seminar becomes relevant: not for the substantive nature of its conclusions, but as a parable of what happens in New Testament scholarship when consensus becomes an over-riding mode of assessing evidence. The Jesus Seminar was founded in 1985 by Robert W. Funk, whose academic degrees came from Butler University, the Christian Theological Seminary, and Vanderbilt University. He also founded the "Westar Institute" in Sonoma, California, as a holding company for what became a rapidly expanding array of activities. Funk was joined as co-chair of the Jesus Seminar by John Dominic Crossan of DePaul University whose scholarly credentials include a D.D. from Maynooth College, the ecclesiastical seminary governed by the Irish Catholic bishops. Thirty original "Fellows" comprised the Jesus Seminar in 1985, and it grew considerably, so that by the early 1990s roughly 100 scholars had been involved at one time or another.[2] The Seminar, through its holding company, came to possess an array of instruments of self-publication: its own publishing house (Polebridge Press), and three periodicals: *The Forum*, its scholarly house organ; *The Fourth R*, a general magazine aimed at promoting "religious literacy"; and the *Seminar Papers*, which were the working papers of the scholars. As far as I can ascertain from talking to members of the Seminar, there was no philanthropic foundation or other financial godfather behind the work of the Seminar. It ran on a shoe-string until the MacMillan Publishing Company signed on to publish *The Five Gospels*, the Seminar's magnum opus. (The "fifth gospel" was the Gospel of Thomas, a

Coptic document that the Seminar's Fellows embraced with an enthusiasm that bordered on fervour.)[3]

The Jesus Seminar's publications were markedly self-vaunting, not least in their description of the academic qualifications of the guild. The glossary of *The Five Gospels* contained this definition:

> Fellows (of the Jesus Seminar). Fellows of the Jesus Seminar have had advanced training in biblical studies. Most of them hold the Ph.D. or equivalent from some of the world's leading graduate institutions.

The Seminar's *The Gospel of Mark. Red Letter Edition* contained a prefatory discussion by Robert W. Funk of the rigours of biblical scholarship. It concluded: "The end product of this process is something called the scholarly consensus. Every scholar aspires to contribute to that consensus and to become a representative of it."[4] Although some historical scholars would rather walk alone than tramp with fools, this consensus position at least is honestly expressed, and says clearly what many other biblical scholars would not feel comfortable expressing openly.

2

So, as its first task, the Jesus Seminar set about developing a definitive edition that would spell out which sayings attributed to Jesus-the-Christ were authentic and which were not.[5] This was to be done democratically and by consensus. The opinion of each Fellow of the Seminar was declared to be equal to that of every other. The Fellows would listen to each other's arguments, to be sure, but in the end each individual's opinion was just as good as anyone else's. This puts one in mind of Spiro Agnew, deposed vice-president of the United States, who reportedly proclaimed that in his life he always tried to find the Golden Mean between right and wrong. As a means of making historical judgements, the Seminar's method was absurd. (What would the consensus of the Astronomy Seminar have been in the days of Copernicus?) But the Jesus Seminar's collective methods were not very much different from the efforts of individual scholars in biblical history (or any other historical field) who search for a "balanced" view of a given topic or for a "synthesis" of previous secondary literature, rather than sorting out the primary evidence, making decisions, and taking responsibility for their own views.

The Jesus Seminar decided that each saying of Jesus-the-Christ reported in the New Testament and in various extra-canonical sources, should be graded according to levels of probability: Jesus certainly said it; he probably did; he probably did not; he certainly did not. Each Fellow voted. This was done by casting one of four coloured balls – red, pink, gray, or black – into a voting box. One can ignore the diverting picture of biblical historians voting for or against the sayings of Jesus, as if they were voting for a candidate for the Papacy, but what cannot be ignored is (1) that, as already mentioned, the consensus method has no discriminatory power as between good and bad historical arguments, and (2) that the four-category method the Seminar employed was so deeply methodologically flawed that they had to fudge heavily the results. This is a matter of statistics, but is not a complicated matter, and it is very instructive indeed on how a "scientific" approach to history can turn into a woozle hunt.

In considering the methods by which the Jesus Seminar determined the opinion of its Fellows, we must keep in mind one axiom of basic and general statistics: an applied statistical description of a problem should not be used to generate data that appear to be more accurate or more specific or more important than those original values one is seeking to interpret. For example, it is actually less genuinely descriptive to say that "over 66.3% of my office's lights malfunctioned," than it is to say "both my desk lamps burned out, but the ceiling light stayed on."

The basic technique the Seminar used to make a judgement was simple. A panel of members ("Fellows") voted on whether a given saying attributed to Jesus was authentic or not. That is uncomplicated, but it has one hidden requirement. The reliability of the method is compromised if the panel of voters is not constant throughout the entire procedure. The panel's being constant does not guarantee the validity of the result, but the panel's not being constant virtually guarantees that the result will be invalid. In the actual event, the panel changed a good deal over time, so the results of the opinions on one section of the scriptures are not comparable with those on another. The Seminar, in publishing its voting results, camouflaged this problem by reporting not the actual number of voters (which would have given away the flux in the panel) but instead reported only the percentage of the (unstated) number who actually voted.[6]

However, for the moment, let us forget that the flux in the panel of experts invalidated their procedures. Pretend that we do not know this fact, and instead follow the obliquely revealing explanation of the Seminar's techniques that was published in *The Gospel of Mark. Red Letter Edition* (pp. xx–xxi). The balls of four different colours were placed in the voting box indicating what each panel member thought of each purported saying of Jesus:

> The Seminar adopted two official interpretations of the four colors. Individuals could elect either one for their own guidance. An unofficial but helpful interpretation of these categories by one member led to this formulation:
> red: That's Jesus!
> pink: Sure sounds like Jesus.

gray: Well, maybe.

black: There's been some mistake.

The Seminar did not insist on uniform standards for balloting.

The ranking of items is determined by weighted vote. Since most Fellows of the Seminar are professors, they are accustomed to grade points and grade point averages. So they decided on the following scheme:

red = 3

pink = 2

gray = 1

black = 0

The points on each ballot are added up and divided by the number of votes in order to determine the weighted average. While the scale is zero to three, it was decided to convert the weighted averages to percentages to employ a scale of 100 rather than a scale of 3.00. The result is a scale divided into four quadrants:

red: .7501 up

pink: .5001 to .7500

gray: .2501 to .5000

black: .0000 to .2500

We instructed the computer to carry the averages out to four decimal places, but we have rounded the numbers off to two decimal places in the voting tables found in an appendix to this volume.

Before considering what all this meant, the Seminar should be rescued from two minor errors in their own terminology. The "weighted average" they refer to is not a weighted average, but simply the average of the number of points the voters gave to each saying of Jesus: it is the total of points divided by the number of voters, and there is no special weighting involved. Also, they refer to "percentages" when they are not actually using percentages, but simply mapping their results on an arbitrary 100-point scale. These are minor matters, but if these two points are not noted, the Seminar's methodological fog lifts rather more slowly than is necessary.

Now, consider the original scale: red (3), pink (2), gray (1) and black (0). On the surface it seems to make sense. For instance, it seems reasonable if, for example, fifty-one members of the Seminar voted red, and forty-nine voted pink, then a purported saying of Jesus would be ruled genuine, since it would have an average score of slightly over the half-way point between red and pink, which is 2.5. (For purposes of this discussion, I am pretending that there were always 100 Fellows of the Seminar voting; the argument works with any number voting, however.) And, at the other end of the scale, say that fifty-one of the Fellows did not believe at all in a given saying and hence they cast the black ball, while forty-nine were not quite so certain and they cast the gray. The result of the vote would be accurately indicated by a score of slightly less than 0.5 and thus the saying would be cast out. Seemingly, then, a valid scale would have the following break points:

Jesus certainly said it.   average of 2.5 and up
Jesus probably said it.   1.5 to 2.49 points
Jesus probably did not say it. 0.5 to 1.49 points
Jesus certainly did not say it. 0.49 points and below.

The problem with this is that the scale does not work. Assume for the moment that there is one ideologue in the Seminar who believes that Jesus said almost nothing in the scriptures, and so, on almost every issue, he votes black. Now go back to the example of a highly probable saying. But now assume that fifty-one Fellows vote red, believing Jesus certainly said it, forty-eight vote pink, and one Fellow votes black. This is the same 51–49 break that, in the earlier example gave the yes-it-is-genuine result, but now the result is pink, because it falls beneath the 2.50 break-line.

Exactly the same thing happens at the bottom end of the scale.

The overall result of this scoring system is to seriously bias the Seminar's reported judgement against the two ends of the scale. (The example I gave was the most modest possible; the reader can easily illustrate much more serious cases of skewing.) In sum, this scoring system misrepresented the opinions of the Fellows by artificially reducing the black and the red categories, ostensibly the most decisive and important ones. In practical terms, the problem was more acute at the top end of the range, because, tough-minded as the scholars wished to be, the Seminar would be in a delicate position if it produced a new edition of the Christian scriptures in which few, if any, sayings of Jesus were adjudged to be genuine.

The Seminar tried to escape from this methodological box by adopting a 100-point scale. They neglected to explain the scoring system they adopted when they moved to the new scale, but it can be reconstructed from their published results. It was as follows:

Red   = 1.00
Pink   = .666
Gray   = .333
Black = 0.0

Take our case of fifty-one Fellows voting red and forty-nine voting pink. The score would be 83.6. This is above the mid point of the range between .666 and 1.00 – which is .833 – so the saying is ruled authentic.

The break points of the new 100-point scale, if one uses the mid-points of each range, are thus, as follows:

Jesus certainly said it.	.833 and up
Jesus probably said it.	.500 to .832
Jesus probably did not say it.	.167 to .499
Jesus certainly did not say it.	.166 and below.

This new scale has exactly the same problems that the scale of "0" to "3" had: it skews everything towards the pink and gray ranges, the muddy middle of the scale. In fact, by this method only twelve out of the 1,544 possibly-authentic sayings of Jesus which the Seminar examined met this test of red-letter authenticity. This dozen, no matter how significant, would have made for a red-letter Bible with very few red letters.

So, the Seminar was in trouble. They had to move the goalposts, so that more sayings of Jesus would be adjudged to be authentic. The positions to which the posts were moved at first glance look as if they must be based on logic or upon probability theory:

Jesus certainly said it.	.7501 and up
Jesus probably said it.	.5001 to .7500
Jesus probably did not say it.	.2501 to .5000
Jesus certainly did not say it.	.0000 to .2500.

That is an optical illusion. Take the top end of the scale. Why was 75.0 chosen as a mid-point between 1.00 and 0.66? It defies logical explanation, as does the goal post at the bottom end of the scale: 0.25, which is employed as a break point between 0.00 and 0.333! In fact, the break points – 25, 50, 75 – look good and, equally importantly, they produce more of the desired results, namely, many sayings that are now said to be certainly authentic, when, under the original system, they had been judged less-than-certain.

In fact, there is no statistical technique and no technique of probability assessment that indicates when, among a given social group (in this case, the Fellows of the Jesus Seminar), one begins to feel confident that some Jesus-sayings either were clearly authentic, or certainly were not. (There is no statistical reason why, for example, .7501 was any more appropriate a cut-off point for red-sayings than .78 would have been, or .70.) Therefore, it must be emphasized that the placing of the goal posts (a) was independent of the scoring scale employed in the original ratings, save that it had to fit within the outside parameters of the original system; (b) was completely arbitrary and had no statistical or probability theory behind it; and (c) was set so as to give a pre-determined desired result: namely, more red and more black results than the use of the mid-points in the scoring ranges provided. These desired results were set externally to the data and were imposed upon them. *The results do not represent what the considered judgement of the Fellows of the Jesus Seminar actually was*, but rather reflected what someone, or some group, wished to see promulgated.

This is a long explanation of one of the Seminar's several fundamental methodological flaws. If the reader prefers a compressed version it is that the Seminar made the fundamental error of assigning a cardinal metric to a set of four options that have no natural shared metric. In this situation, the most sensible thing to have done would have been to report that "X" number of the Fellows voted for category 1, "Y" for category 2, and so on. Assigning common values is a basic no-no.

Was this cascade of hubris-turned-to-folly avoidable? Yes, even within the Seminar's own historical assumptions (which, though I do not accept, I have no objection to seeing dealt with competently). All the Seminar had to do was to forget the voting-by-coloured-ball method and employ a simple two-part vote on each saying: (1) do you think this saying is by Jesus? (2-a) If so, do you think it probably was by Jesus or almost certainly was by him? or, (2-b) if not, do you think it almost certainly was not uttered by Jesus or merely that it probably was not said by him?

That yields the four sectors of opinion the Seminar wished to articulate, and no skewing. Of course, it is simple and lacks self-importance.

NOTES

1 A.A. Milne, *Winnie-the-Pooh* (New York: E.P. Dutton, 1926), 34–43.
2 The early history is repeated in several of the Seminar's publications. See, for example, Robert W. Funk, with Mahlon H. Smith, *The Gospel of Mark. Red Letter Edition* (Sonoma: Polebridge Press, 1991), xiii-xix.
3 Robert W. Funk, Roy W. Hoover, "and the Jesus Seminar," *The Five Gospels. The Search for the Authentic Words of Jesus* (New York: MacMillan Publishing Co., 1993).
4 Funk, *The Gospel of Mark*, xiv.
5 In the discussion of statistical techniques which follows, I have been helped by two econometricians, Chris Ferral of Queen's University and Timothy W. Guinnane of Yale University. I am grateful for their generous assistance.
6 The full lists of "votes" is found in several different formats in *Forum*, one of the Seminar's self-publications. The most useful version is found in vol. 6, March 1990, 4–55. It is this list of votes that I have used to investigate the reporting procedures the Seminar employed.

Appendix B

Hubris and Plasticity in the "Q"-Industry

TO DEAL WITH THE LOGICAL INFRASTRUCTURE OF "Q" IN THE WAY that a professional historian would find recognizable and analysable, we need to go back to basics and sharpen our definition of how "Q" can be defined. It must be in a manner that can be replicated even by those who may, for totally exogenous reasons (such as their theological commitments) have no allegiance to the substance of the hypothetical document being put together. Now *if* one adopts the view that Mark is the earliest of the Synoptic Gospels and *if* one also accepts the relations of the so-called "two source hypothesis" (which, as I explained earlier, splays a bit, into multiple sources) *then* one can develop a version of "Q" that will be acceptable as the *minimum* that "Q" will contain. That "minimum-Q" will have the following characteristics:

1 It will consist only of items found in Matthew and Luke on which there is virtually identical agreement. There is a bit of latitude here, but not much, for abandoning the criterion of verbal agreement destroys the two-source version of the Mark-hypothesis on which the entire "Q" project rests.

2 Items on which there is half-way agreement are out. This must be emphasized, because it is common to find pericopes wherein there is agreement in part of the material, but not in the rest. Unless the material is obviously truncated (that is, not a unified pericope), then the sections in Luke and those in Matthew which are not in close agreement must be excluded from our "minimum-Q." (Compare for instance Matthew 11:20–24 and Luke 10: 12–15. They half-way agree.)

3 No materials that Matthew and Luke share with Mark are to be included. That is an arbitrary rule, but it follows from the two-source version of the Mark-hypothesis, and if one abandons it, then one abandons "Q." In any case, how one would discriminate between those parts of the shared Mark-Luke-Matthew tradition that came from Mark and those that came from "Q," is questionable, and no known method would produce the replicability and general agreement that is here being sought.

4 No matter how compelling the special-case argument, no material that is only in Luke or only in Matthew will be included in "Q." Otherwise the logic of the whole enterprise collapses.

5 "Q" is not permitted to be the source of special (that is, unique) material, found in Matthew or Luke. How one would know that "Q" was the source of material that has a verifiable form only within Matthew or Luke, and nowhere else, defies rational explanation.

6 The convention in "Q" scholarship, that the order of the texts as they occur in Luke is to be employed, will be honoured.[1]

The hypothetical contents of the "minimum-Q" can be replicated by anyone, with only the most minor interpretative disagreements around the edges.

Why then, is there such a large "Q" industry? Because, if played strictly by the rules of historical evidence (that is, by requiring hypothesis testing), the game produces a "Q" that definitely is not going to lead to a real document; the "minimum-Q" is inevitably a sharply restricted hypothetical construct and it can be nothing more. If we had the luxury of a "real-Q" – a document that did not depend upon testable hypotheses, but which instead provided direct physical verification – we well might find:

1 that some of the material that is in Mark and Luke and Matthew and which (by the rules of the two-source version of the Mark-hypothesis) we necessarily assigned to Mark and therefore exclude from the hypothetical "minimum-Q" – actually are found in the "real Q" as well.

2 That some of this material shared with Mark (and with Luke and with Matthew) will have to do with the destruction of the Temple. That would play havoc with the assumption (and it is only an assumption) that the hypothetical "Q" is earlier than Mark. "Q" enthusiasts are not very keen to consider this possibility.

3 And that some items that scholars habitually assign to sources unique to Matthew or Luke (that is, items that are found only in Matthew or Luke) are, in fact, found in the "real Q." These would be materials that Luke accepted and Matthew did not, or vice versa.

If we were ever able to examine the "real Q," we might well find that it was a great barmbrack of a document. That is fine – indeed, it would be wonderful to the point of jubilation if we had a real physical object that testified to such rich characteristics. However, this small exercise in imagining the "real Q" has big implications for our evaluation of the "Q" industry of the present day. Because: if one drops the requirement that the hypothetical-"Q" (the "minimum-Q" we defined earlier) can only consist of items testified to in Matthew and Luke (and not found in Mark), then it can have in it anything that the creators of this new, expanded (and now, non-verifiable) version of

"Q" wish to include. There is no way of defining operational hypotheses and the only boundaries to the scholarly imagination are that the items claimed to be in "expanded-Q" also be items found at least once in Matthew, Luke or Mark. To put it bluntly, unless one sticks to the boundaries set by the original rules for deriving the hypothetical document "minimum-Q," one is caught in a *reductio ad absurdum*: namely, that one might as well posit that the precursor to the Synoptic Gospels was called "Q" and that it included everything that is in Matthew, Mark and Luke, and that the author-editors of each of those texts just fished out from that big sticky fruitcake whatever suited their own situations and interests. That, indeed, is absurd, but it is where one lands if one does not respect as a crash-barrier the original, old-fashioned rules of testable, hypothetically-verifiable "minimum-Q."

So, one is on a cleft stick: the methodologically rigorous "minimum-Q" is an hypothetical document that is not very emotionally satisfying: it turns out to be a list of roughly 45 to 50 sayings of Jesus-the-Christ. However, once one gives up the rules by which the "minimum-Q" was determined, there is no point in logic or in historical method between that minimum and the ridiculous maximum – namely, the inclusion of any or all of the contents of Matthew, Luke and Mark that may take the exegetes' fancy. Some scholarly suggestions might be too outré for the intellectual marketplace to buy, and there may be imaginative leaps that even the keenest enthusiasts cannot sell to themselves, but those are matters of taste and fashion, not of historical method. I repeat: if one abandons the criteria by which "Q" was first brought into hypothetical existence (the "minimum-Q" as derived from the two-source version of the Mark-hypothesis), then there is no operational and replicable way of disproving any of the speculations put forward.

Thus, the present-day "Q" enterprise is a state of mind. There is no ethical problem with that, for at some point the limits of historical evidence and of logic and of sound historical method are reached, and intuition must take over. The only danger is that, like the Jesus Seminar with which it shares some methods and membership, the institutional embodiment of front-edge "Q" scholarship, the "International Q Project,"[2] will eventually produce results that will not be labelled accurately as being educated intuitions. (Let me be clear here: guessing right is the heart of real intelligence; but guesses have to be labelled as such.) And this is the point where the present "Q" industry becomes worrisome: guesses that are intuitive jumps being made outside the tramlines for the hypothetical "minimum-Q" are being presented without sufficient emphasis on the fact that they are not protected by the original operationally-testable assumptions for constituting "Q," and thus have to be assessed on totally different probative grounds.[3]

My specific reservations are, first, that at least in the preliminary material at present available, the standard of verbal identity that is required between Matthew and Luke (for admission to "expanded-Q") seems not to be very high. That is a matter of individual judgement, however, and perhaps I am wrong on that issue. However, secondly, there is no doubt that the front-edge "Q" scholarship affirms that it is all right to assimilate into "expanded-Q" some items that are not found in both Matthew and Luke, but only in one of those Gospels. For example, Helmut Koester accepts as an authentic "Q" saying, Luke 9:61–62 ("No man, having put his hand to the plough, and looking back, is fit for the Almighty God") even though it has no cognate anywhere in Matthew.[4] Other examples of alleged "Q" material found only in one of the two sources are: Luke 11:27–28; 12:13–21; 12:49; 15:8–10; 17:22. In some cases, the explanation is a non-systematic one, relating to the exegete's personal sense of the text; in others, it is because the Lukan text has a parallel in the Gospel of Thomas, although not in the Gospel of Matthew.[5] Note that procedure: inclusion in "Q" is being determined in several instances not by the texts' being in both Luke and Matthew but by their being in both Luke and Thomas.

And one has a third hesitation. One finds in the present expansionist definition of "Q" that *Sondergut* passages are included. That is, some material that is unique either to Matthew or to Luke is placed in "expanded-Q." Thus, "Q" becomes its place-of-origin. That may clean up some messy files, but it is intellectually difficult to defend.[6]

Finally, a fourth reservation, a big one: some material that is found in Mark, Matthew and Luke is also placed in the presently expanding version of "Q." This is a bit hard to fathom, as the entire two-source premise upon which the existence of "Q" (in any form) depends, requires that when an item is found in both Matthew and Luke, and also in Mark, that Mark is taken to be the source. Both Helmut Koester and John S. Kloppenborg assimilate into "Q" a dozen (and perhaps more) instances of the "triple tradition," that is, of material found in all three Synoptic Gospels. This of 68 passages in the standard "Q" version: which is to say that nearly 20 percent of the material in their "Q" seems to violate the basic logic of "Q" construction.[7] There well may be good reasons in each case, yet this sort of idiomorphic argument not only destroys the logic upon which the entire "Q" enterprise was founded in the last century but makes the entire modern "Q" industry vulnerable to a form of blowback that leads to self-immolation: for, if it is somehow proper to assign to "Q" some items of the triple tradition, why not others?

At this point, one hears Helmut Koester's fiat that no narrative material (even that found in Matthew and Luke, but not in Mark) is to be assigned to "Q," with the exception of that concerning John-the-Baptizer, and also the story of Yeshua's healing of the centurion's son.[8] The voice behind the fiat is authoritative, granted, but one really has to ask why does the decree hold? In particular, why should it be the case that if sayings found in Mark (and in Luke and in Matthew) are said to also be found in the "expanded-Q" that today's "Q" scholars mostly favour, then why are narrative events that are found in Mark (and in Luke and in Matthew) to be excluded from "expanded-Q"? By what principle? Obviously the only one is of edict: it has been decided on grounds exterior to the textual stratigraphy that "Q" must be a "sayings Gospel" and thus, apparently purer and more primitive than the Synoptic Gospels which have all those messy events in them. This simply won't do. *If* the "Q" scholars permit into their latest version of "Q" sayings material that comes from Mark, Luke and Matthew conjointly, *then* they have to do the same for narrative material. And if they do that, the usual claim for the purity of "Q" – that it does not contain all those vulgar miracles of Jesus nor things such as the Passion story and the resurrection – vanishes, for, despite loads of minor contradictions, the basic Passion narrative has loads of factual agreements in the "triple tradition."

There is a way for "Q" scholars to get out of this pinch: go back to the strict original rules of "Q" as an hypothetical text, and only include material that is found in common in Matthew and Luke and exclude anything from the "triple tradition"; this leaves a "Q" that is overwhelmingly a sayings text, albeit smaller than the one that is at present being constructed. Even so, one matter of method must be dealt with: why – except on *a priori* grounds – does "Q" have to be a sayings text? Granted, most of the narrative material in Matthew and Luke has an apparent origin in Mark or in *Sondergut*, and if one follows the rules for "minimum Q," the resultant document will be made up of sayings, mostly. *Except* in a few instances: wherein Matthew and Luke have narratives in common that do not come from Mark. Should they be in "Q"? I would say yes, for the logic for including sayings shared by Matthew and Luke should hold for the inclusion of narrative.

But here is the problem: Matthew and Luke contain in common some narrative material that is not in Mark and which is very embarrassing to the religious sensibilities of most of the "Q" scholars. The gravamen of the problem is that the story of the Virgin Birth is told with sufficient agreement in Matthew and Luke to demand its inclusion in any version of "Q" that includes narrative material. Since that inclusion is necessary if one is being anything but arbitrary in including and chucking out bits of "Q," then the present-day "Q" scholars have an immense problem: either "Q" is not very old (post-Mark) or it is pre-Markan and the story of the Virgin Birth is part of the early Yeshua-faith.

Cumulatively, all of these reservations are unsettling. Frankly, I would like "Q" to be a clean, replicable piece of work. Such a case not only would provide some aesthetic joy (good scholarly work is elegant, an art form all its own) but would fit with what I have been arguing earlier was the nature of pre-70 Second Temple Judaism, an era of multiple Judaisms, in which a document like "Q" would float around with ease, one of the scores of pluralistic religious texts that circulated throughout Eretz Israel and, in the case of this Greek text, throughout the Diaspora. But the present (and presently expanding) form of "Q" is false help for my cause. I cannot accept as valid the version that is emerging. It is a huge, vulgar vitrine, in which every bit of old porcelain, alien gee-gaws and bric-a-brac that the "Q" scholars wish to display are put before us, as if they were a unity.

I suspect that it will be at least a generation before the need for a more rigorous definition of "Q" will be successfully asserted. The "Q" endeavour has reached critical mass as an industrial enterprise and it will continue to reproduce itself for the foreseeable future. It has some very talented minds associated with it (for instance, John S. Kloppenborg is one of the supplest writers of expository prose in the field of ancient history). The newly emerging "Q" hits all the right emotional buttons. It has been given a stratigraphy, so that we have not one simple "Q," but actually three, thus providing a deeply satisfying bit of density.[9] This stratigraphy, of course, has the seductive character of implying that, in shovelling back layer after layer (within "Q"), one is getting closer to the words of the historical Yeshua. Downward dating creep is pandemic with "Q" scholars and although (as I pointed out earlier) there is no reason in historical method to posit a date any earlier than the time of Mark, the "consensus dating" of "Q" is about 50 CE and nothing stops enthusiasts from pushing it earlier, into the 40s. By doing that, they are able to declare that "Q" is the earliest Christian text, pre-dating even the letters of Saul of Tarsus[10] which, we must remind ourselves, at least have the virtue of actually existing.

(And, if, as Burton Mack exults, this is as close as we ever will come to the words of Yeshua,[11] it certainly is hard lines that "Q," being reconstructed in Greek, does not contain a single word that one can with confidence assert Yeshua used.) Particularly appealing to many present-day scholars is that the new, expanded version of "Q" can be woven together with other para-gospels – especially the Gospel of Thomas. John Dominic Crossan goes so far as to claim that an even deeper layer of tradition than either Thomas or "Q" can be derived by melting the two of them into a synthetic "Common Sayings Tradition," the *ne plus ultra* of the words the ancient church ascribed to Yeshua.[12] And, even those "Q" scholars who resist this final step, often still will accept an attestation of Thomas and, say, Luke, as equal to that of Luke and Matthew in forming the "Q" text. (Both Koester and Jacobson do this, as noted earlier.)

Och. That it should come to this. Of course "Q" and the Gospel of Thomas are related. Each is derived from the canonical Gospels, Thomas in the second century, "Q" in the late twentieth. Have we become so hypnotized by our own rhetoric that we can actually think that either one can be an independent attestation of the other, or that, taken together and scraped hard, they will produce something close to the words that came out of Yeshua's mouth? The real surprise would have been if the Gospel of Thomas and the "Gospel of Q" did not resemble each other. The whole encephalitic, slowly self-circling dance that produces this sort of reasoning is enough to give the fundamentalists' straight-ahead reading of the New Testament a good name, almost.

NOTES

1 Helpful in framing the testable "minimum-Q" are: Adelbert Denaux, "Criteria for Identifying Q-Passages," *Novum Testamentum*, 37 (1995), 105–30, and Richard A. Edwards, *A Theology of Q. Eschatology, Prophecy. and Wisdom* (Philadelphia: Fortress Press, 1976), 3–10.

2 The international "Q" Project has been much less self-vaunting and of a considerably higher scholarly standard than the Jesus Seminar. Initiated in 1989 by the Society of Biblical Literature and the Institute for Antiquity and Christianity, it met annually (and, once it gained momentum, more often) to discuss specific texts and to develop a data base that includes both textual and evaluative materials. From 1989 through 1996 the International Q Project operated as a colloquium. After that, it entered a new phase by initiating the publication of *Documenta Q* which is to be a self-renewing series of volumes, each of monograph size and each dealing with a relatively small piece of potential "Q" material.(See the periodic reports on the International Q Project published in the *Journal of Biblical Literature*, 109 (1990), 499–501; 110 (1991), 494–8; 111 (1992), 500–08; 112 (1993), 500–06; 113 (1994) 495–9; 114 (1995), 475–85; 116 (1997), 521–5.) At present thirty-one volumes of *Q Documenta* are projected, but it is also suggested that the project will be perpetual. As the preface to the first published volume stated, "from the beginning it was assumed that the project would be open-ended, to stay abreast of ongoing scholarship, much as Bible translations and critical texts of the Greek New Testament are never 'final,' but are no sooner published than the next revision is already underway." (*Documenta Q. Q 11:2b–4*, vii.) The three co-editors of the thirty-one volume project are James M. Robinson, Paul Hoffman and John S. Kloppenborg: Robinson and Kloppenborg having been active in the Jesus Seminar. The intellectual godfather of both the Q Project (in which he was actively engaged) and the Jesus Seminar (in which he participated as a member of the translation panel for *The Complete Gospels. Annotated Scholars Version* [Sonoma: Polebridge Press, sec. Ed., 1994]) is Helmut Koester of Harvard. As James M. Robinson noted concerning Koester, who was a student of Rudolf Bultmann at Marburg: "One of the growing edges of American New Testament scholarship, most visible in the Jesus Seminar of the Westar Institute and the Q Seminar of the Society of Biblical Literature, has built on creative insights he [Koester] developed on the basis of his Bultmannian heritage." (Robinson, "The Q Trajectory: Between John and Matthew via Jesus," in Birgan A. Pearson (ed.), *The Future of Early Christianity* [Minneapolis: Fortress Press, 1991], 173.)

Although the International Q Project and the Jesus Seminar used similar four-point grading systems (A, B, C, D for the Q Project, and 3, 2, 1, 0, for the Jesus Seminar), they should not be assumed to be following the same methods. For the moment, the differences are that (a) the Q Project has not published its voting results and (b) gives no indication of having developed an aggregating method of the sort that crippled the Jesus Seminar's assessment of its own collective opinions. (See Appendix A of the present volume.)

3 Since *Documenta Q* has only just begun and because the material in the annual reports published in the *Journal of Biblical Literature* (see note 2 above) were necessarily truncated, I must here refer to monographs by individual scholars, rather than the collective voice of the International Q Project. However, a serviceable version of "Q," compiled and translated by Arland D. Jacobson, is found in *The Complete Gospels*, 253–300. For a laconic, brilliant, and almost Swiftian review of the first four volumes of the *Documenta Q*, see Michael Goulder, "Self-Contradiction in the IQP," *Journal of Biblical Literature*, 118 (Fall 1999), 506–17.

4 Koester, *Ancient Christian Gospels. Their History and Development* (Philadelphia: Trinity Press International, 1990), 139–40; Jacobson, in his "Q" version in the *Complete Gospels*, 267, also accepts this as an authentic saying.

5 See Koester, *Ancient Christian Gospels*, 135–49, wherein reasons are given for the inclusion of these passages in "Q." Jacobson, in *Complete Gospels* (274, 281, 289, 292–4) follows this pattern of Koester's but assigns no reasons for doing so.

6 *Sondergut* are admirably clearly marked in Kloppenborg's *Q Parallels*, but one wonders by what logic they are included.

7 Compare Koester, *Ancient Gospels*, 133–49 and John S. Kloppenborg, *Q Parallels. Synopsis, Critical Notes and Concordance*, (Sonoma: Polebridge Press, 1988), xxxi–iii. (The passages in question are (giving the Lucan and then the Marcan references): Luke 3:2b–4 (Mark 1:3–5); Luke 3:16–17 (Mark 1:7–8); Luke 10:4–7 (Mark 6:8–13); Luke 11:14–20 (Mark 3:22–26); Luke 11:23 (Mark 9:40); Luke 11:43 (Mark 12:39); Luke 12:8–9 (Mark 8:38); Luke 12:11–12 (Mark 13:9–11); Luke 14:27 (Mark 8:34); Luke 14:34–35 (Mark 9:50); Luke 16:18 (Mark 10: 11–12); Luke 17:33 (Mark 8:35).

8 Koester, *Ancient Christian Gospels*, 134.

9 This is mostly the result of Kloppenborg's *tour de force*, *The Formation of Q. Trajectories in Ancient Wisdom Collections* (Philadelphia: Fortress Press, 1987).

10 Koester, *Ancient Christian Gospels*, 170–1.

11 Burton Mack, *Who Wrote the New Testament? The Making of the Christian Myth* (San Francisco: Harper, 1995), 47.

12 John Dominic Crossan, *The Cross that Spoke. The Origins of the Passion Narrative* (San Francisco: Harper and Row, 1998), 101, 239–56, 407.

Index of Subjects

Index to References
to Ancient Texts